The Ageing of Great Britain

The
Ageing
of
Great
Britain

Grey Nightmare

or Agenda for a Silver Age?

Martin Slattery

Matador
9 Priory Business Park,
Wistow Road, Kibworth Beauchamp,
Leicestershire. LE8 0RX
Tel: 0116 279 2299
Email: books@troubador.co.uk
Web: www.troubador.co.uk/matador
Twitter: @matadorbooks

ISBN 978 1789018 196

British Library Cataloguing in Publication Data.
A catalogue record for this book is available from the British Library.

Printed and bound by CPI Group (UK) Ltd, Croydon, CR0 4YY
Typeset in 11pt Adobe Garamond Pro by Troubador Publishing Ltd, Leicester, UK

Matador is an imprint of Troubador Publishing Ltd

This book is dedicated to:
My parents, Mary & Brian, for giving me a future;
My children & grandchildren, for being the future;

My mother-in-law, Christina, for her vision of the future; and
My wife, Jacqueline, for being my future.

My Thanks too, to:
Victoria Roddam, my publishing consultant, for her professional support
and inspiring ideas on making Ageing more engaging.

Matador Publishing for making self-publishing that much
easier and more enjoyable.

Contents

Part Two
The New Old, The New Young & the Forces for Change

Part Three
Towards a New Age Manifesto & the Ageless Society Ahead

FOREWORD

What on earth inspires someone to think that ageing is a topic of such importance that they not only write a book about it but also try to come up with a 'skeleton' plan (forgive the pun) and manifesto for tackling it?

Who on earth inspires someone to spend four years of their retirement researching and writing about a topic that at first glance would turn most people grey or, worse, frighten them to death (again, forgive the pun) thinking about the three Big Ds: Disability, Dementia and Death?

My family: that's who. They were the inspiration behind this book, and they are my hope for the future, all four generations of them from one to 92.

Parents often inspire, but the inspiration from my parents, Mary and Brian, was exceptional and possibly unparalleled. They not only brought up and nurtured through the years an exceptionally large family of eight post-war baby boomers, all born between 1946 and 1964; but they also gave all of us love and a sense of family that has kept us together to this day.

Parents often inspire; mothers-in-law rarely do. They certainly don't usually inspire reflection, research and writing on a topic like ageing, but my mother-in-law Christina did. Like my parents, Christina was an inspiring figure, a classic character from the Silent Generation, the generation that had fought for and sacrificed so much for the freedoms we now enjoy and who are now sadly dying out. Her inspiration has been hopefully captured in the background narrative to Polly, the central character in this story of ageing; but suffice to say at this stage, her self-sacrifice, her voracious appetite for fighting for better for those around her, and her wisdom in counselling the young are all features embedded throughout this narrative and within the proposed solutions in Part Three.

Grandmothers often inspire; grandchildren always do. Ultimately, this book is about the future of the young rather than the later life of the old, even the new old. My wife Jacqueline and I are fortunate enough to have an ever-expanding army of eight grandchildren, ranging from aged 20 through to toddlers, living in sunny Suffolk in the UK and noisy New Jersey in the US; a wondrous array of youngsters whose appetite for life and joy of learning is an everyday inspiration. Being a grandparent is an immense privilege and a massive antidote to any sense of depression or decline as old age kicks in. They grow so fast, they learn so quickly and they challenge so openly and so honestly that no older person can fail to be enlivened, if not rejuvenated, by their presence and their company. You simply want to do as much for them and enrich as much of their life as you can – and as much as your limbs and their parents will let you. And these personal pleasures, these social transformations, are being mirrored across the world as grandparents begin to outnumber the young and a third of all babies born today live into the 22nd century.

After a hugely rewarding career in education as a classroom teacher, a college principal and a county officer for 14–19-year-olds' education, I began looking for a new project in life that might make a difference. Retirement is a shock after any sort of intense and demanding working life, even if you think you've prepared for it. Returning back home after a life spent working across four counties in a relentless round of meetings, presentations and people 'stops your clock' and leaves you wondering, what next? What does life hold now and how do I organise it? Will it be as fulfilling and meaningful as work was? It certainly has been, what with the 2012 Olympics, travel across SE Asia and America, and the joys of a growing number of grandchildren in the UK and US. Ironically, though, it was the act of actually retiring that raised my consciousness about older age and the phenomenon of ageing, which then inspired my research and writing. What at first glance seemed to be a very dismal and depressing topic, quickly became a personal challenge as I gradually realised that Britain today is sleepwalking into a national crisis of biblical proportions; a crisis of ageing, the likes of which have never been seen before; a crisis of ageing that will profoundly and permanently affect every individual, every family, every community, every arm of the British welfare state from 2020 onwards as the old become nearly a third of the UK's population by 2060. No society can ignore the fundamental implications of everybody living longer, much longer; of having nearly 20% of its population aged 65 and over; and of having more old people than young. But Britain is ignoring it, woefully; and in the case of the government, wilfully. Hence this book!

Any cursory review of the demographics for Great Britain shows that it's an ageing society that's becoming top-heavy with older people and bottom-light with youngsters, whether through our stagnant national birth rate or the likely cut-off of immigrants post-Brexit. This is a fundamental shift in the demography of the UK and in its social and economic structure. Yet there is no national plan for an ageing Great Britain, no national strategy for replanning Britain's economy and social services. There's not even a national debate akin to the EU referendum, Brexit or Scottish devolution. There's no social dialogue equivalent to the long-term planning that informs more progressive societies such as Sweden or the Netherlands; no warnings or support for individuals and families about to be overwhelmed by the Grey Age ahead. As John Harris of *The Guardian* aptly put it in 2018: "*We seem to have a collective aversion to focusing on the realities of an ageing society.*" We only seem to see the dark side of ageing – the half a million people over the age of 60 who, according to Age UK, usually spend each day in complete solitude. "*Our visions of later life are in danger of collapsing into despair, when we ought to be building them on imagination and hope.*" That's the aspiration and ambition of this book. That's the belief that an ageing Britain can be a better Britain, not just for the old but for the young too, but **only if** we plan and prepare for it. The young don't know what it's like to be old; the old know all too well what it was like to be young and would love to go back in time knowing what they know now. This, apparently, was the ambition of Emile Ratelband, a Dutchman born on March 11 1949, who applied recently to the Dutch authorities to be re-aged as 49 instead of 69. He argued that if you can change your name, nationality and gender, why not your age? So far, the Dutch courts have disagreed with him, but imagine the avalanche of re-ageing applications if they did agree.

But ageing isn't just a British challenge. Ageing is a global challenge, a global phenomenon. What Paul Moreland (2019) has called *The Human Tide* is transforming both the developed and developing worlds of the 21st century, restructuring the global economy and shifting the world 'balance of power' away from the West and towards the younger nations of Africa and Asia. Ageing is going to fundamentally change the future of mankind. Whilst the world of the late 20th century may well have been the world of the young, the world of the 21st century is certainly destined to be the world of the old as those aged 60 and older double in number to over two billion by 2050 – and the over-80s, even the centenarians, grow faster still. The world is 'going grey' at sonic speed, and it doesn't even know it.

Ultimately, though, ageing is a personal challenge, a personal challenge facing all of us whatever our age, but one that is particular challenging for those of us approaching older age, however we define it. Certainly, as a baby boomer who recently celebrated his 70th birthday, this was one of the main motivations for writing this book; and as I hope you can see, it's been a personal voyage of discovery through such challenges as retirement, pension planning, health, housing and even reflections on how to depart this life with both grace and a sense of accomplishment. Planning your own funeral and writing a draft obituary are two unusually stimulating exercises for any older person, even if, like making a will, they always seem to find themselves at the bottom of the pile. Certainly, confronting ageing rather than avoiding it is one way of coming to terms with the certainty of death and of turning the life remaining into a force for positive action rather than resigning oneself to inevitable decline and inactivity. In the perceptive words of the French psychologist, Marie de Hennezel (2011): *"It's up to us, the baby boomers, to invent a new art of growing old – which is a paradox, since it means accepting the inevitability of ageing without becoming old."*

It was insights like this that stirred the social scientist in me to look beyond the personal impact of ageing, and to look at the potential response of the new old, my own generation – the post-war baby boomer generation – to ageing and to whether they have the potential to change old age today in the same way they changed adolescence in their youth. Do baby boomers still have a rebellious streak and a social conscience? Are baby boomers potentially the 'advance army of the longevity revolution'? Are they about to create a whole new ambition and lifestyle for later life? And if the government and politicians cannot – or will not – take up the mantle of longevity, maybe baby boomers will do so. Maybe they will use their economic and political clout to drive the national debate on ageing themselves and demand the national plan on ageing that Britain so desperately needs, not just for themselves but for the generations to come. Maybe, in this way, they will be leaving a legacy for our grandchildren to be proud of, one that lasts as long into the 21st century as their revolution of youth lasted in the 20th. They have the historic opportunity not only to redesign old age as we know it but to redesign life itself, to help create a new age-free environment and a new social contract for the benefit of all ages and generations, not least their grandchildren. Whether they have the generational will and the geriatric energy for such a challenge remains to be seen.

So, this became the thesis of this book and the hope behind it. This became the inspiration for my own personal 'journey into ageing'; not just as some personal swansong but as a contribution to the public debate that desperately needs to happen before we all sleepwalk into the ageing world that's already enveloping modern Japan and threatening to *implode* Russia, South Korea and parts of Eastern Europe. With debate and a national plan, we have a chance to turn grey into silver, or even orange; a new era not just for the old but for the younger generations too. Without debate and real action – personal and political – every one of us will suffer, and our families and our grandchildren will inherit a 'lost world', a grey world, a world of lost opportunity with all the costs of ageing and none of the benefits. How will our grandchildren remember us then?

Finally, let me explain the use of *Polly the Politician*, and her family, as the vehicle for conveying this narrative. This was a deliberate shift from the more academic or polemic style normally used in publications such as this. It offered the opportunity to draw the vast array of issues involved in ageing together under one family roof and so make them more personal, immediate and urgent. It, equally, offered the opportunity to politicise as well as personalise an issue that is so fundamental to our collective future that the government has to take the lead. As a politician, Polly is at the heart of government. As a politician, Polly is ideally placed to see not only the electoral potential of ageing but also the political advantage of developing it into a political strategy, incorporating it into her party's manifesto, or even making it a manifesto on its own, advancing both its cause and her career. I hope therefore that, like me, you can identify more easily with Polly and, like her, engage with your family in the debates ahead. Polly and her parliamentary constituency in Suffolk East may be fictional, but the rest of the book is fact – hard fact – and informed opinion. So, I hope too that, like Polly and myself, you not only find this Journey into ageing fascinating, thought-provoking and worthy of wider debate and discussion but also that it inspires action; action by ourselves in galvanising the government; action by the government in galvanising and leading the age debate; action by employers, entrepreneurs and marketers in recognising and responding to the needs and demands of the new consumers of the future; action by the new old and, alongside them, the new young. Even now, our grandchildren need to begin to plan for their longer life ahead; a life that may take some or many of them into the first part of the 22nd century. Now, that's planning ahead; that's stretching the imagination!

Talking of planning ahead, when did you last think about your later life, how long you have to live and what you plan to do with it? Pretty personal questions at any time. Pretty dangerous questions when you're driving at 70mph towards Heathrow airport in the outside lane of the M25 on an icy winter's afternoon. Pretty challenging questions when your wife asks you how long you think you have left to live – and you begin to wonder why she's asking. Fortunately, it was quite an innocent enquiry, as she'd just discovered a longevity app on her phone. Fortunately, the algorithms were with me, and the longevity calculator predicted that at aged 68 I had another 28 years to go, just long enough to coincide with my wife Jacqueline's own life expectancy of 93 (and enjoy the extra life insurance that she'd just persuaded me to take out). Perfectly matched longevity and fortunately no age clash, or car crash – that day at least. It did, however, inspire a slower, more leisurely speed for the rest of the journey and a great deal of reflection by both of us on how we might make the most of the remaining years ahead. This highly personal and ultimately challenging question has motivated both of us ever since, inspired lots of bold new ideas about life in the future, and inspired much of this book.

Enjoy the Journey.

PROLOGUE

———

Polly's story, and her journey from ageing to ageless; from woeful to wonderful; from national blindness to a manifesto for the future.

———

"Trees grow stronger over the years, rivers wider. Likewise, with age, human beings gain immeasurable depth and breadth of experience and wisdom," *he said. "That is why older people should be not only respected and revered; they should be utilised as the rich resource to society that they are."*
Kofi Annan, Secretary-General to the UN (1997–2006)

Polly is a politician; a politician on a mission; a mission to raise the debate within the UK, and within her own political party, on the "Greying" of Great Britain. The nation, as she now sees it, is ageing right before our eyes. Yet apparently, we can't see it, nor can we respond positively and sensitively to the fundamental changes all around us, changes that will affect every individual, every community and every institution in the UK. And the blindest of all seem to be the politicians, in and out of government, charged with leading and steering our society toward a better, more prosperous, safe and even happy future. Despite the obvious need for a national debate and plan on ageing, the best that governments to date seem to have managed has been a series of largely disparate, knee-jerk responses to intense pressures for more cash, be it for pensions, social care or the 'grandmother of all ageing', the NHS.

Ageing today is a political volcano, one that's simmering furiously beneath the social surface, ready to erupt with explosive force in the next five to ten years and, in the process, transform not only the demography of Great Britain but the very shape, structure and nature of British society as we know it.

As Polly discovered from the Office of National Statistics (ONS: 2017/18), Britain is already on the cliff edge of becoming an ageing society in which the old, or at least the older age groups, begin to outnumber the young.

By 2035, there will be:
- Over 21 million people aged 60 and over in the UK; over 40% more than today.
- Over 3 million pensioners aged 85 years and older; double the number today and tripling by 2066.
- Nearly 100,000 centenarians aged 100 years plus; nearly eight times the number today.

By 2050, over a quarter of the UK population will be aged 65 and over, and the dependency ratio – the ratio of old-age dependents to working population – will have fallen from 4:1 today to less than 3:1, with potentially catastrophic effects on the UK economy and welfare spending.

By 2083, it is estimated that one in three of the UK population will be over 60 years old, and nearly one in five people, 20% of the British population, will live to 100 years plus.

Phenomenal predictions in themselves, but what astonished Polly most was the sheer speed of this demographic shift and how it has and will transform the life of each and every one of us hereafter. In 1919, men in Great Britain lived, on average, 52.5 years and women 56.1 years. Today, in 2019, average life expectancy for men in the UK is 79.6 years, and 83.1 years for women; a phenomenal increase of 27 years of extra life in less than 100 years. Truly one of the Great Wonders of the Modern World.

So, Britain is going through a silent revolution, a demographic revolution, that's transforming Great Britain into a 'Grey Britain', permanently and forever; and unless drastic and dramatic action is taken in the years leading up to 2030, Britain faces the prospect of a social and economic meltdown. Our welfare services are already in crisis, our economy is depressed amid the turbulent challenges of Brexit, and our United Kingdom is in danger of fragmenting, even of imploding, if age and the emerging tensions between young and old explode into an 'age war'. As Professor Les Mayhew (2018) has put it, the UK is walking into a *Dependency Trap*; it is "*sleep-walking into a conflict between the competing needs of an ageing population for a decent pension and a working-age* *population that is struggling to save for retirement, with the issues compounded by inequalities in health and income."* And all because of longevity; all because of the explosion of life so vividly described by Professor Rudi Westendorp (2014): *"Within a period of about a hundred years, average life expectancy rose from 40 to 80 years, and the likelihood of reaching the age of 65 increased three-fold from 30 to 90 per cent."* Yet who today brings up their children in the expectation that they are likely to live the **100-Year Life**?

But surely, reflected Polly, the government at least is aware of this demographic revolution and has a strategy to tackle it. Surely, she mused, there must be some sort of national plan to tackle the challenges of an ageing Britain. Surely, the government has a cunning scheme to tackle an 'age earthquake' that the government has been warned about again and again by numerous commissions and official reports over the last 20 years. Surely, the shocking conclusion of the House of Lords Select Committee Report back in 2013, that the government response to ageing to date has been *"woeful"*, jolted even Westminster and Whitehall into action. Apparently not; apparently the Lords Committee considered the subsequent government response so inadequate that they condemned it as *"wilful"* in their follow-up report in 2016, a full three years later.

Such woeful ignorance, such wilful neglect, such monumental failure of leadership by the government, and by political parties generally – her own Labour Party included – shocked Polly to the core. Ageing may not be the sexiest or most high profile of political topics but NHS and social care crises in Great Britain are weekly news as the weight of the ageing population ahead threatens to sink both of them, while pensions and housing are regularly referred to as financial time bombs about to explode under the UK economy. Despite the dominance of Brexit, ageing itself is now the real 'elephant in the political room', ready to begin trampling across British life in the same way that it's currently turning life in modern Japan upside down and on its head. Ageing looks like nothing but doom & gloom, yet in reality it offers the unbelievable opportunity of a longer and better life – but only if we see it and grasp it; a light at the end of the ageing tunnel that currently only a few age charities and think tanks seem able to see. And just wait for the ultimate 'age apocalypse'; the avalanche of dementia hovering on the horizon waiting to hit home – *every* home!

For Polly, however, this void in public debate and this failure of the government response offered the opportunity for a new national debate, a new national agenda that might supersede Brexit, inspire the young as well as the old and, in the process, provide her with a new platform for her own re-election and future ambitions – personal as well as political. After a lifetime of sacrifice and duty to their families, careers and local communities, the old in the UK, reflected Polly, are a vastly underused, if not wasted, resource; a hotbed of talent, experience and wisdom that modern society currently casts aside on retirement into the outreaches of mainstream life and, worse, into isolation. Such thoughts and reflections came to an emotional peak with the death, two years earlier, of her mother, Charlotte, or Lottie as she was known. Like her name, Charlotte was an inspiring figure, a classic character from the Silent Generation, the generation that fought for and sacrificed so much for the freedoms we now enjoy, and who sadly are now dying out. Highly intelligent, full of mischievous fun and a font of earthly wisdom, Charlotte was, nevertheless, a real fighter. She was once a senior figure in the Samaritans, with a very strong sense of social justice, willing to take up any cause she believed in and see it through to the end, however long or bitter the battle might be. She loved to help others and, even in her retirement home, at aged 90, she took on the management team in her own care home on behalf of the other residents there, demanding better treatment, organising trips outside and even engaging the local MP and local council in order to get a pathway – an 'escape route' she called it – for their mobility scooters out to the local shops just so they could enjoy and experience something of normal life. Here was a woman who'd lived through most of the 20th century and who so typified the Silent Generation which had done so much for generations since. She still had so much to offer, even in later life, offering language lessons for schoolchildren and running quizzes for fundraising at aged 90. But the best our society had to offer her was isolation and incarceration in a rest home with tea and TV, watching and waiting to follow her peers into the grave. She deserved better; her generation deserved better after a life dominated by world war and depression. Like many baby boomers contemplating their future in later life, and most especially as a daughter who owed so much of her own passion for social justice and commitment to public service to her mother, Polly vowed then that such treatment of the elderly had to change. She vowed personally to use her political and public platform thereafter to challenge and change the stereotyping, the loss of independence and the loss of dignity that we seem to routinely and casually impose on the elderly today.

Moreover, Polly's reading and research led her to the conclusion that the future of Great Britain lay not in ignoring or even trying to just cope with ageing, but in embracing it, in looking at it full in the face, fears and all, and turning this *Peril* into a *Promise*. Not just the promise of a better future for the old but a better future for the young too; a future where today and tomorrow's new technologies and scientific discoveries might transform the ageing world ahead and so in turn help transform the social, political and even the moral world for the better. Working together, the generations might be able to harness the immense powers of globalisation and new technology in creating a new type of society, a better society for both; a 'silver society' for the old and an 'orange society' for the young. Polly now contemplated the enormous potential of blending the energy, innovation and ambition of the young with the wisdom, experience and resources of the old, with her generation – the new old, the *My Generation* of the 1960s pop group, the Who – leading the way.

What a vision, what a mission, what an ambition. Yet the more Polly thought about it, the more sense it made; the more it gave a focus and a force to her political passions and offered a platform for facing and winning the elections she faced in the future, not least because she was now MP for the newly created constituency of Suffolk East, a constituency that combined Lowestoft, one of the most deprived areas in Europe, with Southwold, one of the most affluent in the UK. Traditional class rhetoric would not work in such a polarised constituency; it would only divide it, not unite it; and with the elderly in Southwold both outnumbering and outvoting the old in Lowestoft, class campaigning would be political suicide. The only issue to date that united these two 'electoral constituencies' was Brexit; and both communities, like most of the East of England, wanted 'out' of the EU. So, Polly had had to completely rethink her political strategy and find a new source of appeal that cut across class lines and united the older populations of both communities in a common cause. No easy task in an area where Labour roots run deep and Conservatism even deeper. No easy task when the traditional political battle lines and social structures that had informed British politics in the late 20th century seemed to be collapsing all round. Polly, however, now saw this as an opportunity rather than an obstacle. She now saw *Age and Stage* as a new policy framework, one that might bridge social divisions rather than incite or exacerbate them, one that might unite the ages, young and old, in common cause in pursuing a better future for all ages. As an ex-teacher and college principal, Polly believed passionately that the young needed to be brought into British politics as a matter of urgency, not excluded or persistently outvoted as at present. After all, mused Polly, the young are the future and if, proportionately, there are going to be less of them than us 'oldies' in the future, we need every one of them to be healthy and happy if they are to pay for our pensions and healthcare – and visit us regularly in later life!

So, this is Polly's story, her journey as a politician, with all its fits and starts, motivations and setbacks towards developing a plan for ageing

Britain; towards developing the headline themes of a national debate this country so desperately needs; and towards developing a political manifesto that might offer a long-term national strategy on active ageing. Her story, her journey, started in her own constituency surgery, listening to the concerns and needs of her older constituents, trying to help them and find solutions to their personal dilemmas but constantly being obstructed or thrown back by attitudes and stereotypes that relegated older people to the back of the queue, to the margins of society and into isolation, on the assumption that they were 'past it' and had nothing more to contribute. Given her own feelings about how her mother could have contributed and enjoyed later life, such assumptions hit a raw nerve for Polly and led her to think about longer-term solutions to the numerous challenges of modern retirement: pensions, health, sexual relations and inevitably death. She began to read numerous government and academic reports, not least those by the House of Lords Select Committee in 2013, and those about ageing elsewhere in the world, how other societies were seeing it and handling it. With a few exceptions – notably the insights and ambitious thinking of the UN/WHO and EU, and the grand plans of the Nordic nations – they made dismal reading. This forced Polly to develop and devise thinking of her own, thinking that led her to see the notion of generation – both her generation of post-war baby boomers and her grandchildren's generation – as the key to mobilising and driving change in Britain and forcing its government to wake up to the potential 'grey nightmare' ahead.

It is, however, a 'journey in progress'; a journey through the 'what, who, why and how' of ageing today; a journey that is only now beginning, given that the British national debate has not even started. Even ideas on what an ageing or ageless society in the future might look like are still but twinkles flickering in the foresights of think tanks and age gurus. No one yet has set out in detail what the world of longevity might actually look like and, given the pace of technological and global change today, that's not really surprising. A new age political manifesto might, however, at least propel ageing up the political agenda and help stir public opinion and media interest. But for manifestos to make a real difference and take society to a new level of social thinking, they need to offer a vision of a future worth fighting for – a new social contract that binds generations rather than divides them, a new social paradigm that offers a better future for all and particularly for generations to come.

As explained in the Foreword, Polly does not actually exist. She is a figment of my political imagination, just like her parliamentary constituency of Suffolk

East – although Lowestoft and Southwold do sit cheek by jowl on the Suffolk coastline. Nevertheless, her political journey into Britain's ageing future and its application to this particular stretch of Greying Britain's 'silver coast' accurately and vividly describe the seismic and very real changes rumbling beneath the surface of British society today and their potential impact on the future for ourselves and our grandchildren. While Part One of this book describes her travelogue across the numerous challenges of ageing in Great Britain today, Parts Two and Three set out her journey towards finding a new age generation and a new age strategy, to bring it to fruition. It is a fascinating story; a story of our time and a story of the ageing world we are all now entering – and that we are about to pass on to our children and grandchildren. I hope, like Polly, that we do our duty and will be remembered fondly and respectfully by the generations to come for the legacy we bequeathed them.

Part One

Grey Britain
&
The Ageing
Challenge Ahead

1 | The Demographics of Ageing: Grey Britain and the Global World Ahead

"The anticipated increase in longevity and resulting ageing populations is the financial equivalent of climate change. We must address it now or accept that its adverse consequences will haunt future generations, putting an impossible strain on our children and grandchildren."

Michael Drexler,
Head of Financial and Infrastructure Systems
at the World Economic Forum (WEF: 2017)

Ageing was increasingly on Polly's mind. The more she looked, the more she saw. The more she thought, the more she realised that not only were the old looking so much younger today but there were masses more of them. And they looked so much healthier and wealthier; a generation full of *HD* colour, pixel bright and brimming with energy compared with the pensioners of the past. The new old looked younger, acted younger and, my goodness, they would go to any length to stay younger and escape being labelled old or thought of as inactive or incapable of looking after themselves. The new old were more likely to drive a sports car than a mobility scooter, be on a cruise than a coach, have a bikini wax than a blue rinse, and listen to Ed Sheeran than Glen Miller. The oldest woman in the UK died in September 2018 at an astonishing 113 years of life. Soon the old would be the majority – or at least the predominant – age group in Great Britain, and the young would be approaching the '100-year life' that so many people had long aspired to but so many now feared.

But first Polly had to get her head around the demographics apparently driving all this change and see for herself where it was all leading. While financiers might need 'to follow the money', politicians need to follow the demographics, not slavishly and uncritically but with the same focus and critical calculation that forensic investigators might employ in pursuing a money trail. However, whichever way Polly looked at the demographic statistics on the future of Great Britain, they all pointed in one direction; the direction of a fundamental shift in the British age pyramid and, with it, a fundamental shift in British society. Great Britain is ageing and ageing fast.

According to the Office of National Statistics (ONS), the total population of the UK is now set to rise from 65.6 million in 2016 to over 74 million by 2039; an astonishing growth of nearly 8 million people, or 12%, in just 23 years, that will leave the UK the largest country in the EU/EFTA area. This is a massive demographic shift in itself; but what really grabbed Polly's attention was the underlying shift in the **balance of ages** that lay beneath: as the old outgrow the young, as the number of those aged 65 and over grows faster than those aged 15 and under. While Britain's working population (16–64) is predicted to decline slowly from some 64% to 58% of the UK population by

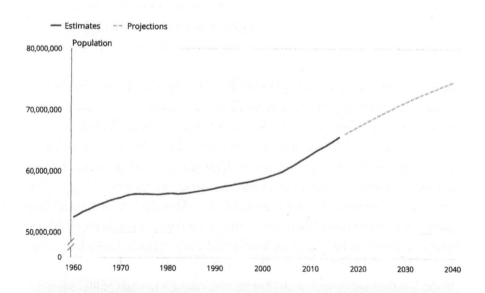

Figure 1: **GB population 1960–2040**
(ONS: July 2017)

2045, the balance between old and young is about to be turned on its head, as those aged 65 years and above are set to nearly double in the next 50 years, while those under 16 are even now shrinking from being 25% of the total population in 1976 to 19% today and falling. Moreover, the old are not only beginning to multiply in droves but also beginning to propagate separate and quite distinct age groups of their own:

- The **New Old**, for example, those aged 65 and over, are projected to rise from nearly 12 million in 2018 to over 20 million by 2066, becoming 26% of the UK population.
- The **Middle Old**, those aged 85 and over, are projected to double by 2041, from 1.6 million currently, to 3.4 million, and treble by 2066 to over 5 million people, or 7% of the population of the UK.
- The **Oldest Old**, those aged 100 and over, are projected to multiply six-fold, rising from nearly 15,000 in 2018 to over 83,000 in 2039. The Queen won't be able to cope with centenarian birthday cards and might have to raise the bar to 110 years or even 120.

Year	0-15 years (%)	16-64 years (%)	aged 65 and over (%)	UK Population
1976	24.5	61.2	14.2	56,216,121
2006	19.2	64.9	15.9	60,827,067
2016	18.9	63.1	18.0	65,648.054
2026	18.8	60.7	20.5	69,843,515
2036	18.0	58.2	23.9	73,360,907
2046	17.7	57.7	24.7	76,342,235

Figure 2a: **Age Distribution of the UK Population: 1976 to 2046**
(Adapted from ONS: July 2017)

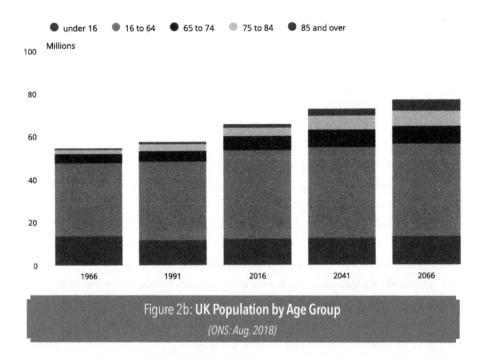

Figure 2b: **UK Population by Age Group**
(ONS: Aug. 2018)

Polly found these headline statistics amazing and quite mind-boggling. She even got her researcher to go away and double-triple check them. While the Brexit debate has conjured up this image of some 300,000 immigrants pouring into the UK each year, no one seems to be aware that twice that amount of 65-year-olds are projected to be pouring into retirement every year between now and 2035, shrinking the British workforce dramatically as they go and putting immense pressure on the British welfare state in the process. The old are reproducing in such numbers that they're spawning whole new generations of old, each outliving the last; each changing fundamentally and permanently the age profile of Great Britain; each having a major impact on the 'ages' below, and on both the British economy and British society in the future. They are fundamentally changing not just the demographic face of Great Britain but the very nature and structure of the society in which we live.

The key shift in Britain's demography, however, is in its **dependency ratio**; the ratio between the dependent age groups pre-16/18 and post-65, and the working age group aged 16-64. This ratio is critical to Britain's economic health and its ability to fund its welfare services, its family life and its political direction. It is predicted to rise dramatically between now and 2035, from 4:1 to less than 3:1; from four workers per dependent, down to three and falling. The strain on the British economy and on the taxpayer is likely to be immense, if not unbearable, as there will be proportionately fewer workers and fewer taxpayers paying for a burgeoning population of elderly. There will be more grandparents than grandchildren, more older voters than young. For a politician like Polly, this shift is fundamental to the future of the UK and, unless tackled very soon and quite radically, could seriously undermine not only the UK economy but the British welfare state as we know it.

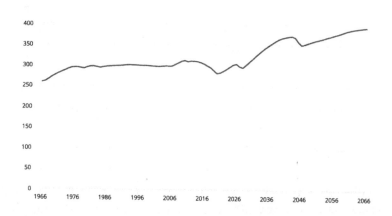

Figure 3: **UK Old Age Dependency Ratio: 1966-2066**
(ONS: Aug. 2018)

And the future ahead looks even more dramatic. According to the Office for National Statistics (ONS: 2018), by 2083, it is estimated that one in three people in the UK will be over 60, and nearly one in five people currently living in the UK will live to 100 years plus. *Read and re-read that again.* In just over 60 years' time, grandchildren born in the last few years will be part of the largest cohort of older people this country has ever seen. How is Britain going to support such an ageing population without an economic revolution in productivity, a transformation in tax revenues and a radical reallocation of resources away from the young and towards the old? This is a political and social choice that Polly prefers not to contemplate, but one that many other commentators are now predicting.

So, what, asked Polly, is driving all this change? What is happening under the surface to transform Great Britain so profoundly and so permanently? What is driving this revolution in age? Longevity, that's what. We are all living longer, much longer than ever before. We're all living 50% longer than 100 years ago, despite the Great Depression, two devastating world wars and a dramatic fall in birth rate. We're all enjoying healthier longer lives, and our children and grandchildren are projected to live even longer – into their 90s and many into their centenaries. Great Britain, like the rest of Europe – and the rest of the world – is facing a revolution in longevity. It is literally being turned on its demographic head. Great Britain is becoming 'Grey Britain'; or, if you prefer, the British Isles are becoming the 'Silver Isles'. Great Britain is facing a demographic revolution, a leap in longevity, as boys born in 2016 are predicted to live on average to nearly 80 years, and girls to nearly 83 years. Even more amazingly, the longer you live, the longer you are likely to live.

According to the ONS (2018):

- **Life expectancy at birth** in the UK is currently 79.2 years for men and 82.9 years for women, rising to 85.7 years and 87.6 years respectively by 2030 as men catch up and, in some areas of the UK, surpass women.
- **Life expectancy from aged 65** today is 18.6 years for men and 20.9 years for women, with nearly 60% of this longer life likely to be in good health.
- **By 2066** baby boys are expected to live to 86.4 years on average, and baby girls to 88.9 years, with **nearly 50%** of this cohort expected to live to 100 years.

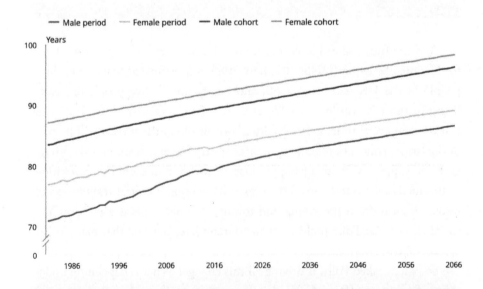

Figure 4a: **Life Expectancy at birth: 1981–2066**
(ONS: Aug. 2018)

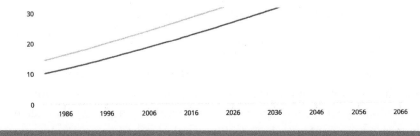

30								
20								
10								
0								
1986	1996	2006	2016	2026	2036	2046	2056	2066

Figure 4b: **Survival to Age 100**
(ONS: Aug. 2018)

As Professor Sarah Harper neatly summed up at the International Longevity Centre (ILC) UK Conference in 2016: *"Death is steadily losing its dominion... In 1850, half the population in England were dead before they reached 46. Now half the population in England are alive at 85; and 8 million people currently alive in the UK will make it to 100 years or more. And if we extrapolate that to Europe, we can say 127 million Europeans are going to live to 100."* Professor Rudi Westendorp (2015) has gone even further. He believes that the first person to reach 135 years of age has already been born.

Polly couldn't help but be astounded at these figures and the amazing message that we are all now living longer than any generation before. Her mother, Charlotte, living to 92, was an exception to that rule for her generation, but Polly's grandchildren have every prospect of living even longer. Moreover, while these figures are breathtaking on their own, they're even more astounding when put against 'healthy longer living'. We're not only living longer but living longer in *good health*, compared to our parents and grandparents. According to the ONS, well over 50% of life after age 65 today will be in *"good health"* in most parts of the UK – but sadly not all of them as shown below.

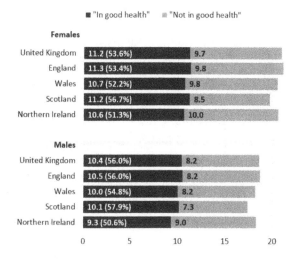

■ "In good health"   ▨ "Not in good health"

Females

United Kingdom	11.2 (53.6%)	9.7
England	11.3 (53.4%)	9.8
Wales	10.7 (52.2%)	9.8
Scotland	11.2 (56.7%)	8.5
Northern Ireland	10.6 (51.3%)	10.0

Males

United Kingdom	10.4 (56.0%)	8.2
England	10.5 (56.0%)	8.2
Wales	10.0 (54.8%)	8.2
Scotland	10.1 (57.9%)	7.3
Northern Ireland	9.3 (50.6%)	9.0

0   5   10   15   20

Figure 5:
Healthy life expectancy at age 65 by sex: 2014-2016
(ONS: 2018)

The true gift of longevity, therefore, is not just longer life itself, but longer, healthier life; life rich in good health even in older age; life to be enjoyed and lived to the full for 10, 20, even 30 years after retirement; a new stage in life; even a new life in itself with a new career, a new partner at home or abroad. **Healthy Life Expectancy** (HLE) is the key to the longevity revolution and the ultimate goal for any advanced and ambitious society or individual in the 21st century, aided and abetted by revolutionary new technologies and dramatic medical advances yet to unfold. We can now anticipate that 80% of life today in the UK is likely to be lived in good health as we increasingly push back the boundaries of morbidity and compress our likely period of ill health and disability into the final stages of life – but only if we continue to live healthy lives ourselves, free from modern and 'self-induced' killer diseases such as obesity and smoking.

Such collective longevity should be cause for national jubilation and celebration. But it isn't, not least because of its disparity and uncertainty. As reports, such as one by Professor Marmot in 2017, have revealed – and as shown in Figure 5 above – there are immense disparities in life expectancy, particularly healthy life expectancy, right across the UK. Where you live and how you live, your social class, gender and your ethnicity all appear to impact directly on how long you live. According to the ONS (2018), the gap in life expectancy between the least and the most deprived areas of England in 2015–17 was 7.4 years for baby girls and 9.4 years for baby boys. In terms of healthy life expectancy, the ONS identified a gap of 19.1 years between the better-off and the most deprived males in England, and a gap of 18.8 years for females in England and 19.4 years for females in Wales. This is a shocking indictment of any civilized country, particularly one as wealthy as the UK but even worse inequality in LE at birth is growing for women as females born in the most deprived areas in England today apparently live 100 days less than three years years ago while their counterparts in better-off areas apparently live 84 days more; an increase in female inequality in LE of some six months.

For Polly, as a socialist, a Labour MP and simply as a human being, such inequalities in longevity are horrifying. They're not only hard to explain but socially and morally impossible to justify, particularly as many of the youngsters Polly had taught in the past, in Lowestoft and elsewhere, are possibly the very youngsters now facing such limited lifespans and poorer prospects for a healthy life later on. Simply from an economic point of view, particularly with the UK's dependency ratio rising rapidly, such huge gaps in LE across both British society and the geography of the UK make no sense. They represent a devastating loss of labour and skill, and a significant long-term cost for the British economy, one that is far less evident in other advanced countries.

Finally, what the ONS reports also showed Polly was that while longevity in the long run in the UK is improving, it's still below the best elsewhere. The Japanese, Scandinavian and the Mediterranean countries are 'years ahead' of us for both men and women, with Scotland still, unfortunately, trailing behind everyone else.

Country	Latest Year	Females		Males	
		At Birth	At Age 65	At Birth	At Age 65
Japan	2015	87.0	24.2	80.8	19.4
Spain	2016	85.8	23.1	80.3	19.1
Switzerland	2016	85.3	22.6	81.5	19.8
France	2017	85.3	23.2	79.5	19.4
Italy	2016	85.0	22.3	80.6	19.1
Norway	2017	84.3	21.6	80.9	19.2
UK	**2015-17**	**82.9**	**20.9**	**79.2**	**18.6**

Figure 6: **International Longevity** (selected countries)
(Source: Adapted from ONS: Sept. 2018)

Worse, longevity in the UK now appears to be slowing down, and not only stalling but falling, especially for women and the poor, and more so, much more so, than the rest of the Western world. Whether this slow-down is due to austerity, as the Marmot Report in 2017 suggested, or the rise in obesity remains a hotly debated topic, but overall, it's a very salutary reminder that longevity cannot be taken for granted and has to be worked on by us all, individually and collectively. As the ONS commented in August 2018, while *"the UK has experienced one of the largest slowdowns in life expectancy at birth and at age 65 for males and females"* across Europe, North America and Australia, Japan has shown that, *"even after a period of slow growth in life expectancy, a country may again return to faster improvements."*

But if the UK is 'going grey' at a rate of knots, the EU is 'going Grecian' at speed, with 23 of the EU's 27 countries' populations ageing even faster than Great Britain's. Germany is soon likely to become the 'oldest' country in Europe, with 31% of its population projected to be aged 65 and over by the year 2035, and Italy is close behind. Ironically, one of the key factors keeping the UK younger than most of Europe is immigration; one of the key reasons Britain voted to leave the EU in 2016.

So, with her political hat firmly on her head, what, asked Polly, is driving the longevity revolution in Britain and elsewhere, and how might we control or change it? The answer from her researcher was fairly obvious but critical, nevertheless, to Polly's analysis. Population growth or decline is down to four key factors: the birth rate, the death rate, longevity and net migration. Populations that are ageing are usually the result of **falling fertility** on one hand and falling mortality and rising longevity on the other. The UK, like most developed nations, has experienced a dramatic fall over the past 40 years in its birth rate, with fertility rates falling below the *natural* replacement level of 2.1 children per woman. In 2014, for example, the total fertility rate (TFR) was 1.83 children per woman, a fall of over 60% on the peak period of 2.93 in 1964. **Falling mortality** in the UK was initially the result of dramatic falls in our infant mortality rate, in the death rate for baby children; now it's the death rate of the older age groups that has fallen dramatically, and it is they who are living longer, much longer, and so creating a dramatic shift in the balance of ages in the UK, reshaping the traditional age shape from a pyramid to a pillar, as illustrated below. As the demographic base of Great Britain – the younger age groups – is proportionately shrinking, so

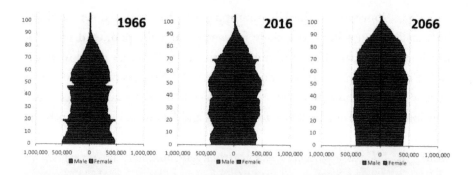

Figure 7: **UK Population Pyramids**
(ONS: 2018)

our social pyramid is becoming top-heavy with older people, bringing the potential for an 'age-overload' on the economy, the welfare services and every family in the UK.

Last but certainly not least, **immigration** has long been a significant force for rebalancing Britain's ageing population, whether it be from the British Commonwealth in the 1950s and 60s, or more recently from the EU. Clearly, though, in the light of Brexit and the intense emotions this topic now inspires in the UK, immigration is no longer the simple 'demographic tap' that Britain can continue to turn on and off in response to manpower shortages in the public or private sectors. Uncontrolled immigration is no longer acceptable to the British public; it has to be a managed process so that no community feels swamped or overrun. Despite public opinion and media headlines, numerous studies, such as one by University College London (UCL) in 2014, have shown that EU immigrants, and immigrants generally, have overwhelmingly been a boon to the British economy, not a drain on its welfare state, contributing over £20 billion to UK public finances in the period 2001–2011 and paying 64% more in taxes than they received in benefits. The Office for Budget Responsibility (OBR) concluded back in 2013 that: "*overall migration has a positive impact on the sustainability of public finances*" and that a complete ban on immigrants would see government borrowing rise by 174% of GDP, while the Manning Report in 2018 concluded that: "*The small overall impacts mean that EEA migration as a whole has had neither the large negative effects claimed by some nor the clear benefits claimed by others.*" Equally, the 'mini baby boom' that the UK enjoyed in the period 2010–2012 (ONS: 2015) was largely down to immigrants rather than British residents. At that time, most people in the UK apparently held a positive attitude towards immigrants but, as the British Social Attitudes Survey back in 2014 began to reveal, a sharp and growing gulf in attitudes was already developing between the young and well-educated under aged 45 and those who left school early aged 65+; a gap in attitudes that, by the time of the 2016 EU Referendum, had become much more prominent and politically powerful. Warnings from authorities like the International Monetary Fund (IMF) (2018), that all advanced countries need to be more open to immigration or risk their economies being overwhelmed by ageing, now cut little ice.

So, the demographic solutions are there, but as Polly was well aware from the Blair era and the Brexit debate, simply pulling demographic levers in isolation without control and the infrastructure to support them might relieve short-term shortages in labour supply, but in the long-run generate social divisions that threaten to destabilise society and produce unforeseen long-term costs and potential conflicts. Germany's humanitarian attempt to relieve the Syrian migration crisis, for example, generated a massive reaction right across Europe that led eventually to borders being closed rather than opened, and to populist/nationalist movements rising in Hungary, Poland and even Sweden. Germany and Italy face a serious demographic implosion and desperately need infusions of 'young blood'; but politically, mass, or even minor, immigration is currently unacceptable. Using demographic levers to control population growth is never easy, and even mighty China has had to abandon its one-child policy, as the population explosion of the young that China feared in the 1960s has now emerged as potentially a population explosion of the old as these same children enter old age.

So, Britain today appears to be 'bursting' with people, old and young; people who will change the 'face of the future' and who might possibly soon make Great Britain the largest nation in Europe. The younger generations are living longer and longer and in so doing, they are generating a demographic revolution that isn't just changing the demographic size and balance within the UK, it's also changing its way of life and even its structure of life. As illustrated in the diagram below, an *age shift* is rippling right across British society as life stages for all ages get longer and longer. Full-time education for today's young, for example, now spans some 18 to 19 years, a fifth of their potential life span,

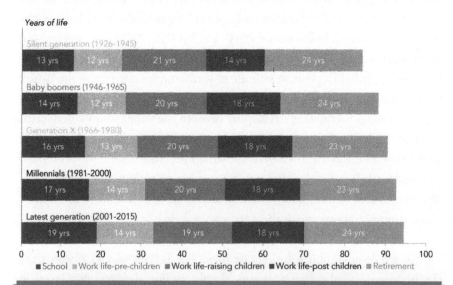

Years of life

Silent generation (1926-1945): 13 yrs | 12 yrs | 21 yrs | 14 yrs | 24 yrs

Baby boomers (1946-1965): 14 yrs | 12 yrs | 20 yrs | 18 yrs | 24 yrs

Generation X (1966-1980): 16 yrs | 13 yrs | 20 yrs | 18 yrs | 23 yrs

Millennials (1981-2000): 17 yrs | 14 yrs | 20 yrs | 18 yrs | 23 yrs

Latest generation (2001-2015): 19 yrs | 14 yrs | 19 yrs | 18 yrs | 24 yrs

0 10 20 30 40 50 60 70 80 90 100

■ School ■ Work life-pre-children ■ Work life-raising children ■ Work life-post children ■ Retirement

Figure 8: **Living even longer: 1926–2015**
(IGC: Live Long and Prosper: 2017)

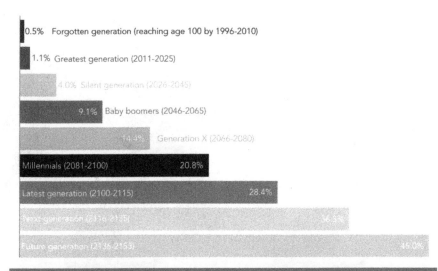

0.5% Forgotten generation (reaching age 100 by 1996-2010)

1.1% Greatest generation (2011-2025)

4.0% Silent generation (2026-2045)

9.1% Baby boomers (2046-2065)

14.4% Generation X (2066-2080)

Millennials (2081-2100)   20.8%

Latest generation (2100-2115)   28.4%

Next generation (2116-2135)   36.3%

Future generation (2136-2155)   46.0%

Figure 9: **Proportion of each generation living to 100 in England & Wales: 1985-2055**
(*IGC: 2017*)

while work, family formation and even retirement are increasingly delayed and proportionately longer than in the past.

A century ago, newborns were expected to live on average to 63; today they are expected to live to 93, with over a third reaching 100. Nearly 50% of future generations are now expected to enjoy, or at least experience, the 100-year life illustrated in Figure 9, so what might happen if we start living to 150 years, as academics like Professor David Sinclair now predict is possible?

For Polly, this demographic tour of Great Britain was eye-opening and mind-boggling. It set out a whole new canvas for her future thinking and speaking, and it generated a whole new perspective on planning British society in the years ahead. Britain's demographic face was clearly an older and an ageing one – more Tom Jones than Ed Sheeran; more Theresa May than Emmanuel Macron. Britain is no longer the country of the young, and more the country of the middle-aged and the middle-spread; a swollen, demographic body perched precariously on increasingly thin young legs; legs that may soon not be able to bear the weight of taxation and eldercare about to bear down on them unless something changes dramatically. The British Isles is fast becoming the 'Silver Isles', with the older ages retiring to the coast and countryside while the young migrate to the cities and the capital, London.

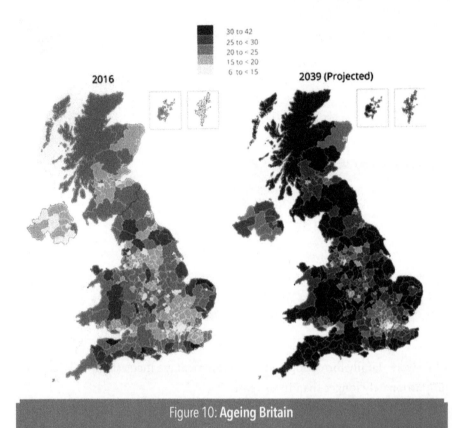

Figure 10: **Ageing Britain**
(ONS Map: 2018)

Global Ageing: But if ageing is transforming the demographic face of Great Britain, what's happening in the rest of the world? Is it, too, 'going grey', or is it just the UK? The answer from the United Nations (UN) and the World Health Organization (WHO) is very clear. The ***globe is going grey,*** and at 'sonic' speed. While the late 20th century saw a population explosion of the young, the last 50 years has seen a population explosion of the old, as those aged 60 and above doubled in number between 1980 and 2017 to 962 million, and they're predicted to double again by 2050 to over 2.1 billion, or 22% of the world's population, and 3.1 billion by 2100. By 2050, 44% of the world's population will live in relatively aged societies where 20% or more of the population are aged 60 years or older. (World Population Ageing Report: 2017)

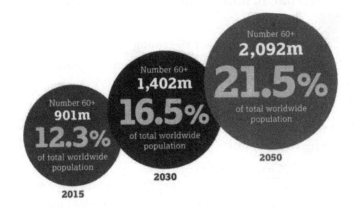

Global population aged 60 years and over, 2015

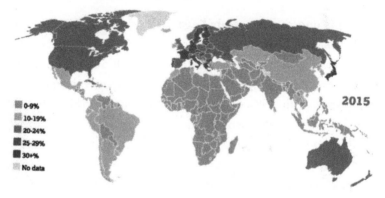

Projected global population aged 60 years and over, 2050

Figure 11: **Global Ageing**
Global AgeWatch/UNDESA: 2015

For the first time in human history:

- **The over-60s will outnumber the young** (those aged ten and under), and by 2050 it is predicted that they will outnumber teenagers and youths aged 10–24.
- **The 'old old',** those aged 80 and above, will become the fastest growing sector of the world's population, tripling from 137 million in 2017 to 425 million by 2050; and then doubling again by 2100 to 909 million, nearly 10% of the world's population.
- **Centenarians,** those over 100 years of age, are predicted to *explode* from just over 300,000 today to 3.2 million by 2050; a tenfold increase in less than 40 years.

The world is undergoing a **global age shift** as the old overtake the young: a population explosion of the old in the early 21st century to match the population explosion of the young after WWII. All continents, except Africa, are already experiencing ageing, and Europe is currently the oldest continent on the planet, with 19% of its total population of 511 million aged 65 or more, and the old-age dependency ratio is set to rise dramatically, from 3.3 workers to pensioners to 2:1 by 2070. Italy and Germany are amongst the oldest countries in the world today, and parts of Eastern Europe are set to 'implode' as their populations shrink according to the 2018 European Commission Ageing Report. By the middle of the century, China alone could have 100 million people over 80 years of age; a phenomenal increase from the 14 million 80-year-olds on the entire planet only a century ago. And it's not only the size of the change that is so dramatic but the **speed**; a 150% increase in 35 years; a seismic shift in world demography undergone at Mach-speed, and one that is likely to see Japan and parts of Europe 'shrink' in population; China, and even India, start to go 'grey'; and younger emerging nations in Africa, such as Nigeria, becoming some of the most populous countries in the world.

Global ageing is about to take off big-time and accelerate at **turbo speed.** And the effect of such a seismic shift in the balance of the world's demography is likely to be equally dramatic, equally explosive, as **dependency ratios** begin to double and a crisis of funding for governments across the world begins to hit home. In Europe and the older advanced economies, for example, the dependency ratio is already beginning to shift from 4:1 to 2:1 and with only two tax-paying workers per dependent, how is it going to be possible for any country to continue funding its welfare state? Worse, some advanced countries, notably Russia and South Korea, are already beginning to **implode** as their populations shrink in the face of a burgeoning older age population, a falling birth rate and the declining desire of its young people to have children. Japan, for example, is predicted to fall from 128 million people today to some 95 million by 2050, while Latvia and Lithuania are currently losing some 14% of their already tiny populations of 2–3 million to Germany and the UK. How will such societies cope economically and socially as the young leave in droves and older people begin to dramatically outnumber the young?

But ageing is not just a **Western** phenomenon, it's a **global phenomenon**, as two-thirds of the world's older people already live in developing regions, and by 2050 that proportion is expected to rise to four-fifths. As Professor Sarah Harper (ILC-UK: 2016) summed it up: "*By 2030, half the population of Western Europe will be over 50, one quarter of the population of the developed world will over 65, and one quarter of the population of Asia will be over 60. This is historically unprecedented. Indeed, it will make the 20th century the last century of youth; the 21st century heralds a new demography – that of maturity.*"

Region	2017 (millions)	2050 (millions)
World	962.3	2080.5
Europe	183.0	247.2
North America	78.4	122.8
Asia	547.2	1273.2
Africa	68.7	228.5
Latin America & Caribbean	76.0	198.2
Oceania	6.9	13.3

Source: Adapted from World Population Prospects: 2017 revision (UN)

Figure 12: **Global Ageing**:
No of people aged 60 years or older in developed & developing world

But demography isn't only transforming the social and economic structure of global society, it's also likely to transform the world balance of power, as the ageing powers of the West shrink demographically and those of Asia, and especially Africa, explode; an astonishing shift in world populations in an astonishingly short period of time. By 2030, predicted Imperial College London and the WHO in 2017, South Korea will have overtaken Japan as the oldest nation on earth, with an average life expectancy exceeding 90 years – over 84 years for baby boys born today, and nearly 91 for baby girls. French women and Swiss men are predicted to be living the longest lives in Europe by 2030, at 88.6 and 84 years respectively, while the UK sits a lowly 21st in this ICL Longevity League Table of the most advanced nations, well behind Japan and Switzerland, and even behind France and Spain. Longevity should be a challenge to galvanise any UK government. Thus should be the league table of all league tables for any government seeking to promote quality of life for all its citizens. The UK should be aiming to be in the top three, commented Polly, not languishing down in the bottom third.

A. Highest Life Expectancy at Birth

Men	Women
1. South Korea: 84.1 years	1. South Korea: 90.8 years
2. Australia: 84 years	2. France: 88.6 years
3. Switzerland: 84 years	3. Japan: 88.4 years
4. Canada: 83.9 years	4. Spain: 88.1 years
5. Netherlands: 83.7 years	5. Switzerland: 87.7 years
14. UK: 82.5 years	**21. UK: 85.3 years**

B. Highest Life Expectancy at Age 65

Men	Women
1. Canada: 22.6 additional years	1. South Korea: 27.5 additional years
2. New Zealand: 22.5 additional years	2. France: 26.1 additional years
3. Australia:22.2 additional years	3. Japan: 25.9 additional years
4. South Korea: 22.0 additional years	4. Spain: 24.8 additional years
5. Ireland: 21.7 additional years	5. Switzerland: 24.6 additional years
12. UK: 20.9 additional years	**22. UK: 22.7 additional years**

Source: Adapted from UCL/Lancet Study:2017

Figure 13: International Longevity in 2030

Finally, ageing is not happening to all countries all at the same time. Many, especially in Europe and SE Asia, are ageing much faster than others and so are already at the 'cliff edge' of ageing; and some are already over the edge, on what the economist, George Magnus (2009), rather dramatically called the "*Demographic Death Row*" – a league table that Britain thankfully rose out of back in the 1980s and 90s, but one she could quite easily rejoin post-Brexit in the aftermath of much more restricted immigration. (See also Bricker & Ibbitson's *The Empty Planet*: 2019 for a detailed description of the depopulation thesis.)

2017	Country	% aged 60 & over	2050	Country	% aged 60 & over
	Japan	33.4		Japan	42.4
	Italy	29.4		Spain	41.9
	Germany	28.0		Portugal	41.7
	Portugal	27.9		Greece	41.6
	Finland	27.8		Korea	41.6
	Bulgaria	27.7		China, Taiwan Province of China	41.3
	Croatia	26.8		China, Hong Kong SAR	40.6
	Greece	26.5		Italy	40.3
	Slovenia	26.3		Singapore	40.1
	Latvia	26.2		Poland	39.5

Source: Adapted from World Population Prospects: 2017 Revision (UN)

Figure 14: Top Ten Super-Ageing Nations: 2017-2050

But ageing isn't happening in isolation. Ageing, according to the McKinsey Global Institute (MGI) (2015), is part of a global transformation, and a global disruption, of the world ahead. It is operating in parallel with, and occasionally in concert with three other all-powerful global forces: globalisation; the internet and new technology; and urbanisation.

Globalisation is clearly reshaping the world's economy, integrating the world into a global capitalist system beyond any government's control, and in the process it's creating a new breed of 'superpower', the 'mega corporation' of the 21st century, and a new breed of global entrepreneur some writers perceive as a new 'power elite'; a power elite with ambitions of world domination – not through military power as in the past, but through economic and technological power, power over world markets and global finance. The tech giants, Amazon, Apple and especially Google, see the world as their oyster and they are in the process of creating their own mini states and centres of power. And behind these 'masters of the universe' are waves of new competitors from the developing nations – the Alibabas of Asia, soon to be followed by those from Africa and South America. The mega corporations of the late 20th century, like Ford, McDonald's, Sony; the giant supermarkets, like Walmart and Tesco; the mega banks, like HSBC and Goldman Sachs; the pharmaceutical giants, such as Pfizer and Allianz, are all under immense pressure from new younger entrepreneurs with the ambition and technology not only to replace them but to transform the very nature of the businesses they're now in. The banks don't fear just competition from other banks, or even new forms of currency such as bitcoin; they fear Amazon and the tech giants and their ability and ambition to transform the banking industry and cream off such lucrative services as credit card transactions. Online delivery is transforming the whole basis of manufacturing and retail businesses, from food and clothing through to entertainment and finance, while digitalisation is transforming every mode of human communication. Google's DeepMind software, for example, is soon to be embedded in the UK's national grid, collecting data on all of us; Alexa is already at home in millions of households, and Amazon boss, Jeff Bezos, is now not only the world's wealthiest man but he's also venturing into food, pharmacy and even world peacekeeping. His dream of Amazon as the 'everything, everywhere, everytime' store is fast becoming a reality and, in the process, whole swathes of industry are being cut out or cut up; and the traditional high street is being decimated, as online buying has taken the legs and lives of companies as diverse as Toys "R" Us, House of Fraser and Poundland.

A new world order is emerging, a new type of global economy is being created, and a new generation of entrepreneurs from both the developing and developed nations is challenging, changing and disrupting the global economy in a fight for control of the markets ahead. Facebook, Amazon and even Google didn't exist 20 years ago, yet now they're the new 'masters of the emerging universe', facing rising Titans from the East, such as Alibaba. They represent a new form of capitalism, one based on ownership of the means of distribution rather than the means of production. Alibaba, the world's largest retailer, for example, owns no warehouses; Uber, the world's largest taxi company, owns no cars; and Airbnb, the world's largest accommodation provider, owns no hotels. As Haskel and Westlake (2017) have argued, we seem to be entering an era of capitalism without capital, as intellectual property and innovative ideas become the most valuable and profitable form of investment in the digital world of tomorrow. And while writers such as Robert Gordon (2016) and Gervais Williams (2017) may well believe that globalisation is slowing down as a result of austerity, setbacks such as Brexit, and the growing backlash against rising inequality that has arisen since 2008, it seems highly unlikely that the underlying trend towards global integration and inequality will stop completely or go into reverse.

Rather, as the MGI reported in 2019, there appears to be a fundamental shift *"in the world's centre of (economic) gravity"* as the Asian Tigers of the East begin to rival the mega-corporations of the West. Asia is coming of economic age and it is *"on track to top 50% of global GDP by 2040 and drive 40% of the world's consumption"*. Such phenomenal economic growth seems to be accompanied by real shifts in Asian living standards, lifestyles, longevity and literacy as hundreds of millions of people are lifted out of extreme poverty and the Asian middle-classes begin to swell to western proportions. Asia's economies are no longer simply a supply source for western nations seeking cheap manufactured goods or low cost labour. Rather they themselves are becoming more economically self-reliant, supplying and trading with each other through regional and continental partnerships and relying less and less on foreign imports even in luxury goods. The Asian Tigers, most of which are state or family owned, now rival their western counterparts in size and profits. Asia now accounts for some 30% of global "superstar" firms and 210 of the world's 500 biggest companies by revenue now come from Asia (Fortune Global 500: 2018). They are led by China but India, Vietnam and even Bangladesh are in hot pursuit. The Asian Tigers are even challenging areas traditionally considered western preserves such as technology and finance as Asia goes fully "on-line" and explodes digitally with 2.2 billion of the world's internet users." China, Japan, South Korea and Singapore are now among the most digitally advanced nations in the world and Asia now accounts for nearly half of global investment attracting venture capital from right across the globe. Globalisation, therefore, seems to be undergoing a fundamental shift in the first half of the 21st century from being a globe-wide trade transaction driven by the West to being an East-West competition for economic supremacy driven by the governments of the East. Self-contained local, regional and continental trade partnerships seem to be replacing transnational trading as automation and AI increasingly replace the low costs of manufacturing in developing countries and as all companies seek to create supply chains that are shorter and more flexible to meet ever-changing consumer demand. Developing nations are starting to "leap-frog" advanced countries through the wholesale adoption of AI and smartphone technology and cashless economies are already appearing in China and India. How, in such a competitive and global economic environment, will Britain prosper after Brexit, alone and outside the European Union that once harboured it? (MGI podcast: June 2019)

W. Brian Arthur of McKinsey Associates (2017) has even argued that digital technologies seem to have created a second economy, a virtual and autonomous economy, that, through algorithms and various forms of artificial intelligence (AI), is creating a new form of intelligence, an automated intelligence, that is external to modern business rather than within it, and one that is increasingly threatening to make human intelligence obsolete. With the advent of 5G, the global economy is now capable of making more than enough for everyone, so the new economic paradigm, he argues, is not about mass production but global distribution, about who gets what and how. Modern computers and software are now capable of 'inter-association', of communicating amongst themselves, of using their sensors and processors to correlate and interrogate vast banks of data in milliseconds and make sense of patterns that human beings alone cannot even see. Moreover, they're increasingly able to communicate amongst themselves and to make decisions without human intervention. The implications of this shift from internal to external intelligence for the human race as a species are monumental. Autonomous intelligent systems are increasingly capable of taking over the organisation and running of vast swathes of the global economy, from transport and banking through to warfare and healthcare, and transforming them. Jobs may disappear as many fear or simply be transformed and relocated within the virtual economy. Jobs may even no longer be the way that humans earn their living; people may no longer need to work as they do today. Instead, the debate may be more about economic distribution than commercial production, more about the distribution of wealth than the creation of wealth; and that, by its very nature, is likely to be more a political debate than an economic one – a competition, Arthur predicts between free market forces of the American model of government compared to the collectivism and loose socialist style of the Scandinavian democracies.

But globalisation has its dark side and downside too. Globalisation has opened up huge new opportunities for cybercrime and terrorism. It has accelerated automation and so threatened future employment for all but the highly skilled and super-rich. This has stimulated the anti-globalisation movement and the surge in distrust of national governments, as reflected in the UK's Brexit vote and, latterly, Donald Trump's US election. There appears to be a deep-seated sense of being forgotten and of losing control of their own countries by voters across the Western world, as globalisation appears to have taken away their jobs and given them to countries abroad or immigrants at home. As David Goodhart (2017) has argued, Western societies seem increasingly to be dividing between the '*Anywheres*', who have enjoyed high levels of material success and mobility in today's open and liberal societies, and so are confident about the future and happy to think and live globally, and the '*Somewheres*', who feel threatened by globalisation and what it's done to their jobs, countries and their future prospects. The latter feel overwhelmed and powerless against the pace and impact of global change, and especially global migration, on themselves and their communities, and distrust the liberal elites in capital cities who have run their countries since 2008. They are, as a consequence, instinctively nationalist in outlook and highly sceptical of global change. Economists such as Stephen King go further and predict the end of globalisation (*Grave New World*: 2017), highlighting the rise in extremism, terrorism and the political and social horrors of mass migration from the poorest parts of the world to the richest, notably Europe, in search of any sort of life as a result of the immense polarisation of global wealth. Add to these global strains, dramatic climate change, ageing populations and the population explosion predicted for Africa, then by 2050 it will be difficult to see how any world order will remain. Certainly, the post-war structures of largely Western leadership are tottering and in a state of siege in trying to cope with, or block out, the new global forces banging on their door. There is a crisis of world leadership, and unless the West reasserts its moral as well as its political authority, the rising powers of Russia and the East will assert theirs, and in the process, chaos may reign over all of us.

The internet is clearly at the heart of globalisation in the 21st century, and in turn transforming world communication and generating revolutions of its own, revolutions of interconnectivity, virtual reality and cyberspace, previously unheard of and undreamt of. It's making possible revolutions in science and technology that will transform human life and both the way we live and how long we live. Artificial intelligence and the rise of the robot have the potential to transform working life and the world economy; biotechnology to transform our bodies and how long we live; algorithms to transform our financial world, and the power of the global corporations to know us better than we do ourselves, to predict our inner desires and control the way we live and what we buy. The **Internet of Things** (IoT) and the rise of **Big Data** represent a data-gathering revolution of immense proportions and unforeseeable consequences. It is the result of the proliferation of data-collecting devices and data services all round us, from GPS, CCTV and physical sensors in our cities and on our roads, through to the explosion in market intelligence about what we buy, what we want, what we think and how we behave. It's creating game-changing opportunities for businesses, big and small, to satisfy our every need, to fulfil our every whim – even before we know them – and transform not only modern manufacturing and retail but also impact on every other sector of society too. Our cities and our transport systems are being transformed as they seek to accommodate, service and mobilise ever-increasing numbers of people from across the world, and increasingly we live in what Marshall McLuhan, back in the 1960s, called the *'global village'*. Through social media such as Facebook, Twitter and Skype, personal relationships and communication are no longer confined by national boundaries, and even the most powerful of dictators can no longer totally exclude the outside world. Grandparents can now keep in contact with their children and grandchildren through Skype and Instagram rather than by letter or phone as in the past, while social media is transforming modern politics, giving a voice to 'the people' and, in the process, helping to bring down ruthless dictatorships in the Middle East, elevating populist politicians such as Donald Trump in the West, and fuelling terrorism and crime across the globe.

The internet is helping to create a global world at a speed and level of interconnectivity never before imagined, and these tidal waves of global connectivity – their volume and their speed – are transforming the developing world as fast as the developed. However, the internet has its dark side too, its Wild West frontier, lawless and out of the control of politicians and security forces, one that Yuval Harari (2015) described as: "*a free and lawless zone that erodes state sovereignty, ignores borders, abolishes privacy and poses perhaps the most formidable global security risk.*" A cyber 9/11 is now a real possibility, as national power grids are hacked and the theft of billions from online accounts or personal identities from corporate data banks are now daily possibilities. Just think how close, and how often, the threat of your credit card being hacked, your airport being put on terrorist alert and even your very identity being stolen now occurs. Big data – your personal details and preferences – is being harvested by every company you now deal with, and sold on to others in the open market, while GPS and CCTV mean that every move you make can be monitored and tracked. 'Big Brother' is alive and very well in the world of the 21st century, with Google and Facebook watching our every move – and predicting the next one, too – while Amazon has even managed to install Alexa in millions of homes, not just as a voice box but as a 'family friend', with Siri, and Google's Home Mini, now on their way too. Data protection is becoming a hope rather than a reality, and fake news seems to have taken over objective debate, with terrorist and foreign security organisations using social media to distort political elections and brainwash young minds. Google and Facebook have a virtual monopoly on digital advertising and so increasingly influence the quality of public debate. 'Big lies' are now much easier to communicate than big truths, and big government seems increasingly unable to control the activities of the new tech giants (Foer: 2018), while the social and psychological repercussions of their activities on human communication and social relationships is only just beginning to emerge. Hackers, meanwhile, are having a field day, and even such technological fortresses as Sony, Yahoo and the National Lottery have proved vulnerable to internet infiltration. Ninety per cent of personal accounts are apparently at risk, and even the security agencies themselves aren't safe from cyber terrorists operating individually, for crime families, terrorist organisations or even for national governments such as Russia and China, as claimed in the recent US elections. Meanwhile, a global power struggle is developing between the American giants of GAFA – Google, Apple, Facebook and Amazon – and their Chinese equivalents, the BATs as some commentators have called them – Baidu, the Chinese search engine, Alibaba, the Chinese marketplace, and Tencent, the Chinese Facebook – competing for the teeming Asian markets ahead.

Urbanisation, meanwhile, is reshaping the 'geography of the world', sweeping away traditional ways of life and instigating a tidal shift of human populations from the country to the city in numbers and at a pace never seen before in developing countries. It is creating megacities, the size of which the world has never seen before and the power of which is outstripping nation states as these supercities become the nerve centres of a global economy that is fast beyond the control of national or even international government. In ten years time, some of the new urban centres, the new megacities of ten million or more people, will be rivalling whole countries, economically and demographically, creating a seismic shift in the world's economic and political landscape. The supercities, the megacities of the developing world, are mushrooming, outstripping the major cities of the West, be they Paris, Berlin or even New York, and in the process shrinking the world as we know it as they increasingly come to control "*nearly half of global GDP growth*". (McKinsey: 2015) However, even they are now being slowly affected by ageing, as the old in both the East and the West start to move in from the countryside and turn their 'bright lights' silver and slow their economic growth rates down to single figures by 2035 according to the MGI Report, *Urban World* (2016).

The global world of the 21ˢᵗ century, therefore, offers both immense opportunity and equally immense uncertainty. The world is becoming a much smaller, much more integrated place, economically and socially; but it's equally becoming a very **disrupted** place, disrupted by the forces above operating at phenomenal speeds: "*10 times the speed and 300 times the impact of the Industrial Revolution*" (McKinsey: 2015). These forces, however, are not operating in harmony, nor are they under anyone's control as part of some grand plan – human or heavenly. These are potentially the 'four forces of the 21ˢᵗ century's apocalypse'. They are transforming life as we know it and creating a radically different world in the century ahead. As the 2008 economic crisis showed, globalisation now has the potential for '**cascading catastrophes**' through 'error or terror' so that what happens in one part of the globe has equally profound effects across the rest of the planet. Hence the fears that globalisation is outstripping itself, outstripping the globe's sustainability and threatening the survival of the planet. Hence the fear about **inequality** and its global backlash. As Pope Francis suggested in his 2015 Lent sermon, the world seems to have developed 'global indifference' to the suffering of millions, if not billions, across the world as they are projected daily on our television screens, be they in Syria and Aleppo or on the shores of the Mediterranean attempting to escape war and poverty. Globalisation, and the worldwide inequality that it is creating, seems to be stimulating the rise of anti-immigrant and anti-globalisation political movements and fuelling recruitment to global terrorism in reaction to the sense of powerlessness, alienation and loss of local and national culture and control that many feel today. We seem to have lost faith in our traditional institutions, our political elites and even in capitalism itself, and its promise to enrich the material lives of all of us, not just the few. So, do we now need a new form of globalisation, a 'smart globalisation', based on new values, sustainable values, that encapsulate inclusion, equity and human rights and new forms of governance that are more genuinely democratic and representative of people themselves, not just the international and national political elites currently in power? Certainly, given the size and potential impact of the dark side of new technology, with even the NHS and Parliament vulnerable to hacking blackmail from cyber criminals or rogue states, there needs to be, argues the MGI, a new societal deal whereby international co-operation supersedes national rivalry in the face of a common foe.

'And what part will **ageing** play in this global, or rather Google, battle of power?' asked Polly of her academic researchers. Will demography be a 'drag' on global growth, or will it actually accelerate growth by creating whole new markets, new 'silver' markets devoted to or inspired by the explosion of older people around the world. *"The developed retiring and elderly will be extraordinarily important to global consumption from 2015 to 2030,"* argued the McKinsey Report on Urbanisation and Global Consumers in 2016, generating, it predicted, some £4.4 trillion and accounting for nearly 60% of consumption growth in Western Europe and North East Asia alone. Such growth would be a sea shift in the global economy and its future direction, but it can only come about if ageing operates in partnership with new technology to offset the catastrophic falls in the dependency ratios predicted for 2030 and beyond – the very strategy that Japan has already adopted in its race to revive its stagnant economy and liberate its ageing people from dependency and isolation.

Finally, this demographic revolution has created a post-war generation – the baby boomers – who have become notorious for their capacity to question and challenge the Establishment, demand personal freedom and create new lifestyles. They arrived as a 'baby boom' after World War II and have impacted on the Western world ever since. In the 1960s they generated a new age of social and political radicalism and created a new and dynamic age of youth culture, mass media and consumerism. And now they're set to descend on old age with the same force and impact that they have generated throughout their lives. Bands like the Rolling Stones are still performing to packed stadiums in their 70s, Glenda Jackson is still performing Shakespeare in her 80s, and David Attenborough is still exploring the planet in his 90s. The hippies of the 1960s are ageing but they are far from ancient and being out to pasture. Active they may be – even hyperactive – but, asked Polly, has this extraordinary generation the power and potential to now lead the age revolution ahead, to check and challenge the global forces above and in the process shape them to their own ambitious demands for an active, engaging and fulfilling later life and an intergenerational legacy to remember?

So, that was Polly's tour of ageing Britain and our greying globe. She now had not only a detailed grasp of the shifting demographics of the UK but also an appreciation of ageing as a global force, transforming our universe, our very way of life and even the balance of world power, all at sonic speed.

Ageing should be at the forefront of every government policy and every party manifesto, but it isn't. Rather, all that most governments to date have done is shift the age goalposts a little by raising the state age of retirement and pouring a few more billion into the NHS and social care. Such piecemeal reaction is clearly no substitute for the long-term planning that is so urgently needed. With planning, Polly now believed, Britain could be entering a new silver dawn of health and longevity. Without planning, Britain is about to sleepwalk into a grey nightmare that will overwhelm our welfare state, suffocate and fragment family life and turn generation against generation in a battle over who gets what, when and how. The choice is ours, concluded Polly, but only if we're aware of it, prepared to grasp it and, like her, determined to act on it. She now saw Great Britain in a very different light, a silver-grey light, depending on which way the sun was shining. She now saw an urgent and critical social, economic and political need, one that represented everything she'd gone into politics for – and one that every one of us is fast approaching. So, while Polly digs deeper into ageing Britain in the next few chapters:

- **How** do you see later life in the UK, and what do you see it offering you?
- **How** long do you expect to live, and how do you expect to live it?
- **Try** using the life-expectancy calculators offered by the ONS, Aviva or Confused.com, and then, like my wife and I, reflect on the life left ahead!

2 | The Retirement Revolution and Our Preparedness for It

Angela worked as a legal secretary for over 20 years. She loved the work, the camaraderie and the sense of fulfilment it brought to her life. Suddenly, however, at aged 61, things changed; and after six weeks off work through stress and ill health as a result of recent redundancies and a doubling of her workload, she finally and reluctantly decided to hand in her notice. She anticipated a happier and more peaceful stage in her life, with more time to spend with her grandchildren, but was shocked to find how much she missed work, the routine and the friendships. She felt miserable and alone, almost a sense of bereavement, at the loss of her old life, and she was left with a sense almost of resentment at having been forced to make such a life-changing decision: 'a permanent feeling of being kicked in the stomach'. John, her brother, on the other hand, revelled in the freedoms of retirement and the opportunity to indulge his passions for golf and trainspotting that lay before him after a working life spent down dark coalmines in Derbyshire and latterly 'dancing to the dictates' of a steel owner in Mumbai. He and his wife Beryl couldn't wait to retire, to spend more time with the grandchildren and tour Britain in their modest motorhome.

Angela is now Polly's office manager – not a big office, not a big job, but more than enough to rejuvenate Angela, restore her sense of self-esteem and purpose; and as a result, she met Simon, remarried and, like her brother John, began travelling and joining local community groups. Suddenly life at 62 years of age has been transformed. Angela is now a new woman, able to look forward to an active later life and a much healthier one, free of the misery and depression that had gone before. Angela's story is for Polly a stark and very personal reminder of the challenges of retirement today and how, while many older people like Angela's brother John relish the freedoms and opportunities of retirement today, others perceive it with dread and apprehension once the certainties and routines of working life fall away. Angela had been lucky; many others of her age had been left behind, alone, and some of them ended up in Polly's Saturday surgery because they had no one else to help them.

Increasingly, as she read the literature and looked around her, Polly came to the conclusion that the traditional model of retirement – the 20th-century model of retirement – was outdated, if not *dead*. In an age of ageing, it no longer accurately described the fundamental changes taking place in the lives of a new generation of retirees. In fact, it didn't even accurately describe Polly's own retirement from a career in teaching and into one in politics. It certainly didn't describe the numbers of 65-year-olds today set out in Chapter 1. Retirees today are far more numerous and living far longer than previous generations of OAPs. According to the ILC-UK report, *When I'm 64* (2017), the numbers of retirees aged 55–69 has increased rapidly, from 8.4 million back in 1995 to 11 million in 2015, and rising to 13 million by 2050, all with an average life expectancy at 65 of 18.5 years for men and an inspiring 21 years for women.

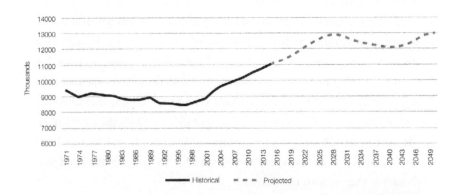

Figure 1a: **Population aged 55-69**
(ILC-UK: 2017)

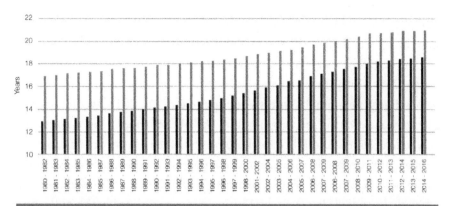

Figure 1b: **Life expectancy at age 65 in UK**
(ILC-UK: 2017)

The traditional model of retirement has increasingly outlived its usefulness, both as a description of modern retirement and as an economic or social framework for government policy. It cannot cope with mass retirement; it cannot cope with the 'retirement boom' of one of the largest generations in British history as some 600,000 baby boomers queue up each year over the next 20 years to leave work and join the ranks of the retired – some 17–20 million pensioners aged 60 to 100 years plus by 2037. The British economy cannot cope with his haemorrhage of manpower, or the escalating costs of pensions, housing and healthcare on this scale solely from public taxation. Nor apparently can the British public cope. As global surveys like those by HSBC in 2013 and Aegon in 2018 have shown, the British in particular, seem ill-prepared for the long-term financial challenge ahead. Only 14% of the UK population at large is regularly putting more into their pensions (Aviva: 2017), and women in particular appear to be even less well prepared for retirement than men, as low wages, part-time work and divorce have severely reduced their lifetime earnings. Female pension pots are on average around £25,000 – a third of men's – and women's pension savings average about £120 per month – half that of mens'. British women are not only the 'poor relations' in retirement compared to men, they are even well behind their counterparts in Europe and the rest of the Western world in terms of both pensions and their length of retirement. While British women today can expect 22.1 years in retirement, their French, Italian and even Australian counterparts can expect much longer – over five years longer.

Even the British pension system apparently cannot cope. Laudable though 'auto enrolment' is proving to be, in encouraging young people to save for the future, it is not enough for a decent pension later this century. Without significantly higher levels of savings in pensions, the Royal London Insurance

Report in 2017 concluded that young people today are likely to still be working into their 70s and 80s. "*We may be witnessing the death of retirement as we know it*", and certainly, a new model, a new way of retiring, is urgently needed, fit for the 21st century, fit for a new, much healthier, much wealthier, much more demanding generation of retirees – young and old. The 2018 Aegon Longevity Report went even further, arguing that the old retirement social contract is "*crumbling*" as responsibility for funding retirement shifts dramatically and permanently from governments and employers to individuals and families. Retirement at 65 is no longer financially viable for many workers, and yet relatively few people in any of the 15 countries surveyed had health or financial plans sufficiently robust to cope with the daunting challenges of the longer retirements ahead. "*It is no exaggeration to say that how we prepare for older age is one of the great challenges of the 21st century.*"

Finally, modern British retirees are nothing like their predecessors in attitude or experience. They are part of the 'freetirement' generation identified by the SIRC/Friends Provident study back in 2007. They are increasingly members of the post-war baby boomer generation, a generation that shocked post-war society in its youth, and 50 years later is now likely to shake up the world of old age. British boomer retirees are healthier, wealthier and growing in number every year into a new age army that will soon constitute more than a quarter of the British population. Moreover, if the past is anything to go by, baby boomers are a generation of retirees with the attitude and ambition to change everything around them. They will demand as active and lively a later life as they had as teenagers. They will change the traditional model of retirement in Britain and create a new one that is active and independent, free from anyone's control and dependent on no one; a model that fits the image and lifestyle of a generation that once declared that it would *never get old* – or at least would die before it did. If these youthful retirees, these 'swinging' 60-year-olds, do to the 2020s what they did to the 1960s, then not only is retirement in Britain going to change completely but Britain itself is in for another age shock, as profound as that in the post-war era and as likely to change the whole way we look at life and look at the old. They are likely to bring the 'rock and roll' of their teenage years to the ambitions they now have for later life: to live later life to the full, to start new careers, to travel the world and even – as many a hippy hoped 50 years ago – to change the world around them, though perhaps this time for their children and grandchildren more than for themselves.

So, while baby boomers have often been portrayed as the most selfish and self-centred of post-war generations, with relatively affluent lifestyles that contrast starkly with the sacrifices and frugality of the Silent Generation before them and the struggles of today's younger 'generation lost', baby boomer retirees do not live in isolation. They are not totally free to fly off to pastures new. They still have families who, although grown up, continue to need support; and they also have new generations of grandchildren emerging out of the multigenerational family that is the 21st century. In fact, instead of there being an 'age of greed', there appears to be an 'age of generosity' as the over-55s not only help out their 'boomerang children' with student debt and housing assistance but equally support, in some way or other, their own ageing parents with care costs and everyday living. This 'generational sandwich' is forcing some older couples to either delay retirement or retire early to care for family members. They've become what Merrill Lynch, the American accountancy firm, in 2013, called *"the meat in the family's sandwich, the banker of last resort and the childcare champion"* all rolled into one, an aspect of retirement planning that few retirees took into account when planning their future.

So, as Polly herself has experienced, a new 'retirement journey' is emerging, a much longer journey, with substantial economic implications and many more personal challenges than could be foreseen earlier. With retirement today now extending for some 20 years or more, patterns of expenditure and consumption amongst the retired now tend to shift from relatively high levels in the early years of retirement, when retirees are younger and healthier, to low levels of consumption and a rise in savings amongst those in their 70s and 80s. This is the time when ill health and care costs begin to kick in, personal consumption of goods and services becomes more modest, and any attempt or desire to leave bequests for children and grandchildren becomes a significant consideration. Such step-change shifts in spending and saving have significant implications, not only for retirees and their own financial security but for government expenditure on this age group and for the wider economy. For example, some £48.7 billion, according to the ILC-UK (2015), is stashed away in low-interest savings accounts that produce little real income for retirees and yet represent significant amounts of capital that could be much better invested in the national or local economy. This is a huge sum, equivalent to 2.8% of the UK's GDP, and it became clear to Polly that unlocking this resource and putting it to effective productive use for the benefit of both older people and their future incomes, and for economic investment in the young and society at large, would be an immense boost for any national economic strategy. It is equally a significant market opportunity – or even a national responsibility – for the financial sector in devising and developing savings and investment products that provide retirees with better returns in early retirement when their expenditure is high and yet secure and sustainable income in the years thereafter when personal spending decreases, but the costs of support and care begin to hit home. A new form of flexible but secure annuity, that is much more cost effective and trustworthy than the old model, may well be one approach; investment in new housing for young and old alike, another. The 'silver economy', in terms of both consumption and saving, offers a treasure trove of opportunities for new businesses and new investments, many of which could dramatically reduce dependency on the state and the family in the years ahead. Such expanding financial opportunities, however, come with risks and, as the Financial Conduct Authority (FCA) Report in 2018 confirmed for Polly, there has never been a greater need for tighter and stronger financial controls and for fuller and more impartial financial advice if this age group is to enjoy the economic benefits of the 'silver economy' and not be faced by yet another round of financial mis-selling, scams and fraud as in the past.

Retirees at the moment are enjoying a 'golden era', even a retirement boom according to the Institute for Fiscal Studies (IFS). Its 2016 Report paints a broadly optimistic picture of retirement in the UK in the near future. It predicts that over the next five to ten years, mortality rates will continue to improve, notably for those over the age of 85; pensioner incomes for those aged 65–74 years will continue to grow; and absolute poverty is projected to fall dramatically, from 20.1% in 2014/15 to 12.7% by 2022/23. These predictions must represent two of the 'great gifts' of the demographic dividend, not only for older couples themselves and the care and companionship they can continue to enjoy in later life, but for society and families at large, in potentially reducing the burden of dependency on them from the old of tomorrow. They are beginning to live the new model of retirement, a more 'ageless' and flexible transition based increasingly on personal choice and circumstance, health and aspirations, rather than the regimented model of the past. They now have the possibility of a 'third age', a 'third stage', even a 'second life'. They now have the opportunity to embark on a new 'silver' career and a new lifestyle far beyond the gold watch and 'grey door' facing retirees in the past.

However, this new stage, this new 'silver door' is not always the 'cradle to cruise' portrayed so attractively in many adverts today. Rather, it is one that is as fraught with the challenges and the uncertainties of life as before retirement. Twenty to thirty years of retirement is a lifetime in itself and has to be managed as such. Dependency on the state or on the family is no longer an option. Living independently and actively has to be the future. As became increasingly clear to Polly and her fellow MPs on the Parliamentary Pensions Working Party (PPWP), as the number of retirees escalates, the costs spiral and the lack of preparedness of the average British retiree becomes increasingly evident, and the national 'car-crash of the future' that many retirement surveys in the UK have long predicted may well come true. Many retirees are ill-equipped to plan ahead for every eventuality – social, psychological and familial, as well as financial – for the 20 to 30 years ahead. They are unlikely to be retiring on their own, as both spouses now live longer; and they are likely to be joined by their elderly parents, as well as the demands and needs of their own children and grandchildren. Retirement in the 21st century is unlikely to be a walk in the park, and the 'care club sandwich' is likely to create stress and sacrifice as well as pleasure and companionship, particularly for the less well-off and their families. While the coalition government of 2010–2015 *liberated* older people's pensions, it did not liberate their later life, or incentivise better later-life saving or planning. The fact that 52% of UK respondents to an HSBC retirement survey as recently as 2017 claimed to have no form of retirement plan for themselves and their families, even 'in their heads', was for Polly one of the most frightening features of all the many reports she read. It became increasingly obvious to her that in the UK we are sleepwalking into a retirement future that might well be heaven for the better-off but hell for the less well-endowed. While life-course management and age planning are apparently 'spreading like wildfire' in Germany and other parts of Europe, the notion of planning for life, even later life, has yet to take off in the UK. Hence the UK's embarrassingly low position of 18th in the international **Global Retirement Index** below, behind countries such as Ireland and even the USA.

Retirement Indices

Country	Health	Finances	Quality of life	Material Well-being	GRI Score
1. Norway	89%	73%	92%	91%	86%
2. Switzerland	87%	77%	92%	81%	84%
3. Iceland	84%	70%	88%	88%	82%
14. Ireland	82%	71%	83%	64%	74%
17. United States	87%	71%	78%	57%	72%
18. UK	**83%**	**58%**	**81%**	**68%**	**72%**
22. Japan	88%	56%	65%	74%	70%

Figure 2: **Adapted from Global Retirement Index (2017)**
(Source: Natixis Investment Managers.)

So, for the PPWP, and for Polly as a national politician in search of a post-Brexit vision, retirement in an ageing UK offers a real and critical political issue with which to confront and rally her new constituents, generate a national debate and frame the beginnings of a new campaign for the elections ahead. Polly's simple question to many of her constituents, *"What's your plan for retirement and how well have you costed it?"* was already provoking an outpouring of need and an upsurge in demand for the sort of help and guidance outlined below. Polly now had the possible touch paper she was looking for to ignite a national debate on retirement; one that might not only generate great fear but equally inspire real hope about retiring in 21st-century Britain; one that might reflect the new social contract for retirement in the 21st century called for by the 2018 Aegon Longevity Report; a contract based on *"the principles of sustainability and solidarity, while providing adequate safety nets that enable people to age with dignity, avoid poverty in old age, and ensure that vulnerable people are not left behind."* The Aegon Report argued that retirement income needed to be raised significantly to some 68% of pre-retirement income through such sources as automatic pension saving schemes and guaranteed lifetime income products, that there needed to be far greater financial literacy and planning that started in school, more accessible and affordable healthcare and a much more positive attitude to ageing in a more age-friendly world generally. High ambitions indeed but increasingly, in Polly's view, essential components of any retirement contract or manifesto for the ageing Britain ahead.

Lord Wei's idea, back in 2013, of a **national retirement service**, a one-stop state-sponsored shop to help all retirees retire 'gracefully' and be properly prepared for the journey ahead, therefore increasingly appealed to the PPWP. It seemed to offer a more comprehensive model and a better balance between the role of the state and the responsibilities of the individual in planning and financing the much longer, more active and challenging later life that now lies ahead. Such an agency, however, would need a much broader brief, a much higher public profile, and far greater resources and expertise than the government retirement services currently offer.

So, what is your retirement plan for later life? Do you and your partner have such a plan? If so, is it on paper or is it just some vague thoughts, some lifetime ambitions, aspirations or dreams yet to be prioritised or costed? Do you have even the vaguest of plans for financing some 20 to 30 years of retirement and the potentially very heavy health costs involved, let alone the potential demands for help from your ageing parents or struggling children? Or like so many retirees today, are you simply hoping that the state pension and NHS will suffice? If so, look below and maybe think again.

What are your retirement priorities?	What is your retirement financial plan?
• Friends	Total Income after tax - £
• Family/grandchildren	Total Expenditure including:
• Partner	Household bills
• New hobby	Travel
• New career/business	Leisure
• New skill	Pets
• Learn a new language/musical instrument	Healthcare
• Travel	Family/grandchildren
• Voluntary work	Contingencies.
• Exercise/sport	Total savings/investments including:
• Reading/theatre/concerts	Healthcare
	Family care
	Death care.

Figure 3: **Retirement, planning ahead**

Do you have a personal/household later-life financial plan based on the following?

- Anticipated remaining life span of 20–25 years
- Anticipated annual income & expenditure
- Anticipated ambitions/later-life adventures or investments
- Unanticipated happenings, incl. death/long-term illness of self or partner

Is it time to make a later-life plan before it's too late?

3 | Modern Work and the Multigenerational Workforce

At aged 62, Charles has just retired from the banking industry after a successful career as a senior manager. He had the good fortune to have successfully weathered the 2008 financial crisis through some shrewd investments – and more than a little luck. Many of his colleagues weren't so fortunate; they'd lost their jobs, their savings and even, in one case, their house. Charles now plans to set up his own financial consultancy in partnership with his daughter-in-law, Emily, an accountancy graduate, so that he can work part-time, spend more time with his family and grandchildren in both the UK and abroad, and travel as far and wide as he did in his gap year after university, while he and his wife Geraldine are still fit and healthy.

Charles thoroughly enjoyed his early career in banking as an old-style branch manager but the constant reorganisations since, the unrelenting pressures to make profit rather than satisfy customers, the never-ending shift to new IT systems, and the new generation of young managers obsessed more with their iPhones and instant promotion than their customers have left him feeling exhausted and disillusioned with an industry he once loved and felt proud to serve. For him the 'soul' had gone out of British banking, the algorithms had taken over, and head office was now in Hong Kong and Mumbai rather than in his hometown of Norwich. Working for himself will, he believes, restore his faith in his own abilities, revive his job satisfaction and dramatically improve his work-life balance as full retirement looms and his wife, too, starts thinking about giving up work. If, however, the opportunity to return to work on a flexible or consultancy basis arose, he would consider it seriously, as he still misses the teamwork and intellectual challenge of professional work.

Charles was Polly's independent financial adviser (IFA). He handled Polly's personal finances and provided the sort of personalised retirement planning proposed in the previous chapter. In discussion on Polly's age manifesto, Charles offered to provide her with a brief resume of the state of the British economy, with a particular focus on the world of work today and tomorrow, an offer Polly readily accepted, particularly as Charles himself was a classic example of the half a million baby boomers each year who would soon be retiring en masse and in shifts. Such senior managers and 'silver workers' will be taking with them 40 years or more of professional skill and expertise and a wealth of talent and expertise that will not only drain British industry but double the UK's dependency ratio; a 'silver brain drain' of substantial size and unprecedented speed, at the same time as the numbers of people of traditional working age (15–64) is expected to fall, or at best stagnate, in the years ahead. The impact on the UK economy, as its old-age dependency ratio (OADR) halves from just under four workers per dependent to nearly two over the next 20 years will be stark and dramatic, as illustrated in Figure 1 below, creating an unsustainable drain on the British economy and a recruitment crisis for British industry.

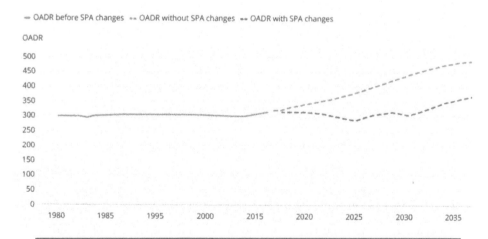

Figure 1: **UK Old Age Dependency Ratio: 1980-2039**
(ONS: 2018)

And if the UK's working population seems to be shrinking at a rate of knots as a result of its rising dependency ratio, other leading economies seem to be about to go into freefall as the old-age support ratio across the Organisation for Economic Co-operation and Development (OECD) is predicted to halve by 2050, as illustrated below.

1. Japan: 1.3	6. Austria: 1.9
2. Portugal: 1.4	7. Finland: 2.0
3. Germany: 1.5	8. Belgium: 2.0
4. Italy: 1.5	9. France: 2.0
5. Greece: 1.5	10. Estonia: 2.1
OECD Average: 2.1	**UK**: 2.3

Figure 2: **Top Ten Old-Age Support Ratios** within the OECD projected for 2050
(Adapted from OECD: 2014)

Numerous reports, notably that by the UK Commission for Employment and Skills (UKCES) in 2014, have highlighted the dramatic and potentially disruptive changes facing the UK economy in the years ahead, changes that range from the upsurge in the employment of women and the advent and impact of big data, through to the global nature of company structures and decision-making, the speed, scale and impact of new technologies, and the quantum leaps on the horizon in areas such as biotechnology and robotics. The aftermath of 2008 is still very evident, and consumers are still very cautious as the world economy stutters towards recovery, and as global competition for scarce resources not only becomes more intense but is part of a dramatic shift from the all-powerful G7 economies of the West over to the 'Asian tigers' and the emerging powerhouses of China, India and the Far East. Add Brexit and the UK's poor record on productivity to this maelstrom and very few economic commentators would feel confident of predicting the future of the British economy now or even ten years hence. As the Oxford Economics report on the UK's economic outlook concluded in February 2017: *"the degree of uncertainty surrounding economic forecasts is virtually without precedent,"* with sterling down and the GDP slowing to around 1.5% per year or lower. The UK's current ranking in the Global Competitiveness Index of 8th, after Switzerland and Sweden, is likely to fall even further after Brexit, predicted the World Economic Forum (WEF) in 2018; and the key to future prosperity for the UK, according to the IMF, is a real and sustained upturn in productivity, an area of economic growth where the UK lags sadly behind the leading economies in Europe.

As Charles's report illustrated, the world is on an economic rollercoaster, with the UK about to plunge up or down in the turmoil and aftermath of Brexit. Globalisation continues relentlessly across the developed and developing worlds but now faces the challenge of 'America First' under President Trump. China continues to surge forward as a leading global force in such fields as robotics and AI with its own tech giants, Baidu, Alibaba and Tencent, rivalling America's Google, Amazon and Facebook, while its Silk Road strategy seeks to open up trade routes right across Asia and Europe. Digitalisation and new technologies, meanwhile, are creating whole new industries and a whole new economic order, one that Professor Klaus Schwab (2016) has dubbed the Fourth Industrial Revolution, so great and profound is the level of economic change involved. An era of increasing complexity, and potentially one of continuous disruption or even economic chaos, is fast emerging, with no one apparently in control. Neither Charles nor his colleagues would feel at home in this new world order, as the impersonal forces of globalisation and new technologies take over, 'shrink' the economic world and leave the workplace of the future under the control of smart machines, algorithms, technological specialists and a management elite living far away in a super-city – or on another planet. Trials are being held to monitor every moment of every employee's working day, to maximise their efficiency, teamwork and all aspects of the way in which they deal with customers, while robots are planning to take over the world of manual work altogether. According to Dr Carl Frey at Oxford University (2017), robots are not only replacing workers in low-skilled repetitive jobs but even quite complex ones, such as insurance underwriting and motor insurance assessing. Even judges, commercial pilots and detectives aren't safe from AI, and the unimaginable is now becoming reality with the advent of driverless vehicles in the taxi and haulage industries, robo-doctors and nurses in hospitals, and Actroids in hotel receptions. No job today seems to be the safe and secure career it once was, and so it's now possible to imagine robo-pilots flying planes and robo-journalists announcing the news. Imagine, too, football managers arguing with a robo-ref, and barristers with a robo-judge, and the level of potential transformation becomes all the more apparent.

According to numerous reports by the MGI in 2017 and 2018, automation – including AI and robotics – has the potential to impact on at least 60% of current occupations and, in the process, transform the modern workplace, generating a shift in the skills required of human workers, from physical and basic skills towards higher cognitive, emotional and social skills. While basic digital skills will become essential for any worker tomorrow, empathy, enterprise, creativity and decision-making will become even more highly prized as routine or manual tasks are replaced by artificial intelligence and robots. Algorithms are already well embedded within our data processing and routine decision-making activities and soon augmentation will sweep through our business routines too, leading towards autonomous automation, towards machines making decisions outside human control. The AI revolution is no longer in its infancy but *"most of its economic impact is yet to come."* AI, ranging from computer vision and natural language through to virtual assistants, robotic automation and advanced machine learning has, according to MGI (2018), the potential to deliver additional economic activity of around $13 trillion to the global economy. It may equally reinforce the 'digital divide' between early and late adopters of AI, and exacerbate world inequality and conflict even more, as countries such as China seek world supremacy and poorer countries get left behind in a 'digital darkness'. Equally, though, new technology has the potential to create new jobs, even whole new industries, as well as destroy or disrupt those that exist today. It is the transition from old industries to new, the disruption to workers and to communities, and the social and cultural transformations that are, in many ways, the real challenges ahead. As dramatic disruption and accelerating technological change becomes the norm and begins to reshape society, increase inequality and outstrip people's capacity to cope, so then the current challenges to democratic political systems are likely to accelerate at the same time as politicians' capacities to assert control are dwindling.

So, as Charles's report amply illustrated, the modern workplace is not only being revolutionised by machines and new technology, it is also undergoing a generational revolution as a result of longevity. A new multigenerational workforce, a new 'spectrum of ages' spanning some four, possibly even five, generations, is emerging, with each generation having its own very different way of communicating and working. As studies like Meister & Willyerds' back in 2009 showed, whereas the baby boomer generation tended to have a highly work-centric, highly focused and even workaholic attitude to their jobs and careers, Generation X apparently has a much more relaxed approach to working life, and a work ethic that places a high premium on family time and a strong sensitivity to work-life balance. Millennials dislike rigid work requirements, they expect flexibility in work schedules, and they have an entrepreneurial spirit in their approach to work. They value freedom and autonomy, and they often prefer to work alone, even at home rather than necessarily in groups or teams. They are much happier using the internet or social media for group discussions and they detest formal meetings, especially 'meetings about meetings'. Generation Y, now in their 20s and 30s, in contrast, is apparently, the 'smart generation' – creative, optimistic and highly achievement-orientated – keen to search out creative challenges and eager for personal growth and meaningful careers. They are tech-savvy, excellent multitaskers and much prefer online communication to face-to-face interaction. As Charles rightly reflected, managing such a multigenerational workforce in the future, spanning some four, even five, generations with a 'time warp' in attitudes to technology and management style, will be a mammoth task in itself. The potential for intergenerational tension and conflict will be as great as the potential for intergenerational collaboration, and the idea of an 'age war' within the future workplace could become a serious possibility!

Even more worrying, though, is the potential for a 'silver brain-drain', or what the consultants Odgers Berndtson (2017) called a *"Talentocalpse"*, as the baby boomer generation – Charles's generation – retires in droves at the very time that the younger population is stagnating or even falling. *"Retiring workers will need to be replaced at an unprecedented rate, yet there will be fewer young people available to meet demand in an already over-heated market."* The 2018 Mercer Report went further and predicted that by 2025, UK business will face a workforce crisis of severe proportions as Britain ages and the overall population grows but the labour force shrinks proportionately as older workers retire. Between 2016 and 2020, the population of those aged 50 to 65 approaching retirement in the UK is expected to leap from 10.1 million to 13.8 million, according to the ONS. During the same period, those aged 16 to 49 years are likely to drop by 700,000 (*Raconteur* magazine: Jan. 2018), particularly among senior management and those sectors such as medicine and engineering where baby boomers are pre eminent but where few employers seem to have drawn up substantial contingency plans for what might become yet another '*demographic time bomb*'. As a result, a **global talent war** might soon erupt, as companies search the globe for the leaders of tomorrow's generations, new types of leaders with high levels of emotional intelligence, interpersonal skills and flexibility, to create the collaborative workforce of the future. The opportunities for the young, ambitious and talented who are prepared to travel and relocate are immense, with women and ethnic minorities potentially the great beneficiaries of this 'talent tournament', and the new styles of national and global management needed to manage the workforces and the businesses of the future. But this search for global talent will not be one-way. The new wave of emerging nations, such as Bangladesh, Egypt, Indonesia, Iran, Mexico, Nigeria, Pakistan, Philippines, Turkey, South Korea and Vietnam, as well as the BRIC countries of Brazil, Russia, India and China, are equally keen to propel their economies into the global arena too. They will be as determined and ruthless in their search for the very best talent that they can find, be it at home or abroad, and so Western nations like the UK may well soon experience '*a wave of reverse migration*' as young talent from the EU, Commonwealth countries or Far East returns home to better job opportunities and increasingly better salaries. This global and gender, 'talent race', however, is equally likely to lead to the emergence of multinational leadership teams, teams drawn from across the globe, living in global cities like London and New York, enjoying lifestyles and living in accommodation distinct from – and separate from – the population at large and in service to the emerging global elite of entrepreneurs and corporate owners rather than to their countries of origin. Charles may even have to work hard to retain Emily, his business partner, as she grows more experienced and ambitious and is attracted by the bright lights of New York, Hong Kong or Singapore. Whatever the outcome, the need for companies to prepare for this dramatic and 'intergenerational transition' is becoming increasingly urgent. More forward-thinking companies are encouraging senior executives about to retire to step back from the business front-line during the final years of their careers and focus instead on mentoring and transferring knowledge to up-and-coming younger executives; a step that Charles might well have embraced had it been offered, particularly as many of the new and emerging industries may well be serving his generation and the 'silver streak' that is rapidly becoming a feature of the world economy; a new silver economy that is predicted to grow in the UK alone from £79 billion to £227 billion, catering for a new older consumer – the baby boomer!

Polly was particularly attracted to the section in Charles's report on government attempts to keep pace with this new age of work. Most governments are now raising the statutory pension age and encouraging much higher levels of labour force participation, particularly from women, as a means of improving productivity. More progressive governments, notably those in Scandinavia, have gone further, developing incentive schemes and workplace environments to enable and encourage later-life working. Finland and Norway, for example, are leading the way in developing part-time pension schemes to encourage 'pensioner working'. The longer-term solution, however, may be in encouraging and supporting silver enterprise so that Charles and his counterparts do not have to retreat from the national economy altogether but have the opportunity to use their business acumen and expertise to serve the emerging silver economy. 'Silver strivers' have doubled in the last 18 years to 1.3 million and, although most of these older workers are in professional and white-collar jobs, blue-collar employment has grown too. The WEF (2018) even cited statistics to show that, overall, older entrepreneurs are generally more successful and last longer than younger counterparts who lack their same level of experience and business contacts, while companies such as Standard Life (2009) have highlighted the emergence of a *"silver enterprise"* revolution. According to the ONS, 40% of those aged 65 and over who are still working are self-employed, and 43% of all self-employed people are over 50. Moreover, the 'British Branson' is not just an older male phenomenon; older women are apparently joining in too, with 80% of the rise in self-employed people between 2008 and 2011 being women (*The Sunday Times* Feb. 2014). The rise of the 'silver entrepreneur', however, is not only a reflection of the later-life ambition of older people to run their own business but also an opportunity for senior managers with extensive business experience to follow in Charles and Emily's footsteps and create a new form of 'family business' – a multigenerational enterprise run by the younger generations and supported by a new form of business investment. The Bank of Mum and Dad, or even Grandad and Grandma, often provides the start-up capital, while the children provide the technology and social media skills that the older generation may lack. (Strathclyde University Global Monitor Survey: 2011). The 2018 Work and the Silver Economy Report clearly illustrated the importance of the family business sector to the UK economy. It showed that the 4.8 million family-run businesses in the UK in 2016 comprised some 88% of all private sector firms, employed 12.2 million people, earnt £1.4 trillion in revenue and contributed £149 billion – or 20% of all government revenue – to the UK Exchequer each year, either directly or indirectly in tax. However, as inspiring as such examples of old age and multi-age enterprise undoubtedly are, prospective silver entrepreneurs in the UK still face major obstacles in starting up new businesses, notably the red tape involved, the restrictive lending practices of the banks and the limited professional support available to help launch this type of business (ILC-UK 2011). As Polly noted, the UK is well behind other countries in nurturing this 'silver streak'; a streak that, according to SAGA, possibly helped save the UK economy in its time of crisis after the financial collapse of 2008. As the Centre for Ageing Better argued in its 2018 Report, ageing is potentially a 'silver lining' for both the UK economy and for intergenerational relations, if – but only if – the government adopts an inter-age work strategy that promotes a more age-friendly workplace and actively promotes and incentivises long-life working; the sort of smart ageing strategy considered by the Irish government in its 2015 Technopolis Report. Although Ireland is a relatively 'young society', the government sees the opportunity to convert **smart ageing** into an economic strategy designed to boost the Irish economy by applying smart technology to industries such as functional and health food, connected health, assisted living, adaptable housing and tourism. As the report explains: "*Smart Ageing is a broad concept that combines innovation and technology to produce products and services to improve the quality of life for people aged 50 and over.*" Ireland already has a strong presence and reputation in these sectors and, although the scale of the global markets is enormous, very few countries have set a 'smart ageing leadership council' to promote and coordinate this strategy, supported by the research and innovation capabilities of a national centre for smart ageing. Is this not, thought Polly, exactly the sort of innovative and forward thinking that the British government should be enthusiastically engaged in, capturing and embracing the spirit and potential of ageing rather than cowering in the Doomsday Book of crisis and denial?

Finally, as Charles concluded in his report, while the obvious solution to the emerging UK talent gap in the past would have been immigration, Brexit has now put that source of labour and enterprise into the melting-pot. As the 2017 Mercer Workforce Monitor report argued, the 143,000 loss of workforce to the UK economy due to retirement and emigration was previously offset by the entry of 147,000 EU and 232,000 non-EU workers in that year. With ageing accelerating and post-Brexit immigration controls tightening, a workforce crisis is arising that will have a potentially devastating effect on such sectors as health and social care, construction and financial services, with London especially exposed. As the 2016 MGI report on global migration and its impact showed, migrants actually represent only 3.4% of the world's population, yet they contribute nearly 10% to global GDP ($6.7 trillion in 2015) – 90% of which goes directly to developed countries. The 2018 World Migration Report equally found no clear evidence that immigration undermines native employment or wages in the UK and instead found that immigrants tend to earn 20–30% less than native-born workers. The real issue, though, isn't immigration itself but the speed and volume of immigrants coming into areas that are unprepared for such 'demographic invasions'. Such areas are ill-prepared to welcome and integrate new migrants successfully, and so local people come to see immigrants as a threat not a solution. Given Britain's rising dependency ratio, yawning skills gap and relative low productivity, any effective economic and ageing policy would have put immigration and integration at the forefront of its strategy. Unfortunately, Brexit has made that strategic option somewhat redundant, at least for the time being; and worse, some of the rhetoric around Brexit has started to make Britain a far less attractive option for young migrants, with sectors like health and social care facing a staffing crisis of major proportions if migrant labour is substantially limited. Even those EU citizens already living in the UK are considering leaving for more welcoming environments elsewhere. As Professor Sarah Harper has somewhat trenchantly put it (ILC-UK Conference: 2017): "*The message from Brexit is if you don't want immigrants, you're going to have to work longer. That's how the sums work out.*" By the late 2030s, the UK's state pension age could be up to 70 according to the Resolution Foundation, and as David Willetts has summed up: "*This decade marks the turning point in a transition to an ageing population in which the population of people aged 65+ is set to grow faster than that of working age.*"

So, the demographic revolution, the retirement of the boomer generation and the explosion of silver enterprise is likely to impact dramatically on the UK economy and the world of work in the first half of the 21st century. The UK workforce is already starting to age dramatically as the number of young employed people falls and the largest age band of workers shifts from 44–46 to 54–56 by 2020. Seventy-seven per cent of the rise in employment in the last ten years has apparently been among workers aged 50 and over and much of the increase has been among older women with the state pension age for them rising from 60 to 65. And with Brexit, the ageing of the UK workforce is likely to accelerate as new young blood from abroad may no longer be so readily available. Meanwhile, as longevity lengthens so too will the UK workforce be more likely to become more multigenerational, with a premium on the leadership skills of a new generation of managers capable of managing such a diversity of talent, attitude and ambition. The 'grey brain drain' is already upon us, and highly skilled workers from the baby-boomer generation, like Charles, are leaving for retirement, leaving behind them large gaps in skill and experience in a huge range of occupations, notably science, technology, engineering and mathematics. Teaching and medicine in the UK are already suffering dramatically from this age-drain, and more's to come yet according to research by the ILC-UK (Dec. 2017) few UK companies have genuinely thought through or begun to address this generational transformation in their workforce. Examples of flexible working, phased retirement and management mentoring are still relatively few, while fear of being labelled ageist seems to have led many firms to steer well wide of targeting older workers in any HR initiative. With record numbers of men and women continuing in work after age 65 – 1.2 million in 2018 – the ONS (2016) has gone as far as to speculate that: *"the [UK] economy may come to rely increasingly on older workers by 2039."* The numbers, however, are still relatively small, more in part-time and casual employment than full-time, and possibly as much a reflection of the ending in 2011 of the compulsory retirement at age 65 as any desire by older people to work longer.

So, as Charles explained, work in the UK – and across the globe – in the 21st century is not only going through a technological revolution but a generational one, and the boomer generation has the opportunity to step away from it *or* be part of it; to be a new generation of businessmen and women, inventors, mentors and coaches rather than CEOs, managers, tradesmen or workers as in the past. These are the sort of intergenerational encore careers that the American third-age evangelist, Marc Freedman, has called for, and the sort of opportunity that Charles and his contemporaries would warmly welcome – provided they kept control of both how they worked and when. In the view of UKCES (2014) and the Centre for Ageing (2018), Charles and his generation are a key, if not *the key*, to future productivity and prosperity in ageing Britain, as both silver entrepreneurs and as silver consumers, sitting alongside: on one hand the new blood, the new talent we need to attract and retain from abroad; and on the other hand, the new technologies and scientific discoveries, particularly the rise of the robot and artificial intelligence. But if British industry doesn't change, and the government continues to ignore the potential of the silver economy and the silver worker in its economic planning, then the UK's dependency ratio is likely to continue to deteriorate and induce the sort of 'economic coma' or 'grey death' that already stalks countries like Japan, with potentially cataclysmic outcomes as the economy implodes, the working population shrinks and the generations 'go to war' over who pays for who and with what. Charles, as an early and well-to-do retiree, may have escaped the 'work-quake' ahead but his children and grandchildren certainly will not.

Polly now had a much fuller and clearer understanding of the world of work in the 21st century and of the radical changes in working practices, manufacturing processes and workforce diversity operating beneath the surface. Globalisation and new technology are revolutionising production and consumption and creating a speed and scope of change that both governments and employers are struggling to cope with. But demography is also playing its part in radically changing the generational composition of the modern workforce, promoting a new form of flexible retirement, necessitating a new approach to managing multigenerational workforces and creating opportunities for new forms of intergenerational business enterprise that combine the traditional values and ethics of the older generation – and their access to capital – with the drive and initiative of the young. As the 2014 study by the UKCES showed, there is a *'seismic'* change occurring under the surface of the British economy, a change driven by demography, ageing and *'attitude'* as the baby boomer generation steps back and Generations X and Y step forward, with women increasingly at the forefront and with global recruitment – and so global migration – a key force. And if that intergenerational mix wasn't enough, just wait for Generation Z – Charles and Polly's grandchildren – to come into the workplace and add their own G-force to globalised working.

4 | The Pensions Revolution and the Financing of Longer Later Life

Polly's Lowestoft surgery had long been characterised by a queue of old age pensioners facing financial difficulties in paying their bills, difficulties with their council tax, or facing the trauma of applying for benefits. She usually referred them on to the local Citizens Advice Service or the relevant section of the housing or benefits office. More recently, though, a trickle and then a stream of older people begun to emerge who were about to retire or who had just retired, and who were patently worried, if not fearful, about living on retirement incomes for the unknown number of years ahead. Many of these constituents had quite generous pensions, and some significant savings or investments, alongside homes that in most cases were now paid for. Nevertheless, their fear of the future was quite palpable. It centred partly on whether they had enough to live on comfortably for another 20 to 30 years, particularly as interest rates on savings currently were so low, while many feared the consequences of another financial collapse like 2008 and the effect on their property values and potential for equity release. It centred, too, on concerns about the future for their children and their continued capacity to help them, particularly as these pensioners moved from independent living into some form of dependency. The overriding fear, though, was the cost and availability of healthcare at a time when the NHS and Social Services seemed to be under intolerable pressure and were less and less able to provide for pensioners' healthcare in the future. Some of her constituents had private health insurance but all of them recognised that a healthy NHS was critical to their own future health and, while they still wholeheartedly supported the principles behind the NHS, they increasingly doubted politicians' commitment to it at a time of life when they might need it most.

Just as work and retirement are being transformed by ageing in the UK, so too, inevitably, is the whole world of pensions and later-life financing. Like retirement today, the 20th-century model of a state pension as a basic income, supplemented by means-tested welfare benefits and a disparate and highly variable range of occupational and private pensions, can no longer cope with the mass retirement of a baby boom generation of some 16 million plus living on average some 20 to 30 years in retirement. The old system was designed for a minority population of old age pensioners projected to live at best into their 60s or 70s on limited incomes and low expectations – and was costed accordingly. The new generation of OAPs have been brought up in a much more healthy and affluent era, with much higher standards of living and expectations of an active and independent later life. The modern pensioner no longer fits the 20th-century stereotype of a 'poor pensioner' surviving on a meagre state pension, hungry, shivering and at home alone. The modern pensioner in the UK is as likely to be rich as poor, healthy as sick, and as likely to be living with their partner into their 90s and beyond as being a female, living alone in isolation and deprivation.

In 1917, King George V sent out 24 100th-birthday telegrams; in 2016, the Queen sent out around 6,000 100th-birthday cards; by 2050, that number is expected to have risen to over 56,000 cards and telegrams. Later life is now mirroring working life and bringing with it all the issues and challenges of financing living in a country as diverse and unequal as British society is today. The modern pensioner cannot rest on his or her pension laurels; she or he must plan their finances for the future much like younger people plan theirs, but without the back-up of a pay rise, promotion or new career. In an age of longevity and a time when the British welfare state seems to be retreating from being the 'provider of first need' to the 'refuge of last resort', this is an immense personal challenge, not only for pensioners but for their families too. As numerous retirement surveys have highlighted, relatively few British pensioners are fully prepared for financing a later life of what might now appear to be unlimited length. The old model of depending on the state for life support after retirement is no longer a sustainable standard of living; it needs to be addressed and planned for throughout working life if personal poverty is to be avoided. Yet swathes of the British public distrust and still fear financial advisers after the mis-selling and scams of the pre-2008 years; and although artificial intelligence has the potential to automate and liberate consumer understanding of pensions and financial management, as Michelle Cracknell of the Pensions Advisory Service highlighted at the ILC Future of

Ageing Conference in 2018, automation can only work when people know the right questions to ask and understand why they need to know the answers. And at present few people do.

As Charles, Polly's IFA, explained, Britain, like the rest of the developed world, faces a potential pensions time bomb in the emerging world of mass ageing, particularly after the financial crisis in 2008 that threatened to take down the whole of the Western world's pension funds, as well its financial system, and whose aftermath continues to constrain government spending even now, some eleven years later. The World Economic Forum (2017) calculated that the six countries with the biggest pensions – the US, UK, Japan, Netherlands, Canada and Australia – along with China and India, are sitting on a global pensions time bomb of $70 trillion, that will escalate to over $400 trillion by 2050 unless action to restrain it is swiftly taken. The UK alone – even with the lowest state pension of any OECD country – has a current shortfall of $8 trillion, rising potentially to $33 trillion by 2050, and its national debt projected by the OBR is set to rise to over 100% of GDP by the 2030s. As the ratings agency Standard & Poor's predicted back in 2010, mass ageing is now *"an irreversible truth"* that is fundamentally shaping national economic health, public finances and public policy making. *"The irreversible rate at which the world is ageing and the escalating costs of Global Ageing threaten to strike at the very heart of the global economy and the global recovery projected for the early part of the 21st Century."*

Warnings about the **British pensions' crisis** and the costs of age-related spending have been no less dire and urgent in recent years. The Government's own financial watchdog, the Office for Budget Responsibility (OBR) warned back in July 2015 that total age-related spending in the UK was likely to rise to 25.1% of GDP by 2063–64, and in its 2018 report it projected that state pension costs alone would rise to 6.9% of GDP in 2067–68 just at a time when national income is projected to plummet and the old age dependency ratio (OADR) is projected to fall dramatically from 4:1 to well below 3:1. So, a crisis in earnings is emerging to match this 'crisis in the costs of ageing', and working adults tomorrow might well face the triple blow of higher taxes, longer working lives and less inherited wealth as their parents are forced to sell property to pay for their future care. Set against these figures, and with the costs of Brexit looming, full economic recovery in an 'age of ageing' looks overwhelming if not impossible, even for a country as wealthy as the UK. Worse, as outlined in Chapter 1, many Britons are ill-prepared for retirement. Eight million over-55s apparently have no savings at all, and nearly 30,000 people aged 60–74 are turning to expensive equity release schemes to pay off loans and credit cards as well as access day-to-day cash. (Key Retirement: 2017) The Pensions Policy Institute (2018) predicts that millions of the poorest UK pensioners will soon have only their state pension of some £7,000 a year – an income below even the national minimum wage – to live on, and the Royal Insurance Report in 2016 warned that without significant increases in pension savings "*we could be witnessing the death of retirement*", as the poorest workers might simply not be able to afford to retire.

Finally, there's no longer a typical or average pensioner as in the past but a spectrum of pensioners as wide as the distribution of wealth in British society at large. At one end, a new 'breed' of wealthy pensioner has emerged, enjoying a comfortable and healthy retirement funded by generous defined benefit final salary schemes, rising property values and a portfolio of investments and savings sufficient to put some into the millionaire class in terms of total assets. At the other end, a sub-strata of poor British pensioners exists – some 1.8 million of them living on one of the lowest state pensions in Europe and facing a bewildering array of means tested benefits that many don't know about, understand or collect. Some £3.7 billion to £5.5 billion in potential pension benefits remains uncollected annually according to Age UK, leaving some 2.7 million pensioners below or just above the poverty line. Women in particular are at a severe disadvantage, often excluded or of secondary importance in a world of pensions that was primarily designed with men in mind. Women are much more likely than men to work part-time and be in low-paid service sector jobs. They have to weave paid work around their caring responsibilities for children, family and elderly parents, and as a result their state pension is often incomplete and their private pension, if any, is paltry. Women have traditionally relied on their husbands, but half of marriages today now end in divorce. So, many women go into retirement on their own, having to rely on minimal pensions, means-tested benefits, and help from others. This enormous and escalating disparity in pensioner incomes – and with it, lifestyles and life opportunities – is well illustrated in Figure 1 overleaf.

In the face of such challenges, explained Charles, the UK pension system is increasingly outdated and desperately needs fundamental reform. The concept of a state pension was initiated by the Liberal Government of 1909, and the post-war state pension system in the UK originated from the Beveridge Report in 1942. It introduced the idea of a simple flat-rate state pension to meet basic income needs and to provide a 'safety net' to relieve poverty in the minority population who, after a gruelling and usually unhealthy working life, managed to survive into old age; most didn't. As *The Guardian* (4 Dec. 2013) explained:

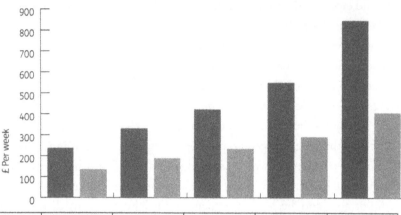

	Poorest fifth	Next fifth	Middle fifth	Next fifth	Richest fifth
Pensioner couples	237	330	420	549	846
Single pensioners	136	189	234	290	406

Figure 1: **Disparities in pensioner incomes**
(Age UK Agenda for Later Life in 2014)

"When David Lloyd George introduced the first state pension, 105 years ago (in 1909), it was worth around 25p a week and could be claimed at the age of 70. At that time, life expectancy was barely 50 years and only one person in four made it to pensionable age." At that time, some 5.2% of the population were over 65. Today that figure is 18% and is projected to rise to 23% by 2033 and 26% by 2065.The resultant leaps in state spending on public pensions are astronomic. According to the ILC-UK, in 1948 the UK spent £4.6 billion on state pensions. By 2013 this had risen to £84.9 billion. State spending in the UK on pensioner benefits alone has nearly tripled since 1978 from £38.9 billion to £113.1 billion in 2013. Moreover, the UK's state pension scheme is not self-financing. Rather, it is based on a pay-as-you-go scheme, with the cost of each generation being borne by the younger generations following them. As the older generation of pensioners grows and the working generations shrink proportionately, so that burden, that dependency ratio, grows too.

Successive governments have built on the 1942 framework and almost *crushed it to death* under the weight of piecemeal amendments and reforms that have created one of the most complex pension systems in the world; one that the Turner Commission in 2004/5 described it as *"not fit for purpose"*. The UK Coalition Government of 2010–2015 did attempt to redesign the British pension system and create a framework fit for *"a State Pension for the 21st century"* (2011) by:

- **Introducing** a new flat-rate pension initially of £144 per week.
- **Raising the state pension age** (SPA) from age 65 to age 67 by 2028, with an independent review every five years.
- **Abolishing the default pension age** and introducing the right to request flexible working.
- **Equalising pension ages for men and women.**
- **Maintaining the triple lock mechanism** to combat inflation.
- **Promoting pension savings** through the introduction of pensioner bonds and increased limits on tax-free ISAs.
- **Promoting occupational pensions** through auto-enrolment schemes such as NEST.
- **Making death benefits** paid to beneficiaries on death before aged 75 tax-free.
- **Liberalising** the whole of the private pensions system and allowing retirees to take their pension pots and invest them as they wished. This radical reform delighted pensioners but sent the annuities market into 'freefall'; a timely reminder to the pensions industry not to take pensioners for granted, and to start developing new, far more cost-effective products.

Welcome and significant as such changes to the UK pension were, they did not constitute the sort of fundamental reform many commentators believe necessary for pensions of the future. They failed to encourage retirees or younger age groups to plan more effectively for later life, and they failed to address the escalating inequalities in pension income and wealth, both between generations and within the pensioner population itself. Raising the state pension age (SPA) to 66 in 2020 and 67 by 2028, for example, may well seem prudent, fair and save the government some £400 billion over the next 50 years. However, as the ILC-UK study in 2014 pointed out, raising the SPA may in practice prove more regressive than progressive; more beneficial and fair to those in comfortable white-collar occupations with good occupational or private pensions and a healthy life expectancy of some 20+ years of retirement to look forward to, than to those in physically demanding jobs with only a limited span of retirement ahead and already suffering signs of disability and chronic illness. For those in unskilled and manual occupations in particular, any increase in SPA could be a 'death sentence' as their health continues to decline, and their period of retirement shrinks to just a few years. The Cridland Commission in 2015 did consider the idea of linking longevity to the state pension age but eventually rejected it as too complex a solution to include in its recommendations.

The Barker Commission in 2014 recommended a much simpler solution, namely that the British state pension be increased to the level of most Western European countries, paid for in part by a ruthless simplification or removal of many, if not all, of the current pensioner benefits. That recommendation, too, has fallen on deaf government ears, despite the fact that the UK has one of the lowest pensions among the nations of the OECD in terms of its income replacement value. At 29%, it's well below the OECD average of 63% and below even Mexico, Poland and Chile, while the replacement value of 90% found in Portugal, Italy and Austria, and the 100% in Holland, seems to put the UK to shame (OECD: 2018).

Percentage of working wage retirees receive around the world

100%	Netherlands–Turkey–India
80%	Denmark–Spain–Cyprus–China
60%	Czech Republic–Latvia–Estonia
40%	Japan–Malta–Ireland
29%	UK–Mexico

OECD Average: 63%

Figure 2: **International pensions league table**
(Adapted from WEF/OECD: 2018)

The UK pension is, in essence, a *'minimum wage for the elderly'*. It leaves millions of elderly in the UK *'suspended just above the poverty line, dangling there'* for the 20 to 30 years ahead and totally dependent on means-tested benefits – if, that is, they collect them. As Ros Altmann, the former pensions minister, has commented: "*We are one of the world's leading economies but our support for the oldest in society is not fit for purpose.*"

So, a perfect 'pensions storm' seems to be brewing for the generations ahead, as increasing numbers of older people retire with ongoing debt, and millions of the young still seem unable to save effectively for the future. As the 2017 UBS report concluded, the UK's combination of a basic state pension even with the new auto-pension system is likely to leave future generations with very low pensions compared to their counterparts in Australia, Singapore and even New York. To achieve a private pension of £20,000 a year, a young person today would have to put away £246 a month at age 25 and £404 at age 53 according to a recent BBC actuarial report. The proposal to extend auto-enrolment to 18-year-olds may help, but as the ex-minister of work and pensions, Steve Webb, commented in December 2017, such a "*proposed pace of change is shockingly lethargic*" and "*risks leaving a whole generation of workers behind*". As Michael Johnson, at the Centre for Policy Studies (Nov. 2017), has argued, the UK state pension seems, "*No longer fit for purpose*" because:

- It is unsustainable. It is paying out more than the National Insurance scheme brings in – £95 billion against £86 billion in 2015/16, so necessitating a £9.6 billion bailout by the Treasury.
- It is unfair as it is the wealthy who live longer and who are therefore effectively being subsidised by the poor who die earlier.
- It is overly complex, and any attempt to personalise pensions to an individual's life expectancy would only twist this tangled web even further.

But it is not just the state pension that is under fire in the UK. **Occupational pensions** are equally in crisis. A stark division of income is emerging between those pensioners who still have comfortable and secure *defined benefit* (DB) pension schemes with guaranteed retirement incomes, and those now relying on *defined contribution* (DC) schemes; schemes that do not guarantee pensions on retirement but depend instead on the uncertainties of the stock market for their final payouts. After the 2008 financial crash, defined benefit pension schemes have in the main been withdrawn by all but a few major employers and the public sector, leaving the majority of future pensioners at the mercy of national and global stock markets, that are as likely to go bust as they are to boom. The pensioner of tomorrow is facing an increasingly risky and uncertain future as both the state and the employer increasingly withdraw from pension provision and leave the individual exposed and alone to navigate his – and especially her – way through a financial market that is notorious for the complexity of its products, its mis-selling techniques and its poor value for money. The government's reputation for effectively policing and regulating the banking and insurance sectors suffered badly from the 2008 crash and has yet to be fully restored. Restoring public trust in the financial markets themselves is a massive challenge for both Western governments and for the industry itself.

As Charles brought home to Polly very clearly and very starkly, the **individual** is now the central figure in any future scheme for funding longer retirement. He, and especially she, can no longer rely solely on a state pension, supplemented by occupational and private pensions on one side and by personal savings on the other. Rather, finances in later life have to be managed just as effectively as they are during working life. There is a growing need for every retiree and retired household to have a personal and/or household retirement financial plan, properly costed for all eventualities – including ill health and incapacity – and all lifestyle ambitions over the forthcoming 20 to 30 years of retirement; a lifetime in itself when the individual is possibly least able to manage it. This is a dramatic and life-changing departure from the traditional model of the 20th-century pensioner free of ongoing worries about assets and income, and for many it's a frightening prospect for which they are ill-prepared. While pension schemes around the world face immense challenges, the greatest potential 'car crash' for the UK would be if pensioners on a mass scale simply ran out of savings and turned en masse to the state – or the family – as so many seem likely to do.

The UK clearly needs a new pensions framework fit for the 21st century, a framework that firstly puts the individual at the heart of its architecture, and secondly puts pensions at the centre of later-life planning, and that clearly reflects its intimate inter-relationship with health, housing and all other aspects of life after 65. Most especially, pensions need to be seen as part of a package that encourages and enables older people to be active and independent, an asset to their local community rather than a burden. Finally, and most importantly, a new pensions framework would need to set out the founding principles for a new pensions contract with future generations. The young, after all, are not only going to have to support it but pay for it! This was a pretty profound and far-reaching proposal, way beyond anything Polly had seen in the numerous pensions' reports commissioned in the UK in recent years. It did, however, reflect the thinking of the Melbourne Mercer Institute, one of the world's foremost authorities on pension design and pension provision and it has proposed the following framework as the basis for any state pension scheme fit for the 21st century:

- A **vision of ageing** in 21st-century Britain and the social aspirations and ambitions behind it in terms of the future for the old and retired and for intergenerational and intragenerational relations.

- A set of **primary aims and objectives** for the overall pensions and retirement income system, including the underlying principles of fairness, equity, adequacy and sustainability, alongside its projected cost and funding, its relationship to the economy at large, its interrelationship to associated social policies, such as healthcare and housing, and its likely effect on the well-being of society, its distribution of wealth, its intergenerational relations and the betterment of the young and of family life, as well as the elderly themselves.

- An **institutional framework**, or **social contract**, that clearly sets out the mutual benefits and responsibilities between retirees and the working population, to ensure equity – and the perception of equity – and to ensure that retirees, and retirees-to-be, are protected from sudden change, by fair warning of changes in the pension system and their likely impact well beforehand, and by a strict, effective and highly accessible regulatory system that enjoys high levels of customer satisfaction.

- A **pension framework** that engages employers and key stakeholders in its design, is seen as an investment, not a cost, and one that adds value to employee recruitment, retention and motivation and to employer-employee relations, as in the best of such schemes in Scandinavia and elsewhere.

- A **pension structure** that incorporates the life cycle of saving before and after retirement, the potential for 'staged retirement' and offers a wide choice of high-quality retirement income products that are effective, efficient and trustworthy.

- A set of **taxation rules** to limit leakage of benefits before retirement which require that at least two-thirds of the accumulated retirement benefit be converted into sustainable and defined income products.

- Compulsory and/or voluntary **tax incentive** schemes to maximise participation.

- **Impartial and high-quality financial education, advice and guidance** at all ages and at all stages, including that designed specifically for the young throughout the '*formative stages of their life cycle*'.

- **Changes and transitory arrangements** that are clear, publicly debated and well explained, with gradual and staged arrangements that do not generate unnecessary shocks to pension planning and give substantive warning of change to those approaching retirement and protection for those in it.

At its heart, concluded the Melbourne Mercer Institute, any state pension system must be **adequate** and provide sufficient retirement income for its pensioner population; **sustainable**, so that the state, through taxation and economic growth, and the private pension industry, through investment, are both capable of paying out pensions in the long-term future; and have **integrity,** so that the populace have trust and confidence in the pensions sector to deliver retirement benefits, and that there is effective regulation to ensure openness, transparency and the prosecution of malpractice. In the view of the Mercer Institute, *"retirees in the 21st Century"* face a *"Retirement Trilemma"*, a retirement dilemma of how to ensure the stability of their retirement income in the face of inflation, stock market volatility and unforeseen costs. There is, in their view, no 'silver bullet' solution but a portfolio of later-life financial products that the individual now has to manage her or himself. Such a radical and wholesale shift of responsibility from employers and the state to the individual has huge implications for any ageing society and its ageing population; and it's scary – very, very scary! It was even more scary for Polly to learn that, on the basis of these principles, the 2017 Melbourne Mercer Institute (MMI) league table of the national pension systems put the UK pension system 15th overall, with a lowly C+ grading, not only behind that of the Dutch and Scandinavians but even below Chile and Columbia. (Note, too, though, the surprisingly low rating for Japan and Korea, the two leading nations in ageing.)

Grading & Score	Country
A 80+	None
B+ 75-80	Denmark-Netherlands-Australia
B 65-75	Norway-Finland-Sweden-Singapore-Switzerland-NZ-Chile-Canada-Ireland
C+ 60-65	Germany-Columbia-**UK**
C 50-60	France-US-Malaysia-Poland-Brazil-Austria-Italy
D 35-50	Japan-India-Korea-China-Indonesia-Mexico-Argentina-S. Africa

Figure 3: Adapted from **Melbourne Mercer Global Pension Index: 2017**

Finally, Charles argued that no pension scheme in the 21st century can be divorced from the national economy at large. Pensions tend to be seen as a drain on the UK economy but, in reality, they are an economic powerhouse, a huge source of both consumer spending and national saving, and likely, as the silver economy grows, to be a global force in the world economy. The **silver economy** in the UK alone is huge, the figures astronomic, with some 600,000 retirees joining it every year and some two million silver entrepreneurs already on its books. (Saga-Cebr: 2015) The UCL report on active ageing in 2012 predicted that spending by older people in the UK would rise from some £76 billion in 2012 to £127 billion by 2030, and the SAGA-Cebr Report in 2014 claimed that it was the over-50s who possibly 'saved' Britain from the worst of the austerity crisis between 2010 and 2014 by continuing to spend sufficiently to maintain the equivalent of 878,000 full-time youth jobs. However, for the silver economy to continue to grow and flourish, the silver sector needs to have its own distinct national plan and financial strategy. It needs to be seen and treated as part of the overall national economy, not as some sideshow or niche market. Pensioner savings alone now amount to some £48.7 billion (ILC-UK: 2015), equivalent to 2.8% of the UK's GDP, and globally some $100 trillion of savings is sloshing around the world's financial systems. Yet such funds are currently languishing in low- or non-interest savings accounts instead of being converted into investment funds desperately needed by British industry. A new pensioner bond, for example, that paid pensioners a decent rate of interest, would not only generate further silver spending but provide urgently needed finance for both private and public investment, all at relatively little extra cost to the Exchequer; a classic and enduring economic win-win. So, in Charles's view, pensions, retirement incomes and the silver economy *all* need to come centre stage in any national economic plan. They need to be part of a radical new way of economic thinking and planning for promoting growth and prosperity in the ageing society of the future. Pensions are not just a social security payment to those no longer able to fend for themselves but a major investment in a critical and emerging economic sector. Pensions are a multi-billion pound industry and so need to be recognised as a key strand of economic policy for any ageing society.

As Charles went on to elaborate, the pensions challenge for the UK, however, is not only about pensions as part of national economic planning; it is equally about the distribution of wealth within and between generations. It is about the young as well as the retired, about their retirement futures as well as those of their ageing relatives. As Paul Johnson, director of the Institute of Fiscal Studies, warned at the ILC-UK Conference in 2016, while the present generation of pensioners may be enjoying a higher standard of living today than when they were working, this '*pensioner bonus*' will not last. Future generations may face pensioner poverty on a widespread scale unless they take a grip of their own pension prospects and plan ahead as governments and employers increasingly withdraw their support and leave them alone to face the retirement challenges of the century ahead. In contrast, the government and its various pension commissions still seem wedded to a very narrow view of retirement and pensions. They still seem to be obsessed with raising the state pension age (SPA) and tinkering with mechanisms, such as the triple-lock, rather than looking at the wider picture of pensions and the silver economy in an era when ageing is fundamentally changing the British economy, its social structure and its lifestyle with it. Moreover, pensioners today and in the future need far greater financial protection than they currently get. They are an increasing target for, and especially vulnerable to, mis-selling, fraud and account hacking. The Financial Conduct Authority (FCA) raised these concerns as a matter of urgency in its 2018 report, warning that the financial, retail and healthcare sectors in particular need to take rigorous measures to protect older customers and to make self-protection much easier and more user-friendly, whether it's in accessing their accounts, understanding the later-life products that they're being sold or in ensuring that third party access to their finances is impartial and conducted solely in the pensioner's interest and no one else's. Given the widespread dangers of account hacking, identity theft and the vulnerability of an ever-growing ageing population to ill health and especially dementia, it would seem that pensioner protection will need to be a priority arena in any future pensions agenda if it's not to become a national scandal.

So, for Polly and her fellow MPs, without reform and radical rethinking the UK pension system is in danger of becoming the financial and social *time bomb* that many commentators fear. With reform and a fundamental redesign, there is some chance that it might not only provide effectively for current and future generations but also prove to be a powerhouse for driving the silver economy and the UK economy with it post-Brexit. However, the UK pension system currently remains a 'financial jungle', a maze of defined and undefined pension systems, a lottery of grossly unequal tax reliefs that few retirees – and even fewer of Polly's own poorer pensioners – seem able to cope with. While Polly's older constituents seem all too aware of this nuclear option, many politicians in Westminster, cushioned by their own gold-plated pension schemes, seem deaf, dumb and blind to the fallout ahead. All their attention is on Brexit rather than challenges closer to home, and few in Whitehall or No 10 seem to appreciate the size of the pensioner economy, its potential power and its growing impact on GDP, nor that it holds within it potential solutions to Britain's need for serious investment in industry and infrastructure.

Such 'economic blindness', however, could be a 'political blessing' to an opposition spokesperson of Polly's stature, drive and commitment. It could constitute the centrepiece of an alternative, even radical, ageing strategy, and Charles's insights had inspired her to start exploring much more innovative ideas for the future, such as the *universal basic income* currently being trialled in Finland, Italy; alongside the notion of a collective defined pension which is somewhere in between the current defined benefit and defined contribution schemes and is now being trialled by the UK Government with the Royal Mail & Communications Union. The Labour Party is also looking seriously at the New Economic Forum (NEF) think-tank proposal to scrap the current personal tax allowance in favour of a 'weekly national allowance" of £48 pw/£2,500 pa. This shift they believe, would dramatically help low-income families and help relieve the inequalities built into a personal allowance that the NEF believes represents "one of the most expensive and regressive public spending initiatives of the 21st century so far." At £111.2 billion, the UK personal allowance costs more than the whole of defence, local government and transport put together and enriches 'the highest income households almost seven times faster than the poorest.'

As the ILC-UK argued in their 2011 Report, *Resuscitating Retirement Savings*, the key to the future lies not just with the old as they approach retirement but in encouraging and incentivising the young to increase their pension saving and prepare for a sustainable retirement from age 70 onwards. As this report argued, financial education should be on every school and college curriculum if Generation Z is not to suffer the same fate as their older brothers and sisters. As Charles calculated, if young people begin saving 12.5% of their income as pension from now on, they could be 'pension millionaires' by the time they're 60; a thought that not only inspired Polly's thinking for how to help her own grandchildren but how to help whole new generations of younger voters think of pension saving as sexy rather than sad; an exciting investment today rather than a thought for tomorrow. What British people of all ages seem to need though, concluded Polly and Charles, is a lifetime personalised pension or financial *dashboard* based on the latest data available, a rigorous and strict regulatory framework, and individualised advice provided by both a financial Alexa and a trusted personal adviser: the sort of auto-advice system that countries such as Estonia have apparently invested in heavily. So, Charles's report had been a wake-up call for Polly and an inspiration for future planning, but as more and more of her constituents – even those from the apparently affluent shores of Southwold – came pouring into her surgery, fearful about their financial health, Polly's fears about the ageing future ahead began to escalate, and her hopes about reforming it began to flicker and fade.

5 | The Healthcare Challenge of Active Living and Eldercare in Later Life

Good health, declared Douglas, is more important than good wealth, and he and his wife Deborah had tried to live their lives by that maxim, working out regularly down at the local gym, eating a Mediterranean-style diet and investing in private health insurance. The news on his 67th birthday that he had prostate cancer was therefore devastating for both of them. It had come out of the blue. None of the annual health tests that he'd had since he turned 60 had picked it up, and now all their retirement plans lay in shreds as he faced the prospect of chemotherapy and possibly surgery. What to do? Carry on with the NHS and the inevitable – and potentially life-threatening – waiting list or put his private health insurance into action with the equally inevitable costs involved. Dougie continued his faith in the NHS, got an urgent referral to Addenbrooke's Hospital in Cambridge and, because he was diagnosed early before the cancer spread, and because Addenbrooke's was developing new surgical techniques through the De Vinci project, he made a full recovery. While world travel was now a distant dream, buying a place in sunny Spain seemed a pretty good, and very healthy, alternative for both him and his wife – and for the grandchildren planning to visit them, including Rosie, their six-year-old granddaughter, recently diagnosed with cerebral palsy.

Douglas is an example of the speed with which new medical research is breaking down old boundaries. His treatment at Addenbrooke's Hospital was cutting edge, and new research by the Institute of Cancer Research is, even now, cracking the genetic code behind prostate cancer to relieve this condition permanently. Douglas was lucky; many other men with life-threatening conditions are not. Much to the consternation of the health sector, men tend to take their health for granted and, especially in later life, are reluctant to go to their doctor and get regularly checked out. Prostate conditions, for example, are now one of the greatest threats to rude health for any man over 60, as urinary problems begin to make daily life increasingly inconvenient (no pun intended) and erectile dysfunction threatens both a couple's sex life and many a man's sense of manhood. Men ignore their testes at their peril, and campaigners are now urging women 'to take matters in hand' and get their partners tested as regularly as they do themselves, for the sort of conditions that can destroy any plans for retirement, however well thought through. Any retirement plan today needs to accommodate ill health as well as actively promote good health, across the whole family, for men as well as women.

Douglas was a patient of Polly's GP husband David and had come through his surgery not hers. Like Polly, David's surgery in Lowestoft served a disproportionate number of older patients, and while the health issues of Britain's ageing population were banging louder and louder on the doors of the NHS, they were now a daily feature of David's medical routine. Polly's growing engagement in the ageing agenda, therefore, resonated very powerfully with David, both professionally and personally. He therefore began to take an increasing interest in Polly's research, not just from a political perspective of how to get more money for the NHS but also in terms of the interrelationship of health to all the other subjects she was now researching, from pensions and housing through to family and even sexual health. More particularly, he, too, increasingly saw the solution not just in increasing state resources but in enabling patients to manage their own health, to develop a healthier lifestyle and diet, and to demand more personalised support from the public healthcare service. Like Douglas, David saw good health at the heart of any ageing strategy but, unlike Douglas, he could see bad health all around him, with Public Health England (2017) estimating that over 80% of 40–60-year-olds in the UK today are overweight and even obese, drink too much alcohol and are physically inactive. So, David began urging all his patients to take the Public Health England quiz '*How Are You*' to find out how drastically people needed to change their lifestyle if they wanted to live their natural lifespan. His surgery was festooned with posters and copies of this quiz to entertain patients while they waited for their appointment. And as David was well aware, waiting in the shadows for at least one in three of his patients is the 'elephant in the surgery',

dementia, a hugely under-funded area of medical research but one that even now is hinting at a possible cure, or at least a delaying factor. Like Polly, David fervently believed in the principles of the NHS but was equally increasingly aware of its shortcomings and the need for fundamental reform. He therefore began to devote more time himself to healthcare research as he saw Polly's embryonic manifesto starting to emerge. So, with help from colleagues at the University of East Anglia, he began the grand tour of healthcare summarised below.

Healthcare is, clearly, at the heart of longevity and any national strategy or personal plan for a better quality, more independent and purposeful retirement. Longer life alone is not the gift of longevity if all it means is more of the same or, worse, a longer life in disability and dependency. The costs to the state and the burden on the family would become intolerable if all longevity brought was millions more elderly people on their last legs, alone at home and needing endless homecare. Longevity in this case would be an economic and social disaster, a living nightmare that would send the UK economy spiralling into a deep depression, burdened by an unsustainable dependency ratio and an age-related tax bill that the young refused to pay and that unleashed an age rage against the elderly that pitted young against old, generation against generation, within and between families and across local communities. This would be the graveyard scenario as Britain sunk into a slow, painful decline as depression and dependency overwhelmed the support services and left the family alone and unaided, the only lifeline for an elderly population with nowhere else to go. The 'caring sandwich' would collapse, the British family would implode and the elderly would engage in a wave of silver suicide similar to that being experienced by more advanced ageing societies such as Japan. Great Britain would become Grey Britain, and the United Kingdom an unhealthy and divided nation facing a future of 'draining dependency' with no relief in sight. Such a scenario may seem extreme, but ageing societies elsewhere are already experiencing the deadly downside of ageing if they've not prepared properly for the onslaught ahead.

Healthcare is equally big business, and the accountancy firm Deloitte (2019) has estimated that the global spend on healthcare by 2022 will be $10 trillion, with dementia becoming a trillion-dollar disease; or worse, a two trillion dollar one by 2030, according to the WEF (2018), if it's not effectively tackled and the numbers world-wide – some 50 million – dramatically reduced. Those societies, however, that adopt the sort of positive health strategy advocated by the World Health Organization, promoting active and independent life for the old with as much vigour and passion as they put into promoting the health and happiness of their young, at least have the opportunity of enjoying the 'silver sunshine scenario' of a healthy ageing society. Healthcare is now a global and expanding industry, with large corporations entering the emerging markets in SE Asia, and the big tech companies, including Google, looking at ways to infiltrate, disrupt and transform this sector through the use of new technology and new models of delivery, as they have done elsewhere.

Everyone – the young as well as the old, the family as well as the employers – clearly has a heavily vested interest in promoting healthy ageing for all ages, but at this point in time the NHS in the UK seems to be fighting just to stay alive, facing what the Red Cross declared in January 2017 as a humanitarian crisis. Such a war-zone depiction of hospitals in England and Wales may be an exaggeration but it does seem to reflect the level of strain that the British system is currently under and its desperate need for fundamental reform. As the health think tank, the King's Fund, declared in 2014, it's Time to Think Differently: "*When the NHS was founded in 1948, 48% of the population died before the age of 65; that figure has now fallen to 14% and life expectancy at 65 is now 21 years for women and 19 years for men. By 2050, one in five people in England will be over 65. This success story for society and for modern medicine has utterly transformed our health and care needs but our health and care services have failed to keep up with this dramatic demographic shift.* As the NHS's then Medical Director, Sir Bruce Keogh, declared back in 2017, the model of delivery and service that we have at the moment "*is not fit for the future*" and, according to the Care Quality Commission in 2016, social services in the UK are about to collapse, with only 60% of adult social care services rated 'good' or 'outstanding'. The UK 2020 Report in 2016 ranked the UK near the bottom of its list of 32 developed countries in terms of survival rates for common cancers and even for pregnancy: "*We all love the concept of the NHS but it is simply not adequate for dealing with the epidemic of chronic disease that is inevitable with an ageing population. A radical shake-up, not just an increase in funding, is needed if we are to catch up with other European countries in the next decade.*" Equally, the May 2017 cyber-attack on the NHS IT systems showed just how vulnerable it, and many other organisations, are to cyber-hacking attacks that can effectively and disastrously disable their whole operations.

The healthcare challenge for ageing England alone is immense and was well summarised in the 2017 Health Profile for England as follows:

- Life expectancy continues to rise, albeit at a much slower rate, with more of this extra time proportionately in ill health.
- While death rates from heart disease and stroke have halved for both men and women, those from dementia and Alzheimer's have increased by 60% since 2001.
- Infectious diseases account for only 8% of all deaths in England, while poor diet, smoking and alcohol are now the major causes of mortality for both men and women, with lower-back and neck pain, skin diseases and depression the highest causes of morbidity or illness in later life.
- Areas of high deprivation and low income tend to have the highest incidence of ill health.
- Climate change, in the form of sudden and dramatic changes in temperature, seems to be generating significant increases in 'excess deaths', while flooding and air pollution appear to now be adding a third and fourth dimension to heat waves and bitter winters.

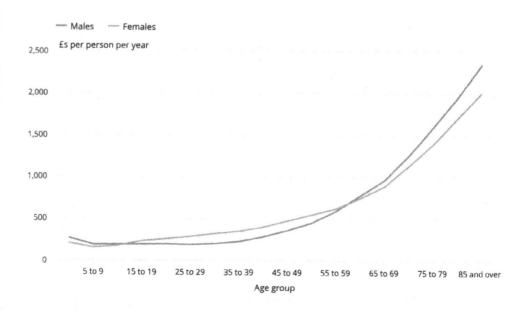

Figure 1: **Healthcare Spending**
(Health Foundation 2018)

Even in terms of **healthcare funding,** the UK has barely kept up with need, let alone demand. According to the IFS (2018), in total we spent over £149 billion in 2016/17 on healthcare in the UK, equivalent to 7.3% of national income – compared with 3% in the early 1960s – with an additional £21 billion on adult social care. While the average increase in health spending in the UK has been well above inflation over the past 60 years, since 2010 and the era of austerity it has slowed down dramatically to a mere 1.3%, despite the continued rise in demand and the ongoing ageing of Britain's population. Collectively, the NHS Trusts have a deficit of over £4.2 billion (2018), and the Nuffield Trust has estimated that by 2021/22 the NHS in England will be facing a funding shortfall of £54 billion, despite government promises of a further £8 billion over the next five years. Meanwhile, adult social care budgets for local authorities have fallen by nearly 10% a year in the same period, contributing to the current crisis of bed-blocking in NHS hospitals and forcing local authorities to raise council tax in 2018/19 by 6% on average to compensate. The UK health and social care system faces what one chief executive has called a *"perfect storm of funding, workforce shortages versus an abundance of patients"*, and the Health Foundation declared in 2018 that: *"national policy and planning for the NHS workforce in England is not fit for purpose."* Recent surveys predict a shortfall of doctors, with more than 350 practices facing closure over 2019 in England alone, according to the Royal College of General Practitioners (RCGP), as GPs retire in droves and the supply of medics from the EU shrinks as a result of Brexit.

The IFS Review in 2018 estimated that just to keep pace with escalating costs, the UK healthcare budget would need to rise by 3.3% a year over the next 15 years; and by 4% a year if it is to have any chance of modernising delivery and performance. Capital spending alone would need to rise by 11% to £5 billion by 2023/24 in funding new or refurbished hospitals and in introducing new technology. This would raise healthcare spending in the UK to 10% of national income, comparable to healthcare spending in countries such as Germany and Sweden, and essential to funding the extra 64,000 hospital doctors and 171,000 nurses now needed to support the UK's growing and ageing population. In response, the Conservative Government in 2018 committed to increasing NHS funding by some £20 billion as part of a ten-year funding plan and, though this may well help stabilise the NHS in the short-term, in the long-term a far more radical reorientation and restructuring of healthcare in the UK will be needed to meet the emerging needs of 21st-century Britain. As John Appleby and his colleagues at the Nuffield Trust have argued, the state alone cannot afford to continue funding the escalating costs of health and social care in the UK; the Individual, too, has to play a part and plan ahead. Extra funding will certainly help but the real issue, in his view, is not funding but "*the underlying (demographic) forces that drive health care spending – a growing and ageing population, rising chronic disease, workforce challenges and expensive new medicines.*" Moreover, the burden of healthcare in the UK may soon have to shift as the over-85s grow, not only in numbers but in disabilities, and in the need for care as they live longer. (Age UK Briefing: 2017.) This may be a shock, not only to the NHS but also to the many elderly people who seem to have made little if any provision for care in later life. Governments of all parties have struggled to come to terms with the cost of long-term care and who pays for it, and Theresa May's attempt to 'cap' such costs in her 2017 election campaign showed just how toxic this issue is and how easily a government can lose electoral support because of it.

The healthcare challenge in the UK, however, is not just a financial one. As David's report highlighted, it is equally a social – and a political – one, as much about the distribution of health as the distribution of wealth. Health inequalities in the UK tend to follow wealth inequalities; and where and how you live in the UK tends to have a dramatic effect on the quality of your healthcare, as well as on your life and the length of it. As official statistics from the ONS in 2017 starkly illustrated, Britain is a highly unequal and highly divided society, with significant health gaps between the North and the South, Scotland and Northern Ireland, compared to England and Wales. Life expectancy for newborn baby boys is highest in the country in Kensington and Chelsea at 83.3 years and lowest in Blackpool at 74.5 years, while for baby girls it's highest in Chiltern at 86.7 years and lowest in Middlesbrough at 79.8 years. The ONS Bulletin (2017) identified a clear and stark gap in life expectancy between the North and South of England – although there's now some evidence of this gap closing. These gender and geographical gaps in life expectancy, however, are dwarfed by those between the most and the least 'advantaged' occupations, between those in manual jobs and those in higher managerial and professional ones. As cited earlier, the ONS report in March 2019 on inequality in healthy life expectancy calculated that: "*Males in the most advantaged areas in England can expect to live **19.1 years** longer in 'Good' health than those in the least advantaged areas as measured by the slope index of inequality while for females this difference is 18.8 years – and growing by as much as half a year over any three year period.*" The Marmot Report (2017) showed that, even within the same area, the gap in socio-economic and occupational life expectancy was vast with, for example, the rich in Kensington and Chelsea living on average 16 years longer than their poorer neighbours. These figures are astonishing, if not scandalous, in a country as wealthy and apparently caring as Great Britain. A 20-year difference in healthy life expectancy between the richest and the poorest in British society is something of a moral as well as a social indictment of the basic principles of the welfare state. It represents a massive waste of human life and potential across the 'classes', and it should provoke political outrage; but it doesn't – partly because, possibly, we are not fully aware of such devastating statistics, partly because we blame the individual given that personal and class lifestyles play a significant part in ill health today. Smokers still seem to be determined to smoke themselves 'to death', while obesity appears to have reached the stage of being declared a national, even global, epidemic, according to the McKinsey Institute in 2016.

As Polly is acutely aware, however, the crisis for the NHS isn't just one of its capacity to meet the demands for good health for all ages in modern Britain but also its ability to retain the nation's faith – and the politicians' – in its founding principles and its future performance. As the 2014 Barker Commission highlighted, although the NHS is still one of the most 'sacred of British cows', whose founding principles still inspire reverence from the British public, severe criticism has grown about the quality of its service and its apparent inability to keep up with best practice elsewhere in Europe.

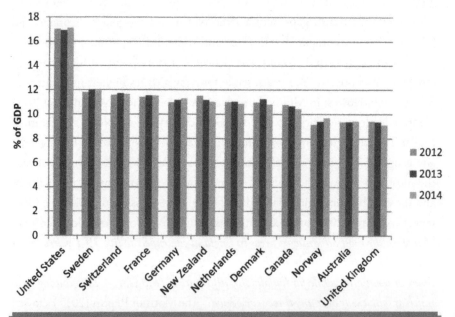

Figure 2: **International Comparisons of Healthcare Spending**
(Age UK: Feb.2017)

Until recently, the UK has spent less on healthcare than all the G7 countries except Italy, and the UK's reputation as 'the sick man of Europe' is equally reflected in its current performance.

In the ILC-UK Health Index in 2016, for example, the British National Health Service came a lowly 11th out of the 24 countries surveyed, below Ireland, Greece and Spain, despite being one of the richest countries in the Western world.

Country	2003	2013	10-year Change
Switzerland	1	1	-
Sweden	4	2	2
Ireland	3	3	-
Spain	16	4	**12**
Iceland	2	5	-3
Norway	6	6	-
Netherlands	8	7	1
Greece	5	8	-3
France	11	9	2
Luxembourg	15	10	5
United Kingdom	10	11	-1

Figure 3: **ILC-UK Health Index (2016)**

And if the NHS appears to be in crisis, the social care sector appears to be approaching meltdown. Spending on adult social care has fallen by nearly 10%, or £770 million, since 2010, with a record 1.2 million pensioners struggling to live independently because they're not being offered the care they need, according to Age UK (2017). The IFS predicted that if nothing changes in the way social care is delivered in the future, then the current budget for social care in England will have to nearly double, from £14.6 billion in 2010/11 to £23 billion by 2025/26, just to keep pace with demand. It estimated in 2018 that social care funding will need to rise by 3.9% just to keep pace with the UK's ageing population and provide, too, for the increasing number of young people living with disabilities.

The 2018 Report by the Care Quality Commission repeated its warning that social care in England had reached a *"tipping point"* as unmet need continues

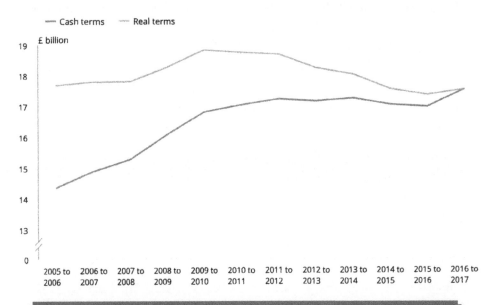

Figure 4: **Adult Social Care Spending**
(ONS: 2018)

to rise, and it highlighted the fact that personal care provision was not only often disjointed but too often an *"integration lottery"* as well as a *"postcode lottery"*. It predicted that unless care collaboration improved, and long-term funding was secured, care injustice in England would increase, particularly for those in most need. The Chief Executive of Care England has described the current social care system as a *"house of cards"* ready to topple over at any moment; the government has now allowed local councils to raise council tax by up to 2% to at least relieve some of this pressure, and promised an additional funding over the next ten years. Social care has long been the 'Cinderella' of the British welfare state, the 'ugly sister' to the 'beauty queen' that is the National Health Service. It has been treated and perceived as merely an adjunct to the NHS rather than an equal partner, despite its critical importance to patient recuperation and care in the community. However, the need for reform of health and social care in England doesn't stop at structure and funding. It also includes culture and community relations. As the Healthcare Ombudsman for England reported to the House of Lords Select Committee in 2012, the NHS *"is failing to treat older people with care, compassion, dignity and respect"*, while reports like that by Professor Francis in 2013 on Mid-Staffordshire

NHS Foundation Trust, illustrated that ill-treatment of the elderly is not only widespread in both hospitals and care homes, but that it has become a national scandal and a mark of shame for a public service specifically created to protect and support the elderly with compassion and dignity. Moreover, the crisis in social care can only escalate as the size and needs of the over-85 age group multiplies, the supply of care homes falls in response to cuts in local authority budgets, and the increasing difficulties of recruiting staff escalates, especially with the restrictions now on importing labour from abroad. According to the Care Quality Commission in 2016, the sustainability of the adult care market is now under threat and, with care home costs for 'self-funders' now nearly £44,000 a year, soon only the wealthiest pensioners will be able to afford such support. As the government's own Care Homes Market Report has identified, local authorities will need *"an extra £1 to £2 billion a year funding by 2025"* just to cope, and a dramatic improvement in their planning and commissioning strategies to build up the supply of care homes and staff to the levels is needed, as nearly 90 people a day – 32,000 adults a year – apparently die while waiting for care to be arranged for them at home, according to the Department of Health & Social Care in December 2018.

And if governments are living in a world of delusion and gross under-estimation as to the true costs of social care, the new old – the baby boomers and their children – are on another planet. According to the 2017 report by the actuarial consultancy, Hyman-Robertson, only 3% of baby boomers and Generation X expect to go into residential care in old age; over half of baby boomers (54%) and nearly half of Generation X (43%) are adamant that they will never save for long-term care; and both generations sadly underestimate quite badly the costs involved. The cost of residential care really is the elephant in the social-care room; and though Theresa May roused it in the 2017 general election, everyone since has sought to put it quietly back to sleep. As the Demos Survey in 2017 revealed, while the majority of the British public tend to agree that paying for care is an individual responsibility rather than the state's, in practice few people seem to be actively preparing for the immense costs involved – some £30–40,000 a year – and instead seem to be putting their faith in downsizing their house or relying on state funding. The dearth of trustworthy and effective insurance products to cover such costs is a monumental omission in government strategy and a serious failure of initiative by the financial sector; one that needs urgent attention. Innovation and step-change thinking are clearly vital to resuscitating the British welfare state. One such proposal from the Friends Provident Foundation, for example, is the creation of a **social care trust fund** paid for by small annual payments from the UK's top 350 companies, a levy on privately owned wealth and a 1p increase on National Insurance contributions. The money raised would be independently managed and globally invested, with an annual target of 4% earnings a year generating in ten years' time, a permanent funding stream of £25 billion for social care needs alone. This is an innovative proposal that clearly reflects the enormity of the care challenge but equally reflects the limitations of government thinking as to the depth and impact an ageing society is likely to have on future generations and on the family if nothing substantive continues to be done. Few families seem to have realised the potential impact on their lives and their finances of this ageing nightmare if the state cannot provide for their parents, nor of the social consequences of loneliness, mental illness and dementia amongst the elderly becoming a national dilemma akin to that in Japan. Here lies one of the most profound and disturbing of intergenerational debates at a time when it's not yet even a national conversation let alone a family one. The case of 'Team Grandad' cited in *The Sunday Times* (30 Dec. 2018) is, however, a shining example of what family support can do when combined with new technology. At aged 81, with the onset of dementia and Parkinson's disease, Albert Powley seemed destined to be consigned to the traditional pathway into a care home. Until that is, his family – all 14 of them – stepped in and pledged to look after him at home, supported by the latest technology to both keep an eye on him and enable him to lead as normal a life as possible. This self-help solution involved little extra cost and generated a great improvement in health and happiness as this particular family clubbed together to pay Albert back for all the care he and his wife had given them when they were young. Albert was fortunate, and deservedly so. Other pensioners may not be so lucky.

As Polly fully appreciated, governments in the UK have acted, almost ritually, to reform and restructure the NHS and social services in the UK, possibly too often and with too little understanding of the deep-seated issues involved. Healthcare, or at least the NHS, has been at the forefront of every political manifesto and every Queen's Speech since the inception of the British welfare state in 1942. The NHS has been subject to numerous attempts to reform and reorganise it, with the most recent attempt by the 2010–2015 Coalition Government claiming to be *"the greatest reorganisation of the National Health Service in England to date."* It took the form of the 2012 **Health and Social Care Act**, designed on one hand to integrate health and care and on the other to devolve it to local authorities through local health and well-being boards. Such boards would be responsible for carrying out a Joint Strategic Needs Assessment (JSNA) of their local population and drawing up a

Joint Health and Wellbeing Strategy (JHWS), prioritising the primary health needs of their area with Clinical Commissioning Groups (CCGs), made up of GPs from local general practices and commissioning the required health services. This was a significant step forward, and this strategic shift in power and responsibility for healthcare, from central to local government, was based on the premise that local authorities know their local populations and health needs best and so will be better able to target resources efficiently and effectively. In particular, local people will feel more in control of their healthcare and more able to demand change or call local services to account. Critics, however, fear that this shift to localism will weaken the NHS as a *national* health service, undermine its political and electoral support and worsen the effects of the current 'postcode lottery' in the delivery and funding of healthcare provision at local level, particularly where local authorities reduce or reprioritise public health as a result of ever tighter budget controls. The subsequent *Care Act of 2014* extended these changes further by undertaking what Age UK has described as "*the most thorough reform of care legislation since 1948*", involving several significant new developments that put local authorities at the heart of managing and monitoring the local 'care market' to assure quality and provide impartial advice and guidance on care options and funding. Increasingly, however, cuts to local government spending have led to an increasing number of care home franchises withdrawing from this market and, although local authorities now have some leeway in raising council taxes, the crisis in care provision is likely to remain.

So, asked Polly, what is the future of the NHS? Can the NHS as we know it even survive? Does it still have a future? As the NHS turns 70, Simon Stevens, the CEO of NHS England, certainly believes it does, and the new NHS five-year plan aims to promote good health as well as treat ill health, to integrate health with social care, and to relocate support services out into the community alongside local GPs. Such a reorganisation would indeed shift the NHS more towards the localised and personalised framework advocated by many for healthcare delivery in the 21st century if, and only if, the historic resistance of the UK health system to change can be overcome, the funding needed for such a radical shift in resources can be found, and the political will for such a long-term reform can be sustained. The record of radical change in the NHS, however, is not strong, and Britain's burgeoning ageing population may not be able to wait patiently for these reforms to be put in place, certainly not if that wait is in a hospital corridor or outside in the back of an ambulance. Greater Manchester appears to be one of the local authorities leading the way in the UK towards a much more integrated and comprehensive healthcare provision for the 2.7 million people and ten local boroughs within its area. Such regional and local leadership, however, at present still seems to be more the exception to the rule than the model for future best practice.

Radical new thinking is equally needed at the national level. The health think tank, the King's Fund, sought to provide such thinking by setting up the Commission on the Future of Health and Social Care in England in 2013 to specifically address the challenges of an ageing Britain. The Barker Commission, as it became known, concluded that the 1948 settlement for health and social care was no longer fit for purpose and needed a new settlement, a more integrated and fairly funded model for health and social care that rebalanced public perceptions and improved the distribution of public funding between the NHS and its ugly-duckling sister, the social care services. "*The NHS is largely free at the point of use. Almost no one has to worry about medical bills. Thanks to the NHS, healthcare bankrupts nobody. Social care, by contrast, can consume large amounts of an individual's or family's income and savings... People with dementia have to pay for their own care while people with cancer don't. There is not equal treatment of equal need.*"

The Commission proposed a single, 'ring-fenced' budget for both health and social care so that patients no longer had to deal with two separate systems. As cited earlier, the Commission also recommended a significant rise in healthcare funding to levels comparable to other advanced countries such as Canada, France and the Netherlands, funded not only from general taxation but by the elderly giving up age-related benefits currently worth over £7 billion, levying NI contributions on private pensions (£350m), and by scrapping the tax-free lump sum (£2.5bn) on existing pensions. As the Commission's report concluded: "*The Prize is huge*", and the reforms proposed would lead to a more integrated and more fully funded National Health and Social Care Service, of equal status and equal funding. However, while a number of these changes have since been adopted, notably the move to integrate health and social care alongside the recent rise in healthcare funding, such changes still tend to be knee-jerk government responses to urgent crises, propping up the existing system rather than rethinking it fundamentally for the century ahead.

Global healthcare planning, in contrast, is streets ahead of the UK. It has moved away from the old-age welfare state model of the mid-20th century, whereby the state provides all, towards a radically new approach pioneered by the WHO back in the 1970s. This model puts the individual rather than the state at the forefront of managing, monitoring and funding personalised healthcare throughout his/her lifetime, not just when they're ill and need treatment but equally when they are well and seek to stay that way mentally as well as physically. This is a much more holistic and forward-looking approach to healthcare, and it has lifestyle and well-being as high on the agenda as illness and treatment. Under this model, the individual, not the medical expert, is in charge, acting as a health consumer and selecting goods and services on how to be healthy, from nutritionists and gymnasts as much as from doctors and psychologists, from a global market as much as their local GP. This paradigm shift in thinking and in defining healthcare can perhaps be traced back to the WHO and its adoption in 1977 of a definition of 'good health' as *"a state of complete physical, mental and social well-being... not merely [as] the absence of disease or infirmity"* but *"as a fundamental human right."* This was a truly radical and ground-breaking step-change in thinking and strategy that took the ideal of good health out of its narrow medical model and placed it firmly and squarely in the broader arena of economic and political policy alongside debates about economic growth and the distribution of wealth and power. It emphasised the importance of mental and psychological health as part of personal and community well-being, and it embraced the ideal of good health as part of its broader vision of social justice.

This definition has underpinned the WHO's approach to global ageing ever since, and in its 2012 report the WHO adopted **active ageing** as its strategy for tackling global healthcare generally, and for all ages, not just the old; a life-course strategy that seeks to promote healthy living in later life by healthy living *throughout* life, so preventing the traditional diseases of old age appearing – or at least appearing so early. For the WHO, the active engagement of the elderly in society and their local community, even their local economy, is central to improving the psychological and spiritual well-being of the elderly themselves as well as reducing the cost and burden of dependent ageing on the rest of the community. The 2015 WHO report on ageing and health took this strategy for 'age liberation' and active ageing to another level by promoting, on one hand, the notion of **age friendliness**, with 'age-friendly cities' as a high profile example, and by attacking **age discrimination** on the other, highlighting its insidious and widespread nature and its profound impact on the elderly and on society at large; an impact as profound and disabling as racism or sexism but one that is less visible and less likely to generate widespread protests and political action. Finally, by declaring **active ageing** to be a human right and drawing up a charter for the rights of the older person, the WHO sought to use age to drive the rights of the old in the 21st century, just as effectively as age was used to drive the rights and the welfare of the young in the 20th.

The WHO approach to ageing in the 21st century, and to global health at large, is indeed **age-defying**, a radical shift in thinking and in the positive promotion of good health as a human right. The WHO has clearly entered the political arena and not only called national governments to task but directly linked population ageing with socio-economic development. The global health debate, therefore, now centres as much around the working of the global economy and the impact of the financial decisions of such international institutions as the World Bank and IMF as it does around individual government strategies to improve national health. The relationship of world health to world wealth was well illustrated when, in the austerity drives that followed the 2008 economic crisis, health budgets across Europe were slashed and ill health and social depression escalated, particularly in countries experiencing the worst of the downturn, such as Greece and Spain. Healthcare today is therefore is as much about **wealth-care** as it is about healthcare, as much about the distribution of global wealth as it is about the distribution of global health. The WHO's torchlight on the economic dimensions of healthcare has highlighted the responsibility of the richer nations for the healthcare and economic development of the poorer ones, not just in preventing global pandemics and the spread of disease but equally in promoting the global economy and, with it, global security. The global economy is now so integrated that ill health in one part of the world can threaten the health and economic well-being of nations across the globe. Global consumers and national workers need to be healthy as well as wealthy if they are to contribute to economic growth, but often the policies of the World Bank, IMF and international stock exchanges – as well as the marketing of the food, drugs and drinks industries – have impacted adversely on national health and on healthy ageing, as the 2008 crisis has so painfully illustrated.

So, while the WHO and the UN have set out the new global agenda for ageing, and while nations across the world struggle to cope with the escalating demand for good health and the escalating cost of ageing, the healthcare industry globally is undergoing a silent revolution of its own; a remodelling, or paradigm change, according to the Economist 2020 study, that involves political, social and ethical issues as much as those involving health and finance; a paradigm change that will increasingly convert any national healthcare system from a *sickness service* to a health service that proactively offers prevention as well as cure in the management of lifelong health; a *medical model* based less on the authority of those at the top – the medical expert, doctor and nurse – and more on the voice and choice of the patient as a consumer with the rights and the power to call the health authorities to account; a *state-run healthcare system* increasingly open to, and working with, market forces; and a *model of delivery* within which hospitals are a last line of treatment not the first port of call. And finally, the shift from a *segregated healthcare system* with separate health and social service systems and funding streams to a fully integrated personalised service, supporting patients throughout their medical journey at all stages and ages of life, from consultation through to diagnosis, treatment and ultimately on to recovery – and longer, healthier life. As the Economist 2020 analysis concluded, healthcare globally is about to enter a new era and be transformed in three critical ways:

1. Medical technology is soon to become simpler, more portable and easy to use 'in the field' and at home, so reducing the need for hospitals and expensive medical expertise and technology at the centre and increasing the capacity for home visits by paramedics and nurses and for home monitoring and self-diagnosis. Telemedicine and e-therapy will enable doctors and specialists to counsel patients at home, and patients to monitor and treat themselves for minor ailments and even chronic disabilities under online supervision and support. Hospitals, currently the costliest form of medical treatment, will become hubs for community care.

2. Developments in genomics and biotechnology are revolutionising our understanding of disease and our capacity to treat it effectively, even to the point of literally transporting drugs to target areas in the body, creating artificial limbs or new organs and personalising drug treatments that match individual needs – "*a pill for every ill delivered to your body part*". Ironically, as the King's Fund warned in its 2012 report, while the pace of innovation is breathtaking, these new developments may, in practice, generate new demands as much as satisfy existing ones and so potentially increase the pressures on healthcare systems rather than relieve them. More urgently, will these new advances be available to all who need them or only to those with the wealth to buy them or the medical clout to demand them?

3. The globalisation of the healthcare industry: Healthcare has already become a global industry through the expansion and integration of multinational companies such as GlaxoSmithKline and AstraZeneca, and through globalisation of the healthcare workforce mainly from the developing to developed nations as Western nations recruit some 70% of their doctors and nurses from Asia and Africa. *Medical tourism* has become a boom industry as the rich – and even the not so rich – travel to South America, India or Asia for treatments unavailable or too costly at home, and outsourcing to call centres or hospital laboratories to faraway continents is now well established. As the European Observatory Report in concluded in 2013: "*The 21ˢᵗ century heralds the era of doctors and patients without borders. The internet, combined with advances in digital technology and affordable international travel, has severed the geographic links between healthcare providers and consumers, offering new options to receive and deliver healthcare services, information and products that were previously unavailable… [However] …This new (global) system lacks both regulation and control.*"

Add to these three transformations, the internet, the digital revolution and modern data management, and the ingredients for a revolution in medical delivery and healthcare are all there. New technology is at the heart, too, of the new NHS five-year plan yet, even now, while over 85% of adults in the UK use the internet for everything else, only 2% apparently use the internet to contact their GP; and the NHS, one of the largest employers in the world, still uses fax machines as one of its main forms of communication. Digital technology is at the heart of modern working life, yet many health and care workers still see it as an intrusion and an additional burden rather than a smart way to relieve their workloads – perhaps not surprising, given the strain they're under.

The healthcare revolution, however, is not only about technology and new medical miracles but also about the liberation of the individual from passive patient to active manager of his or her health, with the capability of self-diagnosis and self-treatment being counterbalanced by healthy living, by regulation and by lifestyles that outlaw the ill health often promoted or induced by the food industry and the over-medication prescribed by doctors and promoted by the drug companies. Such a transformation in medical relationships and in consumer behaviour would represent a power shift away from the current monopoly power of the medical profession over health prescription and provision and back to the ordinary people and the local community, with the patient taking on more of the role of consumer and so gaining far more control of their own health and decisions about it. Certainly there is a growing appetite for self-care created by greater public understanding of the ill health effects of an unhealthy lifestyle, the growth of the health, fitness, and now well-being and mindfulness industries, and possibly a decline in the absolute trust that people once had in doctors and in the NHS as scandals about treatment, misdiagnosis and the spread of viruses within hospitals are regularly headlined in the media and elsewhere. And to encourage such health ownership, the NHS is now undertaking a massive 'moving nation' project to encourage far greater exercise and activity, encouraging patients to get out of bed and exercise rather than, as in the past, recover by resting. As Professor Gray of Oxford University has pithily put it: "*Exercise is a miracle cure. If I could patent it, I would be a billionaire.*" (*The Sunday Times*: 2 Sept. 2018)

The internet in particular has provided people with an array of self-care guides, life-expectancy calculators and the publications of health evangelists such as Patrick Holford (2012), alongside patient forums and peer group blogs to question and challenge traditional medical opinion. The doctor today is no longer God, nor are his words of wisdom accepted without question; rather, the whole Western medical model of health and illness is under scrutiny. Yet at the same time, we in the affluent West – and increasingly the developing East – seem to be killing ourselves through our lifestyles, diet and a lack of positive personal health planning. Hence the Public Health England quiz cited earlier, to try and jump-start public awareness that we are killing ourselves through our own lifestyles rather than being killed by our environments or natural diseases. Hence, too, the shift by health insurance companies to offering lower premiums to clients who exercise regularly and eat nutritionally. Writers such as Lisa Bloch and Kathy Silverman (2012) have gone further, highlighting the hidden, less visible side of human health and well-being, the psychology of health emanating from the male menopause, or '*manopause*' as they call it. As these female writers have sought to show, retirement and withdrawal from the workplace, that traditional source of male status and authority, have a dramatic impact on many men's sense of purpose and self-esteem, and so in turn may impact profoundly on their health, happiness and relationships and on their levels of energy and activity. As Bloch and Silverman observe: "*for most men if their penis is down so are their spirits*". Viagra may not only be restoring men's manhood; it may be restoring their self-esteem.

So, the patient of the 21st century is much more likely to be an active, enlightened and demanding consumer, more aware of and in control of his or her health, and more prepared to demand action than to queue for it. This surge in patient power, aided and abetted by organisations like Healthwatch in the UK, is, however, likely to be more the preserve of the articulate middle classes than the voice of ordinary people, and so likely, potentially, to exacerbate existing health inequalities. As Richard Wilkinson and Kate Pickett so vividly illustrated in 2009, the full step-change in individual health and well-being will only come with a dramatic reduction in inequalities in wealth and income. Britain remains one of the most unequal nations in the Western world, and only a government committed to radical changes in tax and financial controls, as well as in healthcare spending, can seriously impact on the current unequal and unhealthy distribution of healthcare expectancies and provision.

Healthcare in the 21ˢᵗ century: So, where is all this leading? What will healthcare look like in 2030 and beyond? According to Professor Michio Kaku (2012):

- **By 2030** your doctor will have become a robotic animation, your diagnosis will have become a handheld MRI scanner and your computer will be able to accurately profile and diagnose your DNA in 3D. The house will have been 'sensored' to monitor and detect any signs of illness, irregularity or trauma from a fall or an accident. There will be brain food for babies, female Viagra, memory pills, and vaccinations to resist smoking, alcohol and food.

- **By 2070** gene therapy will be standard practice, targeted initially against single mutations but gradually capable of tackling the multiple mutations that cause diabetes, Alzheimer's, Parkinson's and heart disease. Molecular medicine and the Human Genome Project hold the promise of being able to reveal the very 'secrets of life', and in this new era everyone will soon have access to his or her own genome profile, a sort of owner's manual to your body and your health.

Researchers at the Profam laboratory in the UK announced in July 2019 that they believe that they have developed techniques for delaying the menopause for up to twenty years while the CRISPR process opens up the possibility of eliminating or altering serious generic disorders at any stage in their development, from birth to old age. CRISPR is a revolutionary step forward in gene-editing technology, offering the prospect of modifying or editing out defective or life-threatening genes from humans, animals and even crops, and potentially laying to rest many cancers and cardiovascular diseases. It is likely to be big business generating huge profits for the major drug companies, and for investors such as Bill Gates and Larry Page of Google fame. Yet it is relatively cheap, simple and likely soon to be widely available throughout the world's health services. Such availability and ease of application, though, may also open up the possibilities not only of a mass market in designer babies but also the horrors of biohacking and even bioterrorism. Revolutionary developments such as CRISPR even open up the prospect of ever longer life, of eternal youth and even of immortality. According to Nobel Laureate, Richard Feynman: "*By 2100, it might be possible to reverse the effects of aging by accelerating cell repair mechanisms to live well beyond that.*" Professor Robert A. Freitas Jnr has gone even further, with the astonishing prediction that sometime in the near future: "*Using annual check-ups and cleanouts, and some occasional major repairs, your biological age could be restored once a year to the more or less constant physiological age you select. You might still die of accidental causes, but you'll live at least ten times longer than you do now.*"

If correct, then we are truly entering the 'inner sanctum' of nature and all the ethical and moral issues involved. As the secrets of ageing are increasingly unravelled, and unravelled at speed, in decades rather than in centuries, so a new unified theory of ageing may be emerging that will not only explain but also plot and treat any genetic or cellular errors in your DNA. Nano-cars or bodily drones will become bodily 'smart-bombs', targeted to destroy cancer cells, suffocate tumours or kill off viruses. Your body will become a 'battlefield' and genomic medicine will become the hottest field in medical research and medical engineering, a new applied science for renovating and rebuilding the human body. The ethical issues involved will be immense, and given past experience they are likely to be swept away in the gold rush for eternal life, issues involving the ethics of creating, say, designer children, along with critical debates about cloning, brain transplants, cryonics and the freezing of human bodies for life in the future (a facility already provided by the Alcor Life Extension Foundation in Arizona, USA). According to studies such as that by Professor Gordon Lithgow of the Buck Institute for Research on Aging in California, scientists now believe that it's possible to slow down the process of ageing, eliminate diseases such as Parkinson's and Alzheimer's and enable people to live into their 100s and even 120s in *good* health. Truly a new era of geroscience, which at first mesmerised Polly and David but which, on reflection, began to horrify them, given the ethical issues involved and the life-determining decisions that both of them in their respective professions might have to make. Moreover, asked Polly, are we now moving from how best to manage an ageing society towards developing an ageless society where you can live as long as you want and be as young as you want so long as you can pay for it? According to David Kekich of the Maximum Life Foundation: "*We will be able to transform eighty-year-olds into twenty-something's visually and biologically*", while Ian Pearson, a futurologist, believes that by 2050 we will be able to upload our entire brain onto a flash drive, saving our personalities forever. We appear to be moving from a debate about ageing and the *quantity* of life onto one about agelessness and the *quality* of life – and possibly one about man's capacity to play God. As Professor Kaku (2012) gently warns us, while the future may look healthy and long, always be careful what you ask for: "*I once read a story about a genie who offered to grant a man any wish he wanted. He promptly asked to live for 1,000 years. The genie granted his wish and turned him into a tree.*"

So, healthcare nationally and globally is entering a whole new era, a whole new world of unlimited health and apparently unlimited life. Ageing in these futuristic fantasies no longer seems to be an issue. Back on earth, though, people across the globe are ageing, and ageing at incredibly varying rates, that make longevity not only an issue of health but one of international equality and social justice, a monumental gap in life-chance vividly illustrated by Professor Sarah Harper in 2006: "*While a baby girl born in Japan today can expect to live about 85 years, a girl born at the same moment in Sierra Leone has a life expectancy of 36 years. The Japanese girl will receive vaccinations, adequate nutrition and good schooling*" and "*high quality maternity care*" with excellent medical treatment throughout the rest of her long life... "*The girl in Sierra Leone has little chance of receiving immunization and a high probability of being underweight throughout childhood. She will probably marry in adolescence and go on to give birth to six or more children without the assistance of a trained birth attendant. One or more of her babies will die in infancy, and she herself will be at high risk of death in childbirth.*" Medical treatment throughout the rest of her short life will be limited and "*she will die prematurely*".

Patients today are far more demanding, and healthcare is now universally recognised as the key to longer, healthier life. No prize is greater than the demographic dividend of the 21st century, but to gain it we will have to earn it; to see its potential in all its glory and demand its delivery before it's too late. For British baby boomers this is an urgent and, in age terms, a pressing issue, and as a generation they have the need and the power to demand that healthcare in the UK be transformed, be elevated to a new level and to a new model of personalised delivery: a partnership between patients and medical and care professionals. It needs a new social contract that incorporates the ideals of the Beveridge Report, delivered this time through the 'magic' of new scientific discoveries and new technology but with the patient an increasingly active agent at the heart of the system, not as in the past on its periphery. Such a transformation would require the full force of patient power and a properly regulated marketplace for healthcare products and services. It may require a new approach to delivering the NHS that maintains its public control, accountability and leadership but equally develops more efficient and high-quality modes of delivery. It may equally require a much stronger emphasis on community care, as in Holland, where the Dutch are seeking to revolutionise healthcare through '*Buurtzorg*', or neighbourhood care, with nurses acting as health coaches, with minimum bureaucracy and maximum time helping clients keep themselves healthy and active. With claims of a 40% saving in healthcare costs and much higher patient and staff levels of well-being, the Dutch experiment is attracting worldwide attention.

As a generation, the baby boomers, by need and nature, are ideally placed to lead this healthcare revolution if the government will not or cannot. It is this generation that first benefitted from the Beveridge welfare state and its commitment to care from 'cradle to grave'. It is this age group, too, that will now benefit from the step-changes in treatment and cure being offered by these breakthrough discoveries and the transformation in delivery promised by the new technologies. They are equally the most educated and (overall) affluent post-war generation, the most demanding and the most ambitious, the most prepared to use their considerable powers in the political and commercial marketplace, and the least likely to be seduced or swayed by professional techno-speak or commercial promotions, be it by the medical or care professions, the drugs or the food industries. They worked in all these fields, they helped set up these organisations, they invented and deployed these ways of communicating with each other and with the public. They're not going to be easily fooled by them. As the Chief Medical Officer's Report in 2015/16 highlighted: the health needs of the new old, the baby boomer generation, are increasingly immediate and urgent, not only in terms of the size, length and diversity of this demographic, but in the internal split into two distinctly different sub-generations – 1946–55 and 1955–65 – and the likely separation between those living as couples and those living alone. Such challenges include:

• The caring challenge facing baby boomers with ageing parents on one side, and dependent, or even adult, children on the other.
• The health challenge facing this generation in terms of unhealthy lifestyles, with so many baby boomers still smoking, drinking alcohol to excess – with, on average, baby boomer women drinking more alcohol than women 20 years ago – and suffering from obesity, with nearly half of baby boomer men and over a third of baby boomer women overweight.
• The inequalities in health and health provision facing, and dividing, this generation in terms of both class and geography and that currently

separate the northern and rural/coastal regions from the wealthier and heathier South.

- The need to further promote and strengthen screening and immunisation programmes amongst baby boomers, particularly for bowel, prostate and breast cancer, and for pneumococcal and influenza vaccination.

- The rising tide in mental illnesses amongst this age group, notably in male suicide rates, autism, depression and anxiety.

- The challenge of maintaining positive sexual health amongst baby boomers, in tackling sexual dysfunctions such as ED, and yet alerting active oldies to the dangers of sexually transmitted diseases even at their ripe old age as the rate of re-partnering grows.

Such a governmental spotlight on the generational needs and challenges of the emerging old, and the potential to mitigate or alleviate their health burden in old age before it's too late, is clearly a welcome and pro-active approach worthy of much greater drive and communication. It has equally highlighted yet again the dark shadow lurking in the medical room, that of dementia and its potential impact on family and community life in the near future. Over 820,000 people were estimated to be suffering from the onset of dementia in 2010, with an expected rise to one million by 2025 and 1.7 million by 2051. *"Dementia costs the UK approximately £23 billion per year, about twice as much as cancer, yet this country spends nearly twelve times as much on cancer research as on research into dementia."* And hiding behind dementia, less visible but just as damaging, are the age-related social diseases of malnutrition (estimated at 1.3 million over-65s), mental health (estimated at 2 million people aged 65+ in England) and loneliness (estimated at 775,000 older people, or 7% of the over-65s in the UK); social diseases that will overwhelm us very soon if the politicians fail to take a lead or generate the health debate that Britain so desperately needs.

And what about the younger generations, the generations that are going to have to pay so heavily and for so long for the NHS of the future? In a student-led debate in early 2018, researchers from the King's Fund asked exactly those questions, and the young people involved were very clear that *"futureproofing our NHS"* is desperately needed. They wanted to depoliticise the national health landscape by taking it out of politicians' hands and setting up an independent health policy committee modelled on, say, the Monetary Policy Committee, with health champions and health coaches appointed to promote healthcare at all levels across local communities and all ages. They also suggested democratising healthcare through what were called 'normovation pathways' that gave both staff and patients far greater involvement in treatment from start to finish. Radical ideas but invaluable contributions to any healthcare debate if the NHS of the future really is to continue to be a National Health Service for all ages that both the young and the old can believe in and trust.

Finally – be warned – living longer is not a natural right or an inevitability. Douglas apparently led a very healthy lifestyle and appeared to be in rude health. Nevertheless, he was struck down unexpectedly and out of the blue. He was lucky; he was cured and now has to re-plan his health and re-plan his retirement in partnership with his wife, Deborah, according not only to his health and hers but that of his wider family. Was his prostate cancer simply a chance occurrence, or was it genetic and likely to strike Douglas's children, or in the future, his grandchildren? Healthcare today is an immense and potentially very costly challenge, not only for society but for every family and individual. It's the price of longevity but, as Douglas reflected, it's the best possible investment that any ageing couple can make in their future. Ever-lengthening longevity cannot be taken for granted. It has to be worked on, and it can go down as well as up. As ONS data for 2017 has shown, healthy life expectancy at aged 65 has recently shown signs of falling for the first time in 30 years, with a fall for men from 10.6 to 10.3 years and from 11.2 to 10.9 for women in the period 2010–2014 as a result, apparently, of obesity and heavy drinking, as well as failings in elderly healthcare. A warning for all of us – the young too.

Polly and David were exhausted and exhilarated after this walk-through of the medical literature. A whole new world, a bold, and very brave, new world had opened up before them that on one hand had lifted their spirits as well as opened up their horizons about what a forward-looking healthcare strategy might look like and what it could do for their respective constituents and patients; but on the other hand, it had highlighted real dangers for the weak, poor and lonely, and raised immense ethical and political dilemmas that were not readily apparent beneath all the magic and mystery of everlasting life and instant repair. Overall, though, this medical presentation of the future was awe-inspiring and gave both of them real hope for the future. It represented an immense challenge, not least in rejuvenating the principles of the NHS for the world of healthcare needed for the century ahead. Polly's vision of active ageing now became a centrepiece for her embryonic new age manifesto. She could already imagine the response of her own generation, the baby boomer generation, to any prospect of youthful old age, and particularly to everlasting life. They would love it and go for it in a big way. Their determination to live forever is almost written into boomer DNA and is well embodied in the pop songs that gave them life and love in their youth some 50 years ago.

6 | Housing, Homes and the Intergenerational Housing Chain

"England's population is ageing, and fast. By 2030 one in three people are projected to be aged 55 and over. Older people will be a diverse group, ranging from economically powerful 'baby boomers' to over-85s with high care and support needs. How will the housing market respond to this demographic change? Do we have the right kinds of accommodation for older people, in the right places?"

Shelter: A Better Fit (2012)

Lloyd and Lily were in their late 60s. Their three children were all grown up, one working abroad and the other two living locally with their own growing families. Lloyd and Lily lived in a large four-bedroom house in a village just outside Norwich. The house had served them well but it was now too large to manage and too costly to maintain. They needed to downsize to something smaller, possibly in or close to the city, but prices for flats and two-bed properties there were high given the university population and number of young people who stay in Norwich and start families there. Lloyd and Lily also needed to pay off their interest-only mortgage and use the remaining equity to either rent for the rest of their lives or pay for a new, much smaller property. However, few mortgage companies today will lend much beyond age 65, and their own provider had already notified them that their current mortgage had to be redeemed in two years' time. While their income from pensions and savings was adequate, they had ambitions to travel and possibly buy/rent a property abroad in a healthier climate, to relieve Lloyd's arthritis. Hence the need to spread any remaining equity as far as possible. In contrast, their daughter Elaine and her husband Eric were desperate to upsize to something bigger, ideally out in the country, with a sizeable garden and access to better schools. They and their three growing children – aged five, three and 18 months respectively – were simply bursting out of their two-bedroomed terraced house in the city centre, but properties large enough to accommodate three growing children – and a dog – were simply beyond even their joint incomes.

The housing scenario above is a classic example of the housing dilemma facing numerous families across the country at either end of the **housing ladder**. It is a classic example of the many housing dilemmas that walk into Polly's surgery every week. This particular case study, however, was not one of Polly's constituents but one of her fellow MPs in East Anglia, and one example of the many cases confronting the All-Party Committee on Housing that Polly now chairs as it took evidence on the housing crisis that now faces ageing Britain. Recent reports by Shelter have highlighted yet again the dire effects of government inaction and lack of strategic planning and investment in this 'Cinderella sector', despite numerous promises to the contrary.

• The November 2018 Report calculated that although there are at least 307,000 officially homeless people in England today, estimates show that the total figure may well be as high as 1 in 200 across the whole population, as many homeless are hidden by temporary accommodation or 'sofa surfing' with family or friends.

• The January 2019 Report highlighted the dramatic and devastating decline in social house building in England since the 1980s, plummeting from the post-war average of 126,000 per year to just 6,463 in 2018 and generating immense and intense human suffering in its wake.

These reports, and many others, however, all come down to the same thing: the desperate shortage of suitable housing for all ages and all incomes in England today and the endemic failure of government planning and investment in this sector, a shortage that is creating a national crisis and is likely to get even more intense as Britain ages, as baby boomers retire and as the younger generations find themselves either priced out of the UK housing market, stuck in the middle of the housing ladder with an ever-growing family or forced to move back home through escalating rents or unemployment. And that's not to mention the 'housing hothouse' that is London, a housing market fuelled by billionaire buyers from abroad as well as workers not wishing to commute for four hours or more a day. Moreover, until recently, the government has failed to strategically or substantially address the needs of the first-time buyer and has shown even less awareness and understanding of the emerging army of **last-time buyers** – buyers who now have the housing wealth and consumer clout to demand better or force change themselves.

Following the House of Lords Select Committee report on ageing in 2013, Polly's All-Party Committee on Housing was commissioned to look into the later-life housing market in the UK. As the committee became increasingly aware from its numerous submissions, until recently housing hasn't even been on the ageing agenda. Pensions and healthcare have dominated the headlines, while housing has tended to be the 'Cinderella of the silver revolution', relegated by public costs and lower priority to an afterthought. Yet for pensioners like Lloyd and Lily, home is the 'centre of their universe', their 'castle and their keep' in the remaining years ahead and fundamental to their independence and sense of self-control. Moving home, downsizing and especially moving into residential care are, for many, the final stages of life, the last rites in the passage from independence to dependency and departure. The importance of housing, therefore, is often underestimated in debates about ageing; and its value – symbolic as well as financial – to the individual is often seriously overlooked in discussions about later-life and legacy planning. But housing isn't just a personal or family matter. It is equally central to any debate about the UK economy at one level, and intergenerational relations, social justice and inequality at the other. As the scenario above illustrates, it's not just an individual or household matter; it's a family matter too. Lloyd and Lily could quite easily and quite fairly concentrate on sorting out their own housing dilemma. They could equally seek to either help their children move up the UK housing ladder or seek a radically different solution, an intergenerational solution, by, say, all moving in together. Such novel and family sensitive solutions are being adopted by an increasing number of families and they increasingly appeal to Polly, not only as a politician seeking practical solutions and social justice but as a grandmother overseeing an ever-expanding multigenerational family of her own.

As the committee's initial research highlighted, as the UK population ages so an age-related housing crisis is emerging, generated by a serious under-supply of housing for all age groups. The under-supply of housing for the young at a price that they can afford is well known and well researched.

* discontinuity of data 1946-65. Pre-1965 (red) includes Wales. Post-1946 data in blue. Post 2006 data (green) relates to the new builds outlined in the net additional dwellings release this measure is more comprehensive than previous counts.

** data in blue is for calendar years. Data in red and green is for financial years.

Figure 1: **House building since the 1920s**
(DCLG: 2017)

One hundred and eighty-four thousand houses were completed in England in 2016/17, a slight improvement on previous years but nevertheless well below the 250,000 apparently needed, and half the highest recorded figure of 352,540 built in 1968. This dire shortage of housing in turn generates higher house prices that price many first-time buyers out of the market altogether. The under-supply of suitable homes for the older generation, however, is less well recognised and researched. It reflects what the ILC-UK (2013) has called an *"unholy Trinity"* of ageism, self-denial and misinterpretation by policy-makers in the design and development of retirement housing. Such housing is often perceived by planners as only for the frail or those needing specialist care. It is often, therefore, designed to provide comfortable passivity rather than promote active living and community engagement. Even in 2017, only 3% of new housing was granted planning permission specifically for elderly or sheltered accommodation. The Raynsford Review in 2018, Planning 2020, concluded that *"the current planning system in England does not work effectively in the long-term interests of communities or the nation"* and recommended a complete overhaul, particularly as so much of the current system relies on EU directives that will require a thorough review post-Brexit. As numerous lobbying groups argued in their submissions to the committee, the younger generations are becoming increasingly frustrated by their inability to get onto and move up the housing ladder, while older generations cannot easily get down it. House prices are too high, choice is too limited and tight restrictions on mortgage credit in the aftermath of the 2008 credit crisis impact on all age groups. According to the 2016 Spotlight Report, first-time buyers today need deposits equivalent to 76% of their income (in London it's 126%) to even get on the housing ladder, and those that do are often only able to do so with help from their parents (and increasingly grandparents). The London housing market alone rests on £100 billion in deposits funded by the Bank of Mum, Dad and Grandparents. The rest are staying at home or becoming members of **Generation Rent**, possibly for life, and possibly by continuing to live at home, much to their parents' concern and at times frustration as they, too, seek to move on. A sort of intergenerational housing gridlock is developing, with all age groups caught up in the logjam that is the current state of the UK housing market.

Add to this failure of supply of new housing, the **under-occupation** by older couples of larger houses with three or more bedrooms and their apparent refusal or inability to move to smaller properties to allow young families needing more bedroom space to move up and in, and you have even greater intergenerational tension. Officially, the total number of under-occupying households in the UK is some eight million, over half of which are older households. However, according to Savills the estate agents, this is not just a case of older households sitting tight and refusing to move, nor is it a lack of buyers keen and able to purchase larger houses. Rather, the problem seems to be that too many obstacles face older sellers trying to sell, and too few new homes are being built or even designed for the older market at the right price for them to move on to. So, not surprisingly, they stay put, and in so doing ferment the sort of age anger and frustration expressed by the Intergenerational Foundation (IF) in 2016: "*As the proportion of young people 'stuck at home' grows, we have twenty-five million 'spare' bedrooms in larger houses occupied by older people who are unable or unwilling to move to smaller properties.*" Inevitably, "*when aspiration is stifled then envy and resentment are, perhaps understandably, the end result.*"

Add to this deficit of housing provision and design imagination the onslaught of the baby boomer retiree, and you really do have a 'perfect housing storm'; and, worse, a potential age war over property. Baby boomers are homeowners personified, as many of the older members of Polly's committee could personally testify. They grew up as homeowners, grew wealthy as homeowners and now own housing equity in the UK worth some £1 trillion. The over-55s in the UK hold 66% of all housing wealth, equalling about £2.5 trillion. (Knight Frank: 2016.) The post-war baby boomer generation created the private housing market of today and pioneered the very housing ladder that their children are trying to get onto and get up. British baby boomers are *the* market force in housing today, and they're not finished yet as they search for the ultimate happy habitat at home or abroad and revolutionise housing in the 21st century as they do so. Baby boomers are not just a new breed of older householder but a consumer force, with the commercial clout to demand choice, quality and style – and, in some areas, the opportunity to purchase second homes or invest in property as landlords. Just as the baby boomers kick-started the property market in the 1970s and 80s, so they are now at the forefront of redesigning the older housing market – again in their own image and according to their own style. They are still fit and healthy. They are looking for active engagement, fun and adventure. They are not going to downsize to a dreary bedsit, a bungalow or a 'granny stacker'. They expect elegance and style, Wi-Fi and new technology, and spare rooms for their families and their grandchildren.

Demography also appears to be redrawing the age map of Great Britain. On one hand a **geographical segregation** is emerging as the young gravitate to, or stay in, the towns and cities of Great Britain, while the elderly traditionally move out to the retirement towns or villages along the 'silver coasts' in counties such as Norfolk, Suffolk, Devon and Dorset. On the other hand, an 'age contraflow' is gaining momentum as increasing numbers of younger boomers retire into towns and cities in search of the excitement and the facilities of urban life; an urban drift that is now putting baby boomers in direct competition with young house-buyers and, inevitably, pushing urban house prices up even further. Silver cities such as Blackpool and Bournemouth are emerging and expanding, and according to The Future of London report in 2018, even London now faces an age-boom, not this time of the young but of the over-60s and even the over-80s advancing on the capital by 2035. And this silver shift is not just a UK phenomenon; it's becoming a global phenomenon; and the 2018 Grosvenor Report predicted that by 2030 over 30% of the OECD's top 100 cities, including Tokyo, Madrid and Berlin, will be going grey or silver. Such a huge and dramatic age shift will force a radical rethink about the way we design and build cities in the future. Age-friendly design will become imperative, not only in the shift away from high-rise micro-apartments but in the way city services such as transport and shopping are designed. Urban planning internationally will need to move towards creating 'lifetime neighbourhoods' and 'age-proof communities' rather than just building luxury apartments for the rich and young. Add to this urban shift the impact of the boomer generation on house prices and house values in housing hotspots such as London and the South-East, and you have a 'perfect storm'. Whole new classes of older homeowner seem to be emerging, be they the housing millionaires, or 'homillionaires', in London who now own over £836 billion worth of property, the 'smarties', or senior retirement town retirees, occupying cathedral or university towns such as Cambridge, Norwich and Winchester, or the 'gran-lord' baby boomers who have gone into the buy-to-let market as an investment and to supplement their pension, and who are therefore, ironically, becoming the new landlords of their own children's generation – Generation Rent.

So, the 'baby boom' in the housing market is already reverberating right back down the housing chain and fundamentally changing the whole profile of housing demand in the UK in the process. There are nearly 15 million older people and over seven million older households aged 55 years and over in England alone. They constitute nearly a third of all households and, according to the ONS, nearly two-thirds of the projected increase in the number of households from 2008 to 2033 will be headed by someone aged 65 or over. If the government thought they had a problem with building houses for the young, just wait until this older generation of homeowners begin to downsize en masse and threaten to flood the new-build market all together.

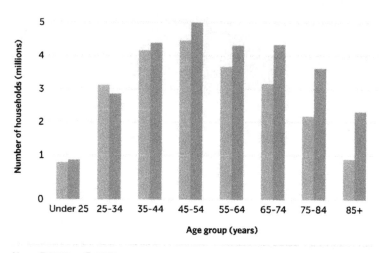

Year: ● 2012 ● 2037

Figure 2: **Housing Demographics by Age**
(Foresight Report: 2016)

Moreover, without a dramatic increase in housing supply and housing type, a stark and potentially permanent housing divide is likely to emerge between an older generation, 77% of whom own their own homes (or more than one), and a younger generation of 25–34-year-olds, only 36% of whom have managed to get on the housing ladder. This is a very stark and telling contrast to homeownership in the 1990s when twice that number of 25–34-year-olds – a whopping 65% – were homeowners. Even worse, competition amongst the generations in the rental market is also apparently 'hotting up' as more and more boomers begin selling up and renting as a way of releasing housing equity for personal use – with rents inevitably escalating as a result. And as more and more baby boomers retire, these demographic divisions and conflicts over the now scarce resource that is housing can only get worse. The silver generation, those aged 65 and over, already control 43% of housing wealth in Britain today – £1.2 trillion's worth, according to Savills – while those under the age of 35 own just 5%; and this disparity is likely to increase dramatically as baby boomers retire in droves. By 2030, predicts the ILC-UK (2017), baby boomers will own nearly 60% of all housing wealth in the UK – a massive £3.3 trillion's worth.

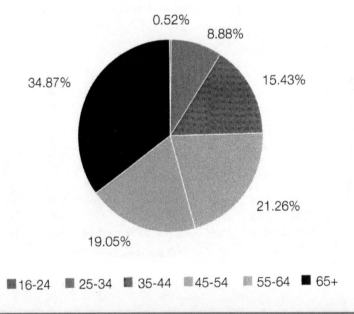

Figure 3: Homeownership by Age: England 2016
(ILC-UK: 2016)

Finally, the UK housing market today needs a radical rethink regarding the range and type of financial product available to fund it. While huge attention has been given by the government and mortgage companies to the financial needs of the first-time buyer, little time or attention has been given to the financial needs of older or last-time buyers seeking to downsize to a smaller property, upsize to a larger, possibly multigenerational, one, or simply age in place. Mortgages, the traditional vehicle for purchasing property in the UK, are still very much directed at the young and first-time buyer. They usually have tight age restrictions on them, and often require some form of secure income stream to finance them other than a pension or interest on savings. Yet such age limits now look increasingly outdated and unnecessarily restrictive. Today's retirees live much longer than in the past and enjoy pensions that are not only generous but guaranteed for the rest of their life. They are often far more secure borrowers than younger buyers facing today's turbulent and insecure job market. A number of mortgage companies are recognising this fundamental shift and some *challenger banks* are now offering mortgages up to age 85, 95 and even 99. Yet the traditional financial products for pensioners, such as equity release, remain increasingly outdated and in many cases highly distrusted by older homeowners. The return on such products has tended to be poor, the interest rates high, and many of these schemes were badly and sadly mis-sold to elderly couples in the past. Moreover, the financial needs of the emerging silver housing market today are much more diverse and wide-ranging. Some older households are asset rich and income poor; some are asset rich and aspiration high, looking to fund holiday homes abroad as well as luxury apartments at home; and others are simply poor, with few assets and only a state pension for daily living. Clearly, these are quite distinct and separate housing markets with very different dynamics – the market demand of the better-off compared to the social need of those in poverty. Moreover, many older couples do not necessarily want to move as such but need to release some capital to fund daily life. Some still have mortgages – including interest-only mortgages; some wish to move or buy abroad; some wish to support their children's first-time house with a deposit or loan.

The UK's housing finance market, concluded many of the committee's members, needs 'liberating'. It needs the sort of dramatic shakeup the annuity market got in 2014, and a fundamental redesign based on the individual or couple's capacity to pay, not on an arbitrary age limit drawn up when average life expectancy was much lower. Many European countries are developing a wide range of later-life mortgages or funding release schemes with inbuilt advice and guarantees, ranging from lifetime mortgages and reverse mortgages to home reversion schemes. Moreover, as research by the ILC-UK showed in May 2017, the mortgage ladder in the UK is already lengthening as borrowing into or in old age is growing, and mortgage debt held by over-65s is now projected to nearly double by 2030 to £39.9 billion. This is partly due to baby boomers extending their own mortgages or entering multigenerational mortgage arrangements to support their children, but it equally reflects the trends above as younger age groups delay entry into the housing market and take on 30-year mortgages when they're already in their 30s or 40s themselves. Government policy itself is a major obstacle, if not a deterrent to moving with stamp duty an eyewatering 8–12% for the more expensive properties in and around London.

So, this is the 'housing challenge' facing ageing Britain; and while Polly and her committee members were profoundly shaken by this chaotic picture of housing in modern Britain, they equally welcomed innovative solutions such as that proposed by the think tank Demos. The Demos researchers argued that instead of thinking of the housing ladder in the UK as two separate ladders, one for the young and one for the old, we should view it as a **single housing chain**, one that is in perpetual motion, with householders stepping on and off as they move up, down and along it at various stages in their life cycle. The researchers argued that by simply releasing older people from large houses they could no longer afford or manage at the top of the housing chain, the government and local authorities could accelerate the movement of young families needing more bedrooms and space up the housing chain, in turn releasing smaller homes for first-time buyers – or for older couples too. Moreover, argued the Demos researchers, the funding for such a revolution in the last-time housing market is already there, locked up in the trillion pounds' worth of assets owned by the older generation across the country. And so, too, is the demand; it simply needs releasing. Demos estimated that if just half of the over-60s in their survey interested in moving were able to do so, this would release around £356 billion' worth of mainly family-sized properties. Potentially, the indirect benefits of unleashing the housing chain in this way would be even greater. It would enhance older people's health and well-being, rejuvenate young people's aspirations and motivations, and it would provide a major boost to the building industry itself and the trades associated with it. In addition, this may help **Generation Rent** move out of rented accommodation or their family home, reduce their costs and get on with their lives. "*A new generation of retirement housing could set off a property chain reaction*" claimed the Demos report; potentially a *"perfect solution to a perfect storm"*; a win-win solution that would, and should, grace any political manifesto, particularly with the grey vote so critical to any election to come. Downsizing on this scale, though, could only occur if smaller and more attractive properties were built specifically for the older buyer and if the financial market suddenly became far more creative and age-friendly in financing such a transition. Otherwise, all that downsizing would do is release hordes of baby boomers onto the already limited supply of new and smaller properties, pushing prices sky-high and even more beyond the reach not only of the young first-time buyer but also of young families seeking two- or three-bedroom accommodation for their growing families.

Recent research by Professor Les Mayhew for the Centre for the Study of Financial Innovation (CSFI: Feb.2019) strongly supports the Demos argument that the *Last-Time Buyer* is the key to Britain's current housing crisis and that potentially downsizing is the lever for shifting the UK housing chain into gear. In Professor Mayhew's view the problem is not a shortage of housing in the UK. Rather it is a shortage of the right type of housing particularly for last-time buyers 'stuck in housing that no longer suits them'. According to his Dwelling Index, the UK's housing stock actually outstrips demand even with the growth in one-person households projected for the future. Rather, the problem is that the obstacles to older people downsizing are still too great to enable or to incentivise them to do so. The costs involved in moving such as stamp duty are exorbitant, the range, cost and security of the financial products currently available is relatively limited and most especially the type, choice and suitability of later-life housing in the UK is restricted in both size and facilities. As the Policy Exchange report in Dec. 2018 concluded, with such a small percentage of older people currently moving home each year – a tiny 8.4% out of the current 10.3 million households aged 55 and over – the aim of government policy has to be to generate 'a societal change in attitude towards downsizing – and for it to be seen as a natural progression in someone's life'. If the government could remove or amend the current restrictions on housing policy, incentivise downsizing in later-life, rental as well as homeownership and require developers to be much more imaginative as well as 'green' in their designs, then there is a real opportunity to kick-start the British housing chain and start 'Building for the Baby Boomers' in a similar fashion to the USA. Just imagine older – and younger – peoples' attitude to downsizing and retirement in the UK if they had anything like vast choice of type and residential mix currently on offer in America.

So, while the concept of housing as a **single chain** appealed enormously to the Commons Housing Committee and led to its recommendation in 2016 of a package of measures to incentivise downsizing – a package that included an equity loan offer, comprehensive financial advice and possibly certain stamp duty exemptions for older people in lower value homes – the government emmeshed in Brexit has yet again failed to respond. Instead as the government's own Foresight Report (2016) concluded, housing in the UK remains in crisis; a perfect storm that continues to price both young and less affluent pensioners out of the housing market altogether; a crisis that is in danger of generating a mass movement 'back home'; back home at aged 20, 30 or even 40, with the additional prospect of older people at 70 and 80 living with sons and daughters, children and grandchildren in some form of 3G or 4G living. The ONS estimates that of the 100,000 millennials now living with their parents, some may never move out, and even worse – or better – they may start moving their partner in with them!

The 2018 House of Commons Communities and Local Government Committee report, *Housing for older people*, recognised many of the issues above. It recognised the need for a national strategy linking health, social care and housing for older people as imperative, and it recommended that the National Planning Policy Framework be amended to ensure that housing for older people be explicitly included under a new 'age-proof' planning classification – C2 – with specific targets for local councils to achieve. Such legislation would clearly support and enhance the housing needs of the older population; and a number of local authorities, such as Birmingham, Essex and Newcastle, are already leading the way in planning and designing suitable housing for their older populations – and for enabling them to *age in place* with the support of new technology as recommended by the Institution of Mechanical Engineers in 2018. The government, in turn, has sought to respond by announcing in February 2017 a major programme of starter-house building including plans to create new types of garden towns and villages in 2017/18. The NHS, meanwhile, has launched an ambitious programme of 'Healthy New Towns' in ten locations across England from Cranbrook in Devon to Darlington in North Durham designed to put healthy living and community life at the heart of town planning even with walking trails that are designed to be dementia-friendly. In 2018 the government allocated £2 billion to support social housing and, more recently, it has sought to relax borrowing rules to allow local councils to embark on more ambitious housing schemes. 'But is all this enough?' asked Polly. Is it all too little and all too late to meet the needs and demands of an army of retirees now considering downsizing and with the wealth and numbers to swamp an already saturated housing market? Has anyone, asked Polly of her committee, seriously looked in detail at the housing needs of all ages, or are we all stumbling blindly into a housing fog?

Moreover, what all these statistics and all these studies showed Polly was that the housing crisis in the UK is not just about building more or even different houses; it's about building an ageing society where longevity is reshaping demography, where longer and longer lifespans are creating new needs, new lifestyles, new intergenerational relationships that the current stock and type of housing in the UK cannot meet. The chances of conflict, of escalating inequality and even of social alienation and isolation is rising daily. An age war over housing is becoming a serious possibility, alongside dramatic increases in pensioner poverty, ill health and early death through inappropriate housing and social isolation. Poor-quality housing costs the NHS £2.5 billion a year and falls by older people alone cost a further £600 million. (Spotlight Report: 2016.) Most appallingly of all, winters in the UK apparently still generate an excess of around 30,000 pensioner deaths due to the thermal inefficiencies of our ageing housing stock. In contrast, new homes offer new life, healthier life, particularly if fitted with smart technology, reducing healthcare costs in the process as well as helping to alleviate the social illnesses of isolation and loneliness that are fast spreading across ageing Britain. The example of Albert Powley and Team Grandad cited in Chapter 4 is but one inspiring case study of what technology and family support can do when working together. With the projected explosion in dementia sufferers from 850,000 today to 3m by 2050, action is urgently needed and the pioneering work by the British Research Establishment (BRE) and Loughborough University in seeking to design dementia-friendly homes is clearly a step in the right direction; homes that include clear lines of sight and natural light throughout, user-friendly technology to monitor and control light, ventilation and sound, familiar features from the past such as colour coded taps and the infrastructure needed to allow the transition from early to late dementia to occur within the same house as memory fades and one-floor living becomes necessary.

The UK housing market clearly needs a radical rethink for all ages, of how the housing market could be liberated, how the housing chain could be integrated and how far greater innovation and imagination could be brought into designing and building homes and houses for an ageing, multigenerational, multi-market society. The need is for the integration, not separation, of services, and for the adaptation and transfer of housing as ageing needs change and as generations of homeowners and tenants move up and down the housing chain and to and from the city and the town to the coast and the countryside. Housing in the future needs to be seen more as a river in flow than a stack of bricks fixed in time and place, with multiple tributaries flowing in and out as people journey through life, change direction as well as location and at times settle down until family and the economy force change. As Polly's research abroad had shown, the UK obsession with homeownership and with houses built from bricks and mortar contrasts starkly with living styles in other parts of the world and even in the materials other countries' housebuilders use and the speed with which they build. Many other countries, for example, use high quality factory-built houses from wood or manmade materials that can be constructed in weeks if not days and transported to locations where land is available and owners wish to live. The announcement by the housing association, Your Housing Group, in 2016, of a £2.5 billion joint venture with a Chinese construction company for the building of some 25,000 factory-built modular homes in 2016 onwards, may possibly help kick-start a similar shift in the UK.

Similarly, other countries seem much more willing to experiment with multigenerational living. The government's 2016 Spotlight Report cites the example of an intergenerational scheme in Alicante in Spain where younger people under 35 years of age and on a low income are offered housing at low rent in residential homes in return for providing companionship and support to the older community living there. The Homeshare scheme, developed in Australia and Europe, now has 24 programmes around the UK whereby young people – students, key public service workers – share homes with the elderly, providing companionship in return for lower rents. Co-housing schemes, like that of the grand ladies of the Older Women's Co-Housing Group (OWCH) in North London, are similarly widespread in Holland and elsewhere in Europe but still very new in the UK. Innovation generally is not a feature of the UK housing industry today, despite the desperate need for a commercial shift to personalised production and the adoption and adaptation of a huge range of new technologies, new materials and new ideas about ways of living. With the baby boomer generation about to bring bank-loads of equity onto the UK housing market, there is a silver – if not golden – opportunity for the government and the UK housing industry to put the British housing economy on a much more sustainable footing and to generate better health and intergenerational relations. It appears to be a no-brainer, with the enormous political credit that any government would potentially earn from across the electorate for incentivising this market, removing planning obstacles and encouraging new ideas in social as well as private housing. It appears to be the perfect solution to the perfect storm. Who, though, will provide the 'perfect push'; who will 'pull the plug', set the housing market in the UK into full flow and so create one of the foundations for a more happy and harmonious ageing society? Are silver co-operatives or retirement villages, owned and run by the residents themselves, a step forward, or is ageing in-place, ageing in the new 'smart' homes described by the ILC-UK in its 2017 Report, with possibly robo-butlers or Actroid housemaids the ultimate solution? Can the banks and finance companies that helped create the 2008 housing crisis now redeem themselves by developing new mortgage products that are far more accessible to all age groups and, like the Barclays Springboard Mortgage, enable the older generations to help the young get on the housing ladder while still protecting and rewarding their savings? Should renting not have a far more prominent and attractive role in later-life housing by offering the sort of controlled rents and security of tenure found across most of Europe; a whole topic in itself and a vital one that Parliament itself is apparently now investigating?

So, as Polly was now crystal clear that, housing cannot be considered in isolation. It needs to come out of the strategic closet and stand proudly alongside health and pensions as the 'third arm' of what she was now contemplating as a triple alliance, a tripartite welfare state at the centre of her emerging ageing strategy. In her view, and that of many on the all-party committee, housing offers the opportunity to integrate elderly health and well-being with intergenerational equity, as well as provide a major boost to the British housebuilding industry and the economy at large. It is potentially a solution in its own right but, more crucially, a key partner in any integrated solution to active ageing and intergenerational harmony. The economic benefits of investing in a new generation of housing for all ages should put housing at the forefront of any political manifesto, but if the government won't act and take the lead then the 'markets' are likely to do so and, in the process, create 'generational chaos' in their wake, with the young and the poor competing for the same limited and over-priced resource while wealthier baby boomers try to downsize and down-cost. The failings of the UK housing system are undermining the harmony of our ageing society, and the market alone is unable to respond. It is effectively leaving Lloyd and Lily, Elaine and Eric locked within their own mortar and bricks, unable to move as they need.

These man-made walls need knocking down if the true potential of longevity is not to be lost; and lurking in the housing background is that 'elephant in the ageing room', the **residential home,** the home for long-term care and who will pay for it, who will run it and in whose interest?

But that's a topic in its own right; that's a topic that as the Local Government Association has argued (LGA: 2017) will require a residential revolution and a dramatic rebuilding programme all of its own to create the 400,000+ units needed by 2035. If this revolution fails to come to pass, then older couples such as Lloyd and Lily may well be condemned to a grey tomb rather than the silver paradise they deserve – unless, of course, by then they can afford to move into one of the late-life luxury apartments now being constructed for super-rich oldies wishing to live by the River Thames or move abroad like so many older Brits to the sunny shores of Spain or the Greek islands. Alternatively, Lloyd and Lily could simply swap houses with their daughter, or all live together in some form of multigenerational property where they all get on together and are happy to share the costs, the lifestyle and, possibly, the childcare – and later the eldercare. The potential options are considerable, and imaginative solutions are slowly beginning to appear but is it all too little and all too late, asked Polly, to meet the needs and demands of an army of retirees already on the move and threatening with their wealth and numbers to swamp an already saturated housing market, leaving younger generations homeless or ageing at home themselves?

Certainly, retirees in the UK have nothing like the range and variety of offer available in the USA where the Senior Living market is big business – very big business with retirement villages and even senior towns offering every possible facility, every type of community imaginable. A veritable paradise of 'later-life living' ranging from golfing and sports communities to those seeking to live within a particular faith or amongst those who are single or younger. These condos and communities, ranging from the sunshine of Florida and California to the mountains of Nevada, are a stark and telling contrast in attitude and culture to the whole notion and image of retiring. In the USA, it is the ultimate 'American Dream'; the first taste of paradise. In the UK, it's more like the last stage in life and the 'first foot in the grave' and the dearth of attractive retirement schemes painfully reflects this cultural void. If developers like McCarthy and Stone could capture the public imagination in the same way that Del Webb did in the USA, then retirement and later-life living in the UK might well leap back to life-and the government's housing dilemma be solved overnight. Just imagine older peoples' attitude to retirement if the

UK had anything like the Laguna Woods Village in California on offer; a gated community located on 2,100 acres of rolling hillsides minutes from the Laguna Beach coastline offering seven clubhouses, five swimming pools, a performing arts theatre and an equestrian centre with over 230 clubs and societies to chose from – a world away from the typical and usual retirement home in the UK but perhaps a sign of things to come?

Finally, some possibly good news for younger house buyers. According to Professor Mayhew's analysis (2019), the housing crisis in the UK may start to subside in the 2020s as the baby boomers begin to die out, pass on their homes and so significantly reduce the demand and the price of housing in the UK. A very sobering thought for boomers but a possible light at the end of the tunnel for their children.

7 | Family, Marriage and the Multigenerational Beanpole

The British Royal Family may not be the typical British family of today, but it might ironically be the family of the future; a model of the extended multigenerational, multinational family of the age of longevity as it comes into its own. The heads of this august family – the Queen and Prince Philip – are now in their 90s, still in robust health, and Her Majesty is still performing a limited number of public duties; their children – the Princes Charles, Andrew and Edward, and Princess Ann – are in their 50s and late 60s; while the grandchildren, ranging from William and Harry through to Beatrice and Eugenie, are in their late 20s, early 30s and starting to have families of their own, with great-grandchildren that include Prince George, Princess Charlotte, Prince Louis and now Harry and Megan's new baby Archie. That is four generations alive today; and before the Queen Mother's death in 2002 at the grand old age of 102, there were five. Add to that the generational network of cousins and nephews across the UK, Europe and elsewhere, and you can see the potential and international spread of the family network of the future, particularly if you add in cohabitation, remarriage, divorce and adoption to the familial equation. Add to that the likelihood that each generation in the future will live on average into their 80s, 90s and beyond, and that the family of the future is likely to mushroom as globally as the internet, then the family network of the future is likely to include four to five generations all alive at the same time, living within the same century or even across centuries, and spread across a global world that is increasingly interconnected. The 'world family' is no longer just a royal prerogative but a growing feature of all our lives in the ageing world ahead.

As a socialist and an MP representing one of the most deprived constituencies in Western Europe, Polly was no great fan of the British monarchy, but she did admire its longevity, its contribution to social stability and the good works of certain of its members. Like many mothers of her age she was enamoured of Prince Harry and his conversion from reckless renegade to crusading campaigner and now happy husband and doting father. She equally admired Charles's Prince's Trust and his crusading for young people and for a greener Britain, while his likely elevation from Prince to King struck Polly as a classic, if somewhat extreme, example of generativity and the encore career that writers such as Marc Freedman so proudly and loudly advocate.

The example of the Royal Family, therefore, led Polly to reflect increasingly on the impact of longevity on her own family network and how, with globalisation and international social mobility, she now had nephews in Australia and Asia, cousins in Wales and Wellington, and grandchildren – and step grandchildren – born of mixed marriages in both Brazil and Costa Rica. Her extended family now stretched across the globe, and she promised herself that immediately on retirement she would sketch out and document this 'world family' of hers – and all four, possibly five, generations therein – and visit them all on some sort of seventieth birthday world tour. If this is the family network now, just imagine what it will look like by 2050… and then try explaining all the ins and outs, the trunks and the branches, the links and the lost relatives of your family tree to your grandchildren; a task Polly attempted one afternoon with her grandchildren and immediately regretted not preparing for it properly as the children interrogated her relentlessly and her daughter phoned up later asking, "*Who the devil is Uncle Albert?*" Soon the world family is likely to be a reality for all, not just the few, as we all become 'royal families' – multigenerational, multinational, multiracial – spread right across a highly connected global world and linked up not just by blood and inter-marriage but by an internet and a Skype that can make family contact a daily reality. Such imaginings left Polly hugely excited on the one hand but deeply troubled on the other as to whether fellow politicians and civil servants today were really aware of the fundamental changes being wrought by ageing and longevity or were they still basing family policy in the UK on the stereotyped images of the past, or, worse, on their own very comfortable family experiences.

As Polly's researches increasingly revealed, the British family of the 21st century is fast becoming a global family in shape and extent. The so-called 'extended family' of the 19th century and the 'nuclear family' of the post-war 20th century are giving way to the **new age families** of the early 21st century: beanpole in shape, multigenerational in character, multi-ethnic in composition, multinational in range and multifamily in structure as divorce and remarriage generate 'stepfamilies' that add immensely to the diversity and complexity of family life in the early 21st century. The traditional stereotypes of family formation, structure and relationships no longer seem to hold true as the British family's structures and lifestyles of the past are swept away by the many and often conflicting forces of the 21st century. The escalating divorce rates of the older generation, the fast-changing roles of men and women at all ages, and the multi-ethnic and multinational interrelationships of many young people today are reshaping British family life at a speed and in a way that few commentators, and even fewer politicians, can keep up with. Cohabitation, for example, seems to have replaced marriage in many Western societies as the primary form of personal and familial relationship for the young, and increasingly the old, while single-parent families and reconstituted stepfamilies have grown dramatically in recent years. Traditional family trees and networks are being redrawn and reshaped by remarriage and less formal forms of relationship. New forms of extended family are being created by global migration, multi-ethnicity and by extended longer life. Marriages today last as long as they did in the past and as Professor Sarah Harper (2006) has pointed out, divorce rather than death is now the way that most modern marriages end. And such changes are not confined solely to the West. As the World Family Map showed in 2015, all nations and all continents, except Africa, are now facing the force of ageing, seeing their family structures shattered and their population pyramids overturned. China's single-child policy created the phenomena of the 4-2-1 family that has now had to be reversed, while mass migration from the countryside into the burgeoning cities has completely undermined the traditional family networks of Asia and South America. Fertility rates across the world are plummeting below the natural replacement rate of 2.1 children in both the developed and developing worlds, increasingly leaving almost all societies with a dearth of new blood and a rapidly rising dependency ratio. Germany and Italy, for example, have fertility rates as low as 1.4 children per childbearing woman. No wonder Angela Merkel tried to welcome over a million migrants into the German Republic. No wonder Hungary is now proposing to offer lifetime exemption from income tax for women who have at least four children.

And as if these forces weren't enough, the young themselves seem to be adding to the speed and impact of this demographic revolution and, in the process, possibly adding to their own burdens in the future. The young today are globally mobile to the point that the move of young people from developing countries across to the West and from the countryside to the city in search of a better life is 'hollowing out' traditional family hierarchies. Many developing nations are becoming 'top heavy', with elderly and dependent children left behind in the countryside while the young and able are working away abroad or in the city. Meanwhile, the advent of international dating through the internet is encouraging romantic migration alongside economic migration, and with it the emergence of the multinational family as young people from the West marry spouses from countries as far afield as Argentina and Thailand. Inevitably, therefore, family life across the world, and with it all the ages and stages of childhood, adulthood and retirement, are undergoing fundamental and global transformation. Even that most basic rite of passage of leaving the family home is being transformed with the emergence of 'boomerang children' in the UK, USA and Europe, as adult 'children' in the West today are increasingly leaving home much later or returning home in their early 20s under the pressures of high house prices and rentals and the devastating rise of youth unemployment across Europe and America that followed the 2008 crash. Finally, and most profoundly, young women today appear to be delaying marriage indefinitely – and in some cases permanently – as they seek to establish themselves in careers rather than in motherhood, and this in turn is leading to a delay in childbirth – or none at all. Japan is a classic example of this delayed or denounced child-bearing and, as a result, is projected to suffer a catastrophic demographic 'implosion' from 128 million people today to 95 million by 2050 and even lower thereafter. On the other side, longer life is enabling people not only to enjoy their first marriage and first family for longer but, through divorce, to remarry and start again – and to hopefully learn from their mistakes.

As the **World Family Map** (2015) summed up, the whole world – developed and developing – is undergoing a social transformation in its family structures and functioning as ageing progresses, and as cohabitation replaces, or at least delays, marriage. Both the 'beanpole' family and the 'rainbow' family are fast emerging as different types of the multigenerational family created by the extended lifespan of the 21st century. Inevitably, too, as the traditional family is shrinking, and in some cases being torn apart, the traditional 'intergenerational family contract' that children have the responsibility of looking after their ageing parents is under severe challenge across the world. Some countries have sought to enforce this social responsibility through legal statute, as in France; or by incentives through pension conditions, as in the Czech Republic; or through housing policies, as in Singapore. Overall, though, this global trend towards fewer children carries with it the profound possibility that, at a time when the numbers of older people needing care are rising, the numbers of children and adults available to care for them are falling. On the other hand, the rise in life expectancy across the world also increases dramatically the likelihood that grandparents today will get to meet, greet and even grow up alongside their grandchildren – and possibly even their great-grandchildren.

'So, how does the **British family** of today and tomorrow compare to the global trends above?' asked Polly. 'Is it evolving into a beanpole with mushrooming branches of 'reconstituted relatives', or is it moving towards the multinational, multiracial 'rainbow' model of the world family above, with branches abroad as well as at home?' As Chair of the All-Party Committee on Housing, Polly needed some answers. As a socialist and a Labour MP with ambitions to gain promotion into the Shadow Cabinet, she needed ideas. As a mother and a grandmother, she needed to know what the future held for her own family. So, through her parliamentary office, and researchers at Oxford University, Polly commissioned an up-to-date review of the modern British family, a review that made fascinating reading and profoundly reshaped Polly's ideas thereafter on family policy in the 21st century.

As the charts opposite show, the traditional British family is changing dramatically and rapidly. Of the 19 million families in 2017 in the UK, the number of cohabiting couple families has increased significantly, from 2.2 million in 2003 to 3.3 million in 2017, while lone parents have

Family type	2017		
	With dependent children	Without dependent children[2]	Total families
Married couple family[1]	4,944	7,890	12,834
Opposite sex married couple family	4,938	7,862	12,800
Same sex married couple family	6	28	34
Civil partner couple family[3]	8	47	55
Cohabiting couple family[1]	1,251	2,040	3,291
Opposite sex cohabiting couple family	1,246	1,943	3,190
Same sex cohabiting couple family	4	97	101
Lone parent family	1,781	1,037	2,817
All families	7,983	11,014	18,997

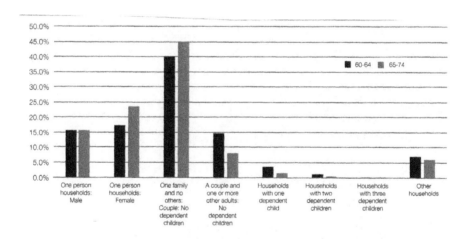

Figure 1: **UK Family type**
(ONS: 2017)

risen by 200,000 in a similar period, to 2.8 million. Of the 27.2 million households in the UK in 2017, nearly 30% consisted of only one person, 20% consisted of four or more people, while multifamily households of two families or more have become the fastest-growing household type of all, rising to 306,000 in 2017. Such families, however, still only represent 1% of all households. More profoundly, the ONS predicts that within the next decade, half of all families in the UK will have only one child as the birth rate in the UK continues to fall dramatically to 1.85 children per woman, well below the 2:1 replacement level needed to maintain our demographic 'age balance' and so stem the ageing of Great Britain and the reshaping of the British family.

Certainly, as the 2018 Modern Family Index has highlighted, the young British family is approaching crisis point, facing intense pressure, as couples, especially young women, seek to maintain their standard of living and their careers while bringing up their children successfully. They face the 'parenthood penalty' of a delayed or broken career, and they often

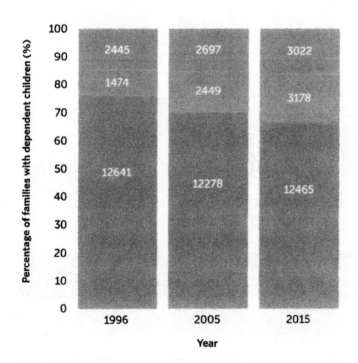

Figure 2: **UK Family structure: 1996, 2005, 2015**
(Foresight: 2016)

lack the support or flexibility to effectively balance childcare and work. Childcare costs alone in the UK are astronomic, and the quality and availability of childcare is something of a lottery. Family break-up in some form or other now seems almost inevitable, and the need for a much more joined-up childcare strategy, engaging fathers, employers and the benefit system, seems crucial if the UK is to liberate and fully mobilise its female workforce and yet ensure that more children are being born to offset the enormous demographic imbalances of an ageing population. Incentivising and supporting grandparents to provide even greater childcare support, while trying to relieve the potential pressures of eldercare on young mothers, would seem essential elements of any effective family strategy for the future.

Meanwhile, marriage is increasingly a 'class affair', the preserve of the affluent and educated, while cohabitation and single-parenthood seem to predominate among the less well-off. Wealthy areas such as Harrow and Wokingham have marriage rates of 88% and 87% respectively, while poorer areas such as Knowsley and Salford have marriage rates as low as 25–27%. Intergenerational living is increasingly forced on families of all social classes with the rise of 'boomerang children' – adult children living or returning home due to the cost of further education, the escalating costs of renting or house purchasing, and even later on by divorce or unemployment – a demographic that the ONS estimates as some 3.3 million young adults today aged between 20 and 34. This is an astonishing and dramatic disparity in marital relations between the poor and better-off in Britain today and, according to the Young Foundation (2017), a major factor in explaining the gulf in both equality and social mobility that lies beneath the surface of modern Britain. Moreover, the foundation's conclusions that: "*A child born in 2017 has only a 50% chance of living with both parents by the time they reach 15*", and that a third of children in one-parent families never see their fathers after three years of separation, are devastating indictments of modern family life. This is also a sociological dilemma that fundamentally undermines one of the central planks of government policy, namely its assumption that the traditional family comprises two parents and that they will take full responsibility for a child's upbringing right through until adulthood. What, asked Polly, are the long-term consequences of an ever-growing number of 'fatherless' families across the UK, and particularly amongst the less well-off? Is Britain, as Iain Duncan Smith claimed in *The Sunday Times* in February 2017, "*a world leader in family break-up*"?; a break-up, he claimed, that is costing the Exchequer some £48 billion. Even parenting itself is under attack as publications such as Lukianoff and Haidt (2018) claim that children today are being overly-protected or mollycoddled to the point that, both psychologically as well as physically, they have become a 'snowflake generation', unable to stand up for themselves, unable to handle conflict or even deal with alternative views in a debate. Hence the author's claim of a rise in anxiety, depression and suicide amongst young people, and a strident student intolerance of alternative views, that has led universities across the Western world to compromise free speech and to ban speakers considered controversial, radical or politically incorrect. *Generation Snowflake* seem to have become used to adults resolving their problems for them; a sort of learned helplessness seems to have set in that leaves them vulnerable in later life.

Finally, the dramatic changes in Britain's ethnic composition are also having a profound effect, not only on the structure and diversity of family life in the UK but on interracial relationships – be they marriage or cohabitation – and on child-rearing. Given the global nature of working life and family life today, an increasing number of young, and older, British men and women are marrying foreign spouses, creating extended family networks that are international and multinational in nature and scope; a scenario sensitively illustrated by this extract from the 2016 Spotlight Report.

"Jane is married with two children aged 9 and 13. Her husband has two grown children from a previous marriage. Jane is a member of the baby boom generation; part of a blended family; supporting her mother who is 78 in a sandwich generation; in an ethnically mixed transnational family. *'My husband's ex-wife's family are in Canada; his family are in the USA; it is unlikely that I or my children would have any contact with them. My children are very close to my husband's daughter from his first marriage (my step-daughter, I suppose). She is definitely family. And his ex-wife is very friendly to my children at special events (e.g. weddings) but she isn't considered family.'"*

But modern family life in Britain is not only under strain and over-stretched by challenges from the young, it is now increasingly under pressure from the old, a pressure rather dramatically summed up in the phrase 'Elderly Parent Responsibility Stress Syndrome' (EPRSS). EPRSS was coined to describe the anxiety and fear many people feel when faced with the need to care for their ageing parents; a phenomenon that appears to be reaching epidemic proportions as the number of older people projected to need care and support reaches 1.7 million by 2025. By the end of 2017 the number of older people needing care will have outstripped the number of working-age family members available to meet that demand. This need is often likely to occur just at the point when the parents thought they were free of childcare as their own children leave home. Inevitably, therefore, eldercare may bring with it some element of resentment, as well as the financial and emotional burden of caring for loved ones now struggling to maintain their sense of independence, self-respect and sanity; a toxic mix that may eat into family life and equally create an overriding sense of guilt for not doing enough. This may well be the reverse side of the traditional family care contract as adult children now return the care and sacrifice that they received from their parents when young, but for many carers it doesn't feel like that, it doesn't feel equally shared amongst all living siblings. Rather, eldercare often falls primarily and overwhelmingly on the member of the family living nearest the elderly parent(s) and on women, so setting the scene for ongoing family tension and possibly even conflict. The 'sandwiched family', and particularly the 'sandwiched woman', is now potentially caught between caring for her beloved mum (or dad), her own children and husband, and her own ambitions for later life. As Amanda Richards (*Good Housekeeping*: 2013) so poignantly put it 'The Guilt Stops Here': "*Six years ago, I delayed returning to work after having children to care for my frail, elderly mother; I battled with hospitals, hospices, home help and nursing homes to find decent care, while bringing up two small children. The worst thing was the constant worry about whether I was doing enough for her, and if the healthcare providers were up to standard.*"

Alongside these profound changes in the family life of the young, the elder population is in a process of reforming and reshaping itself. Older couples are breaking up in record numbers, with silver divorce rates up a staggering 29% in the last 20 years and projected to rise even further by 2037. Secondly, with their children gone and 20 to 30 years of healthy life still ahead of them, many older people are adopting new and alternative later life lifestyles, embarking on new relationships or taking on new challenges or even careers. Silver divorce, cohabitation, late-life dating and single-life living are all emerging as new lifestyles after 50; and while older men may well be enjoying new romances and new freedoms, it's older women, too, who are enjoying and driving this new and elder form of women's liberation. They're choosing to remain single; choosing cohabitation rather than the security, or the 'servitude' of second marriages; choosing to enjoy grandchildren and family life; or choosing to seek new horizons and new adventures abroad. 'Intimacy at a distance' seems to have become the baby boomer relationship of choice for this generation of older women; and with the financial independence of their own pensions or supportive divorce settlements, they're out to explore and exploit their new freedoms and enjoy life to the full, free from the dictates and demands of husbands and children, free to be themselves – at last! **Living alone** – or as Eric Klinenberg (2013) called it *"Going Solo"* – has 'mushroomed' in both the USA and Europe; and according to the ONS, a veritable army of single persons aged between 45 and 64, female and male, has grown in the UK by some 50% since the mid-1990s as almost 2.5 million people now live on their own without any spouse, partner or children.

At one extreme, therefore, older couples are themselves becoming part of the 21st-century beanpole, part of the chain gang of multigenerational families, childcare and eldercare. At the other extreme, they're choosing to go it alone, searching for new adventures, new lifestyles and new forms of relationships. **Late-life liberation** and the joy of being 'alone at last' may be wonderful initially but it does have its price as late-life illness and disability kick in and life becomes restricted to the four walls of their house, flat or even bedroom. 'Grey gloom' is apparently a growing feature of ageing Japan as millions of elderly people experience social isolation and loneliness and 'silver suicide' rates begin to rise. Moreover, this revolution in later-life lifestyles is not without impact on the younger generations, too. ACODs, or Adult Children of Divorced Parents, often get the fallout from silver divorce as their parents turn them into counsellors, confidants and mediators when their marriages break down, rather than protecting them as before. Worse, these adult children then face the prospect of having to care for two lonely, single, elderly parents in later life rather than one married couple. Not surprisingly, many younger people today are extremely cautious about long-term relationships and prefer to cohabit rather than commit to marriage in the first instance.

So, longevity is having a dramatic and profound impact on British family life in the 21st century. It's lengthening the 'chain of family life' and creating serial living, serial marriages and even serial or second lives, as a longer, healthier life creates the opportunity to enjoy extended family life or a new stage of independent living. Family life in ageing societies is no longer linear and longitudinal, predictable and predetermined. It is organic, dynamic – and highly unpredictable. Multigenerational families and multi-stage living are increasingly becoming the norm, with post-war baby boomers and its liberated women leading the way. The family beanpole is fast becoming a global daisy chain as globalisation and international migration encourage the emergence of multinational, multi-ethnic global family networks spread right across the world. As the young join the global economy, move to New York or Mumbai, marry upwardly mobile members of developing societies and have multilingual children with multi-ethnic backgrounds, so the family structure of the 21st century may well be globally transformed in ways that the boomer generation – the grandparents of tomorrow – can barely imagine. Certainly the grandchildren of the 21st century are likely to experience a much more varied and diverse journey through life and marriage than their counterparts in the 20th century did: *"Most will experience old age, most will marry at least once, most will have children, most will have a married child by the time they are in their 50s, and most will have a grandchild before they are 60."* (Harper:2006) Equally, the lengthening of the lifespan is likely to lead to the delaying of the traditional stages of life; the delaying of leaving home, of entry to work, of marriage and childbirth, of retirement, with the related likelihood of relationships breaking down and being reconstructed all along the length of what is now likely to be a very fluid and flexible family tree. The rise of populist movements advocating restrictions on global migration may well stem the speed and flow of the multinational trends above, but through globalisation and the global mobility of young people they are unlikely to stop them.

Such turbulence and turmoil at the heart of British family life left Polly deeply disturbed, extremely fearful for the future of our children and at a loss to see how government policy could keep up with, let alone mitigate, such social and personal instability. That is until her researchers highlighted one sliver of silver light; one possible stabilising influence in this swirling sea of change: the grandparent, the new age grandparent of the 2020s emerging out of the teenage era of the 1960s. As the post-war era heralded the age of the teenager, so the age of longevity seems to be heralding the **age of the grandparent.**

'So, what exactly,' asked Polly, 'does this new generation of grandparents look like and what does it aspire to?' The charity Grandparents Plus estimated in 2009 that that there were 13.6 million grandparents in Britain today: 7.6 million grandmothers and 6 million grandfathers. Thirty per cent of all adult women in Britain are apparently now grandmothers, 25% of men are grandfathers and 44% of grandparents are under 65 years of age. So, grandparents today are not the grandparents of yesterday; they are a distinctly new breed of grandparent – younger, healthier and as likely to be at the centre of family life today as at its periphery. The 2017 ILC-UK report, on t*he Grandparent Army*, calculated that 9 million grandparents in the UK provide some form of childcare and that they spend on average some 8–11 hours a week looking after their grandchildren before and after school, in the school holidays and in giving their grandchildren new experiences, resources and activities whether it be music, sport or simply learning. Grandparents today are increasingly the 'family bank of last resort'. They are providing free childcare – calculated by the 2016 Spotlight Report as £7.3 billion in 2013 – and extensive financial help, whether it be with rent or mortgage deposits, loans or even school or student fees. Grandparental gifts to grandchildren alone apparently totalled almost £333.8 million in England in 2010, with a further £313.8 million put into child trust funds, according to the ILC-UK (2010). And a new form of 'inheritance skipping' is emerging as grandparents pass their wealth onto their grandchildren while they're still alive, wealth currently estimated at £4 billion a year. They are equally and increasingly the 'meat in the caring sandwich', caught between caring for their grandchildren and simultaneously caring for their own ageing parents. With multigenerational families and stepfamilies, grandparents – especially grandmothers – are increasingly caught in the 'club sandwich' of multiple demands and conflicting family pressures, pressures that can often generate a serious 'age strain' amongst older couples, psychologically as well as financially, as they struggle to help their families at the same time as they seek to carve out their own new later life. Such pressures come to a peak when, for a small but growing number of grandparent households, they have to take over full parental responsibility for grandchildren as a result of divorce, bereavement or crisis amongst their own children. Grandparents then become the 'white knights' of contemporary family life, coming to the rescue of families in crisis, and in extreme situations actually taking over the care of their grandchildren themselves. The 2009 Grandparents Plus study *The Poor Relation* calculated that there are some 200,000 to 300,000 children in the UK living with family and friend carers as a result of family crises or individual breakdowns.

So, grandparents today are not a common type or category. They are as diverse as the rest of society, riven by divisions of class, ethnicity, gender and geography as well as age. Social class in particular is emerging as a distinctive feature of both grandparental lifestyles and their capacity to help or support their wider families. Grandparents from higher socio-economic groups, for example, tend to become parents at a later age than less well-off grandparents. They tend to propagate the longer, thinner beanpoles, characteristic of more middle-class families, with large age gaps between the generations and less children per generation. In contrast, working class families are more likely to be quite compact, spread across four (even five) generations but with fewer years in between. As a result, the financial and personal pressures on working class grandparents – and on working class grandmothers in particular – are likely to be more intense and immediate than those on their more affluent middle-class counterparts. Working class grandparents are more likely to be middle-aged or young and head up four generational families, families that are more likely to be poor, single parents and in receipt of benefits. Pressure on such grandparents for both financial help and childcare may mean that they themselves go without. They cannot work, tend to live on lower pensions due to their fractured National Insurance contributions and so often still find themselves 'trapped in poverty' even after retirement. In contrast, grandparents from higher socio-economic groups are more likely to enjoy higher incomes and generous final salary pensions. They are more likely to be part of a dual income household, living with a spouse who has also had a professional career, a good income and a substantive occupational pension. Such affluent grandparents can clearly afford to provide financial support and pay for childcare in a way low-pension grandparents cannot, and research at Oxford University has even shown that there may be a *"grandparent effect"*; that through inheritance, home loans, generation-skipping trusts and assistance with school fees or childcare, middle-class grandparents have the ability to not only help their grandchildren into good universities or jobs but equally to stop them from slipping down the British social hierarchy. So, if the intergenerational cycle of wealth and affluence is still very much alive and well amongst the privileged in the UK, so too with longevity is the intergenerational cycle of poverty and family deprivation amongst the poor and working classes. A new multidimensional, multigenerational picture of poverty in Britain today is emerging that is likely to reinforce inequality and so compound the barriers facing any attempt to break it. It is a feature of Britain today that, according to Grandparents Plus (2009), is somewhat distinct from the rest of Western Europe, where generally pensions are significantly more generous and progressive than in the UK.

On the plus side, grandparents today live longer than grandparents in the past. They have the opportunity of not only seeing their grandchildren grow up but potentially of seeing their great-grandchildren grow up too. Grandparents today are healthier, and wealthier, than in the past and so are more able to actively and physically support their grandchildren: giving advice, driving the school run, providing childcare or financial support, helping with homework, acting as a 'second mum or dad' and providing a haven of peace and quiet for stressed parents and troubled teenagers. Equally, it's a learning experience for grandparents as well as for grandchildren. While in the past the assumption was that grandparents were helping to socialise grandchildren into norms and traditions of society at large, increasingly the modern child is helping the grandparent, introducing them to the intricacies and mysteries of new technology, Facebook and *The X Factor*, as much as they're being socialised into good manners and healthy eating. The modern grandchild has a voice and a presence in today's generational relationships and is not afraid to use it. They are no longer seen but not heard. Rather, they are very much part of the generational dialogue and, according to the small amount of research on this topic, the modern grandchild has considerable influence on contemporary family relations and is well prepared to use it to bind as well as to break the branches of the 'beanpole'. Some older re-partnered men even experience a second fatherhood when their new wife gives birth, at the very time when their adult children from their first marriage have become parents themselves.

Ultimately, however, the extent and nature of grandparent–grandchild relationships depends on the grandparental relationship with the parents and their observation of the 'parental code' – that unspoken expectation that while grandparents may offer help and support, they must not, nay cannot, interfere in the upbringing or disciplining of children, nor seek to impose their own style of childcare on the parents. On the other hand, grandparents, especially grandfathers, don't like to be taken for granted or taken advantage of. Where such family conflicts arise, however, as Dr Robert Schwalbe (2008) has wisely put it, the onus is on the elder to resolve it: "*Their youth is their excuse. You and I are older and more experienced. We have no such excuse.*" With new multigenerational family structures and relationships, new networks of care and support in a multi-age society, the grandparent of the 21st century is emerging not as a peripheral figure in family life but a central one, at the heart of multigenerational life; potentially a new 'superhero'. As Professor Ann Buchanan of Oxford University (2018) has argued, not only are grandparents today playing an increasing role in family life but their contribution significantly increases the well-being and mental health of grandchildren, and so perhaps this 'hidden benefit' should be formally recognised, encouraged and financially rewarded. Ironically, though, just as grandparents are booming in numbers across the world and have more time to become grandparents, the number of grandchildren is falling dramatically. According to the UN (2010), in 1960 there was an average of three children (0–14) for each person aged 65 or over. By 2060, this is projected to reverse to two elderly people for each child – a dramatic and very stark turn-around that is highly indicative of the fundamental changes being wrought by global longevity. If this prediction proves correct, then there will soon be more grandparents than grandchildren, and certainly more grandparents per grandchild than ever before.

So, the grandparents of today, and certainly of tomorrow, are a whole new generation of grandparents, the like of which the world hasn't seen before. They are not an 'extended' version of grandparents in the past, nor of any of the stereotypical images that traditionally come with the title. The grandparent of tomorrow is much more likely to be a baby boomer of the 1960s or 70s, brought up on Dr Spock, rock music, international travel and youthful adventure, keen to explore Disneyland or Legoland with their grandchildren at home or abroad – and with the financial resources to do so. Certainly, the **grandfather of today** is not the grandfather of the past. For one thing, they're still alive; for another, they're relatively healthy. In the past, grandfathers didn't live long into retirement, if they lived to that age at all. In the past, grandfathers didn't engage extensively in the lives of their grandchildren. They were more peripheral or distant figures, remembered more in family photos or family mythology than in real life. In stark contrast, the grandfather of today and tomorrow is much more visible, engaged and active, often enjoying a 'second fatherhood' without all the trials and tribulations that possibly came with the first one. They may even be a step-grandfather, drawn into a new family network by divorce and remarriage, yet expected to play the same role, particularly by their new grandchildren. Mick Jagger may not be a typical grandparent even of the baby boomer generation but amazingly he and Keith Richards are already great-grandparents with the very real prospect that, if they simply keep performing as they are, they could become great-great-grandfathers – highly symbolic of longevity itself, and hugely symbolic of the rock 'n roll generation with which baby boomers tend to identify.

Grandfathers today are expected to take on the role of family counsellor, family coach and family banker; to become the head of the family or at least the family 'godfather'; a role that plays to the skills, experience, and possibly the vanity, of many older males and, at the same time, offers them a critical and fulfilling sense of purpose post-retirement. This new generation of grandfathers are used to 'getting things done', given their previous roles and responsibilities in working life, and so the idea of 'championing' the young may well appeal to many ageing baby boomer's sense of justice, fairness and equal opportunity – ideals many of them fought and campaigned for in the 1960s and 70s. Grandfathers, like their 'sisters-in-arms' grandmothers, may well become part of a new silver army, a new political force, a reserve army of campaigners and volunteers, carers and crusaders, entrepreneurs and innovators that will help transform family and community life, economic and business life in the new century, and force the government of the day, through lobbying and the ballot box, to take ageing seriously and create a new and fairer intergenerational social contract fit for the 21st century.

So, the longevity revolution is transforming family life in modern Britain and across the world. A new age family, a family for and of the 21st century, is emerging, radically different to old-age family types of the past; beanpole in shape, fluid in structure and multigenerational, multiracial, even multinational in relationships. It has become highly organic, adapting to the forces of globalisation and the world economy as well as to the search for personalisation, personal identity and self-fulfilment that now feature in the age of the internet and its companion, social media. And at the forefront of this social revolution is the boomer generation, now as grandparents, searching for a final purpose and an ultimate meaning after a long life of living and family care. The family of the future is on a voyage of discovery, and at the helm or as first mate is the modern grandparent, possibly no longer as physically active a member of the family as anyone else but hopefully with the wisdom of age on their side.

So, as Polly was increasingly asking herself, is the UK government – is any government – up to speed with the extent and type of changes the modern British family is going through, and does it have a policy framework, a new age family strategy, to cope with the fallout that is inevitably likely to follow such a fragile social structure? Does it have, post-Brexit and the likely restrictions on immigration, a strategy for raising the British birth rate back to replacement level to help stem the drift to ageing and to rebalance the UK's dependency ratio through an infusion of new young blood? Does it have a support strategy, for example, for engaging more effectively the army of grandparents, already working in the 'fields of family life', to help cope with the inevitable breakdowns of the delicate beanpole that is family life today? And does the government, or family, of today have a longevity satnav to help steer the child of the 21st century on the voyage of discovery into an *"ever-changing and unknown family formation"* described so poignantly by Professor Sarah Harper (2006): *"An individual born now or late last century has the expectation of a variety of family and household formations. He or she may be born into a consensual union, which then becomes a marital union, which ends in divorce, resulting in a single parent – probably female-led – household. This then becomes a reconstituted family with cohabiting adults, then married adults with a combination of step-siblings within one household."*

'Moreover,' asked Polly, 'has any government any longer got the power to control and plan its family development in an age when the forces of demography are sweeping across the globe, disrupting everything in their path and overturning family life across the world in the process?' Even the 'all-powerful' Chinese government has now had to bow to the inevitable forces of ageing and abandon its one-child policy before an avalanche of elderly descends on modern China. As the migrant crisis of 2015/16 in Europe showed, controlling mass population movement and integrating new cultures and new families into existing society is fast becoming a Herculean task that is beyond the capacity of most governments, even if they had the political will to do so. Global demography is reshaping world society, and with it the British and the world family, as surely and as permanently as global warming is reshaping the planet. But is family life better for the children of tomorrow or worse? Are children happier and better brought up in smaller, multigenerational families with grandparents all around them? Certainly, they don't appear to be in Britain today. As recent UNICEF and OECD surveys have shown, the UK has some of the least happy children and teenagers in the Western world, an indictment that should shock any government into action and inspire as passionate a national debate as intense as anything about the EU or immigration – but it doesn't. And that's an indictment that should set the blood boiling of any true boomer grandparent.

Country Sub-Ranking:	No Poverty	Zero Hunger	Good Health/	Quality Education
1. Norway	1	4	5	9
2. Germany	8	8	4	7
3. Denmark	4	2	21	5
4. Sweden	6	9	13	16
5. Finland	2	15	16	1
12. UK	**16**	**34**	**15**	**20**

Figure 3: **Child Well-being League Table**
(Adapted from UNICEF Report Card 14: 2018)

As illustrated in Figure 4, below, Polly now had a much clearer understanding of the way in which longevity was not only transforming family life in the UK but how it would 'turn it on its head' in the future. She now had her report. She now had her insights. She now had a possible framework for a new paradigm in which the baby boomer grandparent might play a support role or take centre stage in British family life in the near future. But how might the British welfare state transfer and support such responsibilities for family life while itself shrinking its own role? How might politicians like Polly devise strategies and manifestos to encourage, enable and even incentivise many older people to return to the family fold and help nurture, and on occasions prop up, modern family life without over-burdening the younger taxpayer on one hand, and the old on the other, with family pressures that they thought they'd escaped – and may now be less able to cope with. With that political dilemma buzzing around her brain, Polly decided to finish off her tour of family life in ageing Britain with an excursion into love and sexual relationships in later life, an excursion that proved to be much more revealing, seductive and eye-opening than Polly had ever anticipated.

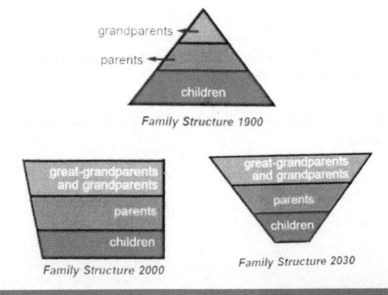

Figure 4: **Age Shift in Family Structure**

8 | Sex, Sexuality and Later-Life Relationships

Ivan and Alwyn had been married for nearly 40 years and were now in their mid-60s. They were both planning to retire but to what? More of the same or something totally different? They had been childhood sweethearts, born and brought up in the Valleys outside Swansea; and although Alwyn had gone on to university, Ivan had followed his father into the steel mills in Port Talbot and, through an apprenticeship, worked his way into management, eventually gaining promotion as a senior accountant. They had married in 1976 after Alwyn graduated as a teacher. They'd had two children, Nigel and Nicola, both married now with families of their own; and they'd enjoyed a good life and an apparently happy home – nothing spectacular, fairly humdrum in many ways, but solid and predictable. That is until Ivan announced, out of the blue, that he'd been having an affair with a woman at work, a woman ten years his junior, and that they were planning to move abroad to Australia. Alwyn's world collapsed. She'd had no idea or even suspicion of Ivan's other, apparently romantic, even tempestuous, side. Certainly, she'd never seen it. And now all she apparently had to look forward to over the next 20 years was a future on her own and maybe a grandchild or two.

Alwyn, however, was a proud Welsh woman brought up to stand up for herself. No way would she be 'dumped' like this or accept a future without promise, even if the divorce settlement had been fairly generous – and rightly so! She was still attractive, enjoyed dressing fashionably and in her teens had been a part-time model. She'd enjoyed a fairly adventurous social life at university in the late 1960s, smoking the occasional bit of pot and marching over Vietnam and women's rights. She often harked back to the friendships, fashions, music and sheer sense of unlimited freedom that era seemed to embody. Life with Ivan the accountant had been fine but adventurous it was not; and Alwyn now had the urge to revisit her youth, to see much more of the world, including her son Nigel and grandchildren in San Francisco, and simply be herself again after all these years as a devoted wife and mother. So, where should she start and, with some 20 years in front of her, where would it all end?

Alwyn is Polly's Welsh cousin. Her break-up with Ivan and their subsequent ambitions to start a new life apart, at ages 64 and 61 respectively, inevitably became a great talking point around the family dinner tables. It equally got Polly thinking about how social mores had changed and how ageing boomers in and outside her constituency might now be facing love and sex in later life very differently to previous generations. Certainly Ivan's, and especially Alwyn's, ambitions for new late-life relationships would have been impossible, if not unthinkable, 60 years ago. Old people after the war simply retired fairly quickly to a care home; very few lived long enough to start a new life or a new relationship, and they probably had to leave town to do so. Certainly, their sexual ambitions seemed to be a lot more restrained than today's baby boomers appear to be; nor could they divorce as easily as today. So, despite her initial reservations, Polly – and for his part, David, her GP husband – began tentatively reading and researching this delicate topic, aided and abetted by Hannah, their 40-year-old daughter and one-time marketer for the health and beauty industry. What they discovered not only tickled their relational fancy but highlighted the fact that in an age of mass ageing, the sexual behaviour and relationships of the new old now have as much social and economic significance as those of the new young.

Today is a new era in ageing and, while the collapse of Ivan and Alwyn's marriage is a tragedy, it's no longer the end of life for either of them. They both now have the time and the ambition to relive life to the full, and as a baby boomer of the late 1960s Alwyn won't be held back by her gender or the social mores of the past. Nevertheless, both Alwyn and Ivan face the challenges of age, the challenges of ageing bodies, where the spirit might well be adventurous and willing but the limbs less lithe and a lot less lively, whether cavorting in the bedroom or striding across the Golden Gate Bridge in San

Francisco. They might both have been children of the swinging 60s but staying sexy when you're 60 and enjoying sex in later life is a whole new challenge, one that either involves an awful lot of work in the gym or an awful amount of money in the beauty parlour. The swinging 60s were one thing; swinging 60- and 70-year-olds are quite another. Just look back to the black and white repeats of *Top of the Pops* – the music, the miniskirts, the hairstyles – and think again. Is this how you want your grandchildren to remember Grandad and Nana, or do we need a new image and a new type of glamour – more sterling silver than golden bling? In an age of ageing, is a new sexual revolution emerging, born of the baby boomers of the 1960s but adapted by and for the old age boomers of the 2020s? Has the Age of Aquarius – of Hair, Woodstock, hippy communes, sexual liberation and free love – given way to the age of Viagra, silver 'splitting' and internet dating? Have the new old given up on sex and settled for a cuddle and a kiss rather than an orgasmic climax, or is a new style of sex life – and with it a new image of the sexy 60-year-old – coming to the surface? As Dr Stephen Nock of Virginia University has boldly put it: *"There's no reason to think that sex will recede in the minds of the baby boomers. It will probably recede in the bodies of the baby boomers, as it does in all older people, but sex will remain an essential part of their sense of self."* And as the ILC-UK report, *How long will I love you? Sex and intimacy in later life* (2017) concluded: *"positive sexuality and intimacy throughout the life-course is linked to higher levels of happiness and well-being – irrespective of age."* The Independent Age survey in 2018 found that 52% of over-65s would like more sex and had no intention of stopping even in their 70s. And despite the alarming rise in STDs amongst this age group, over 10% of respondents claimed to have had multiple sexual partners since turning 65. The sex lives of the older ages is increasingly the subject of journalistic or academic investigations, such as Esther Perel's *State of Affairs* (2017) and Stephanie Theobald's *Sex Drive* (2018), while the 2018 BBC drama *Wanderlust* and its exploration of alternative sexual arrangements for middle-aged couples could have been written about baby boomers as much as any younger generation.

As Polly reflected, the new old certainly don't appear to have given up on sex. They appear to be as determined as ever to 'use it not lose it', determined to generate new passion in old relationships – and old limbs – or old passion in new relationships, well supported now by the booming and diverse sex industry and worldwide websites, be they Ann Summers in the UK or Pleasure Boutique and Good for Her in the States. Films celebrating the sexual re-awakening of the older generations are now widespread; films such as the romantic comedy *It's Complicated* and the sequel to *Fifty Shades of Grey, Fifty Shades Darker,* which starred Kim Basinger, now in her 60s. Erica Jong, now in her 70s, has produced a racy follow-up to her 1970s blockbuster *Fear of Flying* – aptly entitled *Fear of Dying* – and Jilly Cooper's colourful characters continue to romp around the stables and farmyards of her numerous bonk-busters. So, far from sexual activity shrinking amongst 60-year-olds, baby boomers appear to be 'at it again', shedding their clothes and their inhibitions and launching into a whole new era of romantic adventure and sexual experimentation – even with their current partner! The 2011 survey by the Institute for the Advanced Study of Human Sexuality, for example, starkly revealed that sex in all its diverse forms is alive and well amongst older Americans, with two-thirds of respondents admitting that they'd participated in open relationships, with more than a third currently doing so. Eighty-five per cent had engaged in casual sex, 55% of females and 65% of males had had secret affairs and nearly 85% of respondents had used pornographic videos and sex aids. British baby boomers, despite their reputation for reservation, are apparently not far behind with "*the majority reckoning that they were having the best sex of their lives two or three times a week*", indoors and out, and all over the house, with the living room apparently the favoured spot outside the bedroom; and even the potting shed is not apparently out of bounds. (National Survey of Sexual Attitudes and Lifestyles in the UK: 2013; English Longitudinal Study of Ageing: 2015)

So, sex is still the source, and *sauce*, of life that keeps many relationships in later life lasting longer and remaining exciting and romantic. And leading the way, yet again, are women; women like Alwyn in their 60s, free now from the menopause, free from childrearing, free to enjoy their own sexuality to the full, with either their existing partner or through singles sites or LAT relationships ('living alone together'). As Deirdre Fishel and Diana Holtzberg discovered in their study in 2008, women over 60 are not only *Still Doing It* but doing more of "*it*". Few people realise just how many women in their 60s, 70s and 80s today are enjoying alternative relationships and indulging in lifestyles that might shock their children and grandchildren "*by getting together with younger (sometimes much younger) men, dating more than one man at a time, making share-a-man arrangements, or hooking up with another woman for the first time.*" With less time left on this earth, many older women are apparently willing to take risks and open up new doors of possibility. Many women over 60 still want to feel the energy, intimacy and passion of having an active sex life; hence the rise of websites like *Sixty and Me* and, ironically, the rise too of sexual

Figure 1: **FPA adverts**
2010

health warnings like those above, warning of the dangers of unprotected sex for the over-50s by using images from the 1960s to get their message across.

However, while the sex industry may well be tapping into the sexual re-awakening of the older age groups, academia is still some way behind in analysing and explaining this social and cultural revolution. In one of the few academic studies in this arena, Dr Merryn Gott (2005) identified the healthier lifestyles, and healthier bodies, of older people today, along with the rise of the internet, the advent of Viagra and most especially the late-age baby boomers' apparent determination to 'stay young forever', and their rejection, as in their youth, of traditional mores. Later-life divorce and re-marriage rates are escalating, there is a growing trend of intimate but non-cohabiting relationships among older people, and older lesbians and gay men are now more open about their sexuality. A whole new industry is being built up around providing dating services for older people, and new images or stereotypes seem to be emerging for both older men and older women. The 'sexy oldie' is not only a label of description or even admiration but, argues Gott, is fast becoming the new expectation, as older women are encouraged, even expected, to stay sexy, active and attractive as part of the active ageing, even anti-ageing, revolution against the traditional 'grey' or 'blue-rinse' image of older women in the past. Women are under pressure to have sex as a means of remaining young and beautiful and are expected to keep their ageing at bay if they still wish to feel or be valued as glamorous or attractive; a situation the feminist writer Germaine Greer (1991) summed up in her usual strident way, arguing that the middle-aged woman today has a duty to go on being attractive no matter how fed up she is with the whole business. She is not allowed to say, *"Now I shall let myself go'; letting herself go is a capital offence."* Looking young and sexy is at the heart of the health and beauty industry today, and inevitably the food, fashion, media and beauty industries have latched onto the 'older' market using the images, styles and even the icons of the 1960s – Twiggy, Cher and even Jane Fonda (now over 80) – to appeal to today's older women. The Italian actress and model Isabella Rossellini, for example, has recently been reappointed thirty years later as the global ambassador for Lancôme, despite now being in her sixties, as this famous French cosmetic brand seeks to attract back its older clientele.

Sexy at 60 is therefore being redefined, not necessarily by older women themselves but by the young men and women of the media, fashion and pharmaceutical industries seeking to create whole new markets. The Helen Mirrens and the Susan Sarandons of this world, however, are not typical 60/70-year-old women. Rather, they are admired precisely because they are exceptions and seem to have outwitted nature. Inspiring though Judi Dench might be in her 80s and 'hot' as Madonna might still picture herself in her 60s, many women today would be much happier ageing as they wish, plodding into old age at their own pace and style rather than slavishly following stars from the 1960s and 70s, however inspiring and image-changing they might be. As India Knight (2015) has argued, older women are not in decline but in their prime, on a journey from *'Nymph to Nana'*; and after such a rich and hopefully rewarding lifetime, older women need to liberate themselves from the stereotypes of the 1960s and develop and design an image for the 2020s; a new, more mature and imaginative version of the women they are now and the women they aspire to be in the future; a future that now offers a further life ahead, one potentially as full as the last one and one that needs a new Mary Quant or Sophia Loren to create the style and the image that truly reflects the *New Woman of the New Age*. Older women, in her view, must reject the traditional assumption that the only way to look and feel sexy is to look young. Instead, they should celebrate the fact that: *"Older women have it all… wisdom, knowledge and dramatically better sex lives than we did at 20. We're not invisible, and there are millions of us, and we look great. Who needs a youth bus when you can have an age(ing) Bentley?"*; a plea beautifully conveyed by mature models, such as Pamela Lucas (65) in her advertisements for M&S, Maye Musk (68) – the mother of Elon Musk, the PayPal billionaire – modelling for Revlon and Virgin, and by the host of glamorous celebrities, now in their 60s and 70s and still setting new standards of glamour for all ages.

One marketing campaign that really did try to put real women of all ages at the forefront of their advertising was that by the Dove range of beauty products a few years ago. It was an overnight sensation, attracted intense media attention and went viral on social media. It offered a new direction for the health and beauty industry and inspired many older women to feel glamorous and confident even when posing in the nude. Tom Ford, on the other hand, went for the more lusty and longing fantasy about older women in his Facebook advert for elegant jewellery in 2018, an advert that some commentators labelled 'geriatric porn'.

Finally, despite many women's fears and trepidations about their looks and their attractiveness, and their daily battles against ageing, older men are occasionally more perceptive than they're given credit for and can not only see the inner beauty beneath but have the imagination to fantasise about what that might be. In the words of Cosmo Landesman, aged 60 (*The Sunday Times*: 5 July 2015), "*Beauty is very much in the Eye of the Beholder*" and once a woman's beauty has captured a man's heart (and his groin) he tends to stay captured, even if she's now in her 60s or 80s because "*contrary to what the poets tell us, time can't touch your beauty, at least to those who have been touched by your beauty once upon a time in the past.*" Older men's perceptions of older women, however, may equally be down to their failing eyesight and their ability to remember the past much more vividly than the present. Older men, in contrast, have traditionally been allowed to 'grow old gracefully' – and been admired for it. The silver-haired mature male conveys an image of control and authority at the peak of manhood. He can now retreat quietly into retirement – into the study, onto the golf course or off on the cruise ship to faraway places to reminisce about and revisit old conquests or youthful liaisons. However, with the advent of Viagra, spread of fitness centres and the growing demands of boomer women for more active and intimate relationships, boomer men, too, are under pressure to perform against a new standard of mature but 'active' masculinity, to keep pace with and emulate the likes of George Clooney and Alec Baldwin. Some older men respond to such expectations with resignation, and retreat from sex altogether. Others go hell for leather to prove their prowess, proudly displaying symbols of their elder manhood – the sleek-nosed sports car or the sleek and sexy yacht.

So, modern masculinity, too, is no longer safe at 60. Mature men, too, still have to perform in and out of the bedroom, and an active sex life is now considered part of a healthy and happy relationship in older age. Yet, as other studies have argued, a high level of sexual performance is not a statutory requirement. For many older men, with the onset of ageing limbs and diminished testosterone, retirement is the opportunity to relax and enjoy a 'kiss and a cuddle' as much as an orgasm and an orgy. As Arlene Heyman (2016) described it so very vividly in her book *Scary Old Sex*, sex at 70 can be challenging and require as much fore-planning as foreplay. It's like a military campaign *"with plans drawn up, equipment in tip top condition and troops deployed and coordinated meticulously"* as the couple prepare for engagement according to a strict timetable and a ready supply of Vagifem and Viagra beforehand and a nap afterwards to recuperate. As she explains, sexual spontaneity at this age is often difficult, not least when, for example, one participant suffers from acid reflux and has to sit upright, and the other needs clomipramine, an anti-depressant to retard ejaculation. Alternatively, as the French psychologist Marie de Hennezel (2011) has argued, perhaps sex in later life should be more loving than lusty, more emotional intimacy than genital gymnastics – a gentle, more sensual approach to orgasm that may lead to more satisfying and fulfilling relationships for some but lack the physical engagement and adrenalin for others. She cites the Taoist art of love as an approach that many older couples may find more sensual and less stressful, given its core principle of controlled ejaculation (coitus reservatus), the separation for male satisfaction from ejaculation alone. Its strong focus on female orgasm and sexual pleasuring is almost the reverse of the traditional Western model and one born of the belief that men over 50 will gain far greater sexual satisfaction, and live longer, if they ejaculate less and make love more. Under this philosophy, love-making moves from an individual or solo spasm into a whole-body one; a more shared experience that proponents claim is a far more relaxing, erotic and even spiritual experience all round; a new level of love-making designed for a new age, and a new stage in life; a deeper and more enduring experience beyond the brief physical pleasure that ejaculation alone can bring.

Sex after 60, however, is still something of a taboo subject, rarely discussed or openly shared. In the era of the #MeToo campaign, older men risk social condemnation, and worse, for showing any interest in sex or younger women, while older women may be reviled for being attracted to or embarking on sexual relationships with younger men. Terms such as 'dirty old man' or MILF still represent very powerful social stigmas that no respectable older person would wish to bear, particularly in front of their family or children. Yet as Dr Borz of Stanford Medical School argues: *"People that have sex, live longer. Married people live longer. People need people. The more intimate the connection, the more powerful the effects."* And in an era when loneliness is increasingly one of the greatest threats to older people's health and well-being, the social stigmas that condemn or inhibit sexual relationships in later life are likely to increasingly become counter-productive as the cost of elder isolation falls increasingly on society at large and the burden of support on younger families faced with ageing parents living on their own. A positive and healthy society would seek to accept, if not actually applaud, active sex after 60 in the same way and for similar reasons as it promotes it for the young. The health industry would seek to support and enable active and safe sex to help relieve the burden of an ageing population on the NHS, while sex would seem to be a prime target for the silver economy if addressed in a supportive not patronising manner. Perhaps now is the time for a post-60s Kinsey Report to challenge and shatter current sexual stigmas, and for sex shops such as Ann Summers to extend its range of lingerie and sex aids specifically for the amorous oldie, male and female, and possibly introduce a new range of sex furniture to support and re-energise ageing limbs. Certainly, the baby boomer will not tolerate sexual ageism and will probably quite enjoy embarking on a second sexual revolution, shattering all the traditional sexual conventions in their wake, and aided and abetted as before by new treatments to combat physical decline or revive sexual appetites. As Dr Borz has succinctly summed it up: for men *"it is biology or hydraulics"*, while for women *"it's opportunity and availability"*. For both, it may simply be more comfortable positioning, with bouncy beds taking the strain and soothing lubricants removing the pain. As the ILC-UK report, *Sex and intimacy in later life* (2017), argued, sex needs to be seen and even planned as *"a partnered experience"* not just a personal or individual one; part of a shared and mutually enjoyed activity rather than one tolerated, or worse endured, by the other; one that both partners enjoy and look forward to even if their respective pleasures might well be very different – the joy of togetherness and intimate touching as much as physical pleasuring or sexual relief.

And if mature 60-year-olds are still struggling to redefine their sexuality, what of the health practitioner faced by a whole new generation of demanding baby boomers determined to prove themselves again, determined to restore their prowess to that of their youth, anxious to enliven their marriages and to regain the 'joy of sex' that everyone else seems to be raving about. Healthcare policy and practice is still well behind any silver revolution in sexual attitudes and behaviours. GPs apparently still find sexual health a difficult area of consultation, and nurse training is only now beginning to catch up with this new phenomenon. It has generated heated debate within the nursing press in relation to nurse responsibility for addressing the sexual concerns of people with disabilities, assistance that some argue includes putting on a condom, helping them watch pornographic videos, or even helping them to masturbate. As one student nurse responded, she didn't relish the prospect of completing a four-year nursing degree in order to become *"one of the lowest paid prostitutes in the country"*. Should healthcare professionals take sex and sexual relationships into their consultations with older people? Is sex part of any programme for improving health and well-being today? Should doctors and nurses promote and prescribe ways of improving sexual activity amongst older patients in the same way as they promote dieting and medication? Or is this still an area outside of their responsibility and beyond their professional 'comfort zone'?

This dilemma is at its peak for care workers working in residential homes, where the traditional boundaries between public and private space are less evident and less easy to manage. *"Because staff in general do not consider sexuality among elderly clients, there is not an atmosphere in which clients would feel comfortable discussing sexuality and their needs."* In response to this challenge, the Royal College of Nursing (RCN) issued guidance for staff in both 2011 and 2018 that affirms the importance of sexuality in later life, its potential contribution to health, well-being and positive relationships, as well as to patient dignity and sense of independence: *"Sexuality remains a fundamental aspect of who we are as individuals throughout our lives. It influences identity, self-image, self-concept and self-worth. It also affects mental health, social relationships and quality of life."* The 2018 RCN guidance warns staff that advancing age *"in no way prevents older individuals and couples enjoying sexual activity, sexual intimacy or coitus"* and advises staff to ensure that residents have the right environment for intimacy, including access to double beds, sex toys, pornography and Viagra. It even advises staff on how to handle difficult situations, such as two male residents falling in love, competition amongst female residents for the limited number of male residents available, and affairs amongst married residents – even if they can't always remember each other's name. So, sex in the care home is a dilemma, and a growing one as numbers grow and sexually active residents increasingly become the norm. As the 2018 Manchester University study of 7,000 people aged 50 and over discovered, over a quarter of men and one in ten women over 85 were still sexually active. The resulting image of residential homes as 'hotbeds' of sexual activity may initially seem amusing but this is a serious issue of residential management and even human rights, and it is especially difficult and often quite distressing when dealing with older people with dementia – the greatest disease of the 21st century and one of the greatest costs ($60 billion worldwide; £20 billion in the UK alone). At a time when an individual's very 'person-hood' is at stake and their consciousness is disappearing, this "*last taboo*", as the ILC-UK has called it, may be one of the few remnants of individuality still remaining.

Sexuality and sexual behaviour amongst the new old – or even the old old – may seem something of a last frontier, a final fling, even a step too far. However, with the arrival of the baby boomer generation, sex in older age is likely to be a new liberation, a new movement, and with it will generate, if not galvanise, a whole new market in silver sex products and services as the demand for everlasting love runs true – and lasts well in to people's 70s and even 80s. Dating services for the over-50s are widespread, and recently even Debrett's, the bible of formal etiquette, has entered this arena, in partnership with the Ourtime Dating Service. The demand for active sex as part of an active and healthy lifestyle is likely to have a profound impact on the healthcare industry in its treatments and approaches to patient care. It will certainly impact on personal relationships and behaviour amongst the new old and dramatically influence their attitudes to, and expectations of, life and love in later life. As Margaret Manning, editor of the website Sixty and Me, has argued: "*forget the stereotypes, if you ask the 43,000 members of our Sixty and Me community, you will find that they are adventurous, curious, and passionate about living a life that is healthy, wealthy and independent.*"

And almost inevitably, new technology is also getting in on the act, and the advent of the sexbot is likely to add a whole new dimension to human sex lives and relationships. Sexbots, or humanoid robots programmed to be sexually active, are apparently already available, costing as little as £3,000. And according to futurologists like David Levy (2009): "*Love with robots will be as normal as love with humans*" and as a result the "*world will be a much happier place*", particularly for those on their own. Sexbot brothels already exist in cities such as Dortmund in Germany, with German wives apparently dropping their husbands off for a spot of sex while they go off shopping. In Barcelona a home service is on offer, and in Japan these artificial 'passion dolls' are apparently known as 'Dutch wives'. All very convenient, and apparently mutually beneficial, particularly for an ageing population, ageing couples and especially the disabled or isolated. Equally, all very challenging for a culture built on monogamous human relationships and based on personal intimacy, belonging and such emotional bonds as love, loyalty and longing. The whole architecture of this most intimate of human relationships seems to be under threat, and inevitably a strong and passionate Campaign Against Sex Robots has been launched by those fearing such an 'invasion of intimacy', not least as this robot invasion seems to threaten women more than men, whether in attractiveness or availability. In her study, *Sex Robots: The End of Love* (2019), Kathleen Richardson, founder of Campaign Against Sex Robots (CASR), sees sexbots as a new form of male corporate power designed to marginalise women and even replace them in the lives of men and society at large. Other commentators, such as Helen Driscoll of Sunderland University (2016), are less fearful and more sanguine. She believes that sexy robots could significantly enhance, or complement, couple's sexual relationships, making affairs a thing of the past and prostitution obsolete. McArthur and Danaher (2017) see sexbots more as sexual companions, offering novelty and variety rather than replacement and rejection, mitigating any disparities in desire and so enhancing not threatening long-term relationships. So, the notion of an older couple consensually partnering in a threesome with a sexbot may seem the ultimate for a generation that appeared to enjoy free love back in the 1960s; but as Bryan Appleby has argued (*The Sunday Times*: 22 Oct. 2017): "*Sexbots are not just another technological intrusion into our lives but an invasion into the intimacy of our sex lives; and as such an existential challenge to the very notion of what it is to be human, what it is to have sex.*" Just as Alexa is already making friends with our families and beginning to run our households on behalf of Amazon, so the Sexbot is likely to both share our bedroom and transform the very nature and dynamic of this most intimate and personal of human acts; even more so if David

Levy is correct in claiming that within a century sexbots may be able to give birth to children. Equally, sexbots may herald another phase in women's liberation if, as JanetStreet-Porter has refreshingly put it, they could also be trained to do the ironing, cooking and cleaning. This might – just might, she argues – tip the balance for many women and certainly *"The sooner inventors manage to devise a decent robo-man, women everywhere will be reaching for their credit cards."*

And finally, while the older generations appear to be about to embark on a later-life sexual rampage, it appears, according to the British Pregnancy Advisory Service (BPAS) (2018), that teenagers today prefer a quiet life at home in front of a computer screen, texting, sexting and sending romantic or even erotic messages to secret or unknown lovers, rather than venturing out into the reality of an actual date or intimate liaison. Such virtual dating is apparently easier, less physically dangerous and a lot less embarrassing than a fumble in the dark or personal rejection. Despite the widely advertised dangers of internet dating and sexting, *Generation Sensible* seem to be living safer and more responsible lives than previous generations. They drink less, smoke less and are less likely to have unwanted pregnancies. Sexting allows them to enjoy online flirting and even phone sex without commitment or physical effort, as a form of extended foreplay before trying the 'real thing'. Some, however, feel exposed and inadequate on social media and seem to find normal relationships hard to establish or sustain. Some young people, according to the Next Steps Project, are even reverting to celibacy, intimidated or appalled by today's culture of hypersexuality and pressure for sexual perfection, a stark contrast apparently to the wild and outgoing teenage years claimed by their parents.

At first Polly was taken aback, even shocked, by sex even being on the ageing agenda. The thought of including 'sex at 60 or 70' in her campaign speeches initially made her squirm. However, on reflection, she and her husband David realised that sex and relationships have as much importance to older people as to the young; that a healthy sex life in later life could well be a major contributor to living longer, healthier and happier lives, so reducing the possible burden on both the family and the state; and, according to recent research by Salerno University in Italy and Imperial College, London, helping to delay the onset of Parkinson's disease. So from this perspective, sex and personal relationships are not a peripheral issue in any ageing strategy but potentially quite central to it, not only from a health and financial point of view but as a critical factor in any housing policy or care-home provision. If the current rate of 'silver splitting' persists, for example, more and more boomers will be seeking single housing, even if their partner now lives next door. Moreover, good sex and ongoing personal relationships are likely to be a significant source of self-esteem and independence in later life, particularly for older women who are not only likely to live longer alone but be less well off in the process, and increasingly prone to isolation and feelings of no longer being attractive, wanted or needed. Later-life intimacy and sex, internet dating and sexbots may be outside the normal political agenda but with so many people living longer and healthier lives, and determined to live them to the full, Polly was at least now alert to the issues and potential implications both personally and politically. As for Alwyn and Ivan, they were now two 60-year-olds off on a new adventure in life and looking to rejuvenate themselves and their love lives 'for better or worse, from this day forward'. Ivan may hope that a younger woman and a new life 'down under' might rejuvenate him, while Alwyn, liberated from domesticity and home life, is now out to find the 'woman within' and rediscover the adventurous spirit of her youth, personally, sexually and socially, though not perhaps as wildly as Stephanie Theobald's *Road to a Pleasure Revolution* in 2018. Both Alwyn and Ivan have much to look forward to; both have much to look back on; both will hit new horizons but equally new challenges, whether for Ivan it's keeping pace with a woman ten years his junior, or for Alwyn fending for herself until she finds a new soulmate and then has to decide whether to live together or 'live apart together' (LAT). Both may eventually regret separating – and the enduring angst of their children – but ultimately, through the gift of longevity and the joy of longer life, they at least have the opportunity to start again and possibly to do better this time.

9 Death, Dying and the Good Death

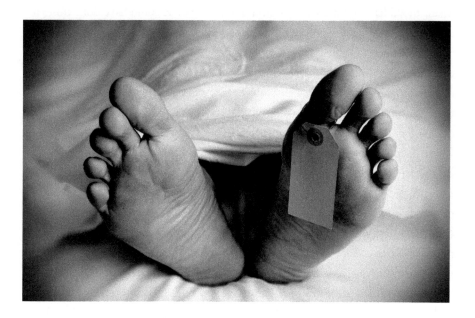

The Dream of Gerontius is a poem written by Blessed John Henry Newman as he converted from Anglicanism to Roman Catholicism in 1865. It depicts a dying man contemplating his past life and seeking redemption through purification in purgatory as the means to saving his soul. A touch over-dramatic, perhaps, for a book on ageing, but one of the joys of longevity – if that is an appropriate expression – is not only that it offers much more time for reflecting on life itself but also the opportunity to reflect on death in the future; on how you want to depart this world; on how you want your family and your world to see you off; and on how you want to be remembered.

Morbid though such a final chapter to Part One might at first seem to be, it is equally a highly fitting finale to the gift that longevity undoubtedly is; the opportunity to contemplate life in the round as well as to live it to the full.

―――――――

Such thoughts had filled Polly's mind when her mother Charlotte had died, and they continued to fill it ever since. Charlotte's words of wisdom often percolated Polly's thoughts and inspired her to think differently or more calmly about challenges – personal or political – that confronted her. She even found herself on occasion talking to her deceased mother, whether at the graveside or over the kitchen sink, and her ideas and strategic thinking about ageing in the 21st century were heavily influenced by her sense of gratitude to her mother's generation for the legacy they'd left, and her sense of guilt that perhaps she could have done more to make Charlotte's later life more fulfilling and liberating than it was.

Polly equally began having thoughts about her own demise, later life and eventual legacy. She had achieved a lot as a teacher and a college principal and was now on a pathway to political eminence, but was that enough? Was there more that she could have done and could do, not only publicly but for her family and her children/grandchildren? In constructing their last will and testament, she and David even began contemplating their own funerals and burial, inspired partly by a recent visit to New Orleans, a community noted not only for having joyful, musical send-offs for the dead but for having family mausoleums to lay generations of the same family altogether in one resting place. This tradition apparently dates back to the days when yellow fever and typhoid swept through the city, necessitating mass burials on a daily basis. However, as a city built on swampland, there was no ground deep enough for traditional burials, so the people of New Orleans built huge family tombs above ground, with space for multiple coffins replaced annually and the remains stored as urns of ashes in the base. The tombs themselves were both large and ornate, and inscribed on the tombstone were whole family histories dating back some hundreds of years; a very fitting memorial for any family, and an environmental solution that other societies might find worth considering. Moreover, funerals in New Orleans are not the sad and sombre affairs we have in the UK. They are a celebration of life rather than a mourning over death, with full accompaniment from New Orleans musicians helping the departed on their way and aiding the living with their grieving. This musical tradition and final act of remembrance so inspired Polly that she and David considered investing in a family mausoleum of their own, back home in Suffolk; the suggestion went down like a lead balloon with other members of the family (though they did like the idea of a jazz band) but the idea stayed with Polly as she contemplated her own passing and remembered the traumas and challenges of burying her mother.

The death business: All this contemplation equally made Polly increasingly aware that the funeral business in the UK is big business, serving a mass market that's about to explode as the boomer generation begins to pass away en masse over the next 20 to 30 years. The UK may even be facing a 'funeral time bomb' as challenging as anything in health or pensions, as the current trough in deaths in the UK is superseded by a dramatic 20% rise thereafter to 627,000 deaths by 2037 – the highest since 1998 with baby boomer deaths alone projected to soar from just under 30,000 in 2019 to well over 100,000 in 2044.

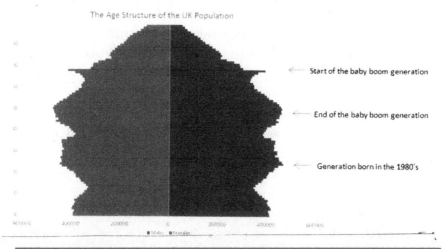

Figures 1: **Age Structure of UK Population**
(ILC-UK: 2014)

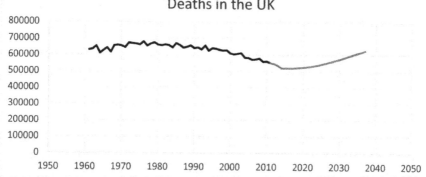

Figures 2: **UK Death Demographics: 1950-2050**
(ILC-UK: 2014)

As the Institute for Policy Research (IPR)/Bath University study showed in 2017, there is a dearth of planning, coordination and forethought at all levels of government, and the current system – if it can be called that at all – is no longer fit for the mass burials of the ageing generations projected ahead. As this study highlighted:

- Death in modern Britain is overwhelmingly now in old age.
- Too many people – almost half – die in hospital unnecessarily.
- Care homes provide the location and care for almost a quarter of all deaths across the UK.
- Organ donation is amongst the lowest in Europe, yet one in ten people will die before they get the transplant they need.
- Nearly two-thirds of the UK population have no will in place and so potentially leave serious chaos and complexity for their relatives to sort out. Equally, family conversations about death and dying rarely take place until serious illness or dementia set in.
- Funerals and burial arrangements are something of a local and national lottery, so intensifying and extending the bereavement and recovery experience for all those remaining.
- The funeral sector is still largely unregulated and under-inspected, so increasing the potential for exploitation and over-charging at a time when those involved, particularly the remaining spouse, are most vulnerable and least able to control the situation and make rational decisions.

The death sector in the UK currently operates in a policy and planning vacuum that will soon be unsustainable as the baby boomer generation 'passes on' over the next 50 years. Even at a personal level, the need to plan ahead, to plan the type and place of the funeral and fund it properly will require a later-life financial plan if the younger generation is not to face a huge cost and a very disruptive legacy that could impact very badly on their own lives and on the broader family relationships that the deceased spent so much of their life building and nurturing. A full funeral may cost upwards of £5,000, a family crypt £35,000+, and even a grave for tomorrow may need booking today given the shortage of places currently available. With the lack of competition within the funeral market, such costs are likely to escalate yet according to the Sun Life survey in 2019, only 23% of respondents had set money aside for their funeral and only 1% had known the deceased's funeral wishes beforehand. Donating your body to the NHS or medical research therefore, may be a cheaper and more communal way to go but this would need to be done quite quickly after death for the organs to still be useful.

Alternatively, as Polly's husband David discovered from a radio phone-in, you can actually organise a funeral yourself. The idea of a DIY funeral might initially sound like black humour, but according to the Natural Death Centre it's all perfectly legal, provided you don't leave the deceased on the side of the public highway or contravene any health and safety regulations. In contrast to many other European nations, Britain is apparently a very liberal society when it comes to burying the dead, and it can all be done quite cheaply, with online companies offering coffins made to order, a civil service conducted by a 'voluntary vicar', and a burial on private ground – or even your own back garden if you so choose provided a police officer is present to validate the death. Certainly attitudes to death are changing quite dramatically with funeral directors reporting a marked shift from 'mourning the dead' with traditional religious ceremonies to 'celebrating their life' carrying the coffin on a milk float or decorating it with the deceased's favourite clothing – a pair of wellies or a racing car helmet (Sun Life: 2019). The *Ideal Death Show* held in Bournemouth in 2018 included designer coffins, a Viking death ship, ash-scattering rockets to send your remains into space, a Death Café and a series of Good Funeral Awards – or 'Death Oscars' – for the gravediggers and coffin makers of the year.

The death debate: So, reflected Polly and David, as the boomers move on through life, are we now entering a new age of dying alongside a new age of living? Are we embarking on a new age conversation but this time about the end of life not the length of it? Such discussion and forward planning, however, does not sit comfortably at present with a society that has traditionally treated death as a taboo topic, and a generation of new old that hoped to die before they got old. Now that they haven't, they're having to come to terms with life in older age, or pretend old age doesn't exist, at least not for them.

However, with the sheer numbers of older persons now living longer, and with public communication now much more open and unrestricted through both traditional and social media, death is no longer a taboo, and the public debate on death and dying is now growing. As boomers get into this arena, and as the funeral business expands, it is likely that the generation, that in the past, has shown its willingness and capacity to challenge and confront tradition, and even overturn it, is just as likely to take on this final stage of life in a very robust and quite radical fashion. Certainly, some leading-edge boomers have begun to speak out, with Joan Bakewell, the age ambassador and journalist, now in her 80s, leading the way.

She is adamant about the need to plan ahead and not just leave it to the doctors and the hustle and bustle of a hospital ward where saying goodbye to loved ones can be a disturbing and badly disrupted event. She cites examples of ambulance services that have now developed provision for taking the dying on one last journey to wherever they wish – the sea, the country and even the Angel of the North – while friends of hers not only invited friends and family to join them in their last moments but ex-girlfriends. (*The Sunday Times*: 11 Dec. 2016.) *"Death, after all, belongs to each of us – not to the medical profession. It's our* [final] *rite of passage, and the more we can shape and plan our own circumstances the better."* Other celebrity boomers, such as Billy Connolly, have sought to express their final feelings before they go, in his case in a letter and a poem to his children.

So, while ageing offers the gift of extended life, it also offers the opportunity to choose and plan one's death, to consider all the options and even to plan a 'good death', however you define it. New technology and new legislation abroad are now offering the opportunity, too, for those with terminal or degenerative diseases to seek the 'right to die', the right to choose the time, place and manner of their death. This right to die, this right to assisted suicide, is certain to grow as a public debate in the years ahead and campaigns involving well-known public figures, such as Chris Woodhead, Terry Pratchett and Iain Banks, have escalated in recent years. As various polls have illustrated, the general public are much more sympathetic to such a significant change in our ethical values, and the 2010 Commission on Assisted Dying declared the current legal status of assisted suicide as inadequate and incoherent. A campaign group, My Death, My Decision (MDMD), has been set up to allow people who are *not* terminally ill to legally end their lives because they believe that the quality of their current life is *"below the level that they are able to accept"*, while Dr Philip Nitschke has apparently developed a suicide machine called the Sarco to enable even the most disabled to end their life if they wish, without human assistance by simply blinking an eye.

Such a debate means challenging, and on occasion even changing, current ethical codes about the process of dying, even if at times this means thinking the unthinkable and speaking the unspeakable. The advert *Symmetry* by the hospice charity, Marie Curie, reflected this new, more open climate, depicting death both sympathetically and graphically, comparing the end of life with the beginning of life, juxtaposing death with birth, and arguing that the two events are just as meaningful and should be treated with the same importance and the same attention to detail so that: *"you exit the planet in a way you choose to"*. Kathryn Mannix's book *With the End in Mind* (2017) is all the more poignant because, as a consultant specialising in palliative care, she is well aware of the current approaches to managing death in and outside the hospital sector and is horrified by much of what she sees. Modern medicine has lengthened life dramatically in the UK but equally it has often lengthened death too and taken it out of the home and into emergency care and hospital wards. In this clinical environment there's no time for ceremony or personal care, simply a professional decision and then a procedure to be followed as the next body is wheeled in. Given the warmth of emotion and compassion expressed when life begins with birth, Dr Mannix was aghast at the coldness of departure when life ends with death. She has therefore devoted her professional life to palliative care and to making death as painless and peaceful for her patients as she can. Her crusade is to persuade everyone to prepare an ***emergency healthcare plan*** that, in discussion with family, decides whether we die in hospital or at home. Ironically, as she records, it is often the young who are most resistant to such conversations and find it most distasteful and disturbing. Consultant Atul Gawande, in his publication *Illness, Medicine and What Matters in the End* (2015), is even more scathing in his indictment of the way modern medicine treats the old and the dying, putting medical considerations first and patient needs, comfort and control a poor second. Terminal patients, in his view, are subjected to *"barbaric procedures"*, designed solely to keep them alive with little consideration of their quality of life in these last stages and, in the process, he argues, deprive death of the human meanings it once had. Dying, today, has become simply a medical procedure to be managed by healthcare professionals with little input from patient and relatives. Such monopoly control, particularly in the final hours, is not likely to be tolerated by a boomer generation used to doing it, and having it, their 'own way'. Dying is rarely easy and yet most of us will end our lives in hospitals or hospices in the care of strangers, with little dignity and no autonomy. As Dr Henry Marsh poignantly summarised it in *The Sunday Times* magazine (1 July 2018): *"Although scientific medicine has brought great and wonderful blessings, it has also brought a curse. Dying, for many of us, has become an unpleasantly prolonged and institutionalised experience."* So, the charity *Living Well, Dying Well* is providing volunteer carers or 'doulas' to help the terminally ill plan their last days while hospices and hospitals in East Anglia are currently looking at ways to give terminal patients a far greater say in their last moments rather than, as at present, simply submitting themselves, and their relatives, to the indignities of the hospital pathway that most people currently have to endure.

And so the debate on death, on a good death, and on ways of dying is likely to grow, fuelled by both the number of baby boomers entering later life and by their appetite for cultural colonisation and for doing it their way, whether through new technology or such innovations as funeral websites and electronic graves as on Facebook. Some councils have even begun to adopt new forms of cremation as a way of solving the shortage of traditional graveyards and environmental issues involved. West Midlands Council, for example, is apparently experimenting with water cremation, liquefying human corpses and then 'flushing them down the drain', out to sea and back to nature.

Living forever and the longevity industry: And finally, boomers being boomers, there are even some in this ever-young, ever-optimistic generation who believe that they can elude death and that they have the right to live forever. As Polly's husband David discovered in his medical researches, there is a growing industry to support this 'ultimate' market. Aubrey de Grey at Cambridge University is one of a number of academics who believe that living forever, or at least to 1,000 years, is a serious possibility through rejuvenation clinics. Companies such as the Alcor Life Extension Foundation in Arizona, USA have been 'freezing' volunteers since 1967 using cryto-protective substances to preserve their bodies for perpetuity. David Kekich of the Maximum Life Foundation has designed a scientific roadmap to reverse ageing using gene restructuring techniques and artificial intelligence to extend youth into pensionable age. "We *think that there is no doubt we'll be able to transform 80-year-olds into 20-somethings again, visually and biologically.*" While such claims at present may seem far-fetched and more scientific fiction than scientific fact, the rate and depth of scientific advance in biological, genetic and medical science is at least raising the very real possibility of even longer, and healthier life for generations to come. The market is certainly there; and even corporate giants, such as Google, are now investing in companies like Calico to develop anti-ageing agents capable of extending the healthspan rather than just the lifespan. The Transhumanism Movement in America is growing in wealth and ambition as it expands amongst the rich and powerful in Silicon Valley, and Elon Musk, co-founder of PayPal and pioneer of electric cars, is apparently investing in the "*pursuit of immortality*" with the Neuralink project to connect human brains with computers capable of downloading and uploading human thoughts. Jesse Karmazin, chief executive of Ambrosia, is seeking to rejuvenate older patients with transfusions of teenage blood as a way of countering dementia and other diseases of ageing, while Ned David, co-founder of Unity Biotechnology, is focusing on eliminating arthritis – that scourge of any ageing body – through attacking decadent senescent cells with senolytic drugs. Silicon Valley billionaires are even offering prizes of $1 million for anyone who can 'hack the code of life'; and they're creating new research centres to promote longer and healthier life through new nanotechnology, 'miracle pills' and even 'reverse engineering' – slowing down and even reversing – such age-related killers as cancer and dementia. While several members of the Alcor project have signed up for 'heads-only' preservation on the basis that they'll be given a new, possibly android or robotic, body later on. Ray Kurzweil, the 'high priest' at Google, believes that mankind is approaching a new Singularity that will transcend biology and elevate mankind into a partnership with artificial intelligence. (See Mark O'Connell: 2017 for a fascinating tour of this brave new world and its claims, fantasies, trials and tribulations.)

So, just as baby boomers transformed post-war society in the name of 'youth', it is just as likely that they will try to transform death too. They entered life with a post-war boom, so are quite likely to go out with a 21st-century bang, but always in their own time and in their own image. They may seek to redefine death and set out a whole new perspective on dying; they may even attempt to take longevity to its ultimate conclusion and seek immortality; they may even create a new funeral march or a rock concert to accompany and to celebrate their 'journey into the next life'. Whatever they do, it will be different. It will be remembered. It will be the end of an era. And it will be a new mass market and a new business opportunity for generations to come. It may be well be **the final farewell**, the ultimate in wish lists or bucket lists. It may be based on principles like those below from the 2000 Millennium Debate of the Age:

- Be able to know when death is coming and understand what can be expected.
- Be able to retain control over what happens.
- Be afforded dignity and privacy in death.
- Have control over who is present and who shares the end.
- Have time to say goodbye.

Such **forward planning** may appear premature, even macabre; but planning your own future in terms of last rites or 'last life', as Polly and David had found, can be quite uplifting and inspiring, injecting new life, new urgency and new energy into the time remaining. The idea of being part of the decision-making about your own death, of contributing to or even drafting your own funeral oration may for some be the ultimate act in living a full life. Writing your own obituary, for example; deciding whether to be cremated or buried and where; deciding who to invite along, what music to play and whether you have a wake, or a funeral party to end all parties, can be quite therapeutic, very engaging and possibly highly entertaining. Equally, by involving your partner and family at this early stage, it can be far less traumatic and stressful for them, and much more likely to avoid the conflict amongst your children and relatives as to who should take responsibility and organise it for you. Such forward planning, even for a generation that planned never to die, is truly in the spirit of the baby boomer age. The generation that was determined to cheat old age may have to settle for simply doing death differently but at least doing it *their way*. Sir Ian McKellen is apparently already rehearsing for his 'final curtain', and preparations are now underway for the funeral of the Queen as the Royal Family once again sets the example for many of us to follow.

Whatever happens, as Polly became increasingly aware, death and dying in the 21st century are entering a new era of cultural change and ethical ambition and, in the process, setting out new challenges for politicians in managing public opinion, and new frontiers for high court judges in balancing the rights of the individual with the norms of society. Such discussions will not only be increasingly dominated by debates about the ethics and methods of dying in an age of ageing but will eventually involve the right of those able to afford it to be reborn again in a later life of their choosing. Longevity is likely to strain, if not stretch, traditional ethical and social boundaries to breaking point, and possibly move legal and social thinking into a new age paradigm about the limits of later life. As Polly reflected, governments and politicians are already being tested about the 'right to die'. They might, equally, now need to also consider the 'right to live forever' growing amongst those with the means to buy everlasting longevity. How far such ambitions will resonate with ageing boomers, and how far they accord with the *Dream of Gerontius*, remains to be seen, but what politician would dare promise everlasting life for all and actually put it in their election manifesto – or on their election bus? Boris Johnson, perhaps? Surely not!

EPILOGUE TO PART ONE

Forward Planning or Wilful Neglect?

The British Government's Response to Ageing and the Ageing World Beyond

So, Polly had had her tour of ageing Britain and the greying globe. She now had a very clear idea of the challenges facing ageing Britain and the demographic shift that is transforming the world of the 21st century. She now had a sense of the size of the age challenge ahead and, as the UN foresaw, a sense of its all-pervasive and all-permanent nature. Britain was never going to be the same again; it was about to be turned on its demographic head. But surely the government with all its resources and civil servants is well-aware of the age shift ahead and planning fervently and proactively for it. Not so, concluded the House of Lords Select Committee in its *Ready for Ageing* report back in 2013. Far from the forward planning called for by such august and authoritative bodies as the UN and WHO ever since 1977, and the agonies of ageing emerging from modern Japan, the committee found "*a collective failure*" at all levels of government in preparing Great Britain for ageing and, worse, that: "*No government so far has had a vision and coherent strategy*" to lead and inform the age debate. Instead, the Lords 2013 report concluded that unless we prepare in earnest in the very near future "*we risk a manageable policy challenge becoming an unmanageable public service crisis*". Britain appears to be walking blindfold into the grey nightmare ahead, and the committee accused the government of *"woeful neglect"* in not preparing the British people for the challenges ahead. It therefore called for two immediate changes to government planning and action on this issue.

Firstly, it called for a fundamental rethink of the post-war Beveridge social contract that underpins today's British welfare state. The committee argued that in the light of ageing, it's no longer fair and sustainable for the young alone to pay in and the old to simply withdraw. The balance between the state and the individual will need to shift, and the older generation with wealth will need to contribute more to the cost of their care, through taxation, through longer working lives and through unlocking some of the wealth that the retired have accumulated through rising property values. A new **Fair Deal** is needed, not only **between** generations but also **within** generations, and between social classes, genders and ethnic minorities. A lasting and sustainable Fair Deal cannot focus solely on the older population. You cannot tackle inequality in older age in isolation from inequality in society as a whole. Over time, inequalities in working life are likely to feed through and be replicated in retirement.

Secondly, the committee called for an urgent and wide-ranging public debate on ageing, its implications and its potential impact on every family and citizen in the United Kingdom. *"The Government should help people be better informed about how long they are likely to live in good health, the size of pension they are likely to receive, the likelihood of needing social care and its costs, and how best to use their own assets… the state needs to make clear what its role will be, and the roles of individuals, families, and employers. This vision or contract needs be well understood and stable so that younger generations can plan for later life."*

The committee hoped that these two recommendations would set alight an urgent and widespread public debate and at least get the coalition government of the day to begin to take the whole issue of ageing more seriously and pro-actively. The response, unfortunately, was so weak and piecemeal that three years later Lord Filkin, the Committee Chair, was forced to declare that while his committee had found Britain *"woefully underprepared"* for ageing, *"with this (lack of) response the Government appears to be wilfully underprepared"*. Such conclusions, such proclamations, particularly from a body as traditionally conservative and august as the House of Lords, were a shocking indictment of past and present government thinking and planning and reflected a litany of lost opportunities to grasp this huge demographic nettle. The New Labour

Government back in 2009 had recognised the importance and potential impact of ageing and had even published an ambitious vision of the **society for all ages** that it hoped to create, but one year later it had fallen from power. The Coalition Government of 2010–15, in turn, sought to liberate pensions and reform healthcare, but then it, too, fell apart. And while both David Cameron and Theresa May propounded ambitious visions of the **big society** and the **shared society**, neither converted such ambitions into anything of substance and both have been superseded by the EU Referendum and the current Brexit debate. Ageing in the UK has been side-lined, if not neglected, by the British political establishment; and while Brexit now dominates the political headlines, the Teutonic plates of ageing grind inexorably on.

Such ignorance and neglect of ageing, however, is not just a British blindness. It is worldwide. The UN and the WHO have been desperately trying to rouse the world to the ageing challenge ahead for the past 40 years, and more recently they've sought to elevate this issue up the world agenda alongside global poverty and global warming. The UN 2012 Report, for example, declared ageing in the 21st century, to be either "*a Peril or a Promise*" and it called on all governments to adopt **active ageing** as the strategic solution to both minimising the economic costs and social impact of increasingly dependent ageing populations, and to maximising the opportunities for making the old more independent, healthy and able to contribute to society at large. More radically still, the UN in 2015 moved on to try and explicitly promote the "*human rights*" of the old as a means to challenging the scourge of ageism and dramatically changing peoples' attitudes towards the elderly and towards ageing generally. It called on all governments to: "*Develop a new rights-based culture of ageing and a change of mind-set and societal attitudes towards ageing and older persons from welfare recipients to active, contributing members of society.*"

In other words:

Help the aged and they help themselves.
Help the aged and you help yourselves!

The EU followed suit. It declared 2012 the European Year of Ageing and issued an active ageing strategy for all EU member states. Yet, even in Europe, the oldest continent in the world with countries such as Germany and Italy now facing demographic collapse, such global warnings and international urgings have not generated the urgency of action or the depth of strategic planning that the challenge of ageing really requires. Few countries appear to have developed comprehensive national plans or even national strategies to support and guide their conversion into ageing societies in the future, and fewer still seem to have instituted a coherent dialogue with their people – young and old – about the implications and likely impact of ageing on them, their families and the nation as a whole. As international league tables on ageing persistently show, while the Netherlands and Scandinavian nations regularly lead the way in terms of such forward planning, Britain regularly lags behind, a middling thirteenth, as shown below. If such low-income countries as Chile, Costa Rica and even Bolivia are capable of creating national plans for ageing, then why can't Britain and all the other so-called advanced and prosperous nations of the Western world?

	Overall rank and value		Income security		Health status		Employment and education		Enabling environment	
	Rank	Value	Rank	Value	Rank	Value	Rank	Value	Rank	Value
Sweden	1	89.9	8	87.0	7	74.8	5	74.3	5	83.3
Norway	2	89.8	3	91.4	13	73.5	1	85.4	22	76.2
Germany	3	89.3	9	86.1	6	75.2	6	73.7	6	82.8
Netherlands	4	88.2	4	90.9	18	71.3	11	66.2	1	85.6
Canada	5	88.0	26	81.1	2	80.3	9	69.6	9	82.3
Switzerland	6	87.9	28	80.6	1	81.3	12	66.1	4	84.0
New Zealand	7	84.5	43	72.7	3	78.7	7	71.1	13	80.2
USA	8	83.8	36	77.9	24	70.1	2	76.6	16	78.2
Iceland	9	83.4	15	84.7	9	74.2	18	58.5	7	82.5
Japan	10	83.1	27	80.7	5	76.9	10	66.2	19	77.2
Austria	11	79.8	5	88.2	17	72.7	42	45.5	2	85.3
Ireland	12	79.5	24	81.9	14	73.1	32	49.4	3	84.0
United Kingdom	13	78.7	10	85.8	19	71.0	24	53.8	17	78.1
Australia	14	77.2	57	57.2	4	78.2	4	76.3	25	73.5
Finland	15	77.1	14	84.8	21	70.8	27	51.4	18	77.4
Luxembourg	16	76.7	1	98.2	16	72.7	55	38.4	11	81.2
Denmark	17	75.9	21	82.3	40	57.5	20	55.7	10	82.2
France	18	75.0	2	93.2	31	63.6	41	45.6	15	78.8
Chile	19	70.6	42	74.2	10	74.2	23	53.9	39	67.1
Slovenia	20	70.5	22	82.0	32	63.2	51	39.3	12	80.7

Figure 1: **Global Age Watch Index:** 2015

Ironically, however, even those nations at the forefront of age planning have yet to grasp the full potential of the **longevity dividend** to set in place structural changes that transform their societies and allow the new old to fully display their potential contribution to the world ahead. One index designed to measure just such a step-change in thinking and planning is the Active Ageing Index (AAI) developed by the UN and the European Union. It attempts to *"point to the untapped potential of older people for more active participation in employment, in social life and for independent living"*. As the architects of this index emphasise, it is only by fully mobilising the potential of both older women and men that the prosperity for all generations in ageing societies will be realised. However, against this standard of age development, few of the 27 EU countries – few even of the Scandinavian nations – apparently achieve even 40% of the full potential of their elder dividend. The UK, in contrast, seems to do quite well, achieving fifth place in the 2014 AA Index overall, just behind Sweden, Denmark, Finland and the Netherlands.

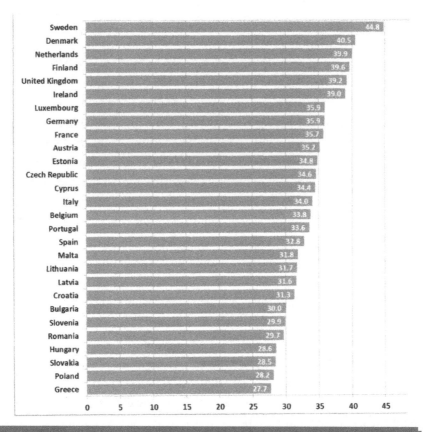

Figure 2: **Active Ageing Index (AAI):** 2014

Overall, though, international preparedness for ageing is at best mixed and at worst inadequate for the challenge ahead. As the authoritative Global Ageing Preparedness (GAP) Index concluded in 2014: "*Ten or fifteen years ago, global aging barely registered as a policy issue. Today, with large age waves looming just over the horizon in most of the world's leading economies, it has become the focus of growing concern... Yet despite the progress, most countries are not ready to meet what is sure to be one of the defining challenges of the twenty-first century.*"

And no index to date, no national or international plan, yet, seems to have factored in the power of this new generation of old, the baby boomer generation, into their analysis or projections of change. While most international league tables have put their faith in national governments, very few have looked to the new old, the baby boomer generation, for salvation. Yet as Dr Alexandre Kalache, President of the ILC in Brazil, has commented: "*Our generation are not going to age like our grandparents, or even our parents... They are going to force society to accept that older people can continue to contribute. I am 65. At this age my grandfather had a walking stick and was walking towards his tomb. I have a completely different prospect ahead of me. We are going to reinvent what ageing is to make it a productive and fulfilling period of our lives.*"

So, ageing is a massive European and world challenge, not just a British one. It's approaching our shores just as surely as it's lurking under the surface of Germany, Italy and Eastern Europe; and like Japan and Korea, we will soon feel the full force of the ageing cyclone. But how could Polly, a lone politician 'whistling in the political wind', possibly do anything about this? How could she shift attitudes in Westminster and Whitehall when even the House of Lords has been resoundingly, and wilfully, ignored? Should she, too, just shrug her shoulders and wait for the inevitable? Or should she take up the cause and campaign for age change just as fervently as she'd canvassed for climate change and human rights; just as passionately as she'd campaigned against inequality and social injustice? This was the resounding view of her husband David; this was the clear view of her daughter Hannah; but most especially it was the overwhelming view of her older grandchildren, who argued so passionately and forcefully that Polly and her fellow parliamentarians had *their* future in their hands that Polly had no option but to take up this cause on their behalf as well as her own. The young, even the very young, fully realise the burden of care created by an exploding population of old, the cost on them as workers and the obstacles to them as employees. They equally appreciate that their grandparents deserve and need better, much better, health, housing and social care if they are to enjoy their later lives. So, they have no doubt about the need for action, and are mystified, if not horrified, that so-called grown-ups, especially in government, are not already planning for the ageing Britain ahead. And it was their reaction, their urging for action, that impacted on Polly most, stirred her socialist soul and galvanised her into action. Ageing today may well be about the new old and their needs but it's also about the new young. It is they who will be most affected by the future and it is they who will inherit the legacy of longevity, good or bad! They cannot be shut out as in the past but must be part of the future; and with this shaft of political insight flashing through her mind, Polly suddenly saw the full political potential of ageing in 21st-century Britain, not just as a political campaign to avert a looming disaster but as a foreword to a whole new political agenda, a headline for a new political manifesto that might help re-galvanise, even rejuvenate, Great Britain after the traumas of Brexit, and in so doing bring the new young as well as the new old generation to the forefront of British politics, joined together in search of a better Britain, an intergenerational Britain working in harmony and mutual support for the elderly and the children of the future.

All very idealistic, but equally all very realistic. All quite essential if the approaching age wave is not to flood British society in a silver tsunami that would soon overwhelm both government and society at large. Moreover, if the British political establishment is deaf, blind and dumb, the British people are not. They can see the challenges of ageing rising up all around them, in the communities that they live and in the households that they inhabit, just as easily as they perceive global warming and globalisation. So, could Polly possibly tap into this undercurrent of British politics, go over the heads of today's politicians and instigate the national debate on ageing that the eminent House of Lords was unable to provoke? The post-war baby boomers, in particular, may be susceptible to political persuasion, not only as the new old of the present and future but as the teenage rebels of the past. They had shown in the 1960s what a huge impact they could have on British society once roused. Could this happen again? Could she enlist their support to the cause of ageing and harness their enormous powers – economically, politically and even morally – to make Britain better not just for the old but for the young too? Could she construct a political manifesto that might not only appeal to the new old but reach out to the new young too? Would a new intergenerational social contract help bind Britain's wounds post-Brexit and help reunite young and old in a common vision of a *United* Kingdom in the 21st century ahead? That became Polly's ambition; that became Polly's mission; and that is what led her to draw together the all-age manifesto and electoral strategy set out in the rest of this publication.

Part Two

The New Old, The New Young

&

The Forces for Change

10 | The New Old and the New Young: The Baby Boomers and Generations X, Y and Z

After her 'grand tour' of ageing Britain, a tour that covered pretty well everything from pensions and healthcare to housing, sex and death, Polly felt extremely well briefed on the age challenge facing Great Britain, and highly sensitised to its growing impact on ordinary people and their families – not least her constituents in Lowestoft and Suffolk East. Her 'age tour' of the UK had given Polly profound insights into ageing Britain today, but it was her parliamentary trip to Japan that took her into 'ageing in the future'. Japan is one of the richest economies in the world but one where the 'grey cloud of ageing' shrouds every aspect of Japanese society, from the queues of elderly people everywhere through to the dragoons of young men and women vehemently rejecting marriage and traditional family life. In stark, or should we say in 'silver', contrast, the bright lights of new technology and the emerging silver markets are already helping to rejuvenate modern Japan's Rising Sun. Robots and new technology are everywhere, with Actroids fast replacing humans in hotels, hospitals and restaurants, while driverless cars, taxis and trains are planned for the near future, and even the toilet seats are designed to help the elderly rise to their feet rather than fall to the ground. In particular, Polly's Far East trip had also brought home to her how the old might be the key driver of change rather than the main obstacle or, worse, the main victim. As their numbers balloon and their fears about their futures escalate, so the older generations in Japan are mobilising, lobbying hard and even taking to the streets, threatening the Japanese political class with a 'grey rebellion' if radical changes to aid ageing are not introduced and executed very soon (see Chapter 16 for detail).

Such displays of age power fuelled Polly's strategic thinking about the potential power of the new old in the UK and how, in the current absence of government leadership, her own generation, the baby boomer generation, might mobilise and structure change just as they had done in the past when young. This is the post-war generation that has a history of radical causes. This is the generation that is fast approaching old age itself and is increasingly aware of what ageing might mean for them personally and for their families in the very near future. Reaching out to this age group, converting them to the age cause and getting them to use their electoral, political and economic muscle to force change in the timescale needed would be a task in itself; but as Brexit had shown, once this 'sleeping political giant' is roused, rallied and driven to the polls, it's capable of making an historic difference. First, however, Polly had to make certain that she had a full understanding of this potential political ally, of what made it tick and what might stir it to action. Once the 'boomer beast' is poked and provoked, there will be no putting it back to sleep; and unless she pressed the right buttons, hit the right nerves and stirred the right ambitions, this engine of change could just as easily become a stubborn obstacle to any reform. Polly had to delve deep into the spirit and soul of baby boomers today, not just into their history of radical change in the past, if she was to stir this silver army out of retirement and mobilise it as a force for change rather than leave it a bulwark of opposition to anything new. And who better to help her craft this strategy than her daughter Hannah, a media expert with extensive experience of the boomer tradition, working for Nielsen, the marketing giant in the USA and leading advocate of the baby boomer marketing strategy. Hannah not only had real insight into the boomer tradition, but she was equally well aware of her mother's aims and ambitions. She was, for Polly, the ideal campaign and strategy manager, and the following chapters reflect many of her findings and recommendations. Such personal support was a great comfort to Polly, particularly as she was already beginning to feel somewhat like Nigel Farage must have felt at the beginning of his Brexit campaign: a voice in the political wilderness, but with a cause others desperately needed to hear. You can imagine just how intensely that irritated her.

British baby boomers

As Hannah's briefings illustrated, British baby boomers, as a generation, come in all sorts of shapes and sizes. They are the 'Liquorice Allsorts' generation that comes in a huge variety of ages, groupings and national flavours, and yet they have certain common features that give them some sense of common character, history and brand identity. They span some 18 years (1946–1964) after the Second World War, and they can usefully be distinguished as almost two sub-generations growing up in two quite distinct post-war eras: the austerity of the late 1940s and the affluence of the 1960s. So, what do these 'generations' of British baby boomers look and feel like as they now shuffle or stride into retirement and begin to transform later life as we've known it? According to the Chief Medical Officer's Annual Report in 2015:

- By 2039, the 1946–49 cohort will be aged 90–94; the 1950–54 cohort, 85–89; the 1955–59 cohort, 80–84 and the 1960–64 cohort, 75–79.
- Baby boomers are overwhelmingly ethnically white, but the percentage identifying themselves as non-white does rise notably between the two generations of boomers, from 5% to 11% in the 1960s, in line with the Windrush wave of immigrants from the Caribbean in 1948 and the influx of Asian Ugandans expelled by Idi Amin in the 1970s.
- Most older boomers aged 60–64 live as a couple without children; most younger boomers still have dependent children living with them, though interestingly, around 20% of 50–59-year-olds are living as a couple with no dependent, adult children; and worryingly, over 13% of 45–49-year-olds are living alone, as do nearly 19% of early 60-year-olds.
- Age at marriage rises between the boomer generations, as does divorce, and though remarriage rates are high amongst baby boomers so, too, is cohabitation in later life.

- Over 30% of baby boomers today live in rural coastal local authorities such as West Somerset and North Norfolk, with the lowest concentrations of boomers in urban areas such as Manchester, Oxford and particularly London.
- Baby boomers are more likely to be working after 60 than previous generations, with increasing numbers going part-time or self-employed, and with employment participation rates in 2014 for ages 50–64 well above the EU average but still well below those of Switzerland, Sweden and Iceland.
- Baby boomers are apparently as eager to embrace new technology as younger ones, with increasing numbers adopting social media too. The boomer generation, however, is still much more wedded to traditional forms of mass media, such as TV and newspapers, than its children, and less likely to be found on Twitter or Instagram.

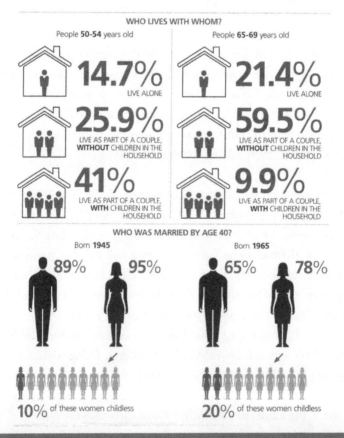

Demography of older adults in England

WHO LIVES WITH WHOM?

People **50-54** years old

14.7% LIVE ALONE

25.9% LIVE AS PART OF A COUPLE, **WITHOUT** CHILDREN IN THE HOUSEHOLD

41% LIVE AS PART OF A COUPLE, **WITH** CHILDREN IN THE HOUSEHOLD

People **65-69** years old

21.4% LIVE ALONE

59.5% LIVE AS PART OF A COUPLE, **WITHOUT** CHILDREN IN THE HOUSEHOLD

9.9% LIVE AS PART OF A COUPLE, **WITH** CHILDREN IN THE HOUSEHOLD

WHO WAS MARRIED BY AGE 40?

Born **1945**

89%   95%

10% of these women childless

Born **1965**

65%   78%

20% of these women childless

Figure 1: **Demography of Older Adults in England**
(ONS 2016)

Baby boomers grew up in the 1960s and 1970s – the era of post-war affluence followed by economic depression, the era of an explosion in youth culture, music and media, alongside the emergence of globalisation and the world economy as we know it today. They are part of what Wikipedia has called "*the wealthiest, most active, and most physically fit generation, and amongst the first to grow up genuinely expecting the world to improve with time… they tend to think of themselves as a special generation, very different from those that had come before.*" However, as Hannah was keen to emphasise, the term 'baby boomer' is much more of an American expression than a British or European one. The post-war baby boom in the USA was a population explosion of some 78 million babies spread over a 20-year period, while other Western countries experienced much smaller post-war baby booms and much shorter ones – more demographic aftershocks than full-blown baby booms. And there are even generations within this generation. While early or 'leading-edge' boomers, born between 1946 and 1955 in the UK, may fit the boomer stereotype as individualists with unrestrained optimism and idealism seeking a life that is both personally fulfilling and socially worthwhile, late boomers tend to be more pragmatic and down to earth. Baby boomers were equally a worldwide phenomenon but with significantly different impacts in different societies.

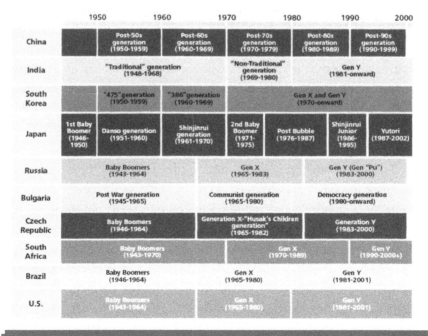

Figure 2: Baby Boomers worldwide

As twins born in 1952, Polly and her twin brother, Donald, were classic examples of leading-edge British boomers, brought up in a post-war Britain that suddenly turned from austerity into affluence, from black and white into colour, from Vera Lynn and Glenn Miller into The Beatles and The Rolling Stones. Pop music and mass media replaced classical music and wartime lyrics, clothing leapt from make-do to make-up, and from hand-me-downs to high fashion. Food moved from rationing and home cooking to fast food and eating out, and politics shifted from fighting fascism in Europe to fighting communism behind the Iron Curtain and across the jungles of Indo-China. The young rose up and protested against every form of social or sexual injustice they could find, be it the war in Vietnam or the liberation of women, and this new generation of teenager was as rebellious at home as they were on the street. They challenged parental authority, went on to university rather than down the pit, and wore clothes to shock rather than keep warm. Scandalising your parents became a new national sport, and Polly had delighted in wearing the shortest of miniskirts along with her hot pants and kinky boots. She had 'burnt her bra' almost as soon as she'd bought one while Donald had happily adopted the classic rocker attire of leather jacket, leather trousers and slicked-back hair, as he and his Triumph motorbike set off every Bank Holiday for battles with the mods on the beaches of Margate and Hastings. *My Generation*, as the pop group, The Who, expressed it, had truly arrived on the British social scene, and the young were no longer to be seen but not heard. Rather, they made their voice heard loud and clear on the streets and on the new university campuses as the world seemed to be about to come to an end with the Cuban Missile Crisis and the creation of the Berlin Wall. The assassinations of President Kennedy, Robert Kennedy and Martin Luther King heralded a new era of post-war politics in which all generations lived under the cloud of the Cold War and nuclear holocaust; a paradoxical era of great affluence, great freedom and great ambition for the future sitting in juxtaposition alongside the threat of 'mutually assured destruction'; a MAD world caught between the global pursuit of affluence and liberation on one hand, and the threat of nuclear annihilation on the other. No wonder many of these early boomers became paranoid about having enough time to live; no wonder the young women of this era were determined to break the social constraints that had tied their mothers and grandmothers to the apron strings of home and domestic servitude for generations before.

As children of the boomer era, Donald and Polly had much to look back on and reflect about in their own lifespans, but were they typical British baby boomers, or just two of the privileged 25% of their generation to go on to grammar school after the 11+, and the 10% who benefitted from the vast expansion, and free fees, of higher education in the 1960s and 70s. They had enjoyed the full flow of post-war meritocracy and the social escalators of this era that had whisked them into high-flying and well-paid careers, that then elevated them up the housing ladder and provided them both with gold-plated pensions and spiralling property values as house prices in the South East of England soared. Their respective children largely followed in their footsteps, though Polly's eldest daughter had a dark period through depression and drug addiction that nearly killed her. In contrast, Donald and Polly's younger brother, Wilfred, aged 61, had not been so fortunate. He stayed in Sunderland and worked for many years in the Tyneside shipyards. He had to endure the massive decline of the steel and shipbuilding industries in this area and the subsequent mass unemployment thereafter, until the arrival of the Nissan car plant and its associated industries resurrected the region. While Wilfred and his wife Wilma enjoyed the 60s as teenagers, thereafter their lives had been more bust than boom and their futures more dependent on the state and its welfare benefits than on work and themselves. They had no private health insurance, no defined benefit pension scheme and had had to rent most of their lives, although, eventually and reluctantly, they took up Mrs Thatcher's offer of buying their own council house. However, despite the gulf in their lifestyles and their life experiences, Donald and Polly and Wilfred and Wilma keep in regular touch as a family, and feel quite a strong affinity as a generation determined, whatever their differences in lifestyle and life-opportunity, to bring all their children and grandchildren together as often as possible and to pass on some of their historic legacy – though, fortunately, not their teenage styles of dress or their *Top of the Pops* style of dancing!

Polly as a politician, and Wilfred as an ardent trade unionist both recognised that the boomer generation, even in Britain, still had something special to offer and that collectively this 'baby generation' was still a force to be reckoned with in the years ahead:

- **They have the numbers,** with 600,000 boomers every year from now until 2030 generating a retired population of some 16 million, or 22% of the British population by then and beyond, living on average much longer and much healthier lives than their parents.

- **They have the wealth,** owning more than 80% of the nation's £12.8 trillion wealth (ONS:2016), and with one in five baby boomers owning a second home.

- **They have the media presence** through celebrities such as Judi Dench, Elton John, Twiggy and Paul McCartney; all stars of the 1960s and 70s, many of whom are still performing.

- **They have the political clout** through voting power that already made its presence felt in the 2015 and 2017 General Elections, and particularly in the momentous 2016 EU Referendum. Boomers will ensure that pensions and healthcare remain very high on any political party manifesto in the future, whether that be in 2022 or before.

As Hannah made plain, by 2040 the over-65s in the UK will constitute nearly a quarter of the UK's total population, outnumbering the combined populations of Scotland, Wales and Northern Ireland and rivalling the populations of such wealthy European nations as Belgium, Sweden and even the Netherlands. What they don't have, as Hannah persistently emphasised, is the voice nor the immense sense of generational affinity evident in countries like the USA, Canada and even Australia. Compared to its American cousin, the British baby boomer is a political 'mouse', hiding in the cupboards of British politics, relatively unknown, relatively invisible, not ready yet to raise its voice or be brought out into the limelight by academia or the media. There is no *British boomer* magazine as such, no *boomer spokesperson*, no *political lobby for the boomer* comparable to the American Association of Retired Persons (AARP) in America or the Canadian Association of Retired Persons (CARP) in Canada. These are age lobbies with immense power within their respective political systems, well beyond that of even the most prominent of age charities in the UK. The AARP, for example, has a membership of some 38 million, a membership that rivals the total population of many European nations, and a lobbying power within the American Congress greater even than the Trades Union Congress (TUC) in the UK. The British boomer in contrast is at present a 'political pygmy', a sleeping giant, but one that once roused and rallied has the potential to transform life in Britain not only for the old but for the young too, as the Brexit vote has so amply displayed.

As Hannah's analysis showed, the full impact of the new old will not be solely in terms of their numbers but much more in terms of their attitudes –

their attitudes to life in general and to society at large. Do these 'children of the age revolution' now have the potential to transform, if not revolutionise, old age in much the same way that they appeared to revolutionise adolescence after the war, or are they a spent force? Did baby boomers actually, and radically, change societies in the Western world, Polly asked Hannah, or was that part of a generational myth? Were they really part of a mass movement, a worldwide movement, for transforming Western capitalist society, for liberating the world, East and West? Or was it all just media hype and historical nostalgia dreamt up and dressed up by those who, having lived in the post-war era, are still alive and young enough to remember it, and celebrate it, aided by a generation of rock stars and film stars who are still performing even in their 60s and 70s? Were they really the centre of the post-war universe or did this Peter Pan generation, who thought they could live forever, just imagine it? Is there even such a thing as a baby boomer generation; is the concept of *generation* a defining characteristic, one strong enough and sustainable enough to seriously explain the behaviour of young people in that era and, most importantly, to potentially explain their behaviour in old age? Do those born and brought up in the post-war era genuinely feel a generational allegiance, a generational consciousness, powerful enough to motivate them to take some form of collective action above and beyond their own self-interest?

In one of the few studies, until recently, of the British boomer, Julia Huber and her colleagues at the think tank Demos set out the distinctive characteristics of what they called these *"Eternal Youths"* and *"The New Old"*. (2003/4) According to these researchers, the boomer generation is now beginning to enjoy the windfall of extra life and the opportunity to live life again, to explore new experiences in terms of travel, food, learning and even sex. They are keen to colonise popular culture and to use their purchasing power to influence and even dictate images and messages in the mass media. In particular, claimed the Demos researchers, they will seek to colonise *the youth culture* that they helped create and adapt it to their own self-image, whether through Harley-Davidson motorbikes or anti-ageing beauty products, fashions or films.

Personal fulfilment is their priority and old age their enemy; and although they're still open and adventurous in ambition and future lifestyle, the retiring British boomer is equally concerned about security for the future. They are staunch defenders of the principles of the welfare state and the free healthcare they've grown up with. They aspire to a good and fulfilling life, and many boomers now aspire to a *'good death'*. Baby boomers detest dependency and isolation with an impassioned zeal, and they fear being a burden to their children even more. Time together – with existing or new partners and their families – is a high priority, yet for many the risks of new careers, new lifestyles and even new relationships are risks worth taking. Ultimately, the quality of life is more important to them than its quantity. All in all, British baby boomers appear to be booming. They are alive, they are well and they have no intention of growing old gracefully.

Such optimism and youthful ambition, however, has its downside. As Harkin and Huber found, British boomers equally display a fear and a loathing of old age, of physical degeneration, of grey hair and wrinkly skin; the possibility of senility and protracted pain raised a chill amongst their respondents. They hate being patronised and talked down to. They distrust authority and demand that all forms of service – public or private – meet their expectations. They dread any loss of independence in old age and want to control their future and even their own death, yet they display a terrifying lack of foresight and future planning in terms of their own finances and their children's possible needs for, say, mortgage support or for inheritance(s). They seem to fail to recognise that for many of this generation the life ahead will not be a continuous 'party' as in their youth but a life alone, particularly for women in their 70s and 80s. They equally display a limited sense of generational solidarity with the current pension and healthcare regimes, likely to perpetuate, and even exacerbate, the two classes of retiree that currently exist: "the *working classes who are rather glad to get out of jobs they didn't enjoy and the middle classes and people with more interesting jobs who are desperate to stay in.*"

The Demos researchers concluded that: "*As they look forward to old age, today's baby boomers do not want to be forced to work until they drop. But they also refuse to see their lives as broken up into linear stages – education, work, parenthood – with retirement the end of the line and the (final) reward. Instead they increasingly prefer to see their life as a never-ending cycle, one which enables them to seamlessly dip in and out of periods of education, work and leisure.*" If society is to capture and exploit the time and talent of this "*Golden Generation*", argued these authors, then time is running out as this generation begins to retire en masse from work and public life and instead become mass consumers, using their financial muscle to demand more high-quality and personalised products and services from both the private and the public sectors.

As Rebecca Leach and her colleagues at Keele University highlighted in 2013, British baby boomers can effectively be sub-divided into two phases or 'waves' – pre and post 1954 – with each wave having a somewhat different and contrasting upbringing and experience. The *first wave* (1945–54) "*broke the* mould" and "*set out a new and distinct course through adult life… one marked by change, challenge and transformation.*" The second wave (1955–64) enjoyed a more settled upbringing and moved into adult life in the 1970s and 80s after the 60s rebellions of their older brothers and sisters, and prior to the economic and political upheavals of the Thatcher era. These two waves, claim the Keele researchers, represent something of a generational bridge with the past as well as a breakthrough into the future: a bridge with their parents and the moral values and ambitions of the Silent Generation in the 1950s, and the breach that was the 1960s, "*when 'everything changed', when materialism exploded and much more relativist values became fashionable.*" Hence, argued these researchers, the high value baby boomers apparently put on quality, durability and value for money when purchasing goods or services, public or private, and the way that they deplore anything that seems at all cheap or shoddy.

As more recent studies of baby boomers, such as Carole Kennedy's *The Ultimate Boomer Generation Guide* (2018), have shown, baby boomers have enjoyed many immense and quite distinct improvements in their lifestyle compared to those of their parents. They live longer, with 78% of post-war boomers likely to live to aged 70 compared to 58% of those born in 1920. Life expectancy at aged 70 has increased by nearly 40% for men and 21% for women since 1990; only 30% of women in their 70s today are widows compared to 49% in 1991; and childlessness for this age group has fallen dramatically from 21% to 9% in the same period (ONS: 2018). Baby boomers are equally much more financially secure and much more likely to own their own home than their parents were. Baby boomers themselves, however, often claim to have more in common with their children's generation in terms of cultural values and lifestyles than that of their own parents. Like the young, boomers look more to the future; like the young, they see themselves as ageless; and like the young, baby boomers remain very conscious of both their looks and their image. According to the McCarthy & Stone 2015 'Colour Report', many boomer women deliberately "*down-age*" by shopping in similar outlets to their daughters – Topshop, Zara and H&M – and boomers are almost as heavily into new technology as the young. They grew up with Amstrad and Sinclair back in the 1980s, and their first mobile phone was the size of a building brick – and about as useful. Baby boomers are avid users of smart technology today. They simply use it differently to younger generations – and possibly less obsessively. Ninety-five per cent of British baby boomers have a mobile phone, and 59% a tablet with Facebook, Skype and various apps as widely used amongst the new old as the new young. Family and friends remain the top priorities for baby boomers but many are equally seeking new relationships in the wake of divorce, separation or widowhood. Rejuvenating existing relationships is equally high on their list of priorities, with most over-60s, and many over-70s, still enjoying healthy sex lives. This is a totally new and different generation of retirees, determined not to be old, determined to lead active, independent and healthy lives in a way that defies ageing. Far from retiring from society, today's late-lifers are ahead of the young and full of ambition for the future – their future. According to the Colour Report, nearly 60% of British boomers feel that their generation was more special and more radical than previous generations, and all of them refused to be stereotyped. They are part of a bright new future for themselves and their families, a silver if not golden future, and they want to feel part of society – inside it, not outside it. They certainly will not tolerate any form of exclusion or ageism.

Moreover, baby boomers are now giving birth to **super-boomers**, leading-edge boomers, now in their 70s, like Charlotte Rampling, Diana Rigg and Marianne Faithful, starring in new films, running new enterprises and even going into political life. The old are no longer old; they are 'shades of grey' with strong silver tints, leading increasingly active and healthy lifestyles with later life as a sort of 'lifestyle crossroads', a bonus life to be lived to the full. While some baby boomers may seem to be reverting back to the rebellious lifestyles of the past as rates of alcoholism, obesity, drug-taking and even sexually transmitted diseases amongst the over-60s appear to be on the increase, overall this 'charmed' generation is much healthier than before and determined to exploit and enjoy to the full the extra life that longevity has bestowed on them, for both their own benefit and that of their children and their grandchildren.

While Donald, with his new yachting business in Marbella, and Polly, with her ongoing political career, are classic examples of the affluent and upwardly mobile boomer described above, Wilfred and Wilma equally personify the fact that many members of this so-called 'charmed generation' did not enjoy such extraordinary advancement and good fortune. And as the researches of the ILC-UK highlighted in 2015, not all post-war baby boomers got a free university education (only 13% of those aged 65–69 today actually have a degree); not all baby boomers have generous pensions (nearly two million people aged 55–64 have no private pension savings at all); and not all baby boomers have benefitted from a giant leap in wealth and assets because of homeownership (less than half of those aged 55–64 own their own homes, and 24% rent). More particularly. and in contrast to the popular image of baby boomers as a selfish and self-interested generation, the ILC-UK report cited the 3.3 million 45–64-year-olds who regularly undertake voluntary work, and the £17 billion that over-65s contribute to society in the form of care and volunteering. Many baby boomers may well be off spending their children's inheritance, assuming children have an automatic right to inheritance anyway, but one-fifth of grandparents aged 50+ have already donated a total of £647 million to their grandchildren prior to writing their wills.

So, as Hannah's report emphasised, far from being a highly homogenous cohort, far from all baby boomers being either affluently healthy or pension poor, they are as diverse and unequal as any other generation in British society today. They may have a common history and many nostalgic memories; but given the social diversity and inequality within their ranks, can they seriously be described as a '*self-conscious generation*' with a common or collective world view or sense of historical mission? Do British baby boomers fit the generational criteria set out by the German sociologist Karl Mannheim in *The Problem of Generations* (1928)? Do they, asked Hannah, have a collective mentality that mirrors "*a dominant view of the world, reflecting similar attitudes and values and providing a basis for shared action*"? Researchers such as Graeme Codrington (2008) believe that baby boomers do have such a "*generational Zeitgeist*", do constitute a distinct generation, do have a particular sense of belonging that can override differences of socio-economic class and geography. He believes that British baby boomers can be considered a generation in their own right and respond accordingly, and that their values and identities, idealism and optimism constitute a coherent generational mindset that, once lifted and led, is capable of responding to some sense of historical mission in leading the nation to "*a better world beyond*". As the American sociologists Strauss & Howe (1997) have argued: "*History creates generations, and generations create history.*" On the other hand, as the AARP highlighted back in 2007, baby boomers everywhere face a very uncertain future. They are unsure of how much longer they will live, and they are increasingly feeling overwhelmed by forces of change that they no longer have any control over. Like all generations today, they too feel increasingly powerless and vulnerable to global forces beyond democratic control, and they grow anxious at the growing divisions within British society and even within their own family and age group. At a time when they would anticipate some peace and tranquillity, they see chaos and conflict. At a time when they might expect to retire from mainstream life, many baby boomers still see the need to exert their voice and their economic and political muscle – if not in their own interest then in that of their grandchildren.

Polly was mightily heartened by Hannah's research and by the potential power baby boomers might still have for converting ageing Britain from grey to silver, from a desert of old-age dependency into a land of active and independent elderhood. However, both Polly and Hannah increasingly concluded that the old alone are not the solution to creating a more age-friendly and age-harmonious silver Britain. Ageing boomers are no longer 'baby' boomers, whatever their therapists might be telling them. The spirit might still be strong but the flesh is weaker and less able to endure the potentially long march ahead. Rousing and mobilising this immensely diverse and disparate generation would be a task in itself; and while Polly was totally committed to the ageing cause, she and Hannah increasingly came to the conclusion that the new old need the new young; they need new, younger allies to bring new blood, new inspiration, new ideas and new drive to the mission ahead. And so they turned their spotlight onto their children, and increasingly onto Polly's grandchildren, as potential allies, both political and generational.

Generations X, Y & Z

Donald and Polly and Wilfred and Wilma do not exist in isolation. Like all baby boomer grandparents, they have children and grandchildren, a mushrooming army of them of all ages and personalities. Boomers live and love, sit and share life with older and younger generations in a multigenerational chain that is growing longer by the decade. Baby boomers like Donald and Polly

may be the '*golden generation*', the 'chosen ones' who enjoyed the post-war welfare revolution of the 20ᵗʰ century, but the ageing revolution of the 21ˢᵗ century is not just about them. It embraces their parents and their children, their grandchildren and even their great-grandchildren in an intergenerational drama that only now is starting to unfold; a sort of 'boomer rather than Bayeux Tapestry' of modern family life. Just as the post-war baby boomers have their own traits and characteristics, priorities and ambitions, so too do the older and the younger generations living either side of them. Just as the older Silent Generation created the post-war society of the 1940s and 50s after fighting and enduring World War II, so the boomers helped create the society of the late 20ᵗʰ and early 21ˢᵗ century.

Tracing the family tree of any family today is no longer the simple task it appeared to be in the past, despite the advent of Google and numerous ancestry websites. Instead of a single tree spouting many branches, the family today is more like a copse, or even an ecosystem, of numerous individual branches interwoven within a complex web of relationships, with numerous roots and historical links, some based on blood and marriage but others increasingly on cohabitation and continental drift. As outlined in Chapter 7, the modern British family is increasingly a multigenerational, multi-ethnic, multinational project with international roots and interlinking family networks under constant recreation through remarriage and reconstitution as well as by blood and genetic legacy. Teasing out the defining characteristics of such overlapping generations is a gargantuan task, an ageing drama to rival *Dallas*, *Downton Abbey* and even the Royal Family; a world-wide web that sits underneath the internet. Polly's attempt to trace her own genealogy and draw it out for her grandchildren swiftly hit a brick wall once she got beyond her own generation and those above and below. Where exactly Uncle Albert fitted into her family tree became something of a familial mystery and the subject of numerous family debates.

Families, however, also represent generations: age bands that cut across family hierarchies and even family ties. Health England's adapted sketch overleaf on page 178 helps to identify and compare some of the main characteristics of the post-war generations of the last 70+ years.

As this generational tapestry shows, there appear to be huge differences in upbringing and childhood experience, attitudes and values, even between generations that are still alive, living in the same society, the same world, in the same century and even possibly in the same family home. Such differences appear to be of such magnitude, strength and impact that

BABY BOOMER (1946–1964)	**GENERATION X (1965–1979)**
I AM AMBITIOUS AND WILL QUESTION EVERYTHING	I AM SELF-RELIANT BUT I LIKE STRUCTURE AND DIRECTION
I want to make a difference	I work to live and want a work-life balance
I am highly motivated and hard working	I work smarter but not harder; can multi-task
I live to work and work well in a crisis	I don't like to be micro-managed
I believe in equality and expect respect	I like rewards and gratification
I will challenge authority and take risks if need be	I can innovate, am tech-savvy and a problem solver
I am driven and experienced and like to see my achievements recognised	Family is important to me
WORK DEFINES ME	I expect to live comfortably
	I AM A PRAGMATIC INDIVIDUALIST
GENERATION Y (1990–1994)	**GENERATION Z (1995–2010)**
I EXPECT SUPPORT TO ACHIEVE	I AM SELF-DIRECTED
I need nurturing, frequent recognition and feedback	I don't fit into a traditional work environment
I am career motivated but not company loyal	Connectivity is as 'important as breathing'
A flexible work-life balance is crucial	I expect everything to be inter-connected
I need to work with you, not for you	I expect to kept informed and involved
My friends are important to me and I want to be liked and have a sense of belonging	I expect to be less well-off than my parents
I earn to spend	I struggle with independent household management
I NEED A SENSE OF PURPOSE AND CONTRIBUTE TO THE GREATER GOOD	PERSONAL FREEDOM IS NON-NEGOTIABLE

Figure 3: **Generational Traits (adapted)**
(Health Education, England Report. Narrowing the Gap: 2017)

they generate distinct modes of behaviour, values, priorities and attitudes to life, different generational consciousness and collective identity that may in turn also generate generation gaps and even generational conflict – at home, at work or even in society at large. As Hannah was fully aware, tapping into such generational traits and world views was a critical part of any contemporary analysis of family, work and especially market research. Certainly, it was a key part of any in-depth understanding of ageing today and the **inter**generational, even **intra**generational, debate that surrounds it. Many millennials from Generation Y, for example, have lived a Peter Pan existence to date, an extended adolescence. They continue to live at home, or boomerang back, well into their 20s and even 30s because their earnings are insufficient to move out and buy their own home. They have burgeoning student debt and, in some cases, it's simply more convenient and less stressful. They may appear very cool and affluent on their Facebook profiles but the anxieties of not being able to fully enter adulthood while subscribing to all the images and pressures of work, peers and the social media is apparently generating increasing levels of anxiety and even mental illhealth amongst many of this age group.

In a fascinating study of generational theory, called *Mind the Gap* (2011), Graeme Codrington and his co-author Sue Grant-Marshall set out to explore the characteristics and attitudes to life of the full gamut of generations since the First World War – their likes and dislikes: heroes and villains, movie stars and politicians; their lifestyles and disasters; their aspirations and attitudes. They highlight the baby boomer generation as a page-changer in the annals of post-war history and in continuing to change life as we know it, not only because they're now entering the portals of retirement but because they still hold the *"levers of power"*. *"The Boomers have impacted this world more than any other generation"* and *"their impact is far from finished"*. They see life as a glass of wine, but half full not half empty. They believe that they are only half done and that there's more to come that's even better. They represent a stark contrast, argue Codrington and Grant-Marshall, to their grandchildren, Generation Z, the 'iFacebook' generation, that is apparently totally immersed in the virtual world of the internet and the social world that is Facebook, rather than in the realities, challenges and opportunities of real life and all it has to offer. Facebook and its subsets Twitter and Instagram seem to be their life, their social persona and their window on a world where connectivity is as crucial today as networking or class was in the past. The new technology of today was but a twinkle in the eyes of inventors and entrepreneurs back in the 1960s; and while it had a growing impact on the working lives of older baby boomers as they grew up, it is engrained in the lifestyles and ways of thinking and working of the generations since. It is part of their generational DNA.

Moreover, the young no longer rely on experience from the past to guide them for the future. Rather, many of the major breakthroughs of the early 21st century have come from 'out of the box' thinking by young people determined to do things differently now that the internet has given them a global perspective and a worldwide market. The tech giants of today – Google, Facebook and Airbnb – were all the 'brain-children' of a new generation of very young entrepreneurs, unconstrained by the past, by existing business models or by traditional structures of power; many of whom, even now, are only in their 30s or 40s. Their generation has transformed and transposed the world economy and put life in the 21st century on a totally new footing; a relatively silent revolution that has led Codrington and Grant-Marshall to cite Strauss and Howe's four-generational cycle and to postulate that if today's iFacebook generation is the generational equivalent of the Silent Generation of WWII, then perhaps the next generation – those soon to be born in the 2020s and 2030s – is the one most likely to resemble the baby boomer generation of today if the global apocalypse predicted for tomorrow, whether it be an ecological disaster, a nuclear or robo-war, or a financial collapse even greater than 2008's, finally hits home. Now, there's a prediction that would stir up a generational debate if all else failed. There is a generational framework of analysis that may well help inform both Polly and Hannah in devising and developing their generational strategy.

The Intergenerational Commission (IGC) was set up by the Resolution Foundation specifically to track generational issues in the UK. It, too, has used a generational perspective as its analytical framework, and its researches provide a fascinating overview of the post-war generations in Great Britain. Its January 2017 report, for example, attempts to track the vast changes in life expectancy between the generations over the last 70–80 years; and in relating such changes in longevity to changing generational lifestyles and attitudes to life, it shows for example that:

- *"Life expectancy has increased by one fifth in just four generations"* as a result of dramatic falls in infant mortality and substantial rises in our standard of living, our healthier lifestyles and much better medical treatments and living conditions. These jumps in generational longevity are awesome and often forgotten. Life expectancy for men born into the Silent Generation (1926–1945) was 52 years and 57 years, for men and women respectively, while the men and women of Generation Z can expect to live to 89 and 93 years, and a third of babies born in the next two years are predicted to live to over 100 years. Baby boomers at age 65 can expect to live on average another 27 years for men and another 30 years for women, virtually twice the post-65 longevity of their parents.

- As life gets longer, the shape of our lives' changes dramatically too, with the traditional staging posts of leaving school, getting married, starting a family and even entering retirement getting significantly later.

- The traditional generation balance of young to old has shifted dramatically too, from a demographic pyramid to an intergenerational pillar, with the older generations outstripping the younger ones and shifting the ratio of dependency dramatically in their favour, from 3 dependents to every worker in 1961 closer to 2:1 by 2065, with an inevitable and intensifying impact on intergenerational relations.

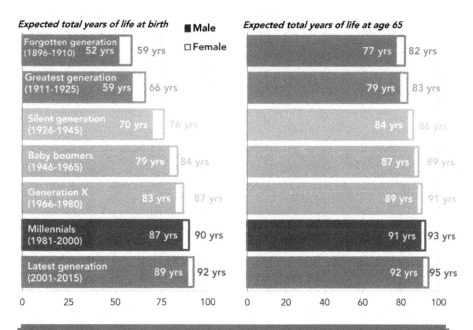

Figure 4: **Living Longer**
(IGC: 2017: Fig.1)

So, all generations today are living healthier and longer lives than ever before, and in so doing each generation is developing a longer and more distinct lifestyle. Traditionally, generational relationships have been relatively happy and apparently harmonious, whatever the *generation gaps* that appeared to emerge in the 1960s and 70s. Recently, however, **intergenerational relations** in the UK, USA and other parts of the Western world have been the subject of intense, and at times bitter, debate as the full implications of longevity emerge and the impact that ageing might have on the younger generations becomes more apparent. Generational conflict or, worse, generational warfare over the distribution of intergenerational wealth, and over who is going to pay for the welfare state of the future, is increasingly becoming a major issue in any political debate, and clearly it has immense implications for any political strategy that's seeking to bring the generations together in common cause. So intense did this intergenerational debate become in the UK that the London School of Economics (LSE) at one point drew up an intergenerational 'charge sheet' against the baby boomer generation and even went so far as to host a 'public trial' at which the baby boomer generation in the UK was accused of violating 'the human rights' of Generations X and Y and of bequeathing a world to the young that: "*is blighted by climate change, record youth unemployment and soaring bills for housing and higher education. They have wrecked the lives of the generations that follow them. Justice demands they pay a price.*"

Much of this debate was sparked off by the then Universities Minister, David Willetts, in 2010 with his book *The Pinch* and its subtitle *How the baby boomers took their children's future – and how they can give it back.* David Willetts' thesis was that the post-war **social contract** in Great Britain between the generations has been broken, or at least that the baby boomer generation seems to have forgotten their obligations to the next generation. The boomer generation has enjoyed unparalleled wealth and success but now their children are facing a much bleaker future. They are finding it harder than ever to get on the housing ladder, find a secure job and settle down with a family. Willetts' book inspired a whole host of critiques of the baby boomer generation, all with withering titles and accusations of gross selfishness, ranging from Francis Beckett's *What Did The Baby Boomers Ever Do For Us? (2010),* through to Ed Howker and Shiv Malik's *Jilted Generation: How Britain has Bankrupted its Youth (2010).* Even senior baby boomers such as Jeremy Paxman joined in this tirade of 'age rage' – or even 'self-rage': "*I am part of the most selfish generation in history and we should be ashamed of ourselves,*" wrote Jeremy Paxman in the *Mail* in October 2011 while, as recently as 2018, Vince Cable, the then newly elected leader of the Liberal Democrats, accused older people who voted to leave the EU of having "*comprehensively* *shafted the young*". In the USA, a similar 'age war' has been reignited with Donald Trump's election, and publications such as Bruce Cannon Gibney's book (2017) have accused American baby boomers of being *"A Generation of Sociopaths"* who have betrayed America, and who through their excessive egotism and reckless self-indulgence have betrayed the younger generations in particular.

In the UK, the Intergenerational Foundation (IF) was created in 2011 to fight this wrong, to promote intergenerational fairness and to challenge the gerontocracy, or 'ruling class', that some IF writers feared the older generation was fast becoming. The IGC, in turn, described millennials as both a *"Stagnation Generation"* in falling behind the incomes and lifestyles of previous generations, and a *"Generation Rent"* in being unable to get on the traditional housing ladder and so having to rent or, worse, continue living at home for far longer than normal. Young people today seem to face a much more uncertain and insecure working life with limited opportunities for normal progression up the housing market or into secure and prosperous careers. Many people have apparently concluded that, contrary to traditional expectations, young people today may well not achieve a better standard of living than their parents.

Powerful and apparently persuasive though such arguments are, they tend to put the blame for all the post-war ills on the shoulders of the boomer generation, ignoring other factors such as globalisation, technology, class and inequality. They tend to ignore boomers' own trials and tribulations in growing up, such as the recessions of the 1970s, the infamous three-day week; the apparent 'class war' as de-industrialisation, trade union militancy and mass unemployment hit home; and the constant struggle with interest rates, rising at one point to 15%, and house prices plunging, many into negative equity, in the 1990s. As Professor Alan Walker argued in the British Academy Debates (2014), the stereotype of the baby boomer generation, as wealthy, selfish, active and independent, is something of a clichéd misrepresentation that fits at best a minority of privileged older people. The vast majority of boomers are not millionaires, or anything like it; and far from baby boomers having stolen their children's future, they have contributed at least what they will receive in pensions, healthcare and other services, with nearly a third of over-65s providing financial support to younger members of their families. British baby boomers, overall, have made positive contributions to life in post-war Britain and can claim some credit for promoting and embracing the full spectrum of human rights, achieving peace in Northern Ireland and in creating the security and quality of contemporary family life.

Moreover, it appears at times that the younger generations today seem to have forgotten that their own upbringing owes much to their parents' sacrifices and investments and that, compared to later generations, baby boomers had far less opportunity for educational qualifications, and relatively few enjoyed substantive inheritances from their parents compared to the 'wall of inheritance' predicted for the children and grandchildren of tomorrow. As David Willetts himself has acknowledged: "*Those born between 1945 and 1965 have turned out to be better parents than we are citizens*", and as James Harkin, one of the Demos researchers, has argued: rather than despising the baby boomer generation, perhaps the young today should admire and look up to them. "*Around the world, the baby boomers disrupted the complacent status quo of the Seventies and set about trying to remake the world in their own image; and they had considerable success. In their heyday, they fought against the Vietnam War, for women's rights and helped repeal segregation laws*" and "*despite all their flaws, the path trodden by the boomers should be an inspiration to us all about the power of ideas to incite political change.*" Moreover, as Jenny Bristow (2017) has pointed out, this blame game may simply encourage young people to adopt a rather fatalistic sense of resentment and powerlessness rather than take action and responsibility themselves – like voting and lobbying in far greater numbers. Finally, as George Magnus (2009) has highlighted, far from the future for today's youngsters being bleak, it is in fact rich in opportunity simply because of ageing; simply because as the populations of older generations explode, the populations of the young are shrinking, making competition for university places, housing or jobs that much easier.

There is nevertheless a very strong sense of pessimism, powerlessness and frustration in the UK about the future for the young, more so than in any other European country despite the fact that young people in Greece or Spain face far higher levels of unemployment and poverty than those in Britain today. In a report for the Foundation for European Progressive Studies (FEPS) (2018), Kate Alexander-Shaw has sought to sum up this intergenerational debate and put it into context as follows:

- Millennials have grown up in a period of exceptional economic uncertainty in which market forces have plunged the Western world into economic chaos and uncertainty and left millennials facing "*a blockage*" in the traditional life cycle – an "*adult purgatory*" that has left them deeply frustrated by their inability to match their parents and grandparents' ascent into adulthood.

- This blockage has generated an intense sense of generational unfairness that is evident across Europe not just in the UK; and that that, it seems, represents a *"great new frontier"* in economic and political policymaking based on cleavages of age as much as wealth or class.

- Such a new political narrative has profound implications for policymaking in the emerging age of ageing when huge swathes of government spending will be directed to the needs of the older populations at the expense – and taxes – of the young. Media images of baby boomers as a privileged and selfish generation who ignored the needs of the young and spent their inheritances may make great headlines but they equally fuel the growing generational conflict that threatens to undermine the social solidarity of the post-war social contract and plunge ageing countries like the UK into an age war where every generation, and every family, loses its sense of community and mutual support. In the 2017 UK election campaigns, for example, the Labour-affiliated campaign group Momentum used the YouTube vision of smug, affluent baby boomers riding on the backs of the young to incite younger voters to register and counter the Tory tendencies of older voters. Increasingly, the older generations live far apart from the young, in quiet coastal and rural communities, and rarely interact with them – or subsequently understand or necessarily sympathise with their needs or ambitions.

- Levels of intergenerational solidarity remain high in the UK but, argues Alexander-Shaw, such familial sentiment cannot be taken for granted; and although generational equity may look like a revamp of previous debates about social justice, such as class and gender, it's opening up new avenues of debate about the distribution of wealth and the type of world the baby boomer generation is bequeathing to its grandchildren. Such a perspective embraces environmental as well as economic issues, such as climate change, and it heightens the moral dilemma of what constitutes fairness in an emerging world where human values are fast being superseded by global forces and the ascendancy of artificial intelligence rather than human intelligence in determining the future of the global economy and even of the planet itself.

- Moreover, the recent and sharp rise in political mobilisation of the young and the shift towards greater age-based campaigning is likely to exacerbate, if not exaggerate, age tensions and so generate a self-fulfilling spiral in which British politics moves from its traditional class-based paradigm onto an age-based one, inciting young against old. As Jeremy Corbyn's Labour looks to mobilise the younger vote to get it into government, the

Conservatives rely increasingly on older voters to stay in power. Is age about to trump class as a political cleavage in Britain, and what might this mean for future intergenerational relations? That may not have happened yet but clearly, given the deep uncertainty around British electoral politics, it is a real possibility for the near future.

The House of Lord's report on Intergenerational Fairness in 2019 sought to draw all these arguments together and recommend legislative action. Like the 2013 Lords report, it put the blame clearly and squarely on *"the failure of successive governments to plan for the future and prepare for social, economic and technological change"*; a failure that in the committee's view is undermining the supportive and affectionate relationship that currently exists between the generations and that threatens to exacerbate emerging tensions in the future. The *"younger generations are not seeing the increase in living standards enjoyed by previous generations"* while the *"older generations face a society that is not prepared for their numbers or their needs as they age."* This report therefore advocated a life-course approach for future government planning and based its six main recommendations on the notion of the 100-year life highlighting in particular the urgent need to radically update an education and training system that is *"ill-equipped for the needs of a rapidly changing labour market"* and the need to promote *"active communities"* to strengthen intergenerational bonds, generate innovative local initiatives and combat loneliness amongst all ages. In particular the report focused on the inadequacies of the government's fiscal and tax and spend policies in directly addressing intergenerational issues of fairness whether in balancing pay progression, social security spending, stamp duty and housing costs or the likely costs of care in old age in the future. It recommended, for example, that the triple lock on the state pension be removed, that older workers continue to pay national insurance, that free television licences over a certain age be phased out and it declared inheritance tax to be *"capricious and not currently fit for purpose."* This was a hard-hitting and precisely directed report that neatly spelt out the issues involved and the actions needed to re-establish a fairer intergenerational balance to government policy and public perception of the most intense and urgent intergenerational issues. And like the IGC proposals in 2018, Polly sought to incorporate their recommendations into her manifesto as part of a fundamental shift in thinking about the 100-year life now facing modern Britain and the need for all government planning to adopt a life-course approach.

The real generational gap today, however, may not be so much **between** the generations, but **within** the boomer generation itself. In raising their own children's aspirations and ladders of opportunity, baby boomers possibly forgot their own generation, or lost the sense of the collective identity, sense of social justice and national purpose that bound and drove their parents in setting up the British welfare state and nationalising industries after the devastation of WWII. Baby boomers often appear to be somewhat indifferent to the enormous gulfs in wealth and life chances within the boomer generation itself and between the generations ever since. As Richard Wilkinson and Kate Pickett argued in 2009, Britain is still a highly unequal society, if not one of the most unequal; one where "***intragenerational inequality***" is far greater than that between generations, and possibly getting worse. As illustrated below, the variations just in pensioner incomes, let alone pensioner wealth, are considerable, and in the view of some writers such as Paul Cann & Malcolm Dean (2009) they represent a new age "*class divide*" just as powerful and significant as that within the country at large.

Moreover, w*ealth begets wealth,* and as the better-off amongst the younger generations inherit not only money from their boomer parents but all the trappings, advantages and lifestyles of a better *start in life,* so the class divides in British society may well widen rather than contract. As middle-class boomer parents help their children and grandchildren up the housing ladder and into top jobs at the expense of less fortunate youngsters from less well-off homes, so the intragenerational inequality gap amongst the younger generations may widen even further. Recent studies, by the Social Mobility (and Child Poverty) Commission, for example, have shown that social mobility amongst the working-class young seems not only to have stalled but to have come to a complete halt as they appear to hit a 'glass ceiling' in the British social system. While researchers at Oxford University have suggested that what might be a glass ceiling for youngsters aspiring to rise up the British social scale is in fact a 'glass floor' by which the better-off families in society hoard opportunity and so not only prevent their own children sliding down the social ladder but actively help propel them back up it, making a mockery in the process of any notion of meritocracy in modern Britain today.

This intragenerational dimension of the generation debate struck a particular nerve for both Polly and Donald. In the pursuit of their own careers and lifestyles, neither of them had seriously considered what life for Wilfred, Wilma and the relatives that they'd left behind in the North East had really been like. They had simply put their own good fortune down to good luck and personal ambition and lost sight of those left behind. Inequality and social immobility for their own generation did not often come into their thinking.

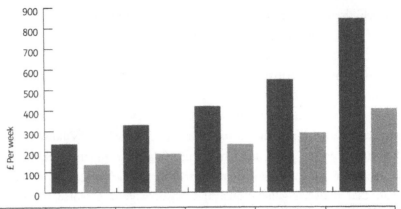

	Poorest fifth	Next fifth	Middle fifth	Next fifth	Richest fifth
■ Pensioner couples	237	330	420	549	846
■ Single pensioners	136	189	234	290	406

Figure 5: **Variations in pensioner incomes**
(Age UK: 2014)

So for Polly, as a teacher, a politician and a socialist, such insights were quite poignant, if not personally quite wounding. While she had challenged inequality and lack of opportunity throughout her career(s), what actually had she – and Donald – done to mitigate such sufferings within their own family, particularly those of their younger brother and his family? As she was well aware, the British welfare state had not delivered the opportunities and benefits for all citizens promised in the Beveridge Report, particularly for communities like Sunderland in the North East. For families like Wilfred and Wilma's, deprivation and lack of opportunity are still the norms of everyday life. Hence the wave of support for Brexit in such areas, even when major employers such as Nissan threatened to pull out of the area.

So, as the IGC concluded, the British social contract hasn't yet collapsed but it certainly *"looks at risk of fraying"*. The answer, the commission believes, though, is not in generational warfare but in generational harmony, with the 'three big players' – the state, the markets and the family – taking the lead on renewing this contract and redesigning it for the century ahead. That is the mission the commission has now set itself; that is the mission that has equally inspired Polly and her pursuit of an intergenerational manifesto for the next general election. In an age of mass ageing, and all that that involves a new **intergenerational (even intragenerational) social contract** would seem to be clearly needed to reunite generations and reinforce the British welfare state of the 21ˢᵗ century in the same way that the Beveridge vision underpinned the post-war settlement in Britain in 1944. The post-war welfare state, however, was designed to support the needs of a minority of old-age pensioners living a relatively small number of years in retirement. It was not designed to cope with the mass retirement of a generation of some 17–20 million highly active pensioners living into their 80s and 90s – and beyond. The 'financial contract' of intergenerational support set up in 1944, and the radical shift in the balance of dependency between the working population and the retired, no longer seems workable or fair. Equally, to continue to allow some 1.8 million pensioners to live on or close to the poverty line seems socially, morally and economically unacceptable in a society as wealthy and fair-minded as Great Britain. A full-scale public debate on ageing offers the opportunity to elevate these issues up the political agenda and encourage a more radical and sustainable foundation for fairness in the UK in support of both the old and the young. Radical thinking is desperately needed to tackle the challenges of ageing and the deep and profound inequalities within and between generations. The creation of the Intergenerational Commission in 2016, specifically to conduct research into intergenerational fairness, was a step in this direction, and Polly sought to incorporate its findings and its recommendations into her draft manifesto.

And finally: What about the generations to come?

What about Donald and Polly's and Wilfred and Wilma's grandchildren – Generation Z? They, too, will soon have the vote and, unlike their older brothers and sisters, may not be so reluctant to use it. As research by The Citizens Foundation (TCF) in 2014 showed, and as a recent Ipsos MORI poll (2018) has confirmed, Generation Z seems to be the most ambitious, career-minded and well-behaved generation of them all. They seem to possess an entrepreneurial spirit that is, apparently, equally matched by their willingness to help people through volunteering, an attitude and ethos that earnt them the ultimate accolade from the think tank Demos in 2017 as **Generation Citizen**. This is the generation that, having grown up in the digital age, now sees new technology as the natural means to their dreams, and the internet as their window on a global world of unlimited opportunity. On the other hand, they do feel under intense pressure to succeed, given the demands at school and the challenges of getting a job that they will enjoy. They fear failure intensely and very personally; and as The Prince's Trust's Youth Index in 2018 found, happiness and confidence amongst young people aged 16–25 in the UK today is at its lowest recorded level, with one in four feeling trapped in a cycle of jobs that they do not want and with relatively few feeling confident about how to break out of this cycle of immobility in the future. Nearly half feel more gloomy about the future, and their futures, than at any time in the past eight years; a quarter don't feel in control of their lives; almost half don't feel that the traditional goals of a good job or owning their own house are realistic; while the advent of Brexit and the election of Donald Trump have, for many, only increased their sense of insecurity and powerlessness. Finally, and most worryingly, according to a *Sunday Times* report in February 2019, the suicide rate amongst teenagers in Britain seems to have doubled in the last eight years at a time when suicide among older age groups seems to have fallen.

Just compare such youthful pessimism about the world today with the boundless optimism that the baby boomer generation had at the same age in the swinging 60s and early 70s. The contrast in world views and perceptions of the future is frightening. Such a gap, if not a chasm, in generational attitudes bodes badly for the years ahead, as the speed of change that is now the 21st century accelerates and leaves all of us, old and young, feeling even more helpless and unable to control the future ahead. That fear, that sense of powerlessness, speculated Polly, may be the common cause that helps bind the generations together instead of pushing them apart, may help all generations see that by working together they could control the future rather than be controlled by it.

11 | The New Old and their Moral Mission: Ageism and Inequality

So, as Polly, in liaison with Hannah, began developing her new age strategy, she knew that she now had the challenge, and potentially the electorate, to drive radical change. She could now see ageing as a possible political manifesto, and she could imagine the potential power of the baby boomer generation to force change. What she could not yet see, however, was how this potential power might be mobilised in practice, nor how a new political manifesto might be formulated around a topic as diverse and long term as ageing sufficiently to get it adopted by her own Labour Party nationally or by her parliamentary constituency locally. She needed, advised Hannah, a cause that would appeal to baby boomers' consciousness, and a plan to convert such ambitions into reality; she needed to appeal to boomers' *hearts* as well as their heads; she needed to stir their memories of the past as well as inspire their aspirations for the future. Though the powers of British baby boomers today are considerable – the silver pound, the grey vote and the bright lights of silver technology – these powers are only a means to an end. They're not an end in themselves. Rather, they need a common cause, a moral mission to underpin and drive them, and a political manifesto to put their ambitions and objectives into practice – a moral mission and an emotional commitment to making ageing Britain a better place to live, not only for older people but one which might equally enhance and open up life for the younger generations too.

So, what might be that cause be? What might be the moral mission of such power and persuasion that it would motivate and inspire millions of older people not only to step into the ballot box but to potentially run onto the streets, not only to lobby for *their* rights and interests but for those of their children and grandchildren, even if it possibly meant giving up some of those benefits in the process and even paying more tax. For Polly, the answer suddenly became quite simple. It was the same moral mission that inspired the Silent Generation to fight World War Two and set up the British welfare state. It was the same moral mission that inspired baby boomers, when much younger, to march for women's rights or against the war in Vietnam; it was the same idealistic fervour, the same principles of fairness and social justice, freedom and human rights that have defined and distinguished the British character and imbued the national spirit ever since; but this time not for any one generation but for all generations. An all-age alliance to liberate the old from ageism, and an intergenerational alliance to create a fairer Britain for young and old alike. These two themes – human rights and social justice – had been at the forefront of boomer activism since they took to the streets in the 1960s and 70s. Could these two themes now motivate and mobilise baby boomers once again into the political lobbies but this time not just on their own behalf but that of their children and grandchildren? Could the scourge of ageism and the injustices of inequality become the new enemies and unite the young and the old in common cause? Would the appeal of a new fairer intergenerational social contract and the vision of an ageless/all-age society reignite the fighting spirit of a generation known for its lust for social justice and its genetic need to leave a historical legacy?

Moreover, reflected Polly and Hannah, was this perhaps the moral mission needed for the 21st century, one that might appeal across today's generations, and also be the means to realising the spirit of generativity proposed by philosophers such as Erik Erikson? Would this moral mission realise and release the underlying spiritual appeal of the gift of longevity, namely the renewed opportunity to "*transcend personal interests and to provide care and concern for (both) younger and older generations*" and, in so doing, leave a lasting legacy that reflects an "*inner desire for immortality*". It was these ideals that Polly now believed would both appeal to the soul of her own generation and to its vanity; its desire to live life, even later life, to the full; and its sense of historic mission to leave a lasting legacy for the generations that followed. Certainly the notion of generativity had a profound impact on Polly's own thinking and political philosophy, not only because its moral message resonated so closely with her own but because the term 'generativity' is now often used not only to describe spiritual and personal awakening but to depict epic technological breakthroughs; paradigm changes in scientific and technological thinking that suddenly open up whole new levels of scientific and commercial opportunity; social and scientific step-changes, such as the advent of the open internet and the cracking of the genetic code. The combination of spiritual and technological meaning within the same term appealed enormously to Polly, and she now believed that the concept of generativity gave her the conceptual and political tool for appealing simultaneously to both the young and the old while at the same time capturing the spirit of the age and the underlying dilemma of the 21st century. At the very time that technological advances seem to offer astonishing material progress, they also seem to be delving deep into the human psyche and giving power over man's destiny to forces beyond most people's control; to forces such as globalisation and new technology and to the new 'masters of the universe', the immensely wealthy owners of the new means of modern production and distribution, the Amazons and Googles of the Western world and the Alibabas of the East. Man's material needs seem to be met now at the click of a mouse but at the price of his and her spiritual soul. In a world where algorithms and big data seem to be dictating all our futures, and with AI and super-robots now on the horizon, humankind seems to face a Faustian dilemma of whether to sell its soul to the comfort and convenience of new technology and material abundance or reassert mankind's need for self-control and spiritual fulfilment, an existential and philosophical dilemma that is chillingly described by Kai Strittmatter in his description of modern China today (2018): a dilemma that is possibly reflected too in Brexiteers call for Britain to 'take back control'.

If Nigel Farage and Boris Johnson could rally and rouse the British electorate, and particularly the older generation, to fight for Brexit and control of our borders, why couldn't Polly rally them to the cause of agelessness and intergenerational equity? These were issues far beyond our relations with the EU, far more fundamental to the future of Britain and far closer to home. If Brexit stirred boomer emotions, surely human rights and social equity would stir their souls, get their blood boiling and resurrect their memories of battles past yet incomplete and give them the moral high ground for rallying people across the political spectrum in common cause against the evils of ageism, inequality and the need for intergenerational justice. But what exactly are these social evils and how deep do they go?

Ageism

Ageism is clearly an issue close to the hearts and minds of the old. It does not look, however, like an issue that might rouse the young. What possibly does it have to do with them and why should they go on the campaign trail for an older generation which doesn't seem to have done a lot for them since they left home? That was Polly and David's initial view too, until that is, Hannah had the inspired idea of bringing in a young person, namely her daughter Laura, to help design and inform the campaign they were creating. Laura, aged 20, was studying Politics and Sociology at the London School of Economics (LSE), and as part of her degree she now had to choose a topic for her dissertation that would both engage her and strengthen her prospects for the first-class honours degree she was aiming for. Laura was an ardent feminist and advocate for women's rights, a leading figure in student union politics and a member of the local Labour Party. The initial theme for her dissertation was women's rights in the third world. Her tutor, however, advised her to look beyond feminism and to consider instead the topic of ageism as an emerging and under-researched source of social prejudice and discrimination in both developed and developing countries. Laura was very sceptical at first. Old people's rights were not the most immediate or sexy topic on the sociological spectrum, nor could she at her age easily identify with them. However, as she read the literature, Laura's blood began to boil and her sense of outrage came to the fore. It brought to life many of the concerns she'd heard and seen about life in old age before her great-grandmother, Charlotte, died. Laura had been devoted to her great-grandmother, and she'd felt strongly that after a long and distinguished career in the health service, and as chief executive of the Samaritans, her great-grandmother deserved more, much more, than to be sent at aged 90 to live in a care home where care seemed to be in short supply and she seemed to spend a lot of time alone. Charlotte's plight tugged at Laura's heartstrings, as did those of the other residents in Charlotte's care home when Laura visited her grandmother. It had helped Laura to see old age and ageism differently; to appreciate that the old were young once too. And it gave her the opportunity to personalise her research thesis by using her great-grandmother as a case study of ageism in an ageing world; an opportunity that infused and inspired her research thereafter.

At first, Laura's grandparents, Polly and David, were very reluctant to involve her in this way, fearing the potential emotional impact on her following her great-grandmother's departure only a few years earlier. Ultimately, however, after long family discussions with Laura's parents, they agreed to let her go ahead, not only because they knew their granddaughter and knew that once roused her passion for human rights and social justice was unquenchable, but also because they would benefit as a family in working together on facing ageing in the future as a team rather than individually. Laura's engagement also opened up the possibility of an intergenerational perspective on ageing, on ways Polly and Hannah might convert young people to the anti-ageist cause, and in so doing provide fresh energy and impetus to the moral bandwagon that Polly was trying to create. Moreover, Polly saw in Laura and her youthful idealism flashbacks to her own crusading days, and if she was excited and energised by her granddaughter then many of her own generation might be equally inspired and motivated to leave their armchairs and follow in the footsteps of their grandchildren rather than fall asleep following the exhortations and sermons of politicians far away in Westminster. As Tessa Harding declared in her farewell speech to Help the Aged in 2006: "*We have hardly yet begun to grasp the scale and impact of age discrimination on our society. We* **expect** *older people to be treated unequally and to be treated worse than their younger counterparts. That is how policies are constructed, how services are shaped and how the environment is arranged. Age discrimination is so integral to our thinking, so much part of the accepted way of doing things and so taken-for-granted in how we see and interpret the world around us, that our judgement is coloured, our perceptions affected and our experiences shaped whatever age we are.*"

This speech summed up many of Polly and David's own daily observations in their surgeries and in their personal experiences particularly when they'd been making arrangements for Charlotte's final retirement. It makes salutary reading, too, for a nation that claims to be caring and to have a special affection and respect for its elderly. It equally highlighted the distance to be travelled and the mountains to be scaled if active ageing was to become reality in a society that many see as inherently and institutionally ageist. Ageism is the heart of the age challenge. It is a challenge that is largely invisible, ignored and virtually built into the fabric of everyday life. The old are assumed to be decrepit, demented and in decline, 'on the way out rather than on the way in', and a burden rather than a benefit to the society ahead. As youngsters, Polly and David had campaigned against every form of social discrimination under the sun, from racism and sexism to the human rights of gay and transgender people, but as they grew older, particularly within their own spheres of work, they became increasingly aware of the insidious nature of ageism; of how it sort of creeps up on you with age; of how it seemed quite natural and expected, with no visible perpetrator or obvious cause that you could point to or blame. That's what makes it so difficult to fight against, why Laura's researches were so critical in bringing it out into the open and why, once exposed, Polly and David believed it would be such a potent force in rousing boomer blood and in mobilising grey power behind the cause of age. Moreover, with longevity, times are changing radically, and so our attitudes to age have to change too. Life no longer ends at 60 or 70. Rather, for most older people today, it's just beginning. Traditional attitudes to age are no longer an aid to life but an obstacle, or worse a social barrier, to the right to life of the older age groups and their capacity to continue to contribute to family, community or economic life. Moreover, ageism is about to face an explosive challenge as the new old refuse to accept or adhere to the stereotypes of the past. The NHS, social services and every institution within and outside the British welfare state will soon face a tidal wave of complaints and resistance from a generation of new old for whom freedom and their rights of self-expression are tablets of stone. They will defy any attempt to restrict their rights or constrain them, nor will they submit to any official or informal assumption or stereotype about what the old of today can or cannot do. No community, no family, will escape the age quake ahead, as the new old break down all ageist barriers and start creating new ones of their own. As a politician and as a community GP, both Polly and David could foresee this 'hurricane on the horizon' and that was why they'd come to see ageism as such a potent force for rallying and radicalising the age cause that they were now promoting. As Archbishop Desmond Tutu proclaimed: *"As we get older, our rights do not change. As we get older, we are no less human and should not become invisible."* (Global AgeWatch: 2015)

But what exactly is ageism? What are these social stereotypes that threaten to suppress and subvert life in the 21st century? As Laura's research brought to light, the term 'ageism' was coined in 1969 by Robert Butler, the first director of the National Institute for Aging in the USA. He defined ageism as: "*a process of systematic stereotyping of and discrimination against people because they are old… old people are categorized as senile, rigid in thought and manner, old-fashioned in morality and skills… Ageism allows the younger generation to see older people as different from themselves; thus they subtly cease to identify with their elders as human beings.*" Unlike sexism or racism, ageism is not lifelong; it is not a permanent feature or physical characteristic from birth. Rather, it 'comes with age' and so is neither easily identifiable nor recognised in the way gender or ethnicity are, even by the victims themselves. It sort of emerges out of the shadows as you approach later-life's landmarks, be they retirement from work or receipt of a pension. In earlier civilisations, old age was venerated and associated with wisdom and authority. The elders of the tribe or clan were a ruling elite responsible for group survival, solidarity and well-being – and for the communication and transmission of its culture and traditions. With industrialisation and modernisation, with the need for fresh talent and young labour, such deference and social hierarchy has been swept aside and the young, the talent of tomorrow, have come to the fore. The elderly, infirm and ageing it is believed, can no longer function as effectively in post-industrial society, and so they're being discarded, retired early and segregated from mainstream society by expectation and by choice at a cost to the UK economy according to government estimates of £31 billion a year (2015, Foresight Future of an Ageing Population project). One survey claimed that ageism in the city of London was more widespread than sexism, and the Royal Society for Public Health (RSPH) survey, as recently as June 2018, found that 30% of millennials held negative perceptions of older people and had virtually written them off. As Geraldine Bedell commented in the *Observer* (8 May 2011): "*Ageism is so deeply ingrained that most of the time we don't even notice it… It is acceptable to speak of old people in a way that would be unthinkable about race or disability.*"

However, unlike other forms of 'ism', ageism is largely invisible and unseen. "*The old can imagine what it is like to be young but the young cannot imagine what it is like to be old, frail, full of loss (of hearing, eyesight, status, loved ones, recognition) and full of memory and the past*" (Nicci Gerrard: 2014). There is an overwhelming and unspoken assumption in most Western societies that after a certain age the old are no longer *fit for purpose*; a burden on society and their families; unhealthy and incapable of living active and independent lives 'within' society; so they are retired to life 'outside' society, dependent on the generosity of the young and support of the middle-aged for their income, healthcare and social support. This medical model of declining physical and mental functioning is reinforced by the financial incentive to retire at a pre-determined age inherent in the state pension system (currently aged 65) and by the public image of the elderly as decaying human beings entering their second childhood and becoming an increasing burden on society and on their families. The old as a cohort, even as a class, face social isolation, segregation and deprivation as powerful and as 'accepted' as any other form of social discrimination, and it seems to be rampant across British society today. After 40 or more years as an employee, professional, societal leader, war hero or super-mum, the elderly retreat, or are pushed, into the *grey mists* of retirement, condemned to a life of leisure and purposeless inactivity; a sort of age resignation that seems inevitable and self-fulfilling as the old themselves accept it as part of the natural order of life and the rightful passage of time.

But ageism is not simply about physical isolation or social exclusion, it's also about psychological exclusion, about the loss of social self-confidence and sense of purpose that leads older people to exclude themselves; and here beauty and fashion are striking examples of how older women in particular are often relegated – and relegate themselves – from centre stage in modern life to the side-lines of society. As the broadcaster, Joan Bakewell, now in her 80s, so poignantly described it, women in particular suffer the double whammy of ageism and ageing bodies: *"while old men are thought to be ruggedly attractive, old women are deemed to be beyond allure, devoid of sexual chemistry, a worn husk of their juicer, former selves."* But men, too, dread the thought of becoming old and physically frail. Men's very identity depends on physical prowess and sexual confidence, so when both begin to disappear, often together, so too does men's sense of manhood. For men, the greatest fear, though, is the fear that as we grow older we will become dependent upon others. Men often don't have the networks of support, the emotional toolkit and fluency of language to articulate and challenge their anxieties. They have been trained from childhood that such an emotional outburst would undermine their manly image and so reinforce their sense of personal inadequacy and rejection. So, at its worst, ageism becomes a self-fulfilling prophecy as the old passively internalise society's stereotype of them and retreat into retirement or a care home.

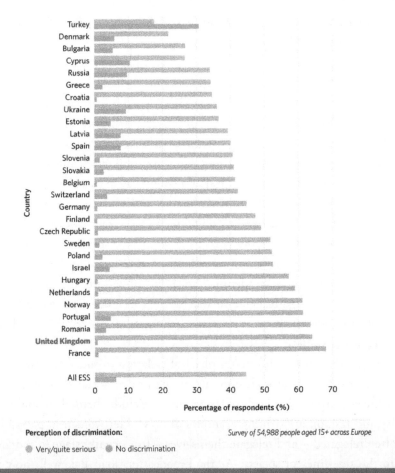

Figure 1: International Perceptions of Age Discrimination
(Foresight Report: 2016)

Worse, as Age UK has persistently highlighted, for many OAPs later life is miserable, not only because of loneliness and isolation but also because of fear – fear of abuse and neglect even by agencies tasked with protecting them. **Elder abuse**, even today, is more widespread and more all-pervasive than anyone cares to admit. The 2013 Eurage Survey concluded that according to the best estimates: *"350,000 older people in the UK are abused in their own homes (primarily by their carers or relatives) and that a further 150,000 are abused in institutional settings."* This amounts to one in 20 of all of us over the age of 65 facing psychological abuse (34%), financial abuse (20%) and even physical abuse (19%). The 2013 English Longitudinal Study of Ageing (ELSA) found similar levels of age discrimination, with the poorer retired apparently at greatest risk, while Age UK estimated that 1.6 million people aged 65 and over in England were chronically lonely. The BBC Radio 5 experiment, in sending out a young female researcher dressed and made up as an older woman, really brought home to her the impact of ageism: *"It was a pretty brutal experience… It made me feel lonely, really invisible. I was overlooked and ignored and I felt like I was being punished because of my age. I only went through it for a few hours but it's left me with a really heavy heart."* Add in sheer neglect and the scale of the problem multiplies exponentially, with that revered institution, the British NHS, the site of some of the worst cases of elder abuse, as the infamous case of Mid-Staffordshire Hospital so poignantly highlighted. According to the Care Quality Commission (CQC: 2017) there has been a 40% rise in serious injuries amongst elderly people in care homes in England in recent years, equivalent to 100 patients a day suffering injury through neglect or negligence, and it has declared one in four care homes in England to be unsafe. Such high-profile cases might, however, only be the tip of an *'age-abuse iceberg'* and be the most visible and extreme. Much more widespread and subtle abuse may lie beneath the social surface in the form of fear, isolation and loneliness (Age UK: 2016). *"Gerald Noble lay dead in his flat for five months before anyone knew about it. With no traceable relatives, his funeral was left to the local authority to organise"* (Royal Voluntary Service).

Ironically and almost perversely, it is in the healthcare industry itself – in David's own profession – that ageism appears to be most virulent and at its worst. Elder healthcare may often be *temporary* rather than permanent; with treatments limited to repair rather than replacement; *over-medicalised* with products prescribed to keep the elderly docile and dependent rather than restoring them to active life; and *reactive* rather than proactive with a focus on remedial treatment rather than using screening or regular monitoring to forestall chronic or fatal diseases by, for example, extending breast cancer screening to women over 65. Such age prejudice is explicitly expressed within the concept of QALYs, or 'quality adjusted life years'. In the view of Professor Sarah Harper (2006): *"QALYs discriminate against older people. Firstly, because older people have lower life expectancies, health interventions in older age generate fewer 'life years' than intervention in younger age groups. Secondly, years lived in disability are given lower weight than years lived in full health. This discriminates against people with chronic disabilities and illness (many of whom are older people). Finally, QALYs do not capture the breadth of outcomes that may be especially important to older people, such as independence, or the impact of intervention on carers or family."* Geriatric medicine itself is not a sexy specialism nor a professional hotspot within the medical profession. It does not have a high profile in medical training, nor is it the market leader in research for miracle cures; while social care is truly the 'Cinderella' profession within the healthcare industry, with the lowest pay and the lowest status. So, not only is the inverse care law alive and well in the distribution of health resources by social class or geography, it is equally active with regard to age. We expect ageism to happen whatever the area of life involved. We accept it as natural that the older you are the less you get (and deserve) and, worse, that this is the natural, right and just way of allocating resources – a perception of *'natural justice'* that often even the elderly themselves subscribe to.

Tackling age discrimination, and uprooting it, concluded Polly, may therefore require a much more forceful, even challenging, approach than social sympathy. It may need a reaffirmation of the basic principle of human rights and legislation that explicitly and rigorously outlaws discrimination against the old as fervently as that against women, gay people or ethnic minorities. While the 20th century was the age of the rights of women and children, the 21st-century needs to become the age of the rights of the elderly, not just for moral or political reasons but as simple economics and self-interest. The idea that societies should invest in children is taken for granted. The idea that societies should invest in older people is an idea ahead of its time, a battle yet to be fought. Yet within the global economy of today, no developed or developing country can afford to lay waste the enormous experience, skill and talent of its older population; no advancing society can afford to lose the active contribution of the elderly nor the vast potential of the emerging army of silver entrepreneurs. The RSPH raised an urgent call for action in June 2018 to coordinate and bring together schools, employers and healthcare professionals in supporting older people, and for the government to expose and challenge ageism right across the media through an independent review. '**Stage not age**' now became Polly's mantra for the ageless society of tomorrow, and 'age rage' the battle cry for baby boomers now entering older age. A new more explicit and more effectively enforced Age Discrimination Act, she now believed, needed to be the focus of any future human rights campaign; and while the WHO has led the way by proposing a convention on the human rights of older people, in the UK, it has been left to the age lobby to campaign for a Bill of Rights for older people. The British government has yet to say a word.

Equal respect

Forget about age – see us as people:

> "We are still seen as second-class citizens [and] a fundamental change in attitudes is needed.
>
> We want opportunities to live better lives and make a contribution; we want equal rights as workers, as consumers and as users of public services; we want to be treated with dignity and respect, especially when times are tough; and we want decisions that affect us to take account of our needs and our views.
>
> We resent being patronised, talked down to and excluded from decision-making. As active, self-confident citizens we expect equality. Yet, despite this, ageism and disrespect remain rife in our society." (2014 Age UK Manifesto)

Such a shift in policy, such a shift in legislation, would dramatically raise the profile of ageism as an issue, enhance public understanding of its extent and insidious nature, outrage public opinion and so hopefully help outlaw it legally and socially in the same way as sexism, racism and homophobia. However, as in all these battles for human rights, traditional stereotypes and traditions about age are deeply held and well embedded in the fabric and even the language of society, so they are very open to covert and low-level perpetuation, whatever the law says. While the state can give a lead and set an example, ultimately responsibility for confronting age discrimination lies with the 'victim' themselves - the new and the 'old' old. As women, black and gay people have shown, it is often in the 'small battles of daily combat' that ageism will slowly be put to rest. However, the *new old* are not a 'minority under the heel of an oppressive majority'. They are a *sizeable minority*, or soon will be and they are not by character or experience a *silent* generation willing to tolerate or accommodate discrimination, particularly of themselves.

So, ageism would be a classic baby boomer *crusade*, given their past history on civil rights as well as their intolerance of any restriction on their own behaviour or activity. Celebrities such as Jane Fonda at 81 and her septuagenarians colleagues have sought to highlight and combat ageism in Hollywood with their film *Book Club*, and others such as Helen Mirren, Judi Dench and Twiggy continue to set the example of older women by not only still working at 70 plus but still looking extremely glamorous. Madonna is now in her 60s and still comfortable exuding sexual confidence, while blogs and Instagram posts from older women that proclaim their ageing beauty are emerging daily. As India Knight has put it (*The Sunday Times* magazine: Sept. 2018), even cool people get old. The way that they stay cool though is "*by embracing oldness*" not running away from it. A silent revolution in ageism maybe slowly be happening under the surface, but for activists such as Baroness Julia Neuberger (2008), evolutionary change is too slow and too late. She has called for a "*Rage Against Age*" and has even proposed that oldies form a 'grey panther' movement to combat age discrimination and liberate older people more forcibly. Angry baby boomers can be a formidable force for change and a vociferous grey army, loud and proud to be old, a force for transforming ageism and all the other barriers to releasing the potential of the new old. Certainly, any anti-ageist campaign that managed to generate an **intergenerational crusade** would elevate this cause from one of generational self-interest to one of intergenerational collaboration, with younger people, too, campaigning for the rights, security and dignity of older people – their grandparents and parents, elderly relatives – as well as for themselves as old people in the future. The platform of an ageless society in which age is no longer a social barrier and in which the old, and the young, are equally respected and held in high esteem would be a bandwagon few political parties could resist, led perhaps by the 'Bin Ageism' slogan developed by the students of Cambridge Heath Sixth Form and older people in Tower Hamlets, East London.

Young Laura had never expected to be so inspired by the notion of ageing nor so outraged at the ill-treatment so casually dished out to old people in a society apparently as civilised as Great Britain. The elderly, according to her research, seemed to have more respect, more protection and more authority in societies far less developed than the UK. They were at the heart of the family in many Mediterranean and developing countries, with legislation, or at least very strict social mores, to ensure that the younger members of the family respect their elders and accept full responsibility for their well-being. The contrast with the UK and the apparently deep-rooted nature of ageism in our society shocked and appalled Laura. It had a profound effect on her choice of future career – a career that took her initially into working and campaigning for Age UK and later on into national politics, following in the footsteps of her grandmother Polly. Polly and David, however, were all too aware of the insidious nature of ageism and its all-pervasive influence on their respective professions, and even the way they themselves often looked at the elderly. They resolved, in the face of Laura's research and her passionate advocacy, that the family adopt an 'age rage' approach to ensuring that her grandmother's contribution to society and to the family be documented and publicised. David undertook a radical review of his medical practice's current approaches to eldercare, gaining in the process a reputation as a particularly age-friendly practice, keen to promote active ageing and be intolerant of any assumption that ageing ailments were automatically either natural or untreatable. Polly, in turn, had had her eyes opened and, besides now being far more rigorous in the standards of care she should have demanded for her mother, she began to believe that maybe she had found one of the key causes that might, just might, bridge the 'class chasm' within her constituency and provide her with the manifesto to return her to Westminster at the next election.

Age and Inequality

If ageism is the great cause for any red-blooded baby boomer, inequality, particularly intergenerational inequality, may be the cause most likely to get the young out of bed and into the ballot box. This might also be the strand that helped draw the two halves of Polly's family together in common cause. Inequality divides families just as powerfully as it divides societies and, as explained earlier, while Donald and Polly had enjoyed relatively affluent lifestyles living and working in the South and East of England, life for Wilfred and his wife Wilma in the North East had been anything but easy. Wilfred, now retired early at aged 61, had worked in the Tyneside shipyards most of his life but moved to Sunderland to work in the Nissan car factory in the late 1990s when the shipbuilding industry across the

UK 'sank' in face of Asian competition. The five years of unemployment that he had had to endure after his redundancy was still etched on his memory and infused his political passion. As a trade union official on Tyneside, he had long campaigned for workers' rights and been active in local Labour Party politics. He detested New Labour, welcomed the election of Jeremy Corbyn and, like so many of his comrades in Sunderland, voted enthusiastically for Brexit despite the warnings at that time from the Nissan management of possibly moving their car plant over to Europe. Wilfred owned his own home – a council house bought, ironically, during the Thatcher era – but otherwise depended on a baseline state pension supplemented with a similar income from his days on Tyneside and at Nissan. His wife Wilma, however, could not retire until she reached 66 years of age, having been born after 1953. Even then, her pension would be meagre given her broken employment record bringing up her children and caring quite recently for her elderly mother. Supplements from her NHS pension as a ward nurse and more recently as a care assistant locally would still leave her below the basic tax threshold in retirement.

As explained earlier, the contrast between Donald the banker, Polly the MP and their respective spouses in equally well-paid jobs in the South and East and Wilfred and Wilma in the North could not be starker, not only in terms of income and lifestyle but in terms of health and likely life expectancy. After years in the docks and later a car factory, living on a fairly basic diet and smoking heavily, Wilfred would be highly unlikely to outlive Donald or Polly, or even his elderly mother, Charlotte, who had lived into her 90s. Donald and Polly had both been to grammar schools in Tyneside where they grew up and then on to universities in London and the South East. Wilfred, however, failed the 11+ examination, went on to a local secondary modern school and then into the shipyards via an apprenticeship. His older son Derek got into Newcastle University to study electronic engineering, while his younger son Gordon followed Wilfred into the Nissan car factory after completing an apprenticeship at Gateshead College of FE. Nevertheless, though Donald, Polly and Wilfred now lived light years apart in terms of geographical distance and lifestyles, they were still quite close as a family and met up every year just before Christmas to exchange presents, catch up and visit their mum when she was alive. Their respective children kept in close contact too, through Facebook and occasional meals in London, and they encouraged the same family spirit in their children. The devotion of their respective grandchildren had enriched and enlivened life for all three of these post-war baby boomers, fuelled their ambitions for later life and, for Wilfred at least, made the social divisions between them that much easier to bear.

The tale of Donald, Polly and Wilfred, and of their emerging multigenerational family network, is but a brief example of the way inequality bites into family life, corrodes and possibly corrupts it. Had Wilfred taken a much harder line about his lot in life and come to resent the prosperity enjoyed by his southern siblings, Polly and Donald, this boomer family could well have been split asunder and grown far apart to the detriment of all ages and branches of this extended family tree.

Equality and equality of opportunity sat alongside each other throughout the 20th century. The search for a fair and just distribution of wealth was the driving force behind the American dream and the Communist utopias of Soviet Russia and Red China. In the global world of the 21st century, inequality has reached new heights and generated a new rich; a global super-rich of individuals and corporations wealthier than individual nations and apparently beyond the reach of national and even international governments. Google, Amazon, PayPal and the like are the new 'masters of the universe'. They seem to have ambitions to 'rule the world', governing from California's Silicon Valley. Apple, today, is the first company in history to be valued at a trillion dollars and Amazon is close behind.

The **super-rich** seem to be getting richer at a time when the vast majority of the world's population is getting poorer, opening up a chasm in wealth and opportunity that is undermining the very legitimacy of global capitalism; a chasm in wealth and opportunity that was starkly and simply illustrated by the 2018 Oxfam Report which identified 42 billionaires whose combined wealth outstripped the poorest half of humanity, men ranging from Bill Gates of Microsoft through to Jeff Bezos of Amazon and Mark Zuckerman of Facebook. And this biblical **inequality gap** is inevitably likely to grow as wealth begets more wealth and their vast investments attract more interest, while the income of the majority of mankind stagnates or even falls. Moreover, according to Oxfam, 82% of the global wealth generated in 2017 went to the most wealthy 1%, while the world's ten biggest corporations have revenues greater than that of 180 countries combined. Moreover, such organisations appear to use their wealth not only to influence government regulation in their favour but to avoid taxation altogether. "*The Economy of the 1%,*" argued Oxfam (2017) "*is working for the super-rich at the expense of the super-poor and, with cronyism so embedded and widespread, the very legitimacy of modern capitalism comes into question.*" Globalisation is leading to a rise in global income inequality, not a trickle-down as many politicians claim; and while billionaires have apparently seen an average increase of 13% in their wealth since 2010, ordinary people have barely kept up with inflation. As the 2016 Credit Suisse Global Wealth Report concluded, though the world was becoming more equal between 2000 and 2008, "*the trend reversed after the financial crisis. Our estimates suggest that the lower half of the global population collectively owns less than 1% of global wealth, while the richest 10% of adults own 89% of all wealth with the top 1% accounting for all global assets.*" Such vast global inequality raises not only questions about the economic and social impact of inequality but moral ones about modern capitalism itself. The encyclopaedic World Inequality Report, authored by Thomas Piketty and his colleagues and updated in 2018, came to similar conclusions. It identified the origins of this huge surge in inequality as coming from the deregulation of global capitalism back in the 1980s, and highlighted, too, its immense variations, with income inequality at its lowest in Europe, highest in the Middle East and rising most rapidly in North America, China, India and Russia. While the middle classes are being 'squeezed' and the rest left behind, private wealth is soaring and public wealth is shrinking. "*Back in the 1970s private wealth apparently represented 300% of national income. Today it has risen to 600% in most rich countries.*" As a result countries may have become richer but governments have become poorer. Hence the rise in government debt and the fall in government spending in most Western countries. Without restraint, global inequality can only increase but with more progressive taxation, believes Piketty, as in modern Europe, governments can not only achieve a fairer distribution of wealth and better fund public services but also reduce the incentives for top earners to use aggressive tax avoidance measures to capture higher shares of growth for themselves. A global financial register of the ownership of all financial assets would, in Piketty's view, "*deal a severe blow to tax evasion, money laundering and rising inequality,*" while more equal access to education and well-paid jobs would substantially enhance social mobility. Thomas Piketty doesn't see closing this wealth gap as impossible but he acknowledges that it will take an exceptional tax on wealth that few governments have the political will or stomach to impose let alone enforce if this vast outflow of public income is to be recouped and public services in countries such as Europe and the UK be properly funded. The need to tax the super-corporations and the super-rich fairly and effectively is clearly critical in restoring a balance of equity and fairness within modern capitalism but, as Apple, Google and the like have clearly shown, global corporations are very resistant to taxation and very adept at avoiding it. Almost 5% of total wealth in the UK, for example – nearly £200 billion – is held offshore according to the IPPR 'Wealth in the twenty-first century' report in 2017, wealth that is apparently beyond the reach even of HMRC. Gabriel Zucman (2015), has calculated that this *"Hidden Wealth of Nations"* amounts to some $8.7 trillion, while John Lancaster argued in *The Sunday Times:* 9 Sept. 2018 that all that governments worldwide have to do is make transactions with tax havens illegal, create a transparent register of assets and crack down on trust structures – simple solutions but only if the political will is there and international co-operation is rigorously enforced. In Nick Shaxson's view (2018), too many banks, businesses and professions today are more concerned with *extracting* wealth from the economy for themselves than *creating* wealth for the economy at large and for their clients and customers – aided and even abetted by the government and the cartel of the four major audit firms in the UK. Big business and big banks take the profit while the public takes the risk: *"Britain owes its pre-eminence as a financial centre to the combination of a strong legal system, which stops people stealing your money, with a weak regulatory one, which allows you to steal other people's."*

Wealth inequality on this scale is astonishing in any age; but in a modern world that has just gone through a global financial crisis that seemed to threaten the very existence of society itself, it seems beyond belief, if not beyond morality, that the global rich have managed to get richer at a time when millions have become poorer. Inequality on this scale doesn't just seem unjust, but obscene, and brings capitalism into dispute if not worldwide condemnation, generating a reaction, an anger, a fury that leads either to mass disillusion with the 'system', or mass protest, and for some mass terrorism. Even the WEF – the think tank for the super-powers – had wealth disparity as one of its top five global risks in 2017; and the OECD concluded back in 2015, and reiterated in 2017, that inequality on this scale is seriously damaging economic growth because significant sectors within the working population are being excluded from the wealth-making and wealth-sharing process through unemployment, or under employment, and low pay. Such forces are dramatically reducing the capacity of the poorest 40% to fully contribute to productivity and to national income earning. Such growing inequalities are also seriously damaging the very fabric and social cohesion of even the most developed of societies today: *"Youths who see no future for themselves feel increasingly disenfranchised. They have now been joined by protesters who believe they are bearing the brunt of a crisis for which they have no responsibility, while people on higher incomes seem to be spared."* (OECD: 2015) From such a perspective, global inequality is not only one of the driving forces behind global terrorism but it also seems to be driving the populist protest movements across both America and Western Europe that led to the

Brexit referendum in the UK and the election of Donald Trump in the USA in a wave of anti-establishment, even nationalist, sentiment.

Moreover, as the OECD highlighted in 2017, ageing is now adding to inequality rather than mitigating it. European societies are *ageing unequally* as the newer generations of old emerge with higher incomes and lower poverty than previous generations. The young are not only replacing the elderly as the age cohort most vulnerable to poverty, but through the life cycle they are likely to continue to be so as a result of increasingly unstable employment conditions, the impact of vast technological changes and the poorer pension provisions as governments cut back on benefits and employers cut back on the defined benefit pension schemes of the past. As the 2016 McKinsey Institute Report concluded, young people today are likely to be "*Poorer than their Parents*"; and although new technology and globalisation are the real forces behind the apparent loss of jobs at home and abroad, immigrants – some 200 million worldwide – have become the easy scapegoat and the target of the simmering frustration and growing anger amongst many ordinary people across the Western economies. For the UN and UNICEF, inequality is now one of the greatest global challenges of the 21st century, not only as an economic challenge but as an ethical and moral one too. As its 2016 report concluded, all this inequality and exclusion emanates from an "*unequal control over assets*" that "*needs to be countered by explicit policies seeking a more equal distribution.*" A conclusion that even Karl Marx might have applauded.

Inequality has had an equally dramatic effect on the UK. Studies, like that of Oxfam's back in 2014, showed that the richest five families in the UK own more wealth than the poorest 20% of the entire population – some 13 million people – and that the most affluent British family – the Grosvenor family – alone own more than the whole of the bottom 10%. The World Inequality Report in 2017 estimated that the richest 1% in the UK control 22% of the country's wealth, a staggering rise from the 15% in 1984, while *The Sunday Times'* annual Rich List in 2019 showed that the wealthiest 1,000 people in Britain were worth a staggering £771 billion, up £48bn on 2018 despite the volatility of the stock market the previous year and equivalent to a third of Britain's GDP. The UK has more billionaires (151) than any other OECD country apart from America and China, with London the billionaires' capital of choice (95) beyond even New York (71) and Hong Kong (61). They are part of a global elite that John Aldridge described in 2016 as: "*a Nation unto themselves, fabulously wealthy and pulling ever further away from the rest of us… living in a trans-global community of peers who have more in common with each other than with their countrymen back home.*" As Professor John Hill concluded in 2013: "*Britain is an unequal country, more so than many other industrial countries and more so than a generation ago"*, and increasingly this wealth gap has an age dimension as the younger generations now seem to be accumulating lower levels of wealth compared to the baby boomer generation at similar ages, according to the IPPR report on 'Wealth in the twenty-first century' (2017).

The IFS Deaton Review launched in May 2019 proposes to undertake one of the most comprehensive reviews of inequality in Great Britain in recent years. Its initial review shows the UK to be one of the most unequal nations internationally with a Gini coefficient that is only just behind the USA, a share of income going to the 1% richest households that has nearly tripled since the 1980s, a rise in 'deaths of despair' (deaths from suicide, drug and alcohol overdose), a sharp rise in loneliness with many amongst the low income and low educated forgoing marriage and stable relationships and leaving 16% of children in 2017 born into households with no father at home. The United Kingsom is fragmenting geographically as well as economically with the divide between London and the rest of the country becoming a chasm in income, lifestyles and opportunities for social mobility while intergenerational inequality threatens on one hand to get worse and on the other to exacerbate the inequalities above as inheritances in the future are likely ot benefit *"those lucky enough to have wealthy parents at the expense of their less well off and less fortunate peers. Each of these individual inequalities are bad enough on their own. Collectively they reinforce each other and culminate in 'myriad forms of privilege and disadvantage'."* Brexit has given voice to an immense and intense dissatisfaction by large swathes of the British electorate, not only with the British political system but with life in Britain today. Inequality – and specific inequalities – *"have sparked world-wide protest movements and been linked to some of the most important political events of our time, including the vote for Brexit and the rise of populism across the developed world."* As Sir Angus Deaton himself has commented: *"As at no other time in my lifetime, people are troubled by inequality."* The taking of wealth seems to have replaced the making of wealth; *"taking rather than making, rent-seeking rather than creating, enriching the few at the expense of the many, taking the free out of free markets, is making a mockery of democracy. In that world, inequality and misery are intimate companions."* The Deaton Review has set itself the mammoth task of delving deeper into these divides as the means to developing *"a comprehensive agenda for change"* – no small task and one that aligns strongly with Polly's intergenerational mission and the draft manifesto that she eventually drew up in chapter 15.

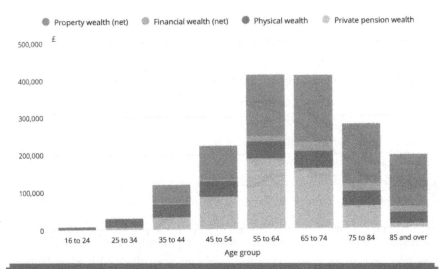

Figure 2: **Distribution of Income in UK**
(ONS: 2017/Equality Trust: 2016)

Country Highest to Lowest	Gini Coefficient for equivalised disposable income
South Africa	62%
China	56%
India	50%
Brazil	47%
USA	39%
Russia	38%
UK	**36%**
Canada	31%
Ireland	30%
Norway	26%

Figure 3: **Distribution of Income Internationally**: 2014
(Adapted from OECD/Commons Library Briefing: Sept 2017)

But inequality is no longer just intergenerational. It is equally **intragenerational**. As the Centre for Ageing Better commented in December 2017: "*Amongst people aged between 46 and 65 years old, those in the highest 20% income bracket have a household income about three times greater than the bottom 20%. For people aged between 66 and 85 the difference is more than double.*" As highlighted in Chapter 4, state pensions in the UK are not only "*the lowest in the developed world*" (OECD: 2017), but as the Royal London Insurance report in March 2018 revealed there is "*a shocking disparity in pension incomes across the UK and even within the same region and borough.*" The City of London, not surprisingly, topped this particular league table with an average pension income of £37,900, while in the same city Barking & Dagenham averaged just £12,900. Outside London, pension income averaged £13,600 in Sunderland, £13,100 in Southampton and a lowly £12,300 in Stoke. In terms of total wealth, the bottom tenth of older households aged 55–64 own less than £28,000, while the top 10% of this age group own over £1.3 million (including pension rights) with the average wealth of women just half that of men. Disparities in intragenerational wealth to the extent shown above are not easy to explain and much less easy to justify. As Professor John Hills (2014) has argued, while the British welfare state appears to be based on the "*Robin Hood*" principle of redistributing wealth from the rich to the poor, in practice it often works the other way round, helping the better-off get richer and institutionalising inequality rather than reversing it. Far from the poor, and the 'welfare scroungers' so beloved of the tabloid press, benefiting most from the British welfare state, it is often the affluent middle classes who do so, through generous pension allowances, longer periods in state education and much greater benefit from the NHS because they simply live longer, much longer, than their poorer peers. Longevity is endorsing inequality; and as the Cass Business School Report in 2016 showed, the richest 5% of men in Britain today are living on average to 96.2 years, 34.2 years longer than the poorest 10% of men, while the richest women live on average even longer than their poorest female counterparts. So, the socio-economic age gap in modern Britain is getting wider the longer you live. **Two 'classes' of pensioner** are therefore starting to emerge, with very different lifestyles and quality of life: those older and poorer pensioners dependent primarily on the state pension for their retirement income, and those, like Donald and Polly, with private pensions, extensive personal and property wealth, and some of the most affluent lifestyles in British history. As the Manchester Institute for Collaborative Research on Ageing (MICRA) Report of 2017 concluded well-being in later life is inversely related to levels of wealth and *"current policy choices simply increase inequalities amongst older people"* and need dramatic rethinking.

So, age is driving both intergenerational and intragenerational inequality and fragmenting Great Britain socially and geographically in the process. According to the government's Social Mobility (and Child Poverty) Commission Reports in 2014 and 2015, Britain is becoming a *"permanently divided nation"* creating in the process a *"Lost Generation of Young"*; a generation of un- or under-employed young people; a generation unable to get on the housing ladder; an alienated generation disillusioned with and resentful of a political system that fails to respond to their needs. Life for many young people today seems oppressive and without meaning; so, all too easily, this generation gap could escalate into an age war that might find expression in the midst of families today as well as on the streets of Britain's cities. In a period of what promises to be one of continuing austerity alongside the economic uncertainties of Brexit, the young and the poor are both likely to be the hardest hit. As the commission concluded in its 2017 State of the Nation Report, Britain's track record on social mobility is *"lamentable"* and there is *"a fracture line running deep through our labour and housing markets and our educational system"* whereby *"those on the wrong side of this divide are losing out and falling behind"*. Although poverty amongst children and pensioners has fallen significantly since the 1990s, the Joseph Rowntree Foundation (JRF) in December 2017 found it to be rising again to 16% for pensioners and 30% for children, while the All-Party Parliamentary Group on Hunger in 2018 found more than one million older people *"withering away in their homes"*. As the poor are trapped by low pay, the aspiring excluded from top universities and top jobs, and the young excluded from owning their own homes, so this divide is not only growing but fracturing the UK socially and geographically through a *"stark social mobility post-code lottery"* that graphically separates London from the rest of the country. London may be both the wealthiest part of the UK and the area with the highest levels of social mobility, even in its poorest boroughs, but according to the commission's Social Mobility Index, social mobility in the isolated rural and coastal communities of the UK is stagnant. The new phenomenon of *"Left-Behind Britain"* leaves the country in the grip of a self-reinforcing spiral of ever-growing division that is *"deeply corrosive of our national cohesion"* and that substantiates the sense of political alienation and social resentment that so many parts of modern Britain now feel. *"Whole communities feel that the benefits of globalisation* have passed them, because they have; and whole sections of society feel that they are not getting a fair chance to succeed, because they are not." Strong words reflecting such deep frustration with government inactivity on these issues that the chair, deputy chair and chief executive of the commission all felt obliged to resign in protest. Add to this stagnation in social mobility, government cuts of over £12 billion to working age welfare benefits due to kick in in the next five years, then according to the Resolution Foundation (2017) we are likely to see *"the biggest rise in inequality since the 1980s."* The IPPR Commission for Economic Justice Report in 2018 went further, arguing that the UK economy today is not working for the majority of the population and needs fundamental reform to restore social justice and far greater fairness to the way it distributes and redistributes wealth. It showed that most people in Britain today are no better off than a decade ago, yet 40% of national income growth over the last 40 years has gone to the richest 10%. *"Economic justice cannot be an afterthought; it must be built into the economy,"* built into the ownership of capital and wealth, the governance of firms, the operation of the financial system and the rules governing market forces. Real change, argues the IPPR report, involves rebalancing economic power from corporate management towards workers and trade unions, from dominant corporations towards innovators and entrepreneurs, from short-term finance towards long-term investment and from Whitehall (and London) towards the nations and regions of the UK. With the 2020s set to be a decade of disruption, the commission argued that the state has to take a more active and purposeful role in promoting prosperity, justice and environmental sustainability *"on behalf of society as a whole"* not in the interests of the few and that this might be achieved through decentralisation of power on one hand and greater social partnership on the other.

The 2018 UN Report into poverty in the UK by Professor Philip Alston was particularly scathing, describing government cuts since 2010 as having inflicted *"unnecessary misery"* in one of the richest countries in the world, torn at its social fabric and replaced the British compassion for those suffering with a mean-spirited and callous approach. *"This is not just a disgrace but a social calamity and an economic disaster all rolled into one."* He identified 14 million people – a fifth of the UK population – living in poverty, a rise in homelessness of 60% and an extra one million children in poverty since 2010. All happening at the very time that the British economy has grown by more than £220 billion. This report was a devastating indictment of the government's austerity strategy, given the very few savings achieved and, add to that, the substantial and growing inequalities in healthy life expectancy described in Chapter one and it is not surprising that the UK came a lowly 21st in the WEF's Inclusive Development Index in 2018, well below New Zealand and Australia. And according to the Centre for Progressive Policy (2019), it is those on middle incomes in Britain today that are being 'squeezed' the most, as the richest 20% – those earning £98,500 a year – have seen their incomes rise by 50% since 1997 and the poorest fifth even more so as a result of the minimum wage and more women working. Aspirations, especially ambitions to rise up the housing ladder, are being blocked and thwarted and 'the great British promise that each generations would do better than the last has been broken.' Moreover, such intergenerational and intragenerational inequality may well escalate in the years ahead as baby boomers begin to gradually hand over a 'wall of wealth' of some £400 billion to their children and grandchildren in the form of gifts or inheritances.

Under such a scenario, the 'affluent oldie' is likely to become a figure of fun if not a focus of generational outrage. Family sentiment may continue to hold the older generation of boomer families like Polly's together but sentiment alone may not moderate or assuage the growing divisions of lifetime opportunities and retirement prospects of the younger generations and so undermine, if not fracture, the delicate nature of the 'beanpole' that appears to be the family structure of the future. As the Church of England bishops wrote to David Cameron prior to the 2015 General Election, inequality in the UK is now becoming an ethical challenge to the moral character of a Britain in which loneliness, alienation and loss of neighbourliness are becoming permanent features. "*Britain is the world's seventh largest economy and yet people are going hungry.*" According to Oxfam (2015), we are facing a "*Tale of Two Britains*", and Professor Danny Dorling concluded in his 2015 study of inequality and the 1% that: "*Gross economic inequality is as vile as racism, misogyny and hatred of the disabled; as damaging in effect; and as dependent on a small group of supporters who believe that just a few should have more because they're worth it.*" Globally, and nationally, we may now be close to the edge of what economic growth can do for us materially, while rampant capitalism and inequality appear to be threatening to undermine the quality of human life rather than enhance and enrich it. As Richard Wilkinson and Kate Pickett argued back in 2009: "*Mainstream politics no longer taps into collective aspirations and it has abandoned the attempt to provide a shared vision capable of inspiring us to create a better society, one in which we have shifted attention from material standards and economic growth onto ways of improving the psychological and social wellbeing of*

Figure 2.2: Ranking of Happiness 2015–2017 (Part 1)

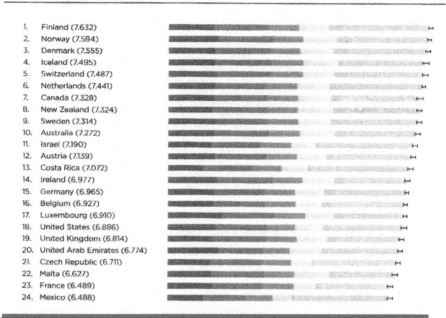

1.	Finland (7.632)
2.	Norway (7.594)
3.	Denmark (7.555)
4.	Iceland (7.495)
5.	Switzerland (7.487)
6.	Netherlands (7.441)
7.	Canada (7.328)
8.	New Zealand (7.324)
9.	Sweden (7.314)
10.	Australia (7.272)
11.	Israel (7.190)
12.	Austria (7.139)
13.	Costa Rica (7.072)
14.	Ireland (6.977)
15.	Germany (6.965)
16.	Belgium (6.927)
17.	Luxembourg (6.910)
18.	United States (6.886)
19.	United Kingdom (6.814)
20.	United Arab Emirates (6.774)
21.	Czech Republic (6.711)
22.	Malta (6.627)
23.	France (6.489)
24.	Mexico (6.488)

Figure 4: Helliwell, J., Layard, R., & Sachs, J. (2018). World Happiness Report 2018, *(New York Sustainable Development Solutions Network)*

whole societies." Egalitarian societies tend to be happier societies, more socially content and more socially united. In contrast, the more unequal societies, such as modern Britain, tend to be the least happy, the more disunited and fragmented, with high levels of social underachievement and profound social problems. It is no coincidence, therefore, that the UK comes a lowly 19th on the World Happiness League table, well below the Dutch and Scandinavian nations and sandwiched between the USA and the United Arab Emirates.

All these reviews of inequality confirmed Polly's emerging view that a one-generational political manifesto that sought to promote the interests and needs of the new old alone would not only be selfish, and seen to be so, but be counter-productive, inspire a political and social reaction from the young and in the long-term be morally and politically indefensible. In thirty or more years, all Britain's baby boomers are likely to be gone, and what would they have left their children and grandchildren but debt and the doubtful duty of having to care for them in old age, assuming, that is, that they are willing to do so? The manifesto for the future, she was now absolutely sure, lay in creating an intergenerational framework, not just a generational one; one that looks to the future for both the new old and the new young; one that builds generational bridges not age barriers; and one that focuses on the quality of life and the quality of society that our grandchildren might inherit, not just on ever more material benefits. It equally brought to the forefront the underlying issue of inheritance and its hidden, profound, and at times insidious, effect on social equality, a question Torsten Bell raised in the *New Statesman* in 2018, a question that has meaning and implications for all of us.

- In your view, is **inheritance** a natural right, a family obligation and a just outcome of a working life or is it a perpetuation of social inequality and as such should be banned or heavily taxed?

- Do you agree with the British multi-millionaire John Caudwell of Phones 4u fame that inheritances are bad for children's health and self-esteem and that the young should make their own way in the world and not depend on their parents?

- Would you go so far as some of the wealthiest people on the planet have done and donate all your final wealth to charities, the poor and the Third World? Bill Gates and his wife Melinda are well-known for their charity work. Warren Buffet, Mark Zuckerberg and 150 other billionaires have signed a giving pledge, pledging to give half or even 90% of their wealth to charity in the future and to fighting inequality at home or abroad. But is such generosity genuine or is it simply a cynical publicity stunt to assuage public anger given that the remaining 50% or even 10% of their wealth is still likely to leave them multi-billionaires?

Interesting questions when put at the personal level; highly pertinent to the debate above when reflecting on social justice and intergenerational fairness. Finland and the Netherlands may not be the biggest economies in the Western world but they seem to be amongst the most egalitarian, and their children appear to be amongst the happiest. British teenagers, however, appear to be some of the least happy, whether at home or in school, of the 72 countries surveyed by the OECD in 2017. If ever there was a case for an intergenerational strategy, this has to be it.

So, Polly now had her moral mission and cause celebre for a generational, even intergenerational, manifesto. Ageism and inequality would clearly provide a moral as well as a political dimension for her campaign, capable of inspiring and uniting both young and old. But if these were to be her political *ends*, what might be her political *means*? What generational powers might she call on in promoting an intergenerational manifesto when the young today apparently feel, and possibly are, so helpless? What special powers do the new old have that might propel ageing to the forefront of national political debate and force the British government to take ageing seriously and plan properly for the ageing world ahead? What economic, political and technological powers do baby boomers actually have that will make age-change the defining force of the early 21ˢᵗ century?

12 | The New Old and Their Economic Power: The Grey Pound and the Silver Economy

Polly was already aware from her reading and research to date that the boomer market was massive; a mass market in its own right and an emerging powerhouse within the British economy. What she hadn't appreciated until now was that it was likely to soon become *the* market of the future in the years ahead. Baby boomers are as voracious consumers in their 60s and 70s as they were as teenagers in the 1960s, yuppies in the 1980s or homeowners in the 1990s. Today, with the advent of the internet, they now have instant access to shops and markets across the world, and they are using it in bucketloads. The silver economy is huge, with the spending power of consumers aged 60+ now estimated by Euromonitor as $15 trillion globally, with healthcare, pharmaceuticals, senior housing, silver tech, travel and tourism the major beneficiaries of this age shift. The international consultants McKinsey have predicted that by 2030 "*The developed world's retiring and elderly will be accounting for nearly 60% of consumption growth in Western Europe and North East Asia alone*" (2016), while the WEF (2015) sees this economic age shift as the "*Great Awakening of the 21st century*" and potentially a virtuous circle, as business leaders, innovators and marketeers begin to design and drive strategies and products that will promote and sustain active ageing. Major companies such as Nestlé and Black Rock, Pfizer and JPMorgan Chase are already investing heavily in this emerging market; the G20 top economies have drafted their "*Principles on the Silver Economy and Active Ageing*," and as cited earlier, countries like Ireland are actively exploring the development of a "*Silver Strategy*" as part of their future economic growth.

So, mused Polly, how might I as a politician both encourage similar development in the UK and harness the British silver economy as part of my generational campaign in the years ahead? On Hannah's advice, Polly turned to Donald's son, Edward, a market researcher who having worked for the advertising giant Nielsen in New York was now seeking to start up his own market research consultancy in the UK specialising in identifying trends in boomer consuming and markets for the new old. Like Polly, Edward was on a mission, a mission to convert British business from the 'altar of youth' to the 'promise of the silver pound', so Polly's request to help her develop an economic strategy that might help underpin her political campaign was manna from heaven and an ideal opportunity to put his experiences in the boomer markets of the USA to good use. He began by outlining some of the current academic research into the emerging phenomenon of the new-age consumer. In 'Ageing in a Consumer Society' (2008), for example, IR Jones and his colleagues had sought to identify the consumption patterns and life-course perceptions of ageing consumers in post-modern society – a society that is increasingly both global and virtual. Jones et al described this new third age as a "*second modernity*", a second stage in modernising contemporary society as the "*golden age*" of the welfare state gives way to a "*silver age*" of the 21st century in which power, risk and responsibility are increasingly shifting from the state and onto the individual and the free market. The near collapse of Western capitalism following the credit crisis of 2008 not only ruptured world markets and world trade but undermined all the taken-for-granted assumptions about full employment, lifelong careers and secure retirement. A new, more fragile and uncertain, life course has emerged in which nothing in life is taken for granted, be it in terms of work, family or even personal relations. Globalisation and new technology are gathering pace and old ways of working or living are being cast aside. New frontiers are being created, and the post-war baby boomers have the opportunity to be at the forefront of this tidal wave of change – or at the back of it. The post-war baby boomer generation represents, in their view, a new type of consumer – affluent, dual income/dual pension older households with high levels of disposable income, high levels of savings and assets, and the backup support in the UK of the National Health Service and social security/social services systems. These wealthier, affluent baby boomers are leading the way in demanding new products, new housing, new lifestyles and a new image as they continue their youthful quest for personal fulfilment. They are not going to passively adopt the old lifestyles and old images of ageing. They are in the business of creating new models and new patterns of consumption all for themselves. The grey pound is currently valued at £300 billion plus, and baby boomers apparently have their sights set on active world travel, property buying, film-going, healthcare and physical fitness. Not only are the great names of the past – be they Jaguar or Harley-Davidson – enjoying a revival but even care homes are having to offer activities such as wheelchair abseiling and tandem parachuting.

The **new old**, therefore, represent a new – possibly a *new form* of – mass market, a distinct but diverse market with ambitions to stay young and beautiful but equally averse to any age-specific products that label them old or inactive, elderly or ancient, *unless* of course they offer the magic cure, the silver bullet, for regeneration and rejuvenation to help them stay active and feel young in spirit as well as in looks. From this marketing perspective, *'ageless'* products, inclusive products, capable of being adapted and adopted by all ages, hold the key to future sales; and this might apply equally to any new technology as to any new home help. We could all benefit from a simpler, integrated remote control that was easier to use; we could all benefit from fewer dials and controls on our car dashboard; and we could all benefit from ring-pulls on tins of beans that don't threaten to slice your fingers in half. However, explained Edward, making this marketing leap, from age-defined to ageless marketing, involves a radical rethink of current marketing strategies and a recognition and appreciation that now there is a *third-age* market in modern life that is growing in wealth and number but doesn't necessarily require age-specific products and services.

Secondly, reaching out to this market will be a challenge in itself. Terms like 'boomer' or 'zoomer' may appeal to marketers in North America but they tend to grate on the British or European ear; tend to sound too brash and too aggressive for the more reserved and sensitive cultural traditions of Western Europe. While Americans in retirement tend to emphasise individual lifestyles and affluent living, their British counterparts tend to play down consumption and self-satisfaction in favour of family and society, citizenship and social contribution. British boomers tend to dislike being labelled or typecast, particularly with American-style labels such as boomer or zoomer. Even the term 'third age' is an inadequate term for describing the diversity and creativity of the new old. Finally, the new old are not passively inhabiting the traditional world of old age but actively creating a new one; one with new images, new lifestyles and new identities. The new old are looking for the 'good life' in older age with as much vigour and ambition as they looked for it in their youth; a DIY, freestyle stage of life is emerging from the boomers' new style of shopping and consuming, one that promotes independence and is ideally free from physical or mental decay; a lifestyle and life stage that is as diverse as boomers care to make it – and the media cares to portray it! This third age, however, is not only a period of continued consumption but, in the view of writers such as Peter Laslett (1965) and Anthony Giddens (1991), it is one of reflection and reorientation, of "*reflexivity*" in coming to terms with life lived so far and the time left to live it further.

Edward's insights were the result of his time working for Nielsen in the US, an agency that has promoted and lauded the boomer market and even coined the phrase 'Boomager' in 2012 to reflect both the attitudes and consumer potential of this emerging mass market as America herself ages. By 2030, the 65+ population in America is predicted to double and to grow by 2050 to nearly 87 million, while the $28 trillion of wealth owned by over-65s is greater than the GDP of many countries in Europe today. And though the tyranny of youth still rules as powerfully in the USA as in the UK – frustrating the AARP so badly that it launched its own marketing agency in 2015 – pioneers of the silver market are growing and their message spreading. Mary Furlong, CEO of Third Age Media, for example, has built her career on trying to turn "*Silver into Gold*" (2007). She believes that not only do the new age markets represent a new gold rush for global businesses but that a more age-friendly marketing strategy might help inspire boomers to use their wealth and their wisdom for doing good and for once again becoming trailblazers, setting out a new roadmap for generations to come in supporting businesses that make a difference and brands that "*have a sense of social purpose as well as business purpose.*" In Mary Furlong's view, new market forces are creating a boomer market that not only includes the usual areas, such as home and lifestyle, travel and adventure, family and child/eldercare, but even the end-of-life market. Mary Furlong believes that boomer women are at the heart of the new economy and that the grandparent market, worth over $30 billion even back in 2007, is the one to watch. As Mary Furlong affectionately concludes, baby boomers are still in love, still as sexually adventurous as they were in their youth, even though they may not be quite as physically pliable as they once were: *"Love for the baby boomer generation isn't about the first time anymore – it's about making love feel like it did the first time… Baby boomers were probably conceived with music playing in the room. They will probably die with music playing in the room, too."*

Consultants, such as Brent Green, have taken these insights further and developed the notion of *Generational Marketing* (2013), of targeting and promoting a collective self-consciousness and a sense of common identity that offers each generation the opportunity for *"reinvention and self-empowerment"*. According to Brent Green's thesis, the baby boomers were the first generation to respond to mass marketing and the first to respond to generational advertising. Baby boomers became the first *"Pepsi Generation"* and straplines like these *"made the consumer – not the product – the hero of its ads, and, in the process, sold viewers this portrait of themselves."* Hence the popularity amongst boomers of images and icons from their past and the nostalgic zeitgeist they seem to evoke. Brands like Levi's jeans, Ben Sherman shirts and Harley-Davidson motor bikes survive and thrive on their power not only to cut across age boundaries but to evoke romantic and rebellious images of the 1960s and 70s; images captured in such films as *Easy Rider*, *Bullitt* and even *Bonny and Clyde*.

However, if the US market is only just waking up to the silver boom, the UK markets are still sound asleep. As Edward's research illustrated, the baby boomer market in the UK is a commercial treasure trove of 17 million plus: *"boomer consumers who already represent over £300 billion in market value per year own 80% of total wealth in the UK and constitute nearly half of total UK household expenditure."* According to the Institute of Customer Service (2016) the UK Silver Economy is worth £43 billion annually with utilities (12.1 bn), travel (£10.6 bn) and insurance (£6.8bn) some of the largest areas of annual spend while spending on health alone is currently estimated at over £8 billion.

But the UK silver economy is tiny in comparison with that of the EU. According to the European Commission study conducted by Oxford Economics and Technopolis in 2018, the European Union's silver economy (still including the UK) is set to expand from 199 million 50+-year-olds in 2015 to over 222 million by 2025 (nearly 43% of the total EU population). It is projected to grow by nearly 50%, from 3.7 trillion euros to 5.7 trillion euros in terms of goods and services consumed, supporting 88 million jobs, representing 31.5% of EU GDP

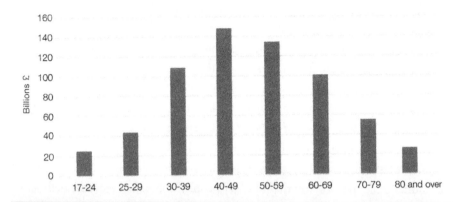

Figure 1: **Aggregate Expenditure by age group**
(ILC-UK Missing Billions: 2016)

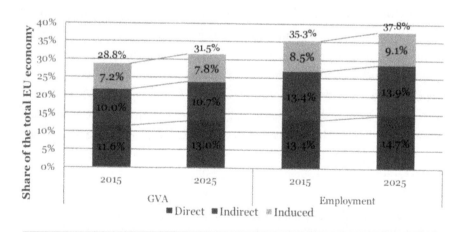

Figure 2: **The EU Silver Economy**
(EUC: 2018)

and becoming in the process *"the third largest economy in the world, behind only the USA and China"*: a phenomenal conclusion yet one very rarely mentioned in the UK Brexit debate; a phenomenal economic opportunity so close to home at a time when the UK is attempting to look to markets elsewhere in the world.

Yet despite such astronomic predictions about the British and European silver economy, survey after survey continues to show that the 50+ generation is at best ignored and at worst patronised, which as Mariella Frostrup commented in *Marketing Week* is quite *"bizarre"* given that by the year 2020 half of the UK population will be 50-plus. Such neglect might just be age blindness on the part of British business but, in the view of Dick Stroud and his colleagues, it verges on ageism. *"We live in a world designed by young people for younger people"*. where the modern marketer is usually young, male, brash and ambitious, steeped in the latest fashion or fad, living in a major city and divorced from the daily drone of ordinary life, particularly that of older people. These marketers are hell-bent, ironically, on pursuing their own age market, the very 18–35 age market that is fast disappearing, that is shrinking in number and is increasingly cash-poor as student debt and heavy mortgages take their toll. Meanwhile, Western societies such as Britain are bulging with boomer consumers with bulging pockets and appetites to match. However, instead of simply converting from millennial marketing to boomer marketing, Stroud and Walker (2013) have advised British companies to develop an all-age marketing strategy based on universal design as both a far more sustainable strategy and a more profitable one. *"Design for the young and you'll exclude the old. Design for the old, and you'll include the young."* Products and services that are age-friendly and age-sensitive, that have universal appeal, will fly out of the shops and showrooms as companies like Samsung and Jaguar have amply illustrated – and as Apple proved in August 2018 when it was the first company to be valued at over one trillion dollars.

So, marketing to the ageing baby boomer, in Dick Stroud's view, should be *"a marketer's delight"*, and marketing to the baby boomer's ageing body should be a *"marketers nirvana"*, offering a whole new set of markets for ageing products, particularly those designed to delay ageing, provide physical support and especially those offering to rejuvenate ageing bodies and tired limbs. Try, for example, opening a tin of beans or a boxed product today, or deciphering the multilingual instructions on a new computer, TV or washing machine. While it is often a nightmare for the able-bodied and able-minded, it's a lost cause for many older consumers, particularly those suffering from arthritis or poor eyesight. Similarly, while the internet and the new social media may well offer avenues for networking and communication for many silver citizens, the way that they are currently designed and presented makes them a no-go area for the ageing technophobe brought up in an era of the old-fashioned telephone and the analogue radio. Modern communication is increasingly overwhelming in its choice, jargon and complexity. Shopping for the elderly should be "*a pleasure to be pursued not a pain to be endured*". Watch any elderly person attempt to navigate a modern supermarket and just feel their pain when products are too high up to reach, labelling is too small to see and staff rush past them not to them. So, in an attempt to get designers and engineers to get into the mindset of our ageing population, the MIT AgeLab developed AGNES, a suit worn by students, product developers, engineers, planners, architects and the like to give them an insight into and an appreciation of the challenges facing older people today. By simulating life as experienced by an older person, the MIT developers hope to help young, physically able engineers and designers to appreciate the monumental difficulties older people often experience in undertaking even the apparently simplest of tasks and so inspire innovative and imaginative solutions to everyday living in an ageing world.

Finally, even this traditional marketing image of the elderly as ageing and disabled is more a stereotype of the old old than an accurate picture of the new old today. The new old – the boomer old – that is emerging from consumer surveys such as the Colour Report in 2015 is as active and vibrant, as fashion-conscious and ardent a shopper, as any of their children. Older women in particular are as well up on the latest fashions as their daughters claim to be and, contrary to popular perception, are far from techno-averse. They often revel in and compete for the adoption of new gadgets, apps and online services, with 95% of those surveyed using a smartphone, 59% a tablet and 26% a smart TV. Boomers are very health-conscious, active exercisers and

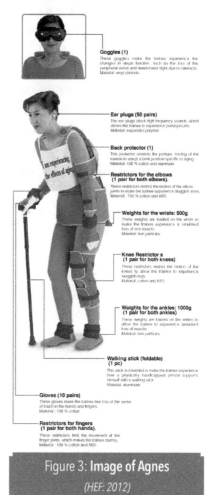

Figure 3: **Image of Agnes**
(HEF: 2012)

devoted dieters, and even 75-year-olds are now members of a gym or sports club. Moreover, many of this age group are not only super-boomers, but what the trade magazine, *Marketing,* called DRAGONS (*Divorced, Rich, Aged-65+, Overseas Traveller, and Networker)* who are "*on the move, on the go, and on the pull*". They are thrill seekers; and their heroes are those who make older age look glamorous and fun, such as Helen Mirren, Judi Dench and Sean Connery. The new old are worlds apart – generational worlds apart – from the old old and the elderly of the past.

So, concluded Edward, the future of marketing *is silver, the boomer is the consumer of the future* and over the next ten years, according to Capital Economics, two-thirds of all retail spending growth will come from those aged 55 and over. The rising influence of this group should see sales shift toward the products and services that they particularly favour, such as health, DIY and home maintenance. Films such as *The Best Exotic Marigold Hotel* are leading the way in the film industry, and older women have even been celebrated in Bond movies with Monica Bellucci, at aged 50, outshining Bond's younger female star. The array of new products and medical breakthroughs aimed specifically at the older market is bedazzling and set to explode, ranging from anti-ageing treatments through to cancer cures, while age-friendly technology now includes the driverless car and the walking stick that has a satnav embedded in its head. However, argued Edward, much of this new approach to marketing is simply an adaptation of old strategies, not a paradigm change in approach. It simply extends the appeal and glamour of the younger new old by a few more years, offering older women in particular a few more years of youthful glamour. It is not the radical change in the image, and self-image, of the new old called for by many feminists. It is not the boomer beauty of the future but the boomer beauty of the past; a facelift from the 1960s rather than a new image of new age for the 2020s. Nor does it reflect the new lifestyles, aspirations and multigenerational family networks that are being created and crafted by this new generation of retiree. Even the beauty industry is now abandoning terms like anti-ageing in favour of more positive straplines such as age-defence or age-reversal. As Helen Mirren, the doyen of ageing glamour, has herself explained, older women don't expect to eradicate all their wrinkles, just soften them and "*look as great as you can on a daily basis*". The 2019 Milan fashion week reflected this dramatic shift by recalling *glamazons* from the 1990s such as Stephanie Seymour (50), Amber Valetta (45) and Eva Herzigova (45) of "wonderbra" fame back to front their catwalks under the strapline "*Imperfection is the new perfection.*" (*The Sunday Times*: Feb.24 2019) And if that wasn't enough to inspire older women why not follow Jerry Hall and other glamorous mothers of the 1960s posing with their daughters and showing that beauty today is intergenerational as well as international.

So, mass marketing clearly has a key role in preparing modern society for ageing and in inspiring, if not designing, new models of living, new lifestyles to encourage and enable the independent and active ageing that is so critical to the ageing world(s) ahead. This age revolution in marketing is as profound and as critical to the British and the world economy as the youth revolution was to the economic boom that exploded across the Western world in the 1960s. We are now entering what marketing strategists call the 'era of post-demographic consumerism', an era in which '*people of all ages are now constructing their own identities more freely than ever before.*' The post-demographic world is an ageless world, according to the market research company Trends, one in which globalisation is transforming consumer behaviour and creating a universal experience of global products that have worldwide appeal, irrespective of any national, or even physical, boundaries. The global brands – Apple, McDonald's, Facebook, IKEA, Sony, Nike, Samsung and those to come – rule the consumer universe of the 21ˢᵗ century, and in marketing terms they have universal appeal across all age boundaries. They are creating a common consumer experience, a common consciousness and a common source of consumer knowledge and information, generating in turn a common and ageless desire for global products across the developing and developed worlds, from 16 to 60, from Brighton to Boston and Beijing. In this new world of global consumption and ageless design, modern marketing must transform itself, argued Edward, and **go age-friendly**; go from assuming that youthful designs and products will appeal to all and any age groups, to recognising that the demographic revolution and the greying of the globe now put the older consumer in all their many shades of grey and silver at the forefront of commercial thinking and marketing. Moreover, the silver market might well be the solution, if not the salvation, for a UK economy seeking to recover and revive after the buffetings of Brexit just as it apparently was after 2008.

So, concluded Polly and Edward, within this new global context, post-war baby boomers once again have the opportunity to take centre stage, to be as much at the heart of the **economic universe** as they were 50 to 60 years ago when they were young teenagers. And at the heart of this boomer consumer revolution, yet again, will be women; older women not only as mass consumers, designers, models and even entrepreneurs but as revolutionaries in a new liberation movement, liberating women this time not from the power of men and the constraints and inequalities of the patriarchal societies of the 20th century but liberating them from their own self-images of womanhood in older age; from the tyranny of youth that pervades modern marketing and design and the monopoly image of feminine beauty that assumes beautiful women can only be young, sylph-like and sensual. As Professor Pat Thane and Dr Lorna Warren summed up in the 2014 British Academy Debates: "*Currently older women increasingly experience double standards in society's attitude towards them. They are expected to follow the ideals of Hollywood and fight or erase all signs of the ageing body, following an impossible ideal of sexualised beauty and youth. The rapidly expanding anti-ageing industry has grown vastly as a result. Women who do not make efforts to conform to this ideal become automatically invisible, can be denied active roles in society and are often subject to abuse.*"

The ageing world is upon us. Marketers have the opportunity to landscape it; baby boomers have the opportunity to lead it; and older women have the opportunity to liberate it, to feminise and personalise it for themselves rather than simply succumb to the whims and wishes of younger designers and marketers. The opportunities are there, the canvas is bare and the choice – whether to engage or exit, to participate or withdraw from this age redesign, or wait for it to be done for us – is *ours*, as older consumers, as ageing individuals and as a generation born to change and to challenge. And if manufacturers and marketers don't change their strategies and campaign paradigms, baby boomers

– even British baby boomers – will change it for them and go to Amazon in the West and Alibaba in the East to search online for what they want – '*what they really, really want*'. Moreover, as more and more baby boomers approach or enter their 70s, their strapline won't be 'we want it tomorrow' but 'we want it today', as tomorrow may never come, *and they know it*!

But boomers are only the frontline in redesign. What is really needed is an intergenerational strategy; a marketing strategy that cuts right across the age-lines not just along them. As KPMG's research in 2017 on global online consumers has highlighted, whatever the differences between the generations in online shopping, the similarities are increasingly stronger as attitudes and appetites converge and as baby boomers colonise areas previously occupied by the younger generations and make them their own. Twitter and Instagram may still be the millennials' preferred platform for social media but baby boomers are heavily into Facebook, and WhatsApp is now virtually an intergenerational medium of communication. As the Institute of Customer Service (ICS) highlighted in 2016, the core values of boomers and millennials are remarkably similar. Both value trust, high, if not excellent, levels of customer service and expect a personalised approach. As Jo Causon, CEO of the ICS put it, "*Business may think that Millennials and Baby Boomers value different things, but the reality is that they share similar desires: the difference is that they want them delivered in different ways.*" Boomers still prefer telephone and face-to-face interaction while millennials are happy to use social media, apps and digital communication.

Finally, while intergenerational marketing may open up new opportunities for British industry, it will equally open up these age markets to the unscrupulous and the criminal. As the Financial Conduct Authority (FCA) has warned, the global market ahead will need much stricter policing if older consumers are not to be exploited and scammed on a massive scale. While the 2018 FCA Report highlighted the immense variety of attitudes, ambitions and appetites that constitute older consumers today, ranging from the well-to-do established investor through to the small-scale saver and poorer pensioner scraping by on a low income and a few savings, its overall message was that all older people now face the serious and sustained dangers of financial exploitation, and that such threats are likely to escalate exponentially as they age – at the very time that their abilities to cope are in decline. The sheer size of this cohort and its latent wealth, estimated by the FCA as £2.9 trillion by 2036 in property alone, makes the silver consumer a highly attractive market for the fraudster and scammer, while bereavement, disability, dementia and deterioration in hearing, eyesight and memory make older consumers especially vulnerable, even when giving over lasting power of attorney (LPA) to trusted relatives. Day-to-day financial management alone becomes increasingly difficult for older consumers, particularly as new technology increasingly shifts shopping and banking online and away from face-to-face interaction; and although new technology is increasingly simplifying such processes and increasing protections with innovations such as fingerprinting or iris recognition, consumers in their 80s and 90s will become increasingly dependent on relatives or trusted others to manage their financial affairs and daily living – a burgeoning burden for younger families and an expanding market for fraudsters and hackers, and for unscrupulous relatives. The FCA is equally fearful about the longer-term realities of funding longer later lives. Older couples may have to refinance their houses and sell their assets as the mounting costs of long-term care draw ever closer. As the FCA has highlighted, the later life markets offer immense opportunities for the commercial and financial sectors, but if they're not strictly regulated, and older consumers fully protected, then the government and families at large are likely to face a financial and social scandal that may dwarf even that of 2008; a salutary but very timely message for Polly and her intergenerational campaign, as such a calamity and failure of government would send shock waves through every generation living and every household in the UK with ageing parents. Their finances will be in disarray, their wills unmade or contested, and fraudsters will be having a field day at their parents' expense.

So, as Polly and Edward concluded, while the new old have immense economic power and marketing potential and while major corporations are slowly recognising the power of the silver pound and the silver economy, converting such economic power into a force for fundamental change, a force for elevating ageing to the top of any marketer's agenda, and for making the future more age-friendly and age-defiant, is still a monumental challenge, however much Edward may relish it and Polly embrace it. It is but one strand in the political strategy slowly emerging from Polly's intergenerational discussions. It is but one strand in what she was now seeing as a tripartite alliance of economic, political and technological power: the silver purse, the grey vote and the shiny new technology that is already burning bright in ageing Japan.

13 | The New Old and Their Political Power: The Grey Vote and the Silver Lobby

As a Labour MP in the East of England, Polly was well aware of the growing power of the grey vote. Her constituency in Suffolk East originally centred on the town of Lowestoft where levels of poverty, deprivation and unemployment were amongst the highest in Europe. However, as a result of a recent boundary change, this constituency now extended across to Southwold and the idyllic Suffolk silver coast, inhabited largely by well-off pensioners looking for peace, quiet and a leisurely retirement. The contrast in her constituents was now quite stark and quite visible, a highly symbolic reminder of the social and economic chasms and schisms that currently divide Great Britain today. The growth of the energy industries, with wind farms springing up like daisies along the coast and the continued development of the Sizewell C power station, offered some prospect of an economic boom for this area, though many of the new jobs being created seemed to be going to EU migrants brought in by the foreign companies now operating these industries. Hence the groundswell of anti-immigrant, anti-EU sentiment that swept UKIP MEPs into office and led this part of the country to vote so wholeheartedly for Brexit. While Lowestoft had traditionally been a staunchly Labour area, the decline of its traditional industries and the ageing of its population had shifted the balance of Polly's vote from the town to the coast as the elderly population there had grown in number and in turnout while the young had stayed in town or migrated down south. However, while both sections of her constituency were strongly for Brexit and stronger controls on Britain's borders, they were fundamentally divided by age, class and geography on virtually everything else. Bridging such contrasting social and economic worlds and creating a political manifesto that both communities would buy into at the next election in 2020 or 2022 now represented the greatest challenge yet of Polly's political career. Polly needed to develop a new agenda that would on one hand unite and mobilise her constituents in common cause, and on the other reflect the core principles and ambitions of the National Labour Party if she was to mobilise any sort of support in Parliament. She needed to develop an all-age, all-class appeal that would inspire both young and old in this area and raise the intergenerational banner above traditional party politics. Such a strategy would require an in-depth appreciation of the shifting geology of British electoral politics and the emerging need of an ageing nation in the throes of Brexit and massive economic change as the UK sought to go it alone. Quite a task, quite a mission and in many ways the central theme of this book as Polly goes in search for a new age paradigm and a new political programme that will unearth the promises of longevity and so offer Great Britain a silver future rather than the grey one predicted by many pundits and feared by communities like Lowestoft.

Grey power in the UK has, until very recently, been a relatively dormant or latent power, a sleeping giant yet to be awakened by any common cause. Self-interest, social class, geography, gender and ethnicity have tended to predominate over age or generational-related issues in determining British elections and voting behaviour. Traditionally, the young and the middle-aged have been the focus of political campaigns in the UK, and it's only in recent years that the power of the grey lobby has begun to be recognised, and then usually only over the *headline* issues of pensions and healthcare. Pollsters such as Robert Worcester, founder of the polling organisation MORI, predicted the electoral shift to the grey vote some 20 years ago, and age charities like Age UK have sought to create their own political manifestos as far back as 2010.

Estimated Share of Votes Cast by People in Later Life

Age Band	2005	2010	2015	2025
65+	25%	27%	28%	31%
55+	43%	44%	44%	49%

Figure 1: **Voting power of older people**
(Age UK:2014)

Britain even has its own grey parties, but none of the size or influence found in other parts of Europe, even though, as UKIP has shown, where the cause is strong enough and where the response from the major political parties is weak enough, then minority parties – protest parties – have the opportunity to take the initiative, rouse the electorate and elevate their cause high up the British political agenda. However, while the influence of older voters in Britain has grown steadily in the last ten years, younger voters seem to have become increasingly disillusioned with a British political system that seems designed not only to ignore them but exclude them as well. As an Economic and Social Research Council (ESRC) study by Nottingham Trent University highlighted in 2012, fewer than one in five young people at that time had a positive view of political parties, and two-thirds of them saw *"past and present UK governments as dishonest and untrustworthy"*, a contrast in attitudes to voting and British politics that culminated in the **2015 British General Election**. Older voters turned out in droves and younger ones in trickles. While 78% of the over-65s voted in 2015, only 43% of the 18–24 age group did; a dramatic 35% points drop in generational voting and a collapse of the youth vote in the UK from the 67% turnout in 1992. Think tanks such as Demos (2014) began talking of a *"Generation Lost"*; and while the grey vote helped the Conservative Party get back into power after five years of coalition government, Labour suffered one of its worst election defeats in post-war history, and the Liberal Democrats were virtually cast into the political wilderness. The SNP swept to power in Scotland, winning all but one of the 57 parliamentary seats, while UKIP gained only one seat from its 1.4 million votes – a stark reflection of the electoral bias built into the UK's first-past-the-post system.

The 2016 EU Referendum, however, saw a significant reversal of this trend, with 53% of 18-24-year-old voters taking part, 73% of whom voted to stay in the EU. In contrast, over 75% of those aged 65+ cast their vote with 60% of those voting, voting to leave. The oldies, it appeared, had won the day; and so on a slim majority of 52/48%, Britain voted to leave the EU rather than stay in it. The electoral age divide, it appeared, had come of age; and as the historian Niall Ferguson declared in *The Sunday Times* (26 June 2016): "*Generation Led Zep has just kicked Britain down the Stairway to Hell*" – and out of the EU.

Age Band	Leave	Remain
18-24	27%	73%
25-34	38%	62%
35-44	48%	52%
45-54	56%	44%
55-64	57%	43%
65+	60%	40%

Figure 2: **EU Referendum Vote by Age**
(Adapted from IG Commission/Ashcroft polls: 2016)

The 2016 EU Referendum sent a shock wave, if not an age wave, through the British political system, leaving the British public stunned and the British political establishment in disarray. The prime minister, David Cameron, resigned to be replaced by Theresa May; the Labour Party suffered mass resignations within the Parliamentary Labour Party (PLP); and the threat of the breakup of the UK was revived as Scotland and even Northern Ireland reconsidered their relationship with England and the EU. But the Brexit vote didn't only send a shock wave through Great Britain; it shocked the European political elites too. It set off the possibility of a domino effect in other EU member countries facing elections in 2017, notably France, Germany and the Netherlands, as anti-immigrant, pro-nationalist feelings burst forth and threatened to overthrow the post-war political order and the liberal consensus that went with it. The shock election of Donald Trump in America in 2016 on a similar surge of national protectionism and anti-establishment sentiment only added to the growing uncertainty about the future direction of world politics and the world order. Age had come of age in democratic politics worldwide, as more than half of those over 64 years of age in America voted for Trump compared to a third of those aged 18–24. Meanwhile, in the UK nearly three years later, the economic shock waves – the falling pound, the stock market panics and the threat of jobs and trade to be lost – are still rumbling beneath the surface and are likely to continue even after the UK formally leaves the EU. So, for the young and old alike in the UK the future looks increasingly uncertain; and for organisations like the Intergenerational Foundation, the Referendum simply confirmed their view that Britain was becoming a gerontocracy, a grey tyranny, ruled *by* the old *for* the old (Craig Berry: 2013).

The 2017 'snap' election called by Theresa May, to cement her parliamentary majority and strengthen her hand in the forthcoming negotiations with the EU, ironically had the opposite effect. While 2015 and even the 2016 Referendum still left the older electorate in the driving seat in British politics, the 2017 election saw a dramatic resurgence of the young and the resurrection of the Labour Party as a potential government. As the post-election analyses by polling companies such as YouGov (2017) showed, while age continued to compete with class, and even gender, as the pre-eminent factor in political voting in the UK, the generational gap in previous elections seemed to have gone into reverse. As illustrated in Figure 3 below, while the young, the better educated and private renters were more likely to vote Labour, the older ages, homeowners and better-off remained staunchly Conservative. As YouGov put it: "*In electoral terms, Age is the new class,*" and according to a 2019 report by the Tory think tank Onward, the Conservative Party is haemorrhaging support from the under-50s at such a rate that it may soon lose "*its ability to govern*". Forty-nine per cent of Tory voters are apparently now age 65 and over and according to this poll only 8% of women aged 18–24 would vote Conservative today.

Vote by Age	Conservative	Labour
18–19	19%	66%
30–39	29%	55%
40–49	39%	44%
70+	69%	19%

Figure 3 **Age Vote in 2017 General Election**
(Adapted from YouGov: 2017)

With a minority government, Theresa May now had to negotiate a deal with the Democratic Unionist Party (DUP) of Northern Ireland to even continue in office, while the Labour vote leapt to over 40%, one of its highest in post-war history. Jeremy Corbyn emerged not only as a potential prime minister but as the poster boy of young people eager now to have their voice heard and the government changed. Jeremy Corbyn's appearance at Glastonbury was greeted by a frenzied outburst of 'Corbynmania' and the unrestrained shrieks of young women wearing 'Jezza' headgear. Age had once again emerged as a major factor in the outcome of a British election, but not this time because of the electoral turnout of the old but because of the turnout of the young, mobilised by *Momentum* and inspired by an ageing socialist whose apparently open style of campaigning and commitment to ending university tuition fees won waves of 18-24-year-olds back into the political fold. 'Generation Snowflake', as *The Sunday Times* called them, registered in record numbers – 1.05 million of them – and voted in constituencies with high student populations, dethroning a number of Conservative or Lib Dem MPs in the process. Labour campaigning, particularly through social media and such Facebook videos as *Tory Britain 2030*, generated a huge upsurge in politics not only amongst young white voters but amongst the black and minority ethnic communities too, while Jeremy Corbyn's street-side rallies had all ages pouring out onto the streets. Had young people voted in such numbers in the 2016 Referendum, the result might well have been somewhat different.

The period since 2017, however, has been dominated politically and socially by the Brexit debate and by Mrs May's government's failure to negotiate a withdrawal agreement with the EU that could attract a parliamentary majority in the House of Commons. This failure led to Britain having to take part in the 2019 European elections in which the Brexit party outstripped all others, the minority parties flew the flag for the Anti-Brexit vote and the two major political parties both suffered humiliating and heavy losses. It equally led to Mrs May's resignation as prime minister and to the turbulence and uncertainty of a Conservative party leadership contest as Britain approached it's second Brexit deadline in October 2019 led ironically now by Boris Johnson, one of the leading figures in the Leave campaign. As Matthew Goodwin (Sunday Times:Aug.2019) has argued the once stable two party system in the UK seems to have imploded and like politics in Europe, become much more "fragmented, populist, chaotic and unpredictable" The old adage that social class is the basis of British party politics no longer holds true. Age has now become the new dividing line with the younger generations struggling to get a life of their own in an age of austerity and the Tory party gaining support among non-graduates and the working class but losing it among young women, ethnic minorities, ascendant middle-class professionals and the young middle-aged. Parliamentary democracy is in the balance and the shape of British politics post-Brexit is now virtually unpredictable.

Devolution and Brexit have opened up deep divisions within the United Kingdom and threatened to undermine its future as a nation. They had laid bare slow burning schisms around generation, class, geography and race, fuelled by slow-burning resentment over inequality and exclusion. As Alan Milburn, previously chair of the Social Mobility Commission, argued in the Sunday Times (July 7th 2019) British politics-and European politics- has swung to the extremes, leaving those who identify with neither the hard left or far right in deep despair as "the new disenfranchised" The new politics, in his view, revolves around three "I"s-identity, immigration and inequality which together "pose an existential threat" to both the post war political order and the global consensus of open markets, free trade and globalisation. Globalisation has overwhelmingly benefitted the rich and better-off with 40% of economic growth in the UK over the past 40 years having gone to the top 10% but only 10% has benefitted the bottom half of the income distribution. "*Poverty, once the preserve of the workless, is now concentrated in working families.*" The poor, the young, the North and more recently the Caribbean immigrants of the Windrush generation continue to feel excluded from power and ignored by the British political establishment and they have reacted by turning inward to old identities and a yearning to "take back control"; a yearning that Brexit suddenly and ironically gave full voice to. As the Joseph Rowntree Foundation declared in 2018: "Britain is a deeply divided country" and although "*The 2017 general election took place in the shadow of Brexit… it also presented more marginalised sectors of British society – voters on low incomes, those in poverty and who are struggling to get by – with a far more meaningful choice than that seen at previous elections.*" The young, at least, seemed to emerge from the 2017 election with a stronger political voice after the successes of the Labour Party two years ago and possibly by the rise of younger political leaders across the globe- Emmanuel Macron (aged 39) in France, Jacinda Ardern in New Zealand (37), Sebastian Kurz in Austria (31), Leo Varadkar in Eire (38), Justin Trudeau in Canada (45) and of course Kim Jong-Un in North Korea (33)-but overall the grey vote generally – and the boomer vote in particular – remains a dominant force that no politician can ignore.

The challenge now for Polly, though, was how, amid all this political turbulence and flux, to convert both younger and older voters to the notion of an intergenerational cause; how to create a political manifesto that combined both their short-term interests and their long-term needs into a multigenerational mission for a better Britain for all ages; how to inspire the age generativity and age generosity so aptly expressed in the Age UK Manifesto in 2015:

"When we vote, it is for everyone's future. We are not a voting bloc with interests set apart from the rest of society. We care about our families' and our grandchildren's futures – from schools to global warming. We know that our well-being depends on a strong economy and strong families. And we know that, whatever age, everyone should be able to expect a happy and secure later life."

Certainly, Polly was quite clear that a one-age strategy, a grey-vote-only campaign would not only be counterproductive, alienating young voters even more, but that it might reinforce an age divide that even Jeremy Corbyn might find difficult to bridge or break down. Reversing the disillusion and alienation that many young people still feel with traditional British politics has to be, in Polly's view, the primary challenge of the next five years if young people's sense of generational injustice is not to escalate and the baby boomers are not to become the new-age enemy. Jeremy Corbyn has shown how to reach out to the young but getting Labour back into government will still take a monumental campaign that encapsulates and embraces all ages. Alan Milburn's proposal for a government of national unity may eventually prove to be a serious alternative.

So now Polly was clearer about her intergenerational cause and two of her intergenerational powerhouses: the silver economy and the grey vote. So, what has new technology possibly got to offer that the other two haven't? asked Polly. Everything, answered Hannah, as she and Edward shone a bright shiny light on the silver technology awaiting to transform later life in the 21st century.

14 | The New Old and Technological Power: New Technology and Silver Liberation

If there is one force that truly holds the promise of liberating older people and realising the true promise – the full fruits of longevity in later life – it's new technology. As Star Wars often promised, the 'Force is with us' but this time, hopefully, with the old as well as the young. New technology is potentially the 21st-century gift to longevity, a global force for age liberation, offering huge new opportunities for 'liberating' older people from the restrictions and constrictions of their ageing bodies and declining memories. Moreover, the elderly of the future are not the elderly of the past. The new old, the post-war baby boomers are a new breed of elderly.

They are eager consumers of new technology, keen to apply its wonders to their homes, their lifestyles and to their personal well-being. Their homes are stuffed full of the latest gadgets from Apple or Amazon; and what they don't know or don't understand, their children or grandchildren can help them with.

But not all older people today are so well endowed. Not all baby boomers enjoy such continued health. All grew up before the advent of the digital revolution and most went to work in an era or an environment where ill health was normal and the work environment hazardous. Many older boomers today face shorter, less healthy and wealthy lives than their better-off counterparts in other parts of the country. As described earlier, this was the situation facing Polly's younger brother Wilfred as he entered retirement early on grounds of ill-health that had accumulated after many long years in the Sunderland shipyards, alongside his addiction to smoking. His wife, Wilma, was in better health overall but she too was now showing signs of early arthritis and back strain from her years in hospitals and care homes, as well as caring for both her elderly mother and for Wilfred's dad, Alfred, still a sprightly 89, living locally in Sunderland but on his own. And that is the challenge that inspired Wilfred's son Derek after he graduated as an electronics engineer. A family dilemma now became a professional opportunity to start his own business and an opportunity to help the millions of other boomers of his parents' generation retire comfortably and as independently as they wished. Here was a golden opportunity to pay back his parents for all the years of loving support and personal sacrifice that had enabled him to go to university and on to a career and a lifestyle well beyond anything that his parents could have aspired to or dreamt of. Equally, it offered the opportunity to work more closely with his 25-year-old daughter Dawn, given her post-graduate research in robotics and artificial intelligence at Bath University, MIT and most recently her work placement with Panasonic in Japan. Derek's technical and business experience, alongside Dawn's specialist skillset, he believed would prove a winning intergenerational combination not only for his parents but for their future too. Uncle Donald was happy to put up the necessary capital to start the business, and his son Edward was keen to provide the market research needed to help open up what appeared to be one of the great silver markets of the future: the 'smart' markets of new technology and the ageing populations of societies East and West in the 21st century. This whole area fascinated Polly. It was 'manna from heaven' both personally and professionally. It not only relieved some of the pressure, and the guilt, she felt in not helping her younger brother earlier, but it offered a magic box for converting her ageing manifesto from a theoretical political promise into a practical and technological solution that potentially could transform the life and living of all ages of old people wherever they lived in Great Britain. New technology, for her, could be the key that unlocked and delivered the full promise of the gift of longevity and, as she had seen on her trip to Japan, transform the UK from a potentially ageing graveyard into a silver paradise for later life. Family visits by her and her GP husband David up to the North East now became a regular event as Polly soaked up Derek and Dawn's visions of the technological world ahead.

And visions there certainly are, as the new technologies of the future begin unveiling a new world of wonder and new frontiers to explore for modern scientific research and development. Previously such visions were no more than figments and fancies in the imaginations of mad scientists, science fiction writers and films like *Star Trek, Star Wars* and *Doctor Who*. 'The force', however, is now with us and the smart new technologies of the 21st century are already beginning to become commonplace, to infiltrate our lives and seep into the very fabric of our homes, our roads – and even our clothing. Amazon's Alexa is already at home in millions of households across the world, co-ordinating the family network and linking it to the World Wide Web (and to the mothership that is Amazon.com). New technology is already connecting most of us to a global world that is both real and virtual; a world in which reality from across the planet can be brought into the home or the workplace; virtual worlds and now augmented worlds that can be created at the touch of a mouse or a swipe of a finger. As the WEF (2016) has argued, new technology is at the heart of the Fourth Industrial Revolution and at the heart of transforming ageing from a social burden into an economic asset, capable of driving rather than impeding economic growth in the 21st century. Moreover, this 21st-century revolution is poised to go into overdrive with 5G mobile internet about to be launched later in 2019. 5G is apparently capable of download speeds up to 20 times faster than today and creating wireless networks capable of supporting driverless cars, revolutionising smart manufacturing and powering smart cities where buildings 'talk' to each other and urban management systems predict and prevent traffic jams and burst water mains before they even happen. Potentially, we are moving from communication between humans to communication between 'things', with massive gains in productivity and huge savings in efficiency and costs.

In what became regular family meetings, Derek, Dawn and Edward began to set out for their boomer parents the enormous range and riches of new technology, technology that represented not only new inventions and applications for everyday life but, in the view of Sarwant Singh (2012), represents "*whole new mega-trends in changing the future*"; mega-trends that are already emerging today; mega-trends that potentially could transform life for the elderly as we know it; megatrends that are already transforming life for Grandad Albert Powley (see Chapter 4):

- **Smart houses** operating at the touch of a remote control and wired up to alert all of the family to any elderly crisis will, he predicts, become the norm. Older people will not need to rely on family visiting or neighbours calling in to look after them; rather the 'house' will do it all for them, through climate control in every room, effortless replenishment of the fridge, bathroom and kitchen, integrated multi-media and home energy management controlling energy use and charging the electric car.

- **Smart phones and Skype-type screens** through which they can communicate with family, friends, grandchildren and the outside world, through which they can order 'driverless' cars to take them shopping and where they wish, through which they, and their families, can monitor their health, order food and clothing and pay bills and purchases automatically.

- **Smart robots who** will be the new companion, slave or maid for the elderly, providing unlimited 24/7 care and companionship as well as monitoring health and happiness. The 'da Vinci' robot, developed for medical operations, for example, has four robotic arms, one for manipulating a video camera and three for precision surgery.

- **Smart healthcare** treatments that will continually monitor elderly health, give early warning of illness, detect cancer and ensure that older people adhere to their medication schedules. Robo-doctors who will not only diagnose patients but treat them too.

As the above examples illustrate, explained Edward, not only is later life being transformed but whole new industries are being created. There is a paradigm shift within virtually every field of elderly healthcare on the horizon; and the psychological, emotional and even spiritual well-being of all people will soon be as much part of the diagnosis as the cure or repair of the 'wobbly bits' that are about to fall off. With longevity, with more and more people living into their 80s, 90s and even beyond, Edward predicted a revolution in thinking and practice in eldercare in the near future as advances in personal technology put the ailing patient at the centre of future healthcare not on the periphery as at present. In the meantime, predicted Derek, 'virtual' and 'augmented' reality will soon open up the possibility of a second or parallel life in retirement. Through the internet and new forms of interactive technology, the elderly of the future will be able to explore the outside world, visit where they wish and meet whoever they want from the comfort of their own armchair and the safety of their own home – aided by the new generation of artificially intelligent 'virtual assistants' like Apple's Siri, Google Voice and Amazon's Alexa. They can shop online, learn online and socialise online, not only with real friends and relatives but with virtual ones and even avatars. The virtual reality of the future offers retirees a whole new world to explore and even the opportunity of a 'second life'. Actroid maids and butlers will soon be available to relieve the old of all household chores and remind them of whatever tablets they have forgotten to take. The ageing body of tomorrow, claimed Derek, is about to be liberated from pain and disability, and older people will soon be enabled by new technology to take as full a part in the outside world as they wish.

Futurologists such as Michio Kaku go even further. Back in 2012 he predicted that the 21st century would see three primary phases of technological transformation, each of which would eventually bring immense benefits not only to the old but to the young too, as the century advanced:

The **near term** (2010–2030), comprising technological developments that in many cases are already with us, such as:

- **The 'driverless' car** capable of navigating all roads, avoiding accidents and traffic jams and responding to the driver's mood even if he or she falls asleep – ideal for drivers over 40 let alone those over 70, and possibly the ultimate solution to that traumatic and decisive moment in any older person's life when their car keys are finally taken away from them and they are subsequently marooned at home.

- **Wall-to-wall internet screens** in older people's homes will allow them to age in a place of safely and to keep in instant contact with family and friends, convene a family reunion or meeting at home, make new friends abroad and even have a romantic evening at home with a 'distant' date.

- **Second-life living** in virtual worlds of their own creation that – possibly with the aid of an avatar – will allow older people to explore any world they wish, including the past; meet new people, real and imaginary; and even date and marry a new spouse of their choice. The world will genuinely be the elder person's oyster, even if they are isolated or house-bound. The elderly of tomorrow will be able, it is claimed, to get out and about without actually leaving home and, if they wish, they will even be able to do some paid or voluntary work from their rocking chair.

By **mid-century** (2030–2070), Professor Kaku believes you will be able to explore the whole universe from the comfort of your armchair, walk on the moon and even enter a fully functional cyber world where the invisible becomes visible. You will be able to see the world in 3-D and create holograms as bright and real as those in such films as *Star Wars* and *Avatar*. And by **far future** (2070–2100) Kaku (2014) predicts that we will control the world simply by thought, through what he calls *"altered consciousness"*. Like Greek Gods, we – or at least our children – will enjoy instant obedience to our every wish from robots, avatars and artificially intelligent computers linked into our every thought and capable, even, of responding to our commands before we actually issue them. Through the power of biotechnology, we will be able to create perfect bodies and extend our lifespans; and through the power of 3D and nanotechnology, we will be able to take an object and turn it into something else, to create something seemingly out of nothing. By 2100, predicts Kaku, we will have replicators, machines the size and shape of a washing machine, capable through nanotechnology and atomisation of converting raw materials into entirely new products at the touch of a button, and at home rather than in a factory thousands of miles away in China or Taiwan, while space elevators will be able to whisk us away to new planets if life on earth gets too much.

Meanwhile, Artificial Intelligence, explained Dawn, is about to take over the universe; preparing to take over the world – the world of work, of transport, of health, of communication and even the world of later life. AI, predicted Dawn, will not only be embedded in all our new gadgets but

inside our daily lives – and probably, increasingly, in our heads. Artificial intelligence is creating a robot revolution; a new breed of robots that is not only highly intelligent but capable of emotional empathy; robots that are capable of becoming receptionists in hotels as well as nurses and even doctors in hospitals and the home. For Japan, and its multinational corporations, robots are the future. They are part of Japan's 'total solution' to the challenge of being the oldest society on the planet. They are Japan's solution to once again being a dominant force economically and technologically in the ageing world ahead. And now China is bounding ahead too, investing billions in transforming itself from being the manufacturing centre of the world into becoming the centre of the AI universe. Artificial intelligence will soon be embedded in every aspect of work and everyday life and, as the Japanese are already doing, personalised in the process. Robots increasingly look and act like humans, and the latest models at the Henn na Hotel in Nagasaki, for example, even look quite glamorous and professional. Such receptionists, as Polly discovered, are brilliant at greeting people and answering routine questions but so far they still need human help in dealing with awkward customers.

The Consumer Electronics Show (CES) in Las Vegas in January 2018 was a showcase of what AI already has to offer, with driverless cars conveying customers around, robot waiters carrying their luggage and bringing them food, and Google's new Assistant coordinating it all. Even Barbie is being updated as a hologram capable of holding conversations with young children; and AI is revolutionising modern medicine, with androids aiding surgeons in the operating theatre, scanning X-rays for signs of lung disease and developing smart phones capable of telling you when you are ill. Robo-doctors are now in actual practice and, unlike humans, can happily and efficiently work all hours, all day with minimal stress or strain. Through 'deep learning' they can access and correlate vast databases of medical information way beyond human capability or even understanding, and do so in seconds. According to Professor McFee of MIT, robots and AI will increasingly replace, and potentially liberate, human labour from routine and repetitive tasks, "*drudgery and toil*", but by working alongside human beings rather than ousting them altogether from the world of work. Uber predicts that robot-taxis will soon be so available, accessible and cheap that there will be no reason to own a car, or need a parking space, while as suggested in Chapter 8, the advent of sexbots may not only wipe out the oldest profession in the world but transform marriage and personal relationships amongst couples of all ages.

The 2017 McKinsey report on analytics, AI and automation identified three key factors driving the current and accelerating pace of robotics and automation. The progress in machine-learning algorithms and the advent of deep learning; the continuing and exponential increase in computing capacity and miniaturisation; the creation and ease of access to vast databanks of information that can be used to teach learning machines, including interchange between ourselves and the likes of Amazon or Google, and between machines themselves: the **Internet of Things**. According to IBM (2017), 90% of the world's current databank has been created just in the last two years, Google's DeepMind AlphaGo defeated the world champion of Go, the world's most complex game, and researchers at Oxford University have created a lip-reading system more accurate than a professional translator. Commercial and financial transactions can be exponentially streamlined and error free, transport machinery can be automated, energy costs dramatically reduced and even checkouts made redundant. AI can equally tackle what McKinsey called "*moonshot*" challenges, such as treatments for incurable diseases such as cancer, or ways to avert or reverse climate change. The 2018 McKinsey report estimated that while "*about 30% of the activities in 60% of all occupations could be automated*", ranging from welders and landscape gardeners to mortgage brokers and CEOs, currently only about 5% of occupations are fully automated. This is partly because AI itself is still under-developed and limited to specific problem-solving rather than the 'general intelligence' of human beings, and partly due, too, to sectors such as education and construction lagging well behind such leading adopters as financial services and the automobile industry. The potential of AI is nevertheless huge in transforming productivity, adding as much as $13 trillion to global GDP and in creating 555 to 890 million new jobs to offset the 400 million workers potentially displaced by automation worldwide. The challenge for governments and employers is in how to invest in and deploy AI while retaining worker trust and public confidence that AI and automation are benefits for the future not threats of today.

Whole new ways of working, whole new ways of making goods and services, and of distributing them, will soon emerge, while futurologists such as Elon Musk are not only designing driverless electric cars and sending people into space but planning to download human memories and develop brain-to-machine communication. His latest company Neuralink, for example, is researching cures for brain conditions such as paralysis and memory loss. Automation and AI are already transforming the world's financial markets as Robotic Process Automation (RPA) reduces the processing time for financial transactions from days to seconds; new challenger banks are undermining the monopoly power of the current Big Four banks, and new finance companies are offering financial products and services never available before. Artificial intelligence will, it seems, soon not only coordinate global financial transactions but take control and communicate financial decisions back to customers through complex algorithms and chat-boxes connected to people's smartphones. Financial start-ups are emerging at an accelerating rate, challenging and transforming traditional ways of banking and insurance

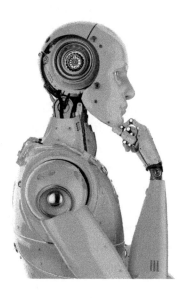

by offering new types of mortgage or rental agreements (*Dlighted*), stress-free conveyancing (*Habito*) and even insurance contracts irrespective of age or illnesses (*Bought By Many*). Blockchain is predicted to totally transform traditional interbank transactions by removing the need for a trusted intermediary such as SWIFT and yet still provide an open and accurate transaction trail that any client or regulator could follow. Modern banking could soon become an exemplar of openness and transparency in stark contrast to its complex and opaque arrangements today. What is wonderful at one level is the way AI could potentially simplify the world today and relieve humans of most of the mundane tasks of working life or day-to-day living. What is fearful about AI at another level is the degree of control and even decision-making being put into the hands of algorithms and automated machines by big business, big government – and by us!

Predictions of a whole new generation of super-robots capable of competing or co-operating directly with human beings as equals or even superior beings, however, raises fundamental questions about the future of the human race. Robots capable of not only out-thinking most human beings but capable of reproducing themselves, and even of cross-breeding with human beings, strikes at the very heart of humankind as a species. Yet, we are already progressing down that pathway as disabled humans seek technological solutions to renovate their bodies – and their humanity.

So, physical ageing may be a thing of the past by the middle or far future. We may have moved from inhabiting an ageing body into living in an ageless one, from living in an autonomous biological body to living in a mechanical body that is linked to a computer and to other people across the planet in a global virtual reality. Free from the physical limitations of the human body and with advanced technology to vastly expand and augment the human mind, the only limitation on human development will be the human imagination. The elders of tomorrow – our grandchildren – will, according to such futurologists, be able to live without fear or constraint, be as young and active as they want to be and able to travel the universe by mind or matter with a robot as an intelligent companion, servant or slave. They will be immortal and unstoppable. Fantastic though such visions might seem, the forces behind this super-scientific revolution – the internet, the global economy, the global media and the new global middle classes – already exist and interplanetary travel is already a real prospect, with Richard Branson, Paul Allen and other tycoons seeking to open up space to the travelling public; while internet billionaire Dmitry Itskov plans to go further and, through his 2045 Initiative, create an avatar or robot with a human personality so he never 'dies' – a latter-day *Iron Man*.

AI, though, is not only a technological and economic force, predicted Derek. It is likely to become a political force too – a new arena for world domination as China invests billions in becoming the AI centre of the world under its Made in China 2025 plan, with its own Silicon Valley northwest of Beijing. The Chinese tech giants Lenovo and Baidu have invested billions of dollars – \$20–\$30 billion in 2016 alone – in robotics, computer vision, language development, machine learning and virtual assistants (McKinsey: 2017). Chinese tech giants such as Huawei are already outstripping the smartphones of their American and Western competitors, and WeChat's 'magic button' apparently records virtually everything any Chinese citizen might do, buy or say. The Chinese State today can '*see everything*', and in the process create personal 'social credit' ratings for rewarding the dutiful and punishing the deviant. As Kai Strittmatter (2018) has described in chilling detail, the Chinese state is fast creating the perfect surveillance society; not only because Big Brother can see all and be everywhere but because through the 'social credit system' on their smartphones the Chinese people seem to submit to self-censorship; to surveying themselves in exchange for economic prosperity and social peace. Through Tencent's WeChat and Alibaba's Alipay, the Chinese people can pay for everything and talk to anyone but with the Chinese State looking over their shoulder and looking into their heads; not only collecting data on what they are currently doing but predicting through advanced algorithms what they might do next – a perfect mix of Orwell's *1984*, Huxley's *Brave New World* and Spielberg's *Minority Report*. Big Brother is alive and well in modern China; and its high-tech companies, its BATs (Baidu-Alibaba-Tencent), have a captive market of over one billion people to sustain them as and when they begin to expand abroad. Vast new shopping malls have apparently been created in China where face recognition allows consumers to pick up goods without formally paying for them at a checkout; and AI analyses of body language allow retailers to spot potential buyers more accurately than their sales staff can. E-bikes, e-commerce, mobile payments and high-speed rail are boom areas as China moves to becoming a cashless society – even for beggars.

Even in the UK, our utility industries are already heavily controlled by computers that can readily predict rises and falls in demand and supply; retailers can already predict consumer choice from past purchases and current browsing; while drones not only man and operate Amazon's massive new warehouses but will soon, apparently, be delivering goods directly to your home. Healthcare may be more resistant at present to AI but patient health-monitoring tools, personalised treatment plans and robo-nurses and doctors are fast appearing in hospitals abroad, so what's next, for example, for schools and education – virtual learning assistants, personalised learning plans and robo-teachers? There is, claims MGI (2017), a sudden and dramatic confluence of technological developments, ranging from a step-

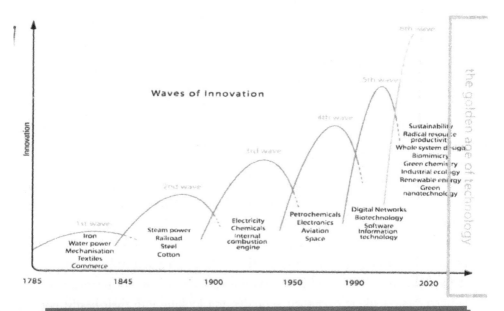

Figure 1: **Long Waves of Technology: (Aguilar-Millan: 2014)**

change increase in computing power to ever-more sophisticated algorithms, that is creating the conditions and toolset for AI to leap into the next digital frontier and not only embed itself firmly in our industries, homes and daily lives but to fundamentally transform the world we live in. So profound are the changes being wrought by globalisation and new technology that the European Futures Observatory, a highly respectable academic organisation not normally given to fanciful speculation, was even moved to raise the possibility of a new **singularity**, of a new and unparalleled stage in the scale of social and economic transformation comparable to the agricultural and Industrial Revolutions the 18th and 19th centuries, but with even more dramatic and devastating effect, with even greater speed and scale, and with the potential for international disruption on a global, even planetary, scale. We may, according to Dr Stephen Aguilar-Millan of the World Future Review, be entering a new stage, a **sixth wave** in the progression of technological and social paradigms; a Fourth Industrial Revolution, as Professor Klaus Schwab (2016) has described it.

So, new technology is advancing at breakneck speed. It offers an immense opportunity to liberate the ageing and the aged from the bonds of their ageing bodies and so enable them to participate actively in the world ahead. The major Japanese corporations are already gearing up for the robot revolution that they see as the next great market opportunity not just in Japan today but across the world. And the baby boomer generation will certainly not be backward in getting their ageing hands on whatever new technology becomes available and redesigning it for their own use and enjoyment; and so, in their own way, contributing to its overall development. Derek and Dawn, with wider family support, are determined to get onto this global bandwagon, to identify and develop a robotic business of their own using ideas and developments from countries as far afield as Japan and South Korea, while using their own parents and grandparents as tech guinea pigs to test out how the older generations might actually respond in practice. Derek was highly entertained, if not inspired, by the film *Robot and Frank*, in which a middle-aged son, concerned about his ageing father's isolation and ill health, buys him a robot of his own, one that looks like something from *Star Wars* or the Honda adverts. At first Frank resents this intrusion into his isolated, rural lifestyle but when he realises that actually the robot is quite intelligent and perfectly capable of learning new tasks, Frank suddenly sees the opportunity for a new lease of life; not a new life for the future but a return to his old life as a jewel thief. So he recruits the robot as his partner in crime, uses his technical skills to hack into computerised security systems and, between them, Frank and the robot set off a crimewave that completely foxes the local police. A new type of partnership was formed, one that gave Frank a whole new purpose in life, even if it wasn't quite the one that Frank's son had intended. Entertaining as this example is, it is nevertheless indicative of how ageing boomers might convert, or in this case subvert, new technology for their own use.

Adaptation, in Derek's view, is the key to future success, and so he has spent considerable time trying to really understand what technology and in what form would be of most benefit to parents who were neither experts nor technophobes. His aim is to engage his ageing parents and grandparents in actively using new technologies for their own use rather than depending on it as part of someone else's grand scheme of how life ought to be used. His thinking here draws heavily on the insights of Joseph F Coughlin (2016) and his view that active ageing in an ageing society needs more than a never-ending toy shop of new wonder gadgets. It is about a new way of life, a new style of life, one that requires the right IT platforms and the proper infrastructure for new technology to become an asset rather than a liability. It is a platform to promote healthy living not only for the elderly but for all ages. We need to move away from focusing on individual developments, such as driverless cars or personalised computers, and look instead to developing technology platforms and infrastructures that are future-proof, that can support and co-ordinate new technology in the long-term and so provide a new way of life for all of us. We need to focus first on **ageing in place**.

We need to think of **the home as a platform**, where we provide or receive care, where we live and work. We need, argues Joseph Coughlin, to invest as much in the infrastructure supporting and co-ordinating the home with the outside world, with family, with carers and local transportation as we do on any new gadgets. Age technology, in his view, will not only support the ageing themselves but hugely benefit society at large in driving innovation, stimulating the economy and resetting the political agenda. It will perhaps inspire a paradigm shift from profit and growth towards healthy living, well-being and the quality of modern life. We need to integrate technology, therefore, into the lifestyles of everyone, not just the elderly, and every home should at least have a health station for all the family. As the MGI report in 2015 highlighted, the distinctive – and the disruptive – feature of new technology and the internet today is the way in which it has become embedded into our lifestyle at a speed that is both awesome and potentially extremely disruptive. It took more than 50 years for the telephone to enter most people's homes and 38 years for radio to attract 50 million listeners. YouTube, Google and Twitter have achieved the same in less than 20 years and are now an integral part of most peoples' lives with billions of users across the planet. Facebook, for example, has more members now than China has inhabitants. As the authors of the MGI report concluded, innovation is spreading at such a rapid rate that it is now *"beyond the power of human intuition to anticipate"*; and as Derek became increasingly aware – and uneasy about – it is potentially becoming beyond the power of humans to control.

As Stephen Hawking commented in his final publication (*Brief Answers to the Big Questions*: 2018): *"Creating AI would be the biggest event in human history. Unfortunately, it might also be the last, unless we learn how to avoid the risks."* When AI becomes better than humans at AI design and it can improve itself without human help then *"we may face an intelligence explosion"* over which we have no control. Mass unemployment and exploitation in the first Industrial Revolution led to fascism, Marxism and revolution. The mass invasion of AI into every aspect of human life opens us up to hackers and the dark side of the net. It equally opens up the prospect of robo-cops, robo-soldiers and robo-wars with robo-politicians controlling weapons of mass destruction. While all this may sound very *1984* and *Brave New World*, possibly the scariest point is that AI may already be slipping out of human control with leading researchers in the Silicon Valley admitting that even they don't know exactly how deep learning works – ***only the robots do***. Robo-doctors may transform modern medicine and hugely relieve the immense pressures on the NHS, but what of the professional and ethical questions of a robo-doctor making a misdiagnosis or error? How can robots be held to account? How might such errors of professional judgement be judged when many human life and death decisions involve emotional intelligence as well as rational analysis? Add to these ethical dilemmas the existential ones arising from the advent of the genome and the revolution in DNA, which is raising not only the prospect of DNA editing to cut out rogue genes but creating CRISPR, the means to redesign life. CRISPR has apparently already created tomatoes that never rot, double-muscle dogs capable of patrolling crowds, and cows without horns. What's next? Children without parents and superhumans with superpowers? Or worse will super intelligent robots simply exterminate the human race, not as Tom Chivers (2019) explains *"out of malice or hatred"* but because we are inconvenient and no longer have any use.

As the McKinsey report on AI in April 2019 noted, while the value of AI is becoming undeniable and its corporate take-up widespread with a projected economic output globally of $13 trillion per year, the risks are escalating beyond current controls. Risks that include data difficulties and violations of privacy regulations, technology problems with software compliance, security snags allowing fraudsters to access and exploit sensitive commercial and personal information, 'models misbehaving' when, say, algorithms target the wrong demographic and interaction issues when automated systems override human judgement or humans mistakenly override their computers and plunge a plane or a self-driving car into catastrophe – not to mention when hackers or terrorist do. Few businesses, however, seem to be fully aware of such risks or organised at every level to "root them out" at source rather than merely respond when they happen.

The WEF (2017) now has AI and robotics firmly within its top ten of global risks; and publications are now pouring out monthly, warning of the dangers ahead, ranging from Jaron Lanier's *Ten Arguments for Deleting Your Social Media Accounts Right Now* (2018) and Mark O'Connell's exposé of transhumanism (*To Be a Machine*: 2018) through to Jamie Bartlett's attempt to reveal *How the Internet is Killing Democracy* (2018) and Roger

McNamee's call for all of us to *Wake Up to the Facebook Catastrophe* (2019). Younger generations, notably Generation Z, have never known life without technology, and many live a split life torn between the simplicities and artificially created identities of virtual reality and the challenges and complexities of real life – and cannot cope. As Jenny McCarthy summed it up in *The Sunday Times* (30 Dec. 2018): "*Technology, that once exciting friend, is turning treacherous: the depictions of lives they see online are often fake, as is much circulating news, doctored imagery and bot-powered web traffic. The feelings that such technology engenders, however, can be painfully real.*" Ironically, while many of the owners of such technologies are apparently either banning smartphones and the like for their own children, or at least severely limiting their use, they are promoting it overtly or covertly for everyone else's. Government investigations into the power and impact of the tech giants have been initiated in America, Europe and the UK, and researchers at the Korean Advanced Institute of Science and Technology (KAIST) have even gone as far as to boycott work on the development of killer robots.

Leading academics have become so concerned about the potential directions of new technology that they created the Centre for the Study of Existential Risk (CSER) at Cambridge University to identify the risks as well as the benefits of globalisation and new technology, and in particular to identify the potential of artificial intelligence to enslave the world as well as to liberate it. There is a danger that the age of man (Anthropocene) will give way to the age of the machine (Technocene) and, according to economists Erik Brynjolfsson and Andrew McAfee (2014), to a second machine age, to an age where machines can think for themselves and who have their own network of communication. In their follow-up publication, *Machine, Platform, Crowd* (2017), Brynjolfsson & McAfee even suggest that not only might AI and the internet create perfect markets as demand and supply are synchronised seamlessly and instantly but that humankind and machines might move into perfect partnerships as each specialises in their particular field – humans in emotional intelligence; machines in rationalising organisation and production, and in solving logical problems. Futurologists predict that by 2040 robots are likely to be capable of conscious, and even independent thinking, initiating dialogue with humans as well as merely responding to questions and to prompts as at present. Robots are apparently already making music and art, beginning to write fiction and poetry, and Amazon's Echo has even been called as a witness to a murder. The global economy of today is likely to give way to a new form of global capitalism, a machine-centric capitalism, where intelligent machines and algorithms are in control rather than humans; where skilled workers and even professions such as lawyers and doctors are under threat, where the traditional middle and working classes evaporate leaving a new hyper-meritocracy of billionaires at the top and poverty-stricken beggars at the bottom, with little in between. Global inequality on this scale is likely to be the ultimate social and economic chasm and one that stretches right across the world.

But it's not change itself that is the issue. It is the **speed** of change and the fact that in the 21ˢᵗ century it seems to be accelerating at a speed beyond man's capacity to understand it, let alone control it. The world, particularly the worlds of the global economy and new technology, seems to be out of anyone's control, except possibly the new 'masters of the universe': the Googles, Amazons, Alibabas and Apples of this world and their successors. Hence the political backlash evident in many Western democracies against the existing political order as people increasingly feel powerless against a world out of their control. Just as new technology and home robots could liberate the elderly of tomorrow, they could equally imprison or enslave them. While the internet seems to offer the means to bring the whole of mankind together as one great global community in perfect harmony and communication, it equally opens up the whole world, particularly the world of the elderly and aged, to the armies of teenage hackers, cyber-attackers and even terrorists lurking on the dark side. Hackers seem to be able to breach the most sophisticated and apparently secure firewalls; cyber-attackers to disrupt even US Presidential elections; and terrorists may soon be adapting Amazon-style drones for deliveries of their own. They will have little trouble hacking into the homes or cars of the elderly, however sophisticated their domestic technology, and taking over their lives and their accounts without them even knowing. As fast as smart technology infiltrates and exposes our personal lives, financial details and purchasing tastes, criminals, terrorists, hackers – malevolent or mischievous – and government agencies will swiftly follow. You may be looking forward to driving a driverless car, but so too are the hackers who have already shown that they can take over its controls from miles away. Certainly, as *The Sunday Times/Raconteur* article on Cybersecurity in February 2019 made abundantly clear, computer hacking has now gone way beyond the early guerrilla warfare of lonely individuals in dark places testing and teasing the firewalls of corporate business and the home security systems of private individuals. Cybercrime is now big business, conservatively estimated to generate some $1.5 trillion in income a year equivalent to the GDP of Russia. Cybercriminals now employ armies of highly trained hackers and use the very latest in artificial intelligence as they seek not only to penetrate and infiltrate the fortress firewalls of national governments and major corporations but to bring them down. We are now engaged in what appears to be a 'Cyber Cold War' where *"AI is both the weapon of mass destruction and part of the sophisticated solution. And the AI arms race is just beginning."* So we may live in a 'smarter' world but it's a far less secure and private one as on one hand companies such as Google, Amazon and Facebook continue data-mining, extracting huge volumes of information or big data from us, to inform their supply chains, their designs, their marketing and our future purchasing power; while on the other hand, cybercriminals seek to steal their data, our identities and everyone's money. The Googles of the future may aspire to be the new Big Brothers, but will the emerging generation of hackers disrupt even their all-powerful universe?

Certainly, as academics such as Professor Tyler Cowen (2013) have argued, it does appear at times that the Googles and Amazons of this world are actually planning world domination. Irwin Stelzer of *The Sunday Times*, for example, has described these young 'Amazonians' as a new breed of young capitalist, a global breed on a mission to systemise and make all the world's knowledge accessible (Google), to connect all the world's people (Facebook), to change the way we shop, read and enjoy music (Amazon and Apple), to move people around cities more efficiently (Uber), and to enable them to chat and gossip incessantly (Twitter). And they are all, as Stelzer puts it, *"Disrupters"*; disrupters on a global scale out to use *"creative destruction"* as *the* means for revolutionising modern capitalism and for creating the greatest material wealth the world has ever seen. These 'high priests' of Silicon Valley – or as they hope to make it soon, the Silicon State – see themselves as above national or even international governments and beyond the usual rules of international commerce; able to circumvent the universe in search of new products, new markets and new inventions; unconstrained by tradition and bureaucracy; and able to move with lightning speed when the opportunity emerges, be it to take over big pharma, the major pharmaceutical companies and their huge databases of patient records, or the mammoths of finance, the big banks, and their failure to adapt to the new types of funding and lending needed for the age ahead. Google, Apple and the other 21st-century corporate creations are out to use the internet to transform the way we work and the way we think, be it about banking, movies, health or even happiness, and in the process replace the 'old guard' through new technology and new business techniques. As Yuval Harari (2015) has put it, while we happily give Google and Facebook all the information about ourselves that they could possibly want, and with Alexa and Google now living in our homes, they will soon not only know everything about us but be able to predict what we are likely to do next. Robotic butlers and housemaids will be soon be able to run your household and organise your lives for you – while happily supplying their respective mothership with every detail of your lifestyle in anticipation of your future needs. That may be great, particularly for the elderly and infirm, lonely and overwhelmed, but without clear checks and balances such benefits could leave the old even more vulnerable to fraud and exploitation, even more powerless against technology they don't understand or control. As Bryan Appleyard has argued (*The Sunday Times*: 28 Oct. 2018), while the world and its governments are now starting to fight back, threatening much stricter regulation and calling these modern day 'robber barons' to account at parliamentary and Senate hearings and through multi-billion tax bills or fines, the existential question remains: namely that in an age when data is the new 'gold rush', the tech giants' primary aim is to mine every last nugget of information out of the human race, turning humanity into "*sacks of machine-readable triviality*", and stealing hours and days of people's time watching endless and pointless advertisements. As James Williams (2018), a senior Google executive, has put it: "*The liberation of human attention may be the defining moral and political struggle of our time.*" With people looking on their phones, on average, every twelve minutes, such attention spans are the very life blood of tech companies whose profits depend on perpetual advertising. Encouraging continuous scrolling and cross referencing to keep users glued to their smartphones for over 40 minutes a session, often on topics and links that they had never originally intended, is at the heart of the Big Tech strategy as increasingly sophisticated algorithms search out your every need and desire. As Tristan Harris, a one-time Google researcher put it "*Your brain has no chance against a supercomputer that's calculating your weaknesses.*" (Sunday Times: July 7th 2019) The idealism of 'open communication' amongst ordinary people that apparently inspired the founders of Facebook and Google initially, now seems to be given over to accumulating and protecting their immense global wealth and to creating surveillance systems that potentially threaten our freedom, democracy – and even our human will. Employees of Microsoft, Google and Amazon in both London and Silicon Valley have already begun walkouts in protest against their companies now bidding for lucrative AI and data management defence, and homeland contracts designed to enhance and increase America's military power and its surveillance capabilities not only over potential terrorists but over illegal immigrants and other potential threats or challenges to the State. "*Our company should not be in the surveillance business; we should not be in the policing business; we should not be in the business of supporting those who monitor and oppress marginalised populations*", argued Amazon employees quoted in *The Sunday Times*. (4 Nov. 2018)

So, the old order of life is being fundamentally challenged, changed and disrupted. High streets are disappearing, traditional media discarded, democracy disrupted – and possibly perverted- and policing redirected from public space into cyberspace as criminality goes digital. The old political order is being overturned, and new smart technology is challenging and changing every aspect of our way of life and, in the process, challenging the very values that many hold dear about the sanctity of human life and our place in the universe. Traditionally, the primary message of capitalism has been that everything has to be sacrificed at the altar of economic growth without which the global world would collapse. The virtue or need for growth is neither obvious nor explained. Rather it is assumed, taken for granted as a necessity of life, and yet it has now reached the stage, some writers believe, of being a threat; a threat to our planet and ecosystem; a threat to our values as human beings; a threat to our sense of social justice as the extent and depth of global inequality reaches grotesque levels beyond all justification and reason, and when the booms and slumps of the global markets threaten to bring down the very financial system that underpins it – and the whole global economy with it. Back in 2003 and again in 2014, the eminent astronomer Lord Rees postulated the idea that the 21st century might be "*Our Final Century*", even 'our final hour' as human beings, as new technology empowers both governments and terrorists, lone individuals or small groups to wreak global havoc: "*The global village will have its village idiots.*" The future prospects for humanity, he believes, are in the balance as inequality undermines our moral superiority, and the short-term and blinkered thinking of our politicians fails to address what life for future generations will be like. With new technology and AI, humanity today may no longer be transformed by natural evolution but by genetic modification and the takeover "*by electronic intelligence*".

Derek and Dawn were, and are, fully aware of all these dangers and, as part of her role, Dawn will have to ensure that the home robot, whether housemaid or butler, chauffeur or companion, never turns from friend to foe, never oversteps its technological mark to become Big Sister or, worse, Big Brother, deciding for Derek's parents what is best for them and making them hostages in their own home in the process. Such fears have to be taken into serious consideration and have to be taken out at the earliest design stage if Derek's parents' retirement is not to turn from a silver dream into a grey nightmare. But for Derek, the goal of using new technology not only to make his parents' retirement comfortable and safe but liberating and active, far outweighs such fears; and inspired by the prospects for his parents and the business opportunities it might bring, Derek and Dawn are now putting all their energies, and those of the wider family, into this inspirational intergenerational project; a project that holds the key not only to his parents' later life but, in turn and in time, to Derek and Dawn's too. Here then lies the future as Derek and Dawn see it, and they are now determined to be at the forefront of it for their parents/grandparents' sake, and for the future of baby boomers everywhere. As Stephen Hawking concluded in 2018: "*Our future is a race between the growing power of technology and the wisdom with which we use it. Let's make sure that wisdom wins.*"

Polly could now see how the power of new technology could be harnessed to her political cause, how it might hold the key to liberating ageing and setting the old free to extend their later life and actively engage with society at large. She was equally alert now to where all this new technology might be leading us, possibly by accident rather than by design, and the ethical, let alone existential, questions that AI and robotics were already forcing humankind to face. With longevity growing ever longer and new technology ever stronger, are we fully preparing our children and grandchildren intellectually, morally and spiritually for a world without limits, and increasingly without frontiers? Or will they, too, be seduced by the promises of abundant materialism and unlimited leisure that brought down previous civilisations? And, if Big Tech cannot control itself because of competition and shareholder pressure for profit, is the answer, as Nick Clegg, now Head of Global Affairs at Facebook, argues, that government takes control and forces Big Tech to act more responsibly?

In the meantime, numerous examples of the new technologies are fast emerging that might well help make the **new age of retirement** an adventure for the future, a voyage of discovery rather than a downhill drift into disability, isolation and old age it has traditionally been. And maybe in the process your grandchildren will be able to explain to you how it all works – and take charge of the family robot!

EPILOGUE TO PART TWO

Generational Power – The Next Great Step

So, Polly now had her cause and her mission, her audience and her powers – moral, economic, political and technological – to design and promote a multigenerational manifesto and to design a strategy for an ageing Britain. What she really needed, though, was **generational power** – the support and mobilisation of the new young as well as the new old. Baby boomers alone would not be enough. Baby boomers alone would generate a political and familial backlash that might well divide ageing Britain rather than unite it.

What was needed, Polly now concluded, was the power of intergenerational collaboration; intergenerational collaboration based on a new social contract designed for the century ahead; an intergenerational social contract based on promoting mutual benefits for all ages. Such a contract, such a manifesto, Polly now believed, would be a much more effective and unstoppable *electoral battle cry* than any campaign based purely on the rights and interests of baby boomers alone. The young would not tolerate inheriting a 21st-century *'retirement'* that they had no part in designing but one that they would still have to pay for. They might, however, embrace a new '**social contract**' that they at least had a say in, that they had helped shape to their own needs as well as moderating its cost financially and socially, and in the process started to think about planning ahead for their own retirement, their own extended life plan, as well as those of their parents and grandparents'. While millennials and Generation Z may now be the ones with the energy and physical capability of 'taking to the political streets', baby boomers still hold the 'keys to power'. They still occupy key positions in government, corporations and the media;

still have the silver pound and the silver vote; still have a tradition of radical change and generational *consciousness*. Separately, the baby boomer generation and Generations X, Y, Z face an impoverished future. Together they have the chance of working together for a 'Better Britain'; together they have the chance of creating a millennium manifesto; together they have at least some chance of controlling the forces of globalisation and new technology and of converting it to the service of humankind rather than being its servants.

That was the challenge that now faced Polly, her boomer siblings, her daughter Hannah and granddaughter Laura and their wider family in coming together as a multi-generational family. That was the challenge that now faced Polly as she sought to unite the 'two worlds' of Suffolk East. That was the **Generational power** that Polly sought to harness and release in the next and final chapters of this book. Polly was now totally committed to giving the young a voice – a loud voice – in designing and developing the ageing Britain ahead. Youngsters such as Laura not only have the energy and charisma to win over Generation Z but also the charm and enthusiasm to win over older voters; to remind grey voters of their own youthful commitment to political change at the same time as reminding them of their continuing responsibility for the future of their children and grandchildren. With that vision in mind, Polly now decided to engage Laura as one of her research assistants for the duration of the summer months ahead. Better, she decided, to have your granddaughter inside the political tent arguing her case than on the outside demanding to come in; better to engage Generation Z within the British political system than have them campaigning on the streets outside or, worse, withdrawing altogether.

Part Three

Towards a New Age Manifesto & the Ageless Society Ahead

15 | Towards a Silver Manifesto and a New Intergenerational Social Contract

"If you landed in Britain today for the first time, you could be forgiven for thinking that we are a country where there is a civil war between the generations. That's what the media and many policymakers would like us to believe as they pit young people against older people and seek to divide the generations. The reality is rather different. Older people are concerned about what is happening to their children, grandchildren and great-grandchildren and their future. Young people are concerned about how their grandparents will fare in old age. We should not be stoking up a war between generations. We should be focusing instead on the distribution of income, wealth and opportunities within and across generations and how we create a society

where people of all ages prosper. Attacks on older and young people are a diversion from the real problems Britain faces and weaken our country."
Stephen Burke, Director, United For All Ages (2012)

So, the scene was set for Polly's new age manifesto. She now had a very clear picture of the challenges facing ageing Britain and the global world in the century ahead. She had clearly identified, in the shape of the British baby boomer, an electoral force capable of leading and forcing through radical change not only on their own behalf but in the long-term interests of generations to come. And finally, she now believed that she had an electoral strategy for constructing and driving an age campaign for the 2020, or 2022, British General Election based not only on the emerging powers of the new old but on their moral mission to try and transform later life for all ages, from ageing grey to shiny silver and autumn orange.

Polly was equally convinced by now that a one-dimensional age strategy – a strategy based solely on the needs and wants of the older generation – would ultimately be counterproductive. It might reap rich rewards initially for Britain's baby boomers in terms of pensions, healthcare and housing but such age gains would be at the expense of the younger generations in terms of the tax bills they would face and the lost opportunities they would experience in terms of employment and steps onto the housing ladder. They would feel as excluded economically as many young people today feel excluded politically, and so the potential for age tensions and even the sort of age war predicted by the Intergenerational Foundation might well erupt over time. An all-age manifesto had the strength, too, to be far more politically appealing, particularly to an electorate still reeling from the momentous decision about leaving the EU and desperate for an uplifting vision that would help reunite the British nation after the bruising referendums on Scotland and the EU. Post-Brexit Britain needed a public debate on ageing and a long-term plan comparable to that in Scandinavia if it was to have any chance of avoiding the age shock that was currently sending tremors throughout ageing Japan and that would soon erupt in the other super-aged nations on George Magnus's *"demographic death row"*. All previous attempts to elevate ageing up the British political agenda had failed. Now it was Polly's turn; and if it worked in Suffolk East then perhaps it might work elsewhere and convert her own party to the electoral possibilities of an all-age strategy; or, like the advent of UKIP, the Brexit Party, it might generate a new political force of its own.

Moreover, it fitted almost perfectly the **dream of generativity** that was now inspiring Polly philosophically and personally. It went much deeper than just developing new ways and new technologies to help the aged. It went to the heart of the human mission: the nurturing of the next generation. So Polly's strategy, too, had to delve deeper, much deeper, than simple generational self-interest. She wanted to draw on the very 'soul' of the boomer generation – its capacity, when challenged and inspired, for selfless generosity and for the idealistic pursuit of a better, fairer society for all; and in the process lay the foundations for a silver society for the old, and an orange one for the younger generations to follow. These foundations, she now believed, could be expressed and enshrined in a new social contract between the generations, one comparable in longevity, commitment and mutual benefit to that enshrined in the Beveridge Report in 1942 and executed by the Labour Government after the Second World War. Britain and the world may no longer be at war, but ageing alongside globalisation, urbanisation and particularly new technology is creating a new world in the 21st century that on one hand offers wondrous change and opportunity but on the other threatens terror and tyranny, leaving ordinary people potentially powerless and grossly unequal.

So, this was the challenge that had faced Polly back in early 2017 when Theresa May suddenly called a snap general election to boost her majority and so strengthen her hand in the forthcoming Brexit negotiations with Brussels. As the Labour candidate for the newly created constituency of Suffolk East, Polly needed to construct a party manifesto and a political platform that might draw together the two sides of her new constituency. She had to create a new political vision in the aftermath of Brexit and publicise a political message that made her constituents feel that this politician at least was listening and responding to their needs in a language that resonated with them, made them feel more in control and think about the future – not only theirs but their children's. While counties like Suffolk might often appear to be sleepy and living in the past, beneath the surface, change, immense change, change created and driven by global forces and big business – the energy and bio-technology industries, tourism and foreign investment – is coming to this coastline. The coast of East Anglia is becoming the largest offshore wind farm in the world; nuclear energy is being expanded through developments in Sizewell C; solar farms are being built on agricultural land; and plans to tame tidal power and build flood protection along a coastline ravaged by the North Sea have now shot up the local political agenda. So, too, have the underlying social issues around inequality, low pay and unemployment in a constituency which seems to be as socially and politically divided as the North and the South of Great Britain. Lowestoft is one of the most deprived towns in Eastern England, and Sunny Southwold is one of the wealthiest, a 'silver El Dorado' where even beach huts fetch nearly £100,000 on the local housing market. The social and political contrast could not be starker nor the age gap greater as the young, skilled and able-bodied move at the first opportunity north to Norwich, south to London or, in an increasing number of cases, abroad in search of new opportunities and new lives. So, how might Polly turn the political divide that characterises her constituency from one of stark contrast and potential conflict into one of dynamic enterprise and open opportunity for all ages and all classes; how do you turn a silver coastline into an orange county, one full of life and intergenerational activity where the older generations not only support the young but where they work for each other for mutual benefit?

However, time was short and Polly had only a skeleton manifesto in mind when she received a last-minute invitation to speak at an ILC-UK conference at the House of Lords on the topic of '*How we can improve the political participation of younger people*'. Very short notice, as the original conference had had to be postponed because of the Westminster terrorist attack in March 2017, but an ideal opportunity nevertheless to test out her initial ideas in front of a prestigious audience of professionals within the field of longevity and an audience of politically minded young people like her granddaughter Laura. In fact, it gave Polly the ideal opportunity to engage Laura herself in the actual presentation and test out the audience reaction to a young person preaching the virtues of an all-age strategy rather than just the usual grey suits and grey hairs. It simply couldn't be a better topic, at a better time and in a better place to trial this agenda before the June election, given the nature and breadth of the audience and the Lords' leadership in promoting the ageing debate back in 2013.

Polly had already settled on the political strapline of a **new common good**, a new intergenerational good based on mutual support that might be enshrined in a new intergenerational, even intragenerational, social contract. At first such an approach might look selfless, highly altruistic and benevolent but, in reality, and beneath the surface, it is highly self-interested. The old of the 21st century, even the fiercely independent boomer generation, need the young even more now than in the past. They need them to support them financially and personally for much longer than previous generations of old, and in greater numbers, but also because the young as workers and taxpayers are declining in numbers and the UK's dependency ratio is likely to rise dramatically in the years ahead, generating in turn immense pressures on state spending. Moreover, as grandparents today, they are likely to live substantially longer than their forebears; and as the modern British family becomes even more multigenerational, so new age grandparents, and even great-grandparents, are likely to be even more engaged in family life, and for longer, as they watch their grandchildren, and even great-grandchildren, grow up into adulthood and even parenthood.

A **new age manifesto based on intergenerational mutual support,** however, might look wonderful on paper but it would be meaningless without practical application and outcomes that people could genuinely believe in both personally and collectively. The Britain of the 2020s and 2030s will be nothing like the Britain of the 1960s or 1970s. It will be an ageing society that will need a new social vision, a new set of social and political priorities and a new economic paradigm to make it work if the full potential of the demographic dividend is to be realised and Britain is not to implode within its own age-quake. It will equally be a very fragile society with an age imbalance even more apparent than today. By then the baby boomers will have all the advantages of retiring, and the young all the burdens of living, whether it be in terms of higher taxes, less housing or greater eldercare. As the OECD briefing in January 2018 reflected, while generational solidarity is currently very high within the developed countries of the OECD, this may change significantly as dependency ratio halve between now and 2050. "*Intergenerational conflict over public resources would be damaging for all age groups and generations. It would imply a breakdown not only in the State's role, but also in the informal nexus of support within and between families which is so vital a complement to the welfare state in providing the essential glue which holds society together.*"

With these crucial insights in mind, Polly and Laura, with a strong steer from Hannah, began to tease out the conceptual framework that might underpin this new social contract in three structured steps. The **first step** was to try and develop a simple overriding message, or vision statement, that summed up and clearly set out what the age mission actually is and upon which a set of policy statements and objectives might be based. The **second step** involved identifying the policy areas and specific changes that might put an ageing and/or intergenerational manifesto into practice. The **third step** would involve the design of a political strategy that would elevate ageing to the top of the British political agenda in time for the 2020 election – or, more probably now, that in 2022. Polly fully appreciated that Brexit was likely to be the dominant issue in June 2017. It was, however, an opportunity to raise ageing up the political flagpole, test the winds of support, get it considered for a future Labour manifesto and use it as a powerful political weapon to chastise the government for its *"woeful and wilful"* neglect of the ageing Britain ahead. The British electorate, even then, was punch-drunk from the turbulence of two referenda and a general election within two years, so any opportunity to look ahead and refocus on life at home would be a welcome relief from Brexit and a look into the future ahead for them all.

Step One: Towards a new age vision: Despite the UN and WHO warnings and numerous reports on the need for a public debate and a national strategy, Hannah and Laura's team found no major party in the UK that had, up to that time, put ageing at the forefront of their election manifesto or policy programme. They found a sub-manifesto, an older people manifesto, published by David Cameron in 2010, but more as a passing invitation for the elderly to join his vision of a 'big society' than as a fully fleshed manifesto for a new later life. What they did find, however, was an age statement developed by the New Labour Government in its last year in office; a *"vision of a society for all ages"* that Polly and Hannah found surprisingly inspiring and quite uplifting:

> "Our Vision is a society for all ages, where people are no longer defined by age and everyone is able to play a full part. This will require a major cultural change"; with the first step being to outlaw "unjustifiable age discrimination".

The vision and the strategic intent behind this statement offered Polly and Hannah the sort of ambition and moral dynamic that they were looking for, particularly the commitment to outlaw age discrimination and to promote age equality. It clearly needed more work and possibly a much stronger intergenerational emphasis or commitment to a new social contract between the generations. Nevertheless, for Polly and Co. it offered a strong starting point, especially as it had come from her own political party and from a government in power, so reflecting both Whitehall and Westminster thinking at that time. More particularly for Polly, this was something of an emotional 'blast from the past', harking back to the political principles that inspired her to join New Labour in the first place back in the late 1990s. It might not be their final vision statement but it offered a valuable starting point.

Step Two: Towards a new age manifesto: Polly initiated the manifesto drafting process by asking Laura and her team to identify the specific needs of the young on one hand, while she and her fellow baby boomers sought to draw up those of the new old on the other. They then pulled these two generational wish lists together, looking for areas of mutual benefit and mutual support. The amount of common ground was quite astonishing, and quite uplifting, and they became the basis of a two-day intergenerational family seminar that they arranged in sunny Suffolk. This proved to be a very lively event, as you can imagine – 'a brainstorm and a barnstormer' – with all three generations hammering out their ideas for the future and revealing in the process their images of each other's generation and their perceived relationships and responsibilities; a new version of the ever-popular *Generation Game*, and one perhaps every family should indulge in once in a while? The home truths and the intergenerational, and intragenerational, aspirations and ambitions all went into the 'generational pot' and produced the final draft of what an intergenerational manifesto for the future might actually look like.

Next, Charles, as Polly's trusted independent adviser, set the scene by drawing on the wide range of research on ageing Britain now emerging from think tanks, commercial organisations and government reports, notably the government's Foresight report on the *Future of an ageing population* in 2016 and the five great challenges it saw facing ageing Britain:

Firstly, the challenge of an ageing workforce as the proportion of those aged 50–64 rises from a quarter of the working population at present to 35% by 2050, an increase of approximately eight million people. Ageing is 'a moving feast'. It has profound implications for the British economy and will impact harshly on post-Brexit Britain.

Secondly, the challenge of ageing households, with the number of households headed by someone aged 85 and over projected to increase by 1.42 million, an increase of 161% in 25 years. The need for suitable housing for the older generations is becoming as urgent as that for the young, but it will need to be very age-friendly, adaptable and community-based if it is to enable older people to be more independent and self-sufficient.

Thirdly, the challenge of the modern British family – its diversity, its fragility and its capacity to provide the quality and quantity of eldercare likely to be needed in a future when long-term care and care of the disabled elderly become urgent issues. Does the British family today have the capacity, or incentives, to cope with this potential crisis in care and/or is it capable and willing to regenerate the UK population with a 21ˢᵗ century-style baby boom at a time when Brexit is likely to cut off the flow of young blood from abroad?

Fourthly, the healthcare challenge of adapting the UK's health and care systems to the chronic and long-term needs of an ageing population by both supporting care in the family and by investing in new medical and assistive technology.

Finally, the challenge of social, physical and technological connectivity in integrating the emerging old into supportive social structures to offset isolation, ill health and, worse, the sort of wave of silver suicide seen in super-aged countries such as Japan.

As this government report concluded, if the opportunities of an ageing population are to be realised, the response has to be coherent and integrated. Ageing cannot be addressed in departmental silos. It must reflect a national strategy that recognises that what happens with the new old has profound implications for all age groups and for all sectors of the economy and society. It is now a lifetime event for all of us whatever our age and one that we must prepare and plan for now, as a matter of urgency.

More recent reports have added flesh to these bones. The Centre for Ageing Better (2018), for example, described in rich detail the sheer variety and diversity amongst both the new old and the new young. It identified six distinct types of baby boomer, ranging from *"Thriving Boomers"* through to those entitled *"Can Do and Connected, Downbeat, Worried and Disconnected, Squeezed Middle Aged, [and] Struggling and Alone"* (sounds like six the Seven Dwarfs, so was Polly to be Snow White?), each with very different life – histories and outlooks on future life – and each dissected by gender, ethnicity, religion and sexual orientation. The Intergenerational Commission, in turn, has provided detailed descriptions of each of the younger generations – from generation X to Z, and from baby boomers to millennials – and described in some detail the fears and dilemmas of the young today in facing a highly uncertain future. Such pessimism is widespread amongst young people in Britain today and appears to be worse in the UK than most nations in the EU, except France, Belgium and Spain. However, according to the Ipsos MORI survey in 2017, such fatalism does not yet appear to have generated high levels of generational antagonism. Quite the opposite; most millennials still see their generation as a victim of circumstances rather than the victim of boomer selfishness, and virtually all the participants in this survey saw the government as capable of resolving these issues if it would only act and act soon, whether it be on growing jobs, improving the scope and availability of healthcare, or increasing the supply and affordability of first-time housing.

The Demos report, *Generational Strains*, back in 2013, had equally found generational altruism and mutual support not only alive and well in modern Britain but growing as baby boomers, both parents and grandparents, increasingly supported their children with childcare, house deposits and tuition fees. However, this report did identify a distinct and critical difference between the generations as to what constitutes any notion of the **common good** in the early 21ˢᵗ century. While older respondents tend to hark back to the post-war principles and social ethos of the original Beveridge Report, younger respondents tend to see the British welfare state in more pragmatic, less emotional and nostalgic terms. They judge it according to its performance rather than its principles and, from that standpoint, even older users have serious misgivings about how well and how fairly the British welfare system actually works. Both generations increasingly view the fairness of welfare distribution in terms of those who through no fault of their own need help, or those who by virtue of their past contributions now have a right to claim support. Hence the common perception of children, the elderly and the disabled as *deserving* or *entitled* beneficiaries while the unemployed and new immigrants are viewed far less favourably, as their contributions to date are far less and their need for help less easily justified. What the Demos report picked up on was a generational shift towards **reciprocity** as the underlying principle of a modern welfare state rather than just need, or perceived need, as in the past; one where the system rewards good behaviour, hard work, honesty and thrift, and punishes cheating and indolence; one where you get back what you put in. Proud though the older generations remain of the British welfare state as a national symbol of British character and care, a generational criticism, if not cynicism, about the way it works has grown up in recent years in the UK that contrasts quite strongly with countries such as Norway and Holland, where contributions are higher but so too are the entitlements – and public support.

As outlined in Chapter 10, there is a growing public awareness, too, of the concept of **intergenerational fairness** and how a fair system of intergenerational distribution of resources and opportunities might actually work. There is an emerging sense that the "*future is becoming a burden on the young*" (Leonardo Quattrucci, WEF: 2018), with resources increasingly being diverted from education and training for the younger ages to pensions and healthcare for the elderly. The traditional social contract seems to be broken, or at least fragmenting, and the young appear to be becoming frustrated with the apparent rise of gerontocracy right across Western societies. Solutions such as incorporating intergenerational equity into national constitutions, as in France and Switzerland, or in creating a ministry of the future, as in Sweden, are gradually gaining wider support. The 2016 House of Commons Work & Pensions Committee Report focused specifically on the issue of whether, in an ageing society where the old are living longer and in greater numbers, it is fair that the younger, working generations alone continue to fund a retired generation of baby boomers that now enjoy a much higher level of income from savings, investments and private pensions and, in addition, attracts a state pension that is protected, triple-locked and enhanced by an array of benefits that many of today's pensioners no longer need. Is it now time, asked the committee, for this older, wealthier generation of retirees not only to contribute more to the benefits they receive but to contribute more to the benefits needed by the young? The committee came to the view that such a generational shift is indeed needed, and its report urged the British welfare state to revert back to its original principles and its mission as a life-long organisation designed to support to better health, social security and housing from cradle to grave for *all ages* not just the elderly; that it develop an integrated and life-course approach to the three giant challenges of health, social care and social security.

So, with Charles's briefing as their backcloth, Polly, Donald and Wilfred set out a baby boomer manifesto designed specifically to address the challenges set out in Part One of this book. Their proposals certainly hit all the 'boomer buttons', and on paper it proposed solutions that would improve life momentously for the new old and ageing elderly in Great Britain today, let alone tomorrow. Raising the state pension to European levels of replacement alone would dramatically improve the quality of later life living, inspire and enable healthier elder lifestyles and possibly make a significant dent in pensioner inequality. Yet such proposals on their own left wide open the question of who and how such elder benefits might be paid for and whether, yet again, selfish oldies might appear to be raiding the British welfare state at the expense of the young. "… *it's alright for the oldies but what about us, the workers having to pay for all this through higher taxes and longer working lives? The baby boomers have made their millions; now it's their turn to pay and give up all these freebies – TV licences, bus passes, free prescriptions and the like. We, the younger generations, need their help – getting jobs, offloading student debt and getting on the housing ladder – more than they need ours. They've had their life;*

now it's our turn". While older voters on both sides of Suffolk East might well come together in support of such an old age manifesto, the price could be an age divide that replaced the class divide evident in many such communities; a divide that Polly was desperate to avoid.

Laura and Co.'s presentation, in contrast, set out the needs and aspirations of the young. It took the family conference by storm, and their energy, idealism and originality lifted everyone's hopes and horizons for the future. More especially, it confirmed for Polly the importance of ensuring that the voice of the young be heard just as loudly as the voice of the old, not only to regain the trust and engagement of the young in the British political process but to stir and inspire boomer consciences and memories of their own youthful idealism and so gain their active involvement and electoral support. Here was the opportunity for all three generations to begin working together on a more age-inclusive approach that would appeal to boomer altruism; to their vanity; to their sense of social justice and historic mission, as well as to their material self-interest; to their sense of responsibility for the young and the very young before they depart this world. It would provide the opportunity and the imperative for boomers to help redesign the social contract that they had inherited from the 20th century. Not alone, not as superiors claiming the wisdom of age as in the past, but in partnership with the young as equals in a common intergenerational project. Presented in this way, Polly was convinced that once the young were offered the opportunity to actively and equally help design a new intergenerational contract, they too would rise to the occasion in great numbers and so at last start to make their mark on British political life and improve it for their generation too.

And so the concept of **mutual support for mutual benefit** was born at the family conference and became the core of the manifesto Polly and her family put together. Mutual support across generations doesn't actually have to be invented because it already exists in bucket-loads through family collaborations such as the Bank of Mum and Dad, family businesses and the chain gang of childcare that exists in most families. It is, however, entirely informal and often unnoticed and underappreciated. It operates entirely through familial ties and social sentiments. It can collapse, and often does, as easily as it is set up. There is no government strategy to strengthen or support it, no policy framework that might take the principles of intergenerational support to the next level and incentivise generational collaborations as part of a national strategy for the future and as a driver for the national and global economy of the 21st century.

Yet the opportunities and the potential for underpinning such generativity, for combatting ageism and for promoting the harmony of an ageless society seem endless and endlessly inspiring. It may even offer the principles needed to inform and inspire an intragenerational strategy for moderating inequality within generations as well as between them; and for shifting generational support from the narrow family orientation evident in most Western societies towards a greater sense of communal responsibility, particularly for children and their overall upbringing. Dutch children, for example, have been described as *The Happiest Kids in the World* by Michele Hutchinson and Rina Mae Acosta (2017), because of the high levels of community support that are a key feature of child-rearing in the Netherlands. Such support, and the lack of it, may well explain why Dutch children regularly top UNICEF surveys about child well-being, while British teenagers seem to be amongst the saddest. Challenging, even to some extent reversing, such family-centredness and developing a more communal culture through the multigenerational family of the future might, just might, felt Polly and David, help overcome many of the darker features of family life in the UK today described in Chapter 7. It might equally be an inspiration for boomer and millennial engagement in a joint campaign to support Generation Z and their baby brothers and sisters at one end of the age spectrum and those elderly members of the Silent Generation still remaining at the other.

So, drawing on the ideas and proposals generated by both the boomers and the youngsters at the Suffolk seminar, Polly, Hannah and Laura came up with the following draft manifesto for an intergenerational future, a manifesto that had as its starting point the **common needs** of the young on one hand and of the old on the other, as summarised below:

The new old (the baby boomers) need policies and programmes to:
- *Keep them healthy and independent* throughout later life and give them the opportunity to continue to contribute positively and pro-actively to the community and family around them and not be a burden to either.
- *Promote the productivity, inclusion and well-being* of the young as the working population funding the British welfare state and as the generation that will care for the boomer generation in old age.

The new young (Generations X, Y and Z) need policies and programmes that:
- *Promote and support their own 'life-long planning'* in terms of employment, health, finance, housing, child/eldercare and their own retirement.

- ***Keep the new old healthy, active and independent*** to reduce the potential burden of age dependency that might otherwise fall on them, their families and the welfare state.

On the blindingly obvious premise that the old need the young as much as the young need the old, the Suffolk seminar began to build an intergenerational manifesto for an intergenerational future that both enshrined and took forward the spirit of Beveridge and many of the core principles behind his post-war social contract. So, with an amended version of New Labour's 2009 age manifesto as their draft vision statement, Polly and family began sketching out the specifics of a draft all-age manifesto.

A. Our vision of a society for all ages and all generations

"Our vision is a society for all ages, where people are no longer defined by age, everyone is able to play a full part and where the spirit of intergenerational collaboration and mutual support that has defined Britain to date is set out in a renewed and refreshed social contract designed for the century ahead. This will require a major cultural change which includes the creation of a national plan for the challenges of ageing facing Britain today; with the first step being to outlaw unjustifiable age discrimination."

This **strategy**:
- For **individuals, families and generations** it will mean early planning for later life so that they can fulfil their ambitions in work, leisure and in their communities.
- For **government** it will mean generating and leading a national debate on ageing and developing a vision and a manifesto for a better Britain for all ages. It will mean supporting individuals, families and generations in doing this but also enabling older people to continue to play an active and important role at the heart of family life and in their local communities in promoting their own well-being and the well-being of the younger generations around them.
- For **businesses** it will mean recognising and engaging the skills, abilities and experiences of older workers, investing in the new silver economy and in promoting silver enterprises and multigenerational projects that might best deliver the goods and services needed by an ageing population.

- For **public services** it will mean working with older people to design services that are right for people of any age, as well as recognising the specific needs that older people often have, for example in healthcare.
- Finally, for the **government and communities** it will mean ensuring that there are safe, accessible and attractive neighbourhoods in which people of all ages can participate and be involved.

B. Our responsibilities as government, society and families

1. Government to:

a. adopt and commit to the principles of active and independent ageing adopted by the UN and EU, and draft a Bill of Rights for the elderly as advocated by the WHO; and

b. appoint a minister to lead and orchestrate a public debate on ageing in Great Britain, and to draw up a national plan and a national strategy for ageing in Britain 2020 and beyond, as advocated by the House of Lords Select Committee, with a specific focus on:

- **The silver market and the silver economy and their integration into national economic planning** with a specific focus on the UK dependency ratio and on the potential for the silver economy to drive all-age employment, enterprise and innovation, particularly after Brexit. This strategy should include a review of current business and financial regulation in terms of its capacity to protect the elderly against fraud, mis-selling, etc. and its ability to promote and protect the silver markets of the future.
- **New technology** and ways to encourage and incentivise the development of technologies, particularly in the fields of biotechnology, robotics and AI, that will encourage and enable active, outgoing and independent later life, offset social isolation and contribute to the growth of the British economy, and in so doing reduce its dependency ratio.
- **Ageism, inequality and intergenerational relations,** requiring city councils, local authorities and devolved nations within the UK to devise and develop their own local and national plans for addressing ageing in their communities in 2020–2030 and beyond.

2. Parliament to introduce intergenerational policies on:

a. Retirement & work

- Raise the age of the state pension in line with longevity rather than just chronological age.
- Incentivise longer working lives through, for example, attractive deferred pension incentives and later-life work schemes with pensionable incentives, health benefits and/or tax breaks particularly in shortage areas such as teaching, nursing, medicine and care.
- Incentivise and support silver entrepreneurs, and particularly intergenerational new businesses, especially in the emerging silver markets.
- Create a comprehensive national retirement service for all ages at all stages of life's transitions: a one-stop shop along the lines proposed by Lord Wei but with a broader brief than just retirement planning for the old with life-long planning for the young too.

b. Pensions & life-long financial planning

- Raise the state pension to 60% of average earnings to equalise income in later life and remove pensioner poverty altogether, funded partly from progressive taxation on wealthier pensioners and partly by the withdrawal of current pension benefits for those under 85 years of age.
- Create more attractive and secure pension saving schemes for the young with, for example, a single tax relief on pensions of, say, 30–35% to encourage long-term pension saving by all young people, not just the better-off.
- Create more attractive pensioner saving schemes for the old to help stabilise pensioner incomes and release billions of pounds in 'zombie' or low-interest savings accounts as new investment funds for such mutually beneficial projects as new-build housing schemes for old and young alike.
- Promote high-quality and fully regulated all-age financial planning advice and guidance, including financial education and entrepreneurship schemes in schools.
- Create a new, all-age pensions and retirement service along the lines proposed by Lord Wei with the brief to advise not only those in and approaching retirement but young people planning ahead.

c. Health & social care

- Raise spending on health and social care by 2%, in line with the GDP spend of leading European nations such as France and the Netherlands, with the emphasis on preventative and active health and on fully funding social care to raise its quality, capacity and ability to relieve pressures on the NHS.

- Fully integrate health and social care on the basis of personalised care plans and budgets, as proposed by the Barker Commission and the King's Fund.
- Raise recruitment and training into geriatric medicine and social care by elevating their pay, professional status and standards accordingly.
- Create healthcare saving schemes with progressive or at least equitable tax relief to incentivise long-term healthcare funding in the same way as pension saving.
- Provide greater promotional and preventive health schemes for all ages, with pensionable incentives for good health, as employed by many private health insurance schemes.
- Set up eldercare incentive schemes for young and middle-age volunteers (e.g. volunteer credits) to reduce pensioner isolation and promote intergenerational support and contact.
- Secure low-cost financial schemes to support the cost of later-life care, with tax relief throughout working life, and into early retirement.
- Redesign the current social care system and care home provision with far stricter regulation and quality standards and much greater innovation and personalisation, to both encourage and support greater active independence in old age and encourage active involvement of families in its development and regulation, as proposed by the ILC-UK.
- Promote investment in new technology for supporting 'ageing in place', active engagement outside the home and for ongoing communication and monitoring of the elderly by the family.
- Set up a national campaign to raise funds to combat age-related diseases, and specifically to raise the status and research funding into dementia as the emerging 'cancer' of the 21st century.

d. Education

- Put ageing and longevity on the school curriculum to promote longer-life planning and early pension saving.
- Promote intergenerational volunteering and support (e.g. in primary schools/residential homes).
- End higher education fees to encourage further education and training for all ages and cut interest rates on existing student loans.

e. **Housing**

- Develop a 'single-chain' housing strategy and associated financial packages, including trustworthy and value-for-money equity release schemes to promote downsizing by the old and enable upsizing by the young, with reduced stamp duty to encourage both.
- Design and develop a 'new generation' of housing schemes for multigenerational living.
- Design saving plans to attract pensioner savings for investment in new-build housing for young and older people alike and so stimulate both ends of the housing chain.
- Promote 'ageing at home' through research, subsidies and planning approvals for new technologies that will support and encourage independent living in old age.

f. **Family**

- Family care schemes to incentivise the young to support older relatives and relieve the 'care sandwich' (e.g. volunteer credits as pension savings and/or offset student loans).
- Grandparent incentive schemes to support family childcare/school travel, to enhance their role in the family and add income to their pensions.
- Visitor/volunteer schemes and incentives to offset the epidemic of loneliness in many residential homes, getting volunteers and families in and pensioners out into the community.
- Legislation, as in other parts of Europe, to encourage and incentivise greater family responsibility for the elderly.

g. **Volunteering**

- Undertake a major overhaul of the charity and community support sector to bring it into the 21st century, to help it develop a more business-like approach, but one that nevertheless retains and strengthens its voluntary mission, spirit and ethos, and develop incentives and simpler schemes to attract the baby boomer retirees and young people during or after formal education and training.
- Create a national volunteer service to mobilise the over-50s, comparable to Marc Freedman's Encore programme in the USA and Lord Wei's ideas in the UK.

h. **Death and dying**

- Generate a national debate on euthanasia, organ donation and the concept of living wills, with legislation to follow.
- Create a policy framework to regulate, stimulate and support the financial market in creating trustworthy and value-for-money insurance packages to support the costs of funerals and the last rites at home or in hospital according to patient wishes.
- Research and regulate the emerging 'everlasting life' industry and its promises of life after death.

This was a pretty comprehensive and dynamic set of age proposals and, although this first draft clearly had a tendency towards benefits for the older generations, the younger members of the family could, after intense discussion, see the long-term benefits for themselves, too, as they progress towards older age. Equally, though, such a long list of demands might well be counter-productive and allow people, especially government officials and the media, to conveniently get lost in the detail and so lose sight of the underlying principles and ultimate aims. So the group set about identifying the core principles that might underpin their policy proposals and, secondly, suggest strategies that might provide single or integrated solutions of the type advocated by the WEF in 2012.

The **core principles** that they eventually agreed upon were the **principles of human rights**, as advocated and applied to ageing by the UN and Ready for Ageing Alliance in the UK. Human rights seemed to provide the power of platform needed for promoting policy improvement across all policy areas but particularly for the ageing generations and their fight against ageism.

The **policy frameworks** that they agreed upon included:

- **Integrating intra-generational** issues such as pensions, healthcare and housing within a single policy area, rather than treating them separately as at present. Such an approach would mirror real life, given that for any ordinary person all three areas are integral to everyday living and, when synchronised, may well have a multiplier effect on each other. For example, a rise in the UK state pension from its current 29% to, say, 60% replacement value as in other European countries, would not only relieve or eliminate pensioner poverty and so improve pensioner health and social engagement but in turn dramatically relieve the pressures on the health and care services and families generally. Similarly, by raising spending on healthcare to European levels and/or dramatically expanding housebuilding to promote both downsizing and ageing in place, you are likely to have more pensioners living healthier, more independent lives at lower cost to the state and to their families.

• **Integrating intergenerational** policy proposals into lifetime or 'cradle to grave' strategies that reflect the emerging 100-year life and that have clear and mutual benefits for all ages: issues such as housing where, for example, the Demos idea of a single intergenerational housing chain linking both first-time and last-time buyers clearly brings to the fore the *common* need for a significant increase in the supply of new bespoke housing for both generations.

Spelt out in this way, the advantages and benefits of an integrated and intergenerational ageing strategy seemed obvious. It would help shift government policy-making from the 'tunnel vision' and fragmented approach that bedevils much of Whitehall thinking today towards the more joined-up strategic thinking called for by the WEF, while simultaneously shifting the generational debate from a generation 'bun-fight' into an intergenerational collaboration.

So, Polly now had an embryonic message and a skeletal manifesto for her June 2017 election campaign. She equally, now, had a full-scale presentation for the forthcoming ILC-UK Conference she had been invited to; an opportunity not only to test out her key themes but also to test out her emerging ideas about intergenerational collaboration and about actually engaging young people like Laura in her forthcoming campaign in Suffolk East. Polly opened her ILC-UK presentation with the quote from Stephen Burke, director of the charity United for All Ages, cited at the beginning of this chapter, and she followed it up by explaining her political as well as personal conversion to the cause of ageing and how, for her, promoting the message of ageing – its opportunities as well as its fears – was now a political mission as well as a parental passion. Most particularly, she argued that the future of Britain as an ageing society lay not simply in creating a silver society but in creating a multigenerational community, an orange opportunity for all ages to grow and flourish, not least her grandchildren and great-grandchildren. Here, she argued, lay the final opportunity for her and her generation to realise the dream of their youth for a more equal and fair society; one that embraced and empowered the contribution of all ages and enshrined that collective spirit in a new intergenerational social contract designed for the 21ˢᵗ century. Then, with her audience now entranced by her vision, ambitions and ideals, she and Hannah briefly set out the manifesto and a multigenerational social contract that she and her family had drafted for this conference, the thinking behind it, the way that she and her family had worked on it and the effect that it had had on them collectively and individually. Finally, Polly emphasised that any all-age manifesto had to be conducted more in the European or Scandinavian style of social debate than the traditional Anglo-Saxon style of Right v Left, good v evil. Brexit had deteriorated into exactly such a gladiatorial or even tribal struggle and look where it had got us – divided and disillusioned with the EU Commission revelling in and exploiting our divisions and indecisiveness with 'leave' and 'remain' turning the debate into one between extremists rather than one based on a national consensus that the country as a whole could rally around. Just like the Brexit debate, the age debate was not ultimately about the generations alive today but the generations of tomorrow.

Ambitious and inspiring as Polly's introduction was, it was Laura and Team Z's presentation that stole the show. Their vision of the age ahead, their ideas and commitment to a new intergenerational social contract and their sheer enthusiasm and idealism lifted the conference 'off its collective feet'. Not only were the older members of the audience captivated, but the younger ones clamoured to join Laura's cause then and in the lobby afterwards. Moreover, the round-table discussions that followed were extremely lively, with participants engaging eagerly in the age debate, following Polly and Laura's lead in thinking 'out of the age box' and coming up with quite innovative and radical new ideas; ideas as far-fetched and adventurous as:

• The **idea of a citizen's income or** universal basic income (UBI), currently being trialled in Canada and Italy and under consideration by the British Labour Party, whereby every adult receives a basic income, or citizen's wage, so that no one, in theory, falls into poverty, and the huge cost, and stigma, of the current benefit system is dramatically reduced.

• The **idea of pensioner investment packages** that would attract the billions of pensioners' savings currently buried in very low-interest accounts so that such monies could be invested in the new housing so desperately needed for both first-time buyers and for older people wishing to downsize, and equally provide pensioners with a more secure stream of income.

- The **idea of a British robot revolution** equivalent to the national drive in Japan and with the potential not only to enhance life for the old at home but to transform productivity at work and take the UK economy on to a new level of wealth creation.

- The **idea of an intergenerational support & caring programme** building on pilot schemes in Exeter and North Wales, where students or toddlers mix regularly with old-age pensioners to the mutual benefit of both. Or the development of a 'dementia curriculum' for both secondary and primary schools designed to raise pupil – and teacher and parental – awareness and understanding of dementia and the ways to handle it.

- The **idea of intergenerational living** based on experiments in Helsinki and Alicante in Spain, where university students enjoy low rents in local care homes in return for five hours a week socialising with their elderly residents.

With ideas such as these flying around the conference room, Polly had to work hard to bring their particular presentation to an end while Laura encouraged participants to keep sending new ideas to the website and video link that her team had set up and invited anyone who might wish to, to sign up to help with the canvassing in Suffolk East. Finally, Polly brought their presentation to a close by repeating Professor Sarah Harper's quote to the ILC-UK conference in November 2016: "*We have a wonderful opportunity with all these generations being alive at the same time for the experience and understanding of older generations to be passed down to younger generations. Imagine being able to draw on the experience of five generations at the same time.*"

The snap general election in June 2017 gave Polly the chance to road-test her new age manifesto. Inevitably this actual election proved a far more challenging experience than her presentation to the ILC-UK conference. The electorate by then was soundly disillusioned with elections. They had had enough of grand visions, whether it was David Cameron's Big Society or Theresa May's Shared Society. They simply wanted action: action on Brexit; action on the NHS; action on housing; and action on the economy. They were well aware of the challenges of ageing – most of them were living with them – but they had other more pressing priorities and saw ageing from vastly different perspectives depending on their income, age or ethnicity. Simply getting ageing on to the British political agenda, let alone giving it a platform, was clearly going to be an immense challenge. As Claire Turner of the Joseph

Rowntree Trust had declared back in October 2014: 'Is Anyone Listening': "*I do think that the ageing population debate has a higher profile than ever before but I'm not sure the message has reached the mainstream. It still feels like ageing experts talking to ageing experts about older people – how do we widen the debate to get a wider group of people (inside and outside government) to care about this stuff?*"

Whatever Polly's own electoral experience that summer, the June 2017 election certainly brought both 'heaven and hell' for Britain's political parties. **Heaven** for a Labour Party fearing an electoral 'hammering' after the disastrous outcome in 2015, but now revelling in Jeremy Corbyn's confirmation as a Labour Leader with youth appeal and even serious consideration as a future PM. **Hell** for a Tory Party losing its parliamentary majority and having to broker a deal with the DUP just to stay in power, let alone negotiate with the whole of the EU. The 2017 election, though, equally brought age to the forefront of British politics, with Labour enjoying a sudden surge in its youth vote by promising to abolish university tuition fees, while Theresa May's attempt to cap care home costs backfired badly. Polly, too, benefitted from the upsurge in support amongst young people in Suffolk East inspired by Jeremy Corbyn, but equally found growing support from older voters for her embryonic age manifesto. Certainly Laura's 'Band of Angels' proved as popular in Lowestoft and Southwold as they had at the ILC-UK conference, and she even had groups of grannies parading up and down Southwold pier with placards calling for student fees to be abolished. But, as Polly reflected afterwards, placards and poster promises were not enough. A full-blown national debate on ageing that generated a national plan to tackle it would need another level of political, even philosophical, thinking about what an all-age or ageless society might actually look like if politicians and voters were to be convinced of its vision and its value. Certainly, the hard-bitten and weary constituents of Suffolk East would need a lot more convincing if their constituency was to become a haven of generational harmony and a model of age-friendly practice.

Conceiving of a society beyond the present, one based on generativity, agelessness and intergenerational collaboration, however, is a different order of philosophical, social and political change to an election manifesto simply offering new policies and material benefits of the sort already available. It is a task in itself and one for the next chapter. Suffice to say that at this point in our narrative, that policy proposals on intergenerational fairness are at least the subject now of high-powered commissions and parliamentary reports. The age debate is slowly beginning to percolate into the public consciousness, and the Intergenerational Commission's recommendations below provide an interesting contrast to the age manifesto outlined earlier in this chapter. However, while there is substantial overlap and common ground, the IGC's recommendations are inevitably limited in scope compared to Polly's grand vision of an ageless society *of and for* the future. They focus much more on intergenerational fairness and set out proposals for improving life for the younger generations that in places represent significant sacrifices by, or losses to, the baby boomers and the old. As the commission argues, the fallout from the financial crisis alongside deeper structural shifts in the labour, housing and pensions markets *"means that 21ˢᵗ-century Britain is not living up to its promises for younger generations"*. In particular, the commission's proposal about inheritances and its recognition that many *"inequalities* within *generations are larger than those* between *generations"* resonated powerfully with Polly's own perceptions about generational inequality as a source and force for engaging all generations in her emerging age campaign. The commission's focus on the needs of the young is nevertheless a powerful and timely contribution to the debate on intergenerational relations in an ageing society, and it offers an invaluable contribution towards an intergenerational social contract for the future. *"If we once again step up to the challenge of keeping the intergenerational contract strong, we will not only have a better Britain but a more united one."*

> ## Figure 1: **Intergenerational Commission's Ten Main Recommendations**
> *(IGC: 2017)*

1. Increase public funding for social care by more than £2 billion from a reformed taxation of property that includes taxing the housing wealth of the older generations but through a new but restricted form of council tax so that *"no one can be asked to contribute more than a quarter of their wealth for their own care"*.

2. Introduce a £2.3 billion NHS levy by reasserting NI contributions on working pensioners, alongside a limited NI contribution on occupational pensions – a tax regime that is likely to raise 80% of any extra funds from the richest fifth of pensioners, so offsetting the imbalance in tax relief the better-off currently enjoy on their pensions.

3. Introduce the right to a regular contract for those doing regular hours on zero-hours contracts, extended statutory rights for the self-employed and minimum notice for shifts, to reduce the current levels of job insecurity.

4. Introduce a £1 billion better jobs deal to support young people seeking work and training, and £1.5 billion to support the development of high-quality technical education funded by cancelling 1p of the forthcoming corporation tax cut.

5. Make indeterminate tenancies the sole form of private rental contract, with rent increases limited to inflation for three-year periods and disputes settled by a new housing tribunal.

6. Replace council tax with progressive property tax, with surcharges on second and empty properties; halve stamp duty to encourage moving; and introduce a time-limited capital gains tax to incentivise owners of additional properties to sell to first-time buyers.

7. Pilot community land auctions to increase the supply of housebuilding land, alongside stronger compulsory purchase orders and a £1.7 billion building precept to help local authorities raise funds for local housebuilding.

8. Lower the earnings threshold for auto-enrolment; increase savings amongst low and middle earners by flattening rates of pension tax relief (currently overwhelmingly benefitting the very highest earners) to, say, 28% for all, and exempting them from NI contributions; require firms contracting self-employed labour to make pension contributions. Possibly reconsider the current ratio of state pension to median earnings, which at 32% is half the EU and OECD averages.

9. Develop a legislative framework for a new 'collective defined' pension scheme to reduce risk for younger workers and develop a guaranteed income product purchased at aged 80.

10. Abolish inheritance tax, replacing it with a lifetime receipts tax that generates sufficient revenue to support a £10,000 citizens' inheritance for all young adults from aged 25, to support skills, entrepreneurship, housing and pension saving.

The 2017 General Election and the 2018 Intergenerational Commission Report were significant steps forward for Polly's age campaign in pushing age and ageing up the political agenda and in stirring the age debate within her own party. So, the proposal by Torsten Bell, the Director of the Resolution

Foundation, that the Labour Party ought to adopt the notion of a fairer social contract as part of its next manifesto, was truly music to her ears, not least as he was a former adviser to Labour and so well positioned to make this actually happen. Hugely encouraged, Polly was now more determined than ever to tease out what an ageing or, better, an ageless society might actually look like and how it might work. As Joseph F Coughlin, Director of Technology for Healthy Living at MIT, commented back in the year 2000, societies today face a "*longevity paradox*"; a paradox whereby although billions of dollars have been invested to enable us to live longer, healthier and fitter lives, we have not prepared for what an ageing society might actually look like and be like: "… *we are not prepared, because we did not expect all of that investment, be it public or private, to actually work. Now that we are living longer, we have not even begun to think about the physical infrastructure of an aging society. Perhaps today will be the beginning.*"

16 | Towards a New Age Paradigm and an Ageless Society

Designing a new age manifesto was one thing. Defining or designing a new age society is quite another. However, after much soul searching and political agonising, that is what Polly and her family agreed they had to do if the ageing project was to have any sustainable political or public credibility. Any experienced politician or policymaker knows only too well that when floating any new social vision, whether it be the Big Society or the Shared Society, that almost the first questions will be: "*What will it look like?*" and "*What difference will it make?*" Grand, sweeping, blue-sky statements will not do. Today's journalists and social media commentators will expect instant answers in the minutest detail before they'll even begin to listen to anymore, let alone begin to have faith that the ideas being presented are realistic and achievable, while local constituents are even more challenging and sceptical. They have to see for themselves that such a paradigm shift would truly be beneficial for them and their neighbours and not just another fancy soundbite or political banner for the politician promoting it. Equally, Polly herself needed to understand the level of change involved if she was to develop and promote policies that might truly transform new age Britain and fundamentally prepare British society for the challenges ahead.

Polly and her family knew only too well that they had neither the time nor intellectual expertise to develop a full-blown theory of the ageing, let alone ageless, Britain ahead, but they did need at least a sketch outline – an 'Aunt Sally', or 'Uncle Albert' – that they could use to promote and provoke further ideas and extend the emerging public debate beyond just generational fairness.

After much thought and reflection, Polly asked her daughter Hannah, the media specialist, to undertake this assignment, aided and abetted yet again by Polly's granddaughter Laura and Donald's son Edward, the market researcher. The inclusion of youngsters from the very inception of this project was to prove a masterstroke, not only because of their enthusiasm and enterprise but because it would be their generations that would both inherit the social contract that eventually emerged and bear the cost of funding 21st-century Britain as it aged thereafter. To have the young, the very young, lead on the campaign ahead would not only defuse claims of generational greed or self-interest but win over the hearts as well as the minds of many battle-hardened boomer voters who had seen it all before, heard every political promise under the sun, and now believed none of them. A campaign led and supported by their own grandchildren, and even great-grandchildren, however, was a different matter. It would remind baby boomers of their own youthful ambition and passion for radical change. It would remind them of their own need to challenge the established order, their own need to make a mark, as well as their own underlying and enduring desire to make life better for generations to come, not just materially but spiritually and socially too. Here was a generational ambition above and beyond the self-interest that seemed to pervade and drive modern societies today. Here was a generational opportunity to engage with the young rather than disengage from them, and in the process create a fairer future for all.

Hannah and Laura assembled a team of young people across the generational age bands, suitably entitled Team Z, that included Tim, Donald's grandson and now a young civil servant working at the Home Office; and Dawn, Wilfred's granddaughter working up in the North East with her father, Derek, on the robotics project. Team Z now began their first steps in constructing a new age paradigm, a vision of a new age society, an ageless society, in the future. As they started examining and then deconstructing the current 20th-century paradigm of age, they quickly realised what a mammoth task they had taken on.

Stage 1: Developing a new age paradigm, or social framework

What would a new age paradigm look like? What is wrong with simply tweaking the existing old age paradigm? asked Polly.

Firstly, replied Hannah and Team Z, the age paradigm of the 20th century has largely been based on *age* as *the* defining characteristic behind the key stages in human development, behaviour and social expectation. These stages of life – childhood, adulthood, retirement – have in modern industrial society generally been defined by chronology; by specific ages for specific stages in the human life-course; and by appropriate rites of passage, such as becoming an adult at 18 or retiring at 65. Such age-based stages are not natural or inevitable. They are manmade, and as such movable. Retirement, for example, can simply be delayed by extending the state pension age to, say, 70 years; or adulthood extended by simply lowering the age of voting to 16. Such age tweaks, however, fail to even begin to reflect the radical changes in lifespan and lifestyle offered by longevity and its potential to generate a 'second life' or even a Third Age. As Andrew Scott (WEF: 2018) has highlighted, biology and chronology are no longer in sync. Today's 75-year-old is more like the 65-year-old of 50 years ago, and today's 65-year-old is a new man or new woman altogether in terms of their health and longevity. **Stage not age** is likely be the new mantra for the life-course of the future; and as new technology transforms modern living, so the full potential of the demographic dividend may more clearly emerge and require a new vision of life, a new social paradigm and a new dynamic, not just of later life but of the whole of life in the future. If, as Professor Westendorp (2014) predicts, people will now start living to 135 years of age, it cannot mean that they will also retire at 65 or 70 and be entitled to enjoy, or endure, some 50–60 years in retirement. Moreover, scientists today are even challenging the notion that there is a natural ceiling to human life; a "*mortality plateau*" beyond which we cannot go. Professor David Sinclair, for example, believes that with today's medical discoveries "*people could live to 150*" by the end of the century, while Aubrey Grey at Cambridge University believes life in the future is unlimited. Such claims clearly carry profound ethical and practical questions, not least whether people today would wish to live so long; or are such existential ambitions purely for the birds or, worse, the super-rich?

Such questions would have been unthinkable even 20 years ago but now, with ever-extending longevity, researchers are not only asking such questions but looking at ways to organise it. As Professor Laura Carstensen (WEF: 2018) has argued, we need a fresh 'map of life' that reflects the gift that is longevity and that allows us to move away from the current two-stage mad-cap run through work and family, to the sudden and life-ending halt on reaching retirement. We need a life plan that is more measured, staged and staggered, one that allows us to step on and off the treadmill that is life today, and instead experience life in the future more as a journey to be enjoyed than a marathon to be endured.

Secondly, the traditional age paradigm is based on and assumes a stable and predictable social structure, particularly around the family and the other traditional social institutions such as the welfare state. As explained in Part One, virtually every area, aspect and assumption about social life in Britain today is under challenge, from the onset of ageing, from retirement and pensions, through to housing and even death and dying. That most fundamental of social institutions, the family, is being fragmented and reconstituted as a multigenerational beanpole by cohabitation, divorce, remarriage and now longevity. The new age family is likely to have the new age grandparents at its heart rather than at its periphery. New age grandchildren are likely to enjoy the whole of their childhood and much of their adulthood not only with both their grandparents but even their great-grandparents. Generational relationships and social structures are being transformed right before our eyes but not always in the old images we expect. As Graeme Codrington (2018) has argued, we need to plan for the 100-year life and shift our mindset and social planning accordingly, with a more multi-stage approach to life that puts much greater emphasis on the resilience, health and financial capability needed to cope successfully with such a longer life, and that seeks to eliminate, or at least moderate, the ill health and inequalities at all ages in life that so drain and divide the resources, resilience and community spirit that will be essential to the life ahead.

Thirdly, the traditional age paradigm has tended to depict the elderly as passive and voiceless victims, past their sell-by date, inactive and incapable of acting independently. Like children, the old are often 'spoken for' by their carer, the family or the state, rather than having a voice of their own. They are no longer seen as adults capable of making their own decisions, but rather stereotyped as incapable of looking after themselves, and saturated with either sympathy or disdain. Within this context, ageism tends to flourish, and the rights of the aged today are but a 'twinkle in the sky' compared to the rights of children and the young. The new old, argued Hannah, the emerging army of retired baby boomers, however, are not likely to take kindly to such treatment. They will not tolerate being patronised, forgotten or mistreated, and they will fight for their rights at home, in the streets and in Parliament with the same fervour they displayed 50 years ago. This post-war generation of retirees will not only demand change, they will *make* change, and make it happen in their own image, not someone else's. They will rewrite the *'age script'* and in the process transform ageing as we currently know it.

Finally, while the 20th-century paradigm has focused largely on profit, the creation and distribution of wealth and on our material standard of living, in the age of the machine, the 21st-century paradigm is more likely to focus on the quality of life than the quantity; on well-being and happiness than on material wealth; on the meaning of life and the preservation of the planet rather than simply material growth, growth and more growth. As the 2018 Origins of Happiness Report concluded, real happiness may lie not just in the pursuit of wealth but in the pursuit of well-being; a very different social and personal objective that resonates strongly with many of the new young, reflects much of the generative philosophy that has so attracted Polly and fits well with the UK's emerging and urgent need for greater harmony at both a national and a personal level.

The 21st-century paradigm of age, therefore, needs to reflect a new level of thinking, a new stage in human development and philosophical ambition. Fifty years on, the world and its priorities are very different; 50 years on, life is longer – much longer and much fuller – and not only are people ageing, but so too are societies. Within this environment, society cannot afford to discard the old, to simply put them out to pasture. The young need the old to contribute and to be an economic and social asset. Society cannot afford the liability of a mass population of dependent pensioners; cannot afford an ever-rising dependency ratio where the old begin to outstrip the young. Moreover, the *new old, argued Hannah,* do not want to retire in the traditional sense, do not want to suddenly withdraw and be a burden on the young. The new old still have much to contribute in a world where ageing is accelerating; where the elderly are becoming a major *minority;* and where Japan, that great world leader in technology, is using the very latest in artificial intelligence and robotics to lead the way into the silver world ahead.

Life in the future will not only be longer but involve longer *stages of life;* multiple stages alongside the multigenerational family, the multigenerational workplace and the multiple careers that are increasingly becoming key features of ageing societies in the 21st century. It equally offers the possibility of *higher stages of life;* stages when, freed from the demands and the constraints of everyday living involving working, earning and simply surviving, men and women can reflect on and redesign their life, review its meaning and its purpose, and as a result possibly redirect it, change direction or change values, change priorities and adopt or search for a new lifestyle, even a higher 'cause' or vocation in life knowing you have the time to undertake it, to make a difference and to leave a mark, a memory or even a legacy. *"If we continue to view the life course as our ancestors did and simply tack added years on at the end, we face sure calamity. If instead we begin to modify the life course and build infrastructures that support long life, societies can begin to utilize the strengths of older people and support the real vulnerabilities advanced age brings."* It should not just be about adding years to life *"but adding life to years"* as the Acton Institute/Global Aging Coalition sought to illustrate in 2010.

Traditional Linear Life Plan

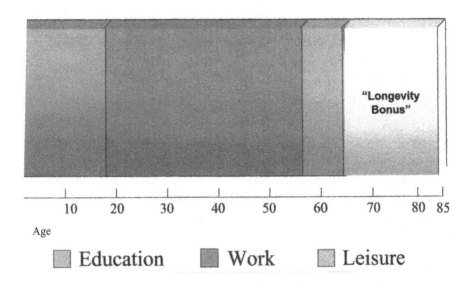

Changing the Paradigm: A New Intergrated Life Course of Learning and Financial Security

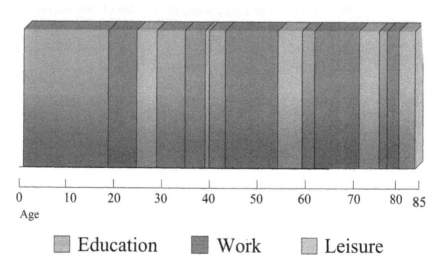

Figure 1: Images of Reconstructed Life span
(Acton Institute/Global Coalition on Aging: 2010)

Such a reconception of modern life and modern society would, Hannah and Team Z concluded, therefore involve:

- **A redefinition of age** and the underlying assumptions and perceptions behind it; rethinking how we use the concept of **age** and move away from it, even downgrade it, as a social definition capable of describing specific types of characteristics and behaviours at any given age, be it those of the young, old or middle-aged. The key to age in the future, is **not age but stage,** and ageism needs to be outlawed.

- **A redefinition of the life-course** and the traditional stages defined by chronological age, distinct lifestyles and social expectations ranging from childhood through to adulthood and retirement.

- **A redefinition and a redesign of the current notion of retirement** and all its underlying assumptions about work and leisure, lifestyle and engagement with society at large.

- **A redefinition of the role of the state** within an ageing or ageless society, and the extent to which the state can or should bear all the cost and responsibility for leading and supporting the burden of dependency.

- **A redefinition and re-examination** of the role of family in a multigenerational society, and of the employer with a multigenerational workforce.

- **A redefinition of the social contract** that currently underpins post-war democracies and their various welfare states.

- **A redefinition of the current notions of social equity and social fairness** as part of the drive to eliminate, or at least moderate, intergenerational and intragenerational inequality and conflict.

Such redefinitions might, just might, begin to realise and release the full potential of the **longevity dividend** to:

- **Transform healthcare** and our current notions of good health, keeping the elderly active and independent and enjoying happiness in their later life. As explained earlier, the key to healthy life *after* 60 is healthy living *before* 60, and a *"life-long commitment to healthy living throughout life before obesity becomes the global epidemic many fear." (McKinsey: 2014)*

- **Transform the workplace** and our current concepts of career and employment. Employers can no longer afford to casually toss the skills and experience, the leadership and the management of the older worker on to the scrap heap of retirement in favour of the young – increasingly there are too many of the second and too few of the first! The *multigenerational workplace* needs rethinking and the older workforce re-recruiting, blending the skills and energies of youth with the experience and wisdom of age as companies today face the intense competition ahead for survival in the global economy of tomorrow.

- **Transform our environment** and make it far more age-friendly, and far less age-threatening, enabling older people to get out more and feel part of mainstream society rather than cowering at home with only the TV for company.

- **Transform technology** through *gerontechnology;* through age technology that might make life more age-friendly; through universal design and the development of products that do not depend on physical strength or perfect sight and that help older people lead more independent lives: smart homes, tele-health, assistive technology, driverless cars, and of course age-friendly robots.

- **Transform our cities** and make them more age-friendly and age-accessible; make transport, shopping and even walking more comfortable and welcoming, not only for the elderly but for the disabled in a wheelchair or the young mother with a buggy. As the McKinsey study in 2016 highlighted, cities are becoming the powerhouses of growth in the 21st century, and the old as much as the young will be the power consumers of tomorrow.

- **Transform our financial services** and make their products simpler, fairer and more able to protect the elderly than exploit them. The current range of financial products available to older age groups are generally complex, poor value and the source of numerous scandals or mis-selling in recent years.

- **Transform the role and status of the senior citizen** from the senile and the segregated to the wise and the caring – the family godfathers, grandfathers and grandmothers of future life – whose words of wisdom and lessons on life are taken as important and considered worthy of listening to, and whose contribution to family or community life is taken as essential and beneficial, to be neither ignored nor patronised.

We need world leaders of wisdom and insight into the human condition, capable of providing spiritual and moral leadership as well as political and economic understanding and experience. Equally, at ground level, at the community and work level, we still need older people, older workers, older managers with everyday down-to-earth wisdom and an experience of life and work that the young cannot yet have learnt, and that robots and artificial intelligence cannot yet replicate. They represent the *'grey brain-drain'*, the loss of age and experience that many major corporations fear and that the national and global economies will soon regret. They represent the results of institutionalised ageism.

Stage 2. Imagining life in an ageless society

Redesigning an ageing society and campaigning for an age-free or ageless one, is one level of imagination. Imagining living in an ageless society where living to 100 is normal is quite another, but that is exactly the challenge that Lynda Gratton and Andrew Scott set themselves in their study of *The 100-Year Life* (2017). In a fascinating run-through of living and working in an age of longevity, Gratton and Scott sought to examine the challenges of living the 100-year life predicted for our grandchildren. They echo the primary concern of this book, that "*We are in the midst of an extraordinary transition that few of us are prepared for. If we get it right it will be a real gift; to ignore and fail to prepare will be a curse.*" Life, 100 years down the line, will no longer be a set pathway from childhood and education into a career for life and a pensionable retirement at the end. It is likely to be a highly unpredictable, multi-stage life more akin to a voyage into the unknown than a drive down the motorway; more *Star Trek* than career-trek, with you at the helm as Captain Kirk tries to steer a safe course through the asteroids to the planets beyond but this time without having your parents and teachers there to point you in the right direction and catch you if you fall. A long life means more changes, more choices, more decisions and more chances that you will make mistake upon mistake, particularly if you don't plan ahead and decide now not only where you want to go and how to get there but who you want *to be* at the end of it. Truly a new way of looking at life; truly exciting and forward thinking but oh so risky. The past is no longer a predictor of the future; and to grasp the gift of longer life fully, even in retirement, we now have to plan ahead rather than simply look back. The world at present is already in the midst of tumultuous and radical change in the form of new technology, globalisation and climate change. But it won't then stand still. Such changes, such technological and social revolutions, will become normal and generate new revolutions, new paradigms, in their wake that will change human life even further, not in millennia or even centuries but in decades or less, as the advent of high tech and social media has already shown, and as the advent of robotics, AI and biotechnology will do in the future.

To illustrate their thesis, the authors outline in some detail the lifespans and life stages of three characters – Jimmy, Jane and Jack – and how the traditional 3.0 stage life cycle no longer works even in financial terms, let alone personally or socially. Under their present savings and pension plans, both Jimmy and Jane will be out of money by the later stages of retirement on the relatively low replacement level of 50% of their late-life earnings. Worse, not having invested in continuous retraining, even in their own occupational specialisms, they will have run out of skill to obtain later-life work. In a fast-changing, technological world, old skills learnt during formal education in a person's 20s are likely to be obsolete 40 years later. Retraining in later life (Scenario 3.5) is one solution for those brave enough; retraining throughout life to extend your current occupation or to prepare for a new one or even to start your own business in later life is a better solution (Scenario 4.0) for both coping with future life and exploiting it to the full. A 100-year life, though, requires a new approach to life as well as regular re-planning. It requires a youthfulness and plasticity or adaptability that the authors refer to as *"juvenescence"* – a sort of older person's adolescence or rebirth, alongside an eager anticipation of future change; embracing change rather than fearing and withdrawing from it. This multi-stage, juvenescent approach to longer life, the authors postulate, may also help reverse the contemporary segregation of the generations and help restore the multigenerational lifestyles that used to be a central feature of societies in the past.

Finally, Gratton and Scott highlight the massive challenge of inequality to the quality of life in any age of longevity. They identify two key sources of inequality: the huge variances in the length of life enjoyed by the well-to-do compared to the poor; and the inequalities in terms of skill, education and social networks inherited by the richer sections of society that enable them to take full advantage of later-life opportunities while their poorer counterparts languish in shorter lives, poorer lives, lacking the skills or opportunities to offset their limited savings and low earnings earlier on in life. Future society in an age of longevity could be a Hobbesian horror of a war of all against all, just as easily as one of the reflection and harmony aspired to by advocates of generativity and all-age living. Which vision prevails, which pathway we follow, will depend as much on the quality of government leadership and employer foresight as on action by ordinary people on the ground. Either way, hope Gratton and Scott, life with longevity will be lively, exciting and a whole new experiment in human living but only if we start discussing it now. And to help that particular conversation, they have set up a website of their own. (www.100yearlife.com)

Stage 3. Creating and articulating a new age vision

Theoretical frameworks and even descriptions of life in an age of longevity are extremely helpful but, argued Hannah, what is really needed to raise public consciousness above national self-interest and propel ageing up the global and national agenda is a vision; a compelling and inspiring vision of a better future; a better Britain that will inspire millions of people, young and old – and especially the new old – to act, mobilise and campaign for government leadership and for a national plan for ageing Britain. That will take an exceptional message delivered by exceptional communicators, and at present Britain doesn't have many, if any. In fact, **age visionaries** across the world are few and far between. Age is not the sexiest of topics nor the most uplifting of messages. Few prominent figures and no political party in the UK or Europe have taken up the issue of ageing with any great gusto, and none has yet sought to promote it as a political cause. Contrast this absence of public debate and even awareness in Great Britain and Europe with the USA, where the issue of ageing is not only big business but the source of mass mobilisation. Age gurus such as Marc Freedman and Ken Dychtwald have inspired millions of Americans to sign up to their visions of a new age of ageing, and they have even managed to promote it as the new American frontier.

Marc Freedman, for example, has sought to set out the 'dream' of longevity as virtually the reincarnation or extension of the American dream, as a 'second life' or a Third Age and, in so doing, sought to inspire his generation, the post-war American boomer generation, to rise up and take up an encore career in later life. He is inspired by the concept of generativity embodied in the ideas

and ideals of the psychologist and philosopher Erik Erikson and his notion of a **third act**: an active and adventurous final stage in life; a climax and an accumulation of everything that has gone before, not in self-service but in service to the wider community. **Generativity**, therefore, takes longer living to the higher moral plain of service to the community, and particularly to improving the quality of life for the generations ahead. We have the opportunity through generativity of using our experience of life and the wisdom learnt from a lifetime of work and living to rise to a higher level of thinking and personal development; a state of being all that you can be. As Erik Erikson himself put it: "*The only thing that can save us as a species, is seeing how we're thinking about future generations in the way we live.*" And the beauty of this concept is that it allows you to think of life after death, of living on through your grandchildren, even though you yourself have passed away. In Marc Freedman's view:

- **We fear** the future, instead of embracing and engaging in it.
- **We fear** mortality and remain obsessed with youthfulness, our own youthfulness rather than that of future generations and the future of humankind.
- **We fear** the loss of life and the time ebbing away, rather than planning for a 'new life'; a life free of daily demands and material needs; a life free to explore our true selves and the world around us; a time to look forward with hope and renewed ambition rather than with nostalgia and longing for 'times past'. We worry about our children and our grandchildren and the 'state' of the world they are about to inhabit instead of looking forward to it.

To convert these ideals into practice and give them real meaning, Marc Freedman focused on volunteering as the means to realising the generative dream. In a series of publications, including *Prime Time* (1999), *Encore* (2007) and *The Big Shift* (2011), Freedman has sought to elevate **volunteering** from simply being a charitable exercise to becoming a social movement; a new stage in human development, a stage where wisdom and compassion, self-realisation and self-fulfilment combine in the service of society; a stage when generational conflict can be converted into intergenerational collaboration and mutual benefit; a stage when instead of being a burden on society the retired become an asset, even a saving grace, helping young and old to realise the full potential of the American dream. For Freedman, volunteering is one way, if not *the* way, to confront and refute the claims by many in America that the ageing population is the cause of all its ills and that boomers are a particularly selfish generation, threatening to undermine the American way of life instead of cementing and celebrating it.

Freedman, however, is not talking about volunteering as an occasional or casual exercise. He is advocating it as a mass movement, a national 'call to arms' for the 78 million American boomers projected in the years ahead. From this framework, within this philosophy, retirement is not a **final** phase in life but an elevation into a **higher** stage, whereby the individual seeks to both repay and revitalise the society of the future, to give something back through an 'encore career', through voluntary work devoid of personal profit or self-interest but immensely satisfying and fulfilling in its own right, as service to society rather than, as previously, service to self. Such selfless service, Freedman believes, would form the foundation for a new type of **intergenerational compact**. And leading the age revolution, this *"big shift"*, believes Freedman, will be the boomer generation; a unique generation with the appetite and the energy for selfless service but only if they can step outside *"their generational tendency toward self-centredness and wield this power with wisdom and generativity"*. In this way, and only in this way, *"when the boomers' time on earth is over, perhaps they will be remembered not just as the 'largest' generation in history, but the finest."* As he puts it –*"**THE CHOICE is OURS and the MOMENT is OURS**"*. There will be no second chance this time and soon we will be too old to march, too old to lobby, too old to make a difference. The title of Marc Freedman's most recent book pretty well sums up his philosophy of *"How to Live Forever"* and his social mission in seeking to use the *"Enduring Power of Connecting the Generations"* as the means to ultimate human happiness and fulfilment.

Hannah and Edward's research into the current state of Britain's third sector, however, cast serious doubt on the UK's ability to replicate

Freedman's revolution in Great Britain. The NPC/ILC-UK report on *Ageing and the Voluntary Sector* in 2014, for example, showed that volunteering in the UK is big business, worth over £24 billion a year to the charities involved and employing some 23 million volunteers annually. It is a mass market and one that is likely to grow exponentially as the over-65 age group in the UK rises rapidly from 16% of Britain's population in 2010 to 23% by 2030, with the over-80s set to double in number and centenarians projected to grow fivefold in the same period.

With the government outsourcing so much of its work as part of its austerity strategy, and with ageing accelerating, the third sector is set to grow massively. It is already undergoing seismic restructuring, and the NPC Commission predicted that by 2033, while big charities with over £10 million turnover are likely to expand to nearly 60% of the sector, small charities will have to become more specialist and age-niche at the local level if they are to survive. The past ten years alone have seen voluntary sector income from government contracts soar from £9.1 billion in 2000/01 to £14.2 billion in 2010/11. A three-way relationship is emerging between the public, private and voluntary sectors as the public sector steps back and uses commissioning and outsourcing rather than providing local services itself. This strategy is creating a highly competitive and quite intense marketplace for the provision of social services, one where relationships are quite blurred through corporate alliances and contract co-operation, and through the rise of social enterprises which have strict not-for-profit rules but nonetheless earn income through trading. With the ageing of the British population, this process is likely to accelerate and expand into areas as diverse as education and training, healthcare support, disability support, poverty relief, housing, community development, religion, environment, heritage and conservation, and overseas aid.

However, while the market for charity work is expanding, the UK voluntary sector seems to be stuck in the past, stuck in the Victorian era of philanthropy and paternalistic concern for the elderly and the poor, and so is ill-equipped to meet the challenges of an ageing Britain of the future. The charity shop, the reserve army of old ladies, the coffee morning, the food bank, the Third World appeal still predominate and reflect what the commission called "a *collective failure of imagination and innovation*" to meet the age of opportunity that longevity is now creating. The NPC Commission, therefore, called for a sea change in strategy and approach, a call to arms by the voluntary sector in mobilising the next generations, young and old, into active volunteering. There needs to be, in its view, a radical rethink of the role, image and whole organisation of volunteering in the UK to make it fit to meet the changing needs of an ageing Britain. Such a paradigm shift in strategy, structure and performance would, in the commission's view, involve a much more professional and business-like approach, particularly to fundraising and to relations with employers, a dramatic and much more up-market image and reputation, and a much more appealing offer to potential recruits, especially to baby boomers with so much else on offer to engage their time. The *volunteering buzz* that currently inspires and sustains volunteers needs to be turned into a *volunteering bug*, into an urgent and infectious lifelong commitment, an ongoing desire to help others; one that generates that very special and uniquely uplifting sense of personal fulfilment and human purpose, that sense of achievement and emotional well-being, that sense of having made a difference that is gained from helping others, and the overwhelming gratitude it often generates in response.

Most especially, the commission argued, the voluntary sector needs to move away from the current firefighting and doom and gloom approaches to longer life and instead promote the benefits of active ageing as a whole-life approach that enables people in their mid-life or early 60s to take control of their later years and stay healthy and active both physically and financially. We will need an all-age charity provision for an all-age society, and in particular a charity provision for mid-life, the 'rush hour of life'. These are new opportunities, new markets for the voluntary sector to develop and expand into in an age of government cutbacks and greater responsibility being thrust on the individual, opportunities that include taking a lead responsibility in the prevention of disease and in the aftercare of treatment, personalising the social services to give them the 'human face', time and attention that patients often need and that increasingly seems to be disappearing in the modern welfare state. It needs to raise funds, engage industry and commerce, and generate mass sponsorship, to promote intergenerational voluntary work through mentoring and collaborative teamwork and to promote new ways of working and new approaches to community life.

As Polly fully appreciated, the challenge for the voluntary sector of moving from a Victorian model of mission, role and responsibility to a business model fit for the 21st century is a gargantuan one. The idea that a sector built on 19th-century ideals of selfless, community service now enter the mainstream of 21st-century business, competing with and working alongside huge corporations like Capita, with global reach and multiple incomes, seems like economic suicide as well as an ethical sell-out. But, argued Hannah, does it actually have any choice, if it and its ideals are even to survive, let alone thrive, in the competitive world ahead? Rather than step back, argued Hannah and Edward, the voluntary sector now has the opportunity to step forward, lead the age revolution and set its tone for the future. The voluntary sector has a special place in people's perceptions and affections, a unique identity in the British way of life that symbolises the very values and ideals of intergenerational and intragenerational public service that Polly is trying to promote and publicise. It has a unique market position and a public image of respectable innocence, unquestioned integrity and traditional honesty that no private company can compete with, though some try to emulate. It has a real future, they argued, not by copying big business but by contrasting with it. Charities can continue to embody the ideals of selfless public service and non-profit-making, but to survive they have to become far more business-like in their practices and strategic planning.

Moreover, charities offer ideal partners for any business seeking to open up the older age markets and the new silver sectors that ageing is likely to generate. They may even make ideal partners for sectors such as finance and banking desperate to reform their reputations and salvage their public images after years of bad practice and corporate greed. 'Getting into bed' with big business, however, can be a dangerous and counterproductive strategy that could divert, even distort, voluntary work from its primary mission. It could put profit before people and in the process corrode both the ethos of voluntary work and the public trust that is its lifeblood and USP (unique selling point) for both the people donating and the people volunteering. '*Supping with the Devil*' can turn even the saintliest into sinners, as charities such as Age UK have found to their cost in endorsing financial products that failed to fulfil all their promises. More particularly, as Oxfam and the leading aid charities found in 2018, growth brings greater public attention to standards of corporate behaviour and, for charities at least, being whiter than white isn't only an ethical requirement but essential to business survival. Oxfam lost millions in donations after revelations about aid workers in disaster areas consorting with local prostitutes.

So, the opportunity for the British voluntary sector to grow and to become big business is there in the ageing world ahead. Retaining its USP, retaining its spiritual soul within the soulless world of competitive capitalism, however, will be a huge challenge if it is to rekindle the spirit of giving and generativity within the new and growing generation of retirees; a boomer generation looking for life before death, looking to leave a lifetime legacy that will be remembered and revered rather than reviled and relegated to the dustbins of history. Such a transformation in image and ambition, in ethos and energy requires a whole new business model, new outstanding leadership and more innovative and intergenerational programmes of enterprise and employment, like those of the

Prince's Trust and its work with young people, of *Now Teach* as it attracts senior staff out of corporate boardroom and into the classroom, and of the new NHS *Helpforce* as it attempts to provide the personal touch for hospital patients that its professional staff no longer have the time to give.

The government appears, at last, to be showing some support and encouragement for this shift from the public to the voluntary sector. Its Civil Society Strategy in August 2018 promised to *"build stronger communities"* by helping to bring together businesses, charities and the public sector to work alongside the government's Industrial Strategy through new types of local democracy and leadership; working together in seeking to *"grow the economy, while creating an environment where people and communities are at the heart of decision-making"*. The National Council for Voluntary Organisations (NCVO) has welcomed this initiative but said that much more is needed than the £20 million proposed. Others have been much more critical, contrasting this relaunch of the Conservative Big Society with the swingeing cuts facing all council budgets as a result of ongoing austerity – a combined shortfall in funding of some £6 billion. As *The Guardian* (Oct. 2018) bitingly put it: *"There is something sad and ridiculous in the launch of a civil society strategy imagining new institutions to support local communities when the existing political structures, the democratically mandated authorities that have always fulfilled that purpose are collapsing in a fiscal famine imposed with ideological motive by central government."*

A much more practical and personalised approach to promoting voluntarism might have been for the Government to have set up and funded the sort of comprehensive national retirement service envisaged by Lord Wei; a service that might encourage, support and mobilise the new old, the baby boomer generation, into working in their local communities, and so enable them *"to live the life that they dreamed of while at the same time connect them with opportunities that can help all of us"* (Lord Wei: *The Telegraph*: 30 June 2012). Should we be considering the idea of a National Voluntary Service for both old and young rewarded by tax credits or additional tax relief on their pensions now or in the future? Do we in Britain today need a call to arms akin to that of President JFK's to the American people in his Inaugural Address in 1961: *"Ask not what your country can do for you – ask what you can do for your country."*? Is this the sort of call for generativity and volunteering that might really inspire British baby boomers and truly convert them from a #MeToo into a We-Too generation? And if so, do we have any politician in Britain today with the charisma and common touch to inspire British people of all ages to look outward and to look forward in search of common purpose rather than in pursuit of self-interest? And if no such British politician exists today, does this task fall back on celebrity boomers like Joanna Lumley to do it for them – and for us. As Anthony Seddon has argued (*The Sunday Times*: 23 Nov. 2014), **don't forget the young** when promoting volunteering: "*Young people have a palpable appetite to help and they recognise that the benefits this brings are not just to their communities but also to themselves.*"

So, Hannah and Team Z had done their job well. Polly now had not only a theoretical outline of the key features of an ageless society and some idea of what a 100-year life would look like, but also a vision of at least one very positive and practical way to get there that would benefit all generations and make full use of baby boomers' undoubted skills, experience – and possibly their wisdom: *the voluntary way* and its potential appeal to the altruism and generativity of the new old. She, equally, had a draft manifesto and revived intergenerational social contract, a vision of a Britain greater than today and a strategy for raising the age debate within her own party and up the national agenda. A 'project hope' to counter the 'project doom and gloom' surrounding so much of the media portrayal of the ageing world ahead; a silver frame for a new age of intergenerational support and collaboration. In particular, she now had a new faith; a faith in the young, inspired by her granddaughter Laura and Team Z, that they were the future; that they needed to take a joint lead in this age campaign and be instrumental in designing the British age manifesto and in campaigning for a 21st-century social contract. Shifting the ownership in this way and engaging the younger generation from the start was to prove Polly's masterstroke in propelling this manifesto forward, in engaging all ages, in winning over older voters resistant to change, and in convincing her parliamentary colleagues and party leader that here was something fresh, something special, something for the future. So, perhaps what the Ageing Agenda needs is a Greta Thunberg to propel Ageing on to the international stage with the same passion and force as climate change.

Polly even set up a competition for local schoolchildren as to what they thought an ageless world might look like. As you can imagine some of the sketches and descriptions, poems and pictures defied belief and provided a rare – and highly amusing – insight into how the very young see the old and what we ought to do with them. The moon proved to be a popular retirement home in the view of many schoolchildren while one budding economist suggested that post-Brexit Britain reduce the demographic imbalance between itself and the developing world by trading a percentage of its elderly population with twenty-year-olds from Africa and South America. In that way, he argued, developing countries gained the wisdom and experience of our retirees; the UK gained the energy and ambition of young

Africans and Latin Americans – alongside a boost to its birth rate – while our elderly got the opportunity to retire to warmer and healthier climates abroad and to live even longer. Apparently, a win-win proposal despite the numerous ethical and political issues involved and certainly one that caused much amusement at Prime Minister's Question Time when Polly used it as an example of what very young people thought the government might do about ageing.

An ageing world; a super-ageing society

What Polly didn't have, and what she now needed, was experience herself of an ageing society; what it actually looked and felt like. She had read about ageing societies but never actually been to one. She had imagined life in an ageing society but never lived in one. And where better to visit than ageing Japan – still one of the top five economies in the world but now also the oldest nation on the planet, and one facing the monumental challenges of both ageing elders and an 'imploding' population. Japan today is literally shrinking and shrinking fast. It is 'super-ageing' at a startling rate and is predicted to shrink from its current 127 million people down to a mere 95 million in the next 30 years. It is currently looking like the 'grey nightmare' feared by so many in an age of ageing, but through government action and technological innovation it is now being slowly transformed into the first rays of what might be "***the dawn of a silver age.***" Japan is becoming something of an international laboratory for the age revolution ahead and, as such, an ideal 'silver or grey' hot-spot to visit for the parliamentary working party on ageing that Polly had managed to put together. And what a visit it proved to be; what an insight into the grey and silver world ahead; and what a warning to a complacent Great Britain if and when it and its politicians ever wake up to the horrors and hopes ahead. This was to be the third act in Polly's journey into ageing. This was to prove the ultimate inspiration for her own encore career as a politician and as a preacher for the gift of longevity.

Japan is often described as the Land of the Rising Sun but now, as the oldest nation on earth, Japan is working desperately towards transforming itself into the '*Land of the Silver Sun*' rather than the world's first 'grey graveyard'. Japan today has a population of some 127 million people, and this is projected to fall to 95.2 million by 2050 and 87 million by 2060 – a fall in population of some 31% or one million people a year over the next 36 years. This is the **demographic collapse** of volcanic proportions that economists at Tokyo University have called a "*countdown to national extinction*". Japan currently has the highest proportion of those aged 65 and over (26%) and the lowest ratio of those under 15 years old (12.8%) in the world. By 2060, those aged 65 and over are projected to rise to

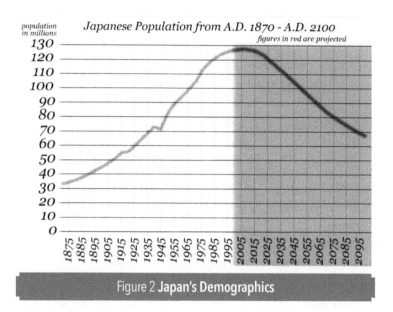

Figure 2 **Japan's Demographics**

40% of the total population, turning the Japanese population pyramid almost literally on its head in less than 100 years, and dramatically overturning in the process all the normal demographics of population planning. Between 2010 and 2060, the percentage of over-75-year-olds is predicted to more than double, from 11% to 27%, and Japan already has over 68,000 people over 100 years of age. And the working population in Japan is projected to shrink to 53.6% of its population by 2050, from 66 million in 2013 to 38 million by 2060, creating a dependency ratio of 1:3 dependents to workers.

So, Japan faces an ageing Armageddon, a **population implosion** of catastrophic dimensions, with its over-65 population threatening to swamp its working population and so reduce Japan from the world's third largest economy into an economic backwater. It has the world's highest life expectancy at 84 years, combined with one of the world's lowest fertility rates. Demographically and economically, Japan is facing implosion and stagnation; and the government is now having to decide between raising its state retirement age to 77 and/or accepting net immigration into Japan of some 17 million 'foreigners' by 2050.

So, Japan today faces monumental challenges that include:

How to respond to hyper-ageing: How to raise the birth rate and rebalance the population in a society where the birth rate is currently is even now only 1.43 children per woman, well below replacement level.

How to change social behaviour, particularly of the young: Young women, for example, currently delay child-rearing on average until aged 28–30, and one in five have apparently decided to stay single for life as a means of enjoying high levels of disposable income. They live at home and focus on their careers rather than seek marriage. These single women are often labelled 'parasites' by the Japanese media, while young men are often referred to as 'herbivores' because they too seem equally determined to stay single and equally reluctant to engage in marriage, long-term relationships – or even sex. Marital roles are still highly segmented, with few men taking childcare leave or undertaking childcare responsibilities. Surveys have revealed that over 40% of fathers have never changed a nappy or put the children to bed. The cost of childcare, schooling and even pregnancy is not covered by healthcare insurance, so adding to the numerous obstacles to promoting fertility.

How to meet the escalating costs of a hyper-ageing population, with pension costs escalating and social expenditure projected to rise from 18% of national income in 1992 to 27% by 2025.

How to rebalance the dependency ratio as it approaches 3:1 by 2025. The working population is shrinking but there is a national aversion to immigration as a replacement source of labour. Immigrants are seen as a threat to the purity of Japanese culture. It is difficult for foreigners to become Japanese citizens, although two million foreigners live in Japan currently. A UN study in 2000 found that Japan would need to admit ten million immigrants annually to maintain its current 'worker to retirees' ratio.

How to engage and reactivate the elderly as they retire from work and live apart in the mushrooming towns and cities or live alone and abandoned in the countryside. While the Japanese elderly are living longer, many of them are living alone and giving up on life. Japan has grown old psychologically, and much of the media is focused on death and dying. The Japanese monthly magazine *Takarajima* (which means Treasure Island), for example, featured an article in December 2013 entitled, 'Japan: Suicide Archipelago', as people over 60 now account for some 37.8% of all suicides. Shoplifting and senior-citizen crime have equally soared, tenfold in the past 20 years, and one in five inmates in Japanese prisons is elderly, many of whom have deliberately sought incarceration in preference to the loneliness of life outside.

As *The Japan Times* explains: "*Japan is an elderly country. Twenty-three percent of its population is 65 or over. By 2050, nearly forty percent will be. Nothing like these demographics has ever been seen before, here or anywhere… But there is another dimension to it. Japan has grown psychologically old. Old age has reshaped the mental landscape… For 13 straight years, suicide has claimed more than 30,000 Japanese lives annually, carnage worthy of a civil war,*" and nearly 40 per cent of these suicides have been by those aged 60 and over. Shop-lifting has "*soared ten-fold in the past 20 years among the elderly, twice the rate among those 19 and under*" (*The Japan Times*: Nov. 2011).

The government's response has largely centred around the following:

Abenomics – the economic strategy launched in 2013 by the new Japanese Prime Minister Shinzo Abe to resurrect the Japanese economy after two decades of low growth and the financial crash of the early 1990s. According to Linda Yueh of BBC News (18 Dec. 2013), Abenomics is based on three key strategies: reflating the economy through quantitative easing or cash injections; investing in infrastructure to stimulate employment and consumption; and deregulation to free up Japanese markets and encourage foreign investment. In particular, the government aims to raise the working population by encouraging higher labour participation by women, encouraging the newly retired back to work and even by reconsidering the country's retirement age of 60. Japan's female labour participation rate is amongst the lowest in the advanced economies at 50%, compared with 60% in the US and UK. It reflects both the priority given by families to childcare – and now eldercare – the impact of a male-dominated working culture and the glass ceiling facing Japanese women seeking entry to the top professions. Finally, and very reluctantly given the traditional Japanese resistance to immigration, the government has recently relaxed its immigration control laws to allow a limited number of manual labourers from abroad to enter the country.

Childbirth initiatives. In 1994–1999 the Japanese government launched the Angel Plan, with the aim of trying to improve work-life balance and so encourage couples to have more children by improving childcare and improving family life. However, this failed to stem the country's declining fertility rate, which fell dramatically from the 2.07 in the 1970s to a record low of 1.26 in 2005 and even now is only 1.43, as child-support payments remain low but fees for education and health remain high.

Promoting the silver economy. Japan's elderly, in contrast, are spending 'like there's no tomorrow'. Japan's pensioners are buying luxury goods, travelling abroad and indulging their tastes for expensive food. They are no longer saving to support their children financially, and parents now have few inhibitions about spending their children's inheritance. The unspoken family contract is no longer as firm as it once was.

Transforming national healthcare. Up until the year 2000, it was assumed that the family would look after older relatives, as part of the Confucian ethic of filial piety, and as part of the duties expected of children. However, with Japan's economic miracle and the economic boom of the 1970s, healthcare expanded but so too did the nuclear family and the rise in female labour participation. Traditional values were under threat as the young started to enjoy new opportunities; and the abuse and poor treatment of elderly relatives created a crisis in care, which included the abandonment of elderly parents in hospitals and residential homes. The shame of this pattern of behaviour led, in the year 2000, to Japan introducing a new compulsory long-term-care insurance system with the motto '*Our family Our society*'; a new form of social contract through which everyone pays healthcare insurance. This brought long-term peace of mind and a sense of security to the elderly alongside, inevitably, a dramatic expansion in service use and a reduced burden on family carers. The demand for improvements in the quality and level of care, however, soon led to increases in both taxation and insurance premiums. In 2005 the government introduced measures like means-testing to ensure that the new system was more sustainable, comprehensive and proactive. The system of healthcare for women became one of the most generous and inclusive in the world, and it has created a profound shift in attitude towards care for older people. It is now accepted that care is a collective social responsibility led by the state and funded by taxation. It is equally recognised that isolation is one of the greatest dangers of ageing; to that end, the number of residential homes is severely restricted, to encourage care in and by the community, mainly by volunteers, many of whom are pensioners themselves, as part of an 'age circle of care'. Inevitably, however, as costs rise so do taxes, while shortages of nursing homes and care staff are creating inequalities in provision and putting a heavy burden still on poorer families. Japan now has an age tax levied on every worker over 40, paid, too, by pensioners, to fund long-term care – a strategy that the UK government, amongst others, is currently looking into and could well learn much from according to the Nuffield Trust (2018).

Creating age-friendly communities designed by and for the residents with everything at hand, with transport well integrated and with families close by to support active ageing and ageing in place, such as Yukarigaoka in the city of Sakura. Japan is now developing self-driving robot shuttle buses in rural communities and highway rest stops to ferry the elderly to and from medical, retail and banking services.

Investing in new technology and the robot revolution as the key to raising productivity and the national GDP. New technology is being developed to service the rapidly expanding elder market, with products as wide-ranging as intelligent toilets that can literally lift the elderly up off the loo, analyse their waste and report to their GP; intelligent cars with enlarged dashboards and computer controls that can curb erratic or dangerous driving; and 'care-beds' that can transform into wheelchairs or even turn the sleeper over during the night. Japan's Institute of Physical and Chemical Research has developed Ruba, a nursing robot that can lift the elderly out of bed; a robot bath that can enclose an elderly person in a tub and put them through a wash and rinse cycle; and walking sticks with inbuilt satnavs to guide the elderly home or alert carers in the event of any falls they may have. Japanese mega-corporations such as Panasonic are aiming to develop the **total solution** to the silver society, not only for Japan but for the ageing world at large. For many in Japan, robots are the ultimate solution, whether as workers or servants, pets or partners, in the battle to raise productivity for the young and combat loneliness and isolation for the old. Paro, for example is a furry white baby seal that many elderly Japanese have adopted as their companion as well as their pet; and Toreo is a red panda that apparently barks out exercise instructions to get the elderly to be more active. Japan now has twice as many pets as children and "*in a society that remains resolutely anti-immigration, robotic technology is seen as the answer to the lack of human beings.*" Companion robots have not yet led to dramatic reductions in healthcare costs, but they do apparently boost the morale and sense of community of both care-home residents and their staff. Many elderly find robots like RoBoHoN – an eight-inch tall black and white figure with a cute monkey-like face – much easier to talk to than humans, and even more soothing in reducing anxiety and depression, as described in Camilla Cavendish's new book *Extra Time: 10 Lessons for an Ageing Society* (2019).

Japan may be the oldest nation on the planet today with 20% of the world's centenarians but others are now close behind, notably Korea, China and Hong Kong in Asia, and Germany, Italy and Sweden in Europe. Some, like Seoul, Korea's capital city, have started to develop a 50+ strategy in preparation for the 100-year life ahead, but currently Japan still leads the way in seeking to solve this immense demographic conundrum. Its experiences and solutions could and should make it a 'silver research laboratory' for every other society facing the age of ageing that is the 21ˢᵗ century. Japan's challenge, however, is twofold. It is ageing faster than any other society on the planet, and its population is imploding at the same time; an ageing double whammy of immense proportions and one that will take a social and a technological revolution to even begin to come to grips with.

Polly's visit to Japan had a profound impact not only on her own political thinking but on her own philosophy of life. Wowed as she was by all the technological wizardry that the Japanese government and corporations were throwing at the ageing challenge, what stayed with her most was the attitude and demeanour of the Japanese people and most especially the older and elder ones she met. Her visit to the ancient people of the island of Okinawa, for example, introduced her to the concept of ***ikigai,*** the Japanese word meaning '*having a reason to live; having a reason for being*', and to a way of life where self-realisation and a sense of oneness or commitment to the group underpin every aspect of this community's way of life. Here the people enjoy exceptionally long lives living on a very healthy diet, and they specialise as master craftsmen in skills that collectively contribute to the way of life of the whole community, whether it be as master fishermen, farmers or karate experts. Polly found their sense of purpose and their community spirit truly moving and, given that many of this island's inhabitants were over 100 years old, their example of positive and purposeful ageing stayed with Polly thereafter and heavily influenced her ideas on generativity and the ageing societies of the future. Okinawa, however, is not alone. It is one of the growing number of *Blue Zones* around the world that includes Barbagia in Sardinia and the Nicoya peninsula in Costa Rica, where communal living based on healthy natural eating and communal rituals that include destressing exercises underpin some of the longest and healthiest lifespans in the world. Dan Buettner, Blue Zones founder, has now attempted to set up Blue Zone projects within urban environments in the US to try and combat the hectic, stressful and unhealthy lifestyles that such manmade environments seem to generate. The results, he claims (WEF: 2017), have been dramatic, with local people living nearly three years longer, healthcare claims falling by 49% and absenteeism from work declining by some 20%. Changing the lifestyle of a whole nation, however, may prove another challenge altogether, but at least such Blue Zone living offers an alternative model for arriving in later life fit enough to enjoy it – particularly for ageing hippies harking back to the communal lifestyles of their youth. And while Britain may not have any Blue Zones of its own, towns like Rushmoor in Hampshire and my own Leigh-on-Sea in Essex have been identified by the ONS (2018) as some of the happiest places to live in the UK. Perhaps 'happiness' ought to be the new mantra, the new philosophy for life, the new measure of life in ageing Britain, for all of us in the years ahead, too.

So, Polly returned to Britain mightily impressed by both the technology of ageing that Japan is now developing and the philosophy of ageing life that she saw and experienced in Okinawa. It led her to reflect not only on the lessons for the UK but equally those for Europe, currently the oldest continent in the world – and unlike Japan, not a world away but just a tunnel away geographically and culturally. Britain may be leaving the EU but what happens there still has immense implications for us in the UK. Yet, as described in Appendix A, with the notable exception of the Netherlands and Scandinavian nations, most European countries seem to be as '*woefully*' underprepared for ageing as Great Britain. The tiny nations of Latvia and Lithuania are already being demographically drained as their young migrate to Germany and the UK, while Chancellor Merkel's attempt to attract a million refugees from North Africa and the Middle East into ageing Germany not only backfired domestically but provoked the rest of Europe into shutting its doors to migrants. Britain may be still be a younger country than most in Europe, it may still be growing in population, but beneath the surface it too faces a demographic shift of monumental proportions that will soon gather pace and impact right across its social and political structures, a shift that Brexit may ironically accelerate rather than derail.

Welcome, thought Polly, to the wonders of ageing and to the challenges ahead.

EPILOGUE TO PART THREE

Unfinished Business – We've not even started!

An African proverb says: *"The world was not left to us by our parents. It was lent to us by our children. What survives of me are the world's children, for whose sake I act today. It is as if the most generative people among us most readily envisage the future's children, as if they see the baby watching them. Innocent and dependent on our own efforts of care, the future looks to each of us with hope."*

From 'Generativity: The new definition of success'
in the journal *Spirituality and Health* (2001)

So, Polly had now seen for herself the impact of ageing. She now had personal experience of the realities of living in an ageing society – a super ageing world – where the old are exploding in number and the young are shrinking in size. She had seen first-hand how one of the richest nations on earth is using the latest technology and the most *human* of robots to tackle the greatest challenge to the future of Japan since WWII. She had equally come across a philosophy of life, a silver philosophy of life, practised in the mushrooming communities of the Blue Zones, that had offered inspiration not only for how to live to 100 or more but why to do so and with what purpose. It had been a life-changing experience as well as a fact-finding expedition that had not only profoundly affected Polly but influenced all of her fellow MPs.

Coming home to the UK and to all the trials and tribulations of Brexit, therefore, was quite a shock. Important as Brexit is as a national debate, it is a relatively temporal one compared to the long-term impact of ageing on British society. In contrast to the furore over Brexit and the intensity of its debate, ageing is a national silence broken by the occasional headline about bed-blocking in the NHS, the care crisis in residential homes or think-tank reports whose doom and gloom prophecies now outstrip anything put out by project fear. The renowned think-tank, the ILC-UK, for example, presented a worst-case scenario at its 2017 Future of Ageing conference of '*too little for too many*' that was quite horrific in terms of the escalating costs and numbers of elderly that will soon face Britain's health and social care services, housing supply and family structures. The post-Brexit scenario presented by the Institute for Public Policy's report in late 2016 entitled *Future proof: Britain in the 2020s* was even more disturbing in its conclusions. It argued that in the aftershock of Brexit, slow global economic growth and escalating inequality:

- **Britain in the 2020s** will have reached a demographic tipping point as the fastest growing country in Europe, with its 65+ population growing by 33% between 2016 and 2030, notably amongst the over-85s. It will have become almost as ethnically diverse as the USA is today, with the non-white population expected to rise from 14% to 21% by 2030 and 33% by 2050, with immigration slowing after Brexit but remaining high due to the need for younger labour from abroad.

- **Britain in the 2030s** will be part of a brave new world in which the economy is likely to see manufacturing, administration and public services shrink, while the service sector grows with creative and care work surging and even the space sector taking off; in which work will become more insecure, more polarised and more freelance, with intelligent automation radically changing the way we work and supercharging inequality with middle- and lower-income households struggling to cope while the super-rich grow ever richer. Human work may not disappear, but it will become increasingly obsolete with the relentless advance of automation and AI. The state will shrink in size and importance, and public services will be under enormous strain as delivery and funding are increasingly devolved to local authorities, while the tax gap between receipts and expenditure is forecast to grow as the population ages, the workforces shrinks, and Brexit diminishes public finances.

- **British democracy by 2030** will be in distress in the aftermath of Brexit. The British political system and its first-past-the-post electoral system will struggle to reflect and accurately represent the growing diversity and growing inequalities in British society, particularly those of age. Attitudes to immigration and globalisation will become the new dividing line, and trust in Westminster government and the British political class will decline even further. Devolution, emergent nationalism and Brexit are likely to fragment the United Kingdom even more while "*The whole of society will have become a single office and a single factory*" as a result of globalisation. The data revolution and the Internet of Things will generate even greater wealth and power for whoever controls it, and democracy will be under threat from either big government or big tech. Worse, the brave new world of AI may lead to the surveillance society feared long ago by George Orwell, this time not in the hands of the human masters of the universe at Facebook or Google but in those of supercomputers serving robot rulers. Finally, intergenerational relations will be under serious strain as generational differences over income and housing reach a peak as millennials threaten to become the first post-war generation with lower total lifetime earnings than the generations before, and with the cohorts now entering work struggling to find employment, earning less than their predecessors and being unable to afford a home of their own. By 2030, almost 40% of under-40s are forecast to be living at home – with powerful political and economic consequences in the future. As the institute concludes: "*Without reform, our political and fiscal system will struggle to build a more democratic, healthy society in the decades ahead, even as Brexit accelerates us towards a radically different institutional landscape.*"

So, Britain – and the world – desperately needs a big debate on ageing, not just one in Suffolk East or just in the UK. It needs a new social contract to reassert and reaffirm the contract between the generations that is at the heart of any harmonious or integrated society. It clearly needs leadership and a new age movement to support it, with both the new old and the new campaigning in the Westminster lobbies and on the streets of Britain. The state alone cannot bear the ageing burden or create the ageless society. It can only lead the way. Ultimate responsibility falls to the individual, the family, the employer and the markets. What the state *can* do is instigate, lead and orchestrate such a public debate and set out the principles for planning a fundamental shift in the structure of British society upon which long-term planning in the interests of all generations in the multigenerational society of the future might be based. Realising the gift of longevity, maximising the full potential of the longer life ahead in the 21st century, is a huge challenge but one that is vital to the health and future of our children and grandchildren if our generation is not to become their burden; if our generation is to realise its mission as a generative and generous generation and not go down in history as a greedy and self-obsessed one; and if Laura's generation and thereafter are to enjoy the future we would want for them.

That was the mission that Polly had set herself; that was the national debate that she was calling for. Polly was aware, however, that in many ways she was swimming against the tide of contemporary political movements. *"Identity politics and Nationalism seemed to be replacing class politics – or any other form of organised collective consciousness and action – as the key forces for social change and political action"* (Francis Fukuyama: 2018). #MeToo, Black Lives Matter and transgender campaigns now dominate much political campaigning in the USA and UK, while 'Take Back Control' and 'America First' have become the hymn sheets of the Brexiteers in Britain and Donald Trump supporters in America. The dispossessed and disenfranchised seem to be fighting back against the established political order, and democratic societies seem to be fragmenting along the lines of identity and status rather than class, ethnicity or even gender – a fragmentation that the existing electoral systems and political parties struggle to represent, reflect or contain. So the challenge for Polly, and for any like-minded politician now or hereafter, is how and where to sow the seed of intergenerational reunion and how to grow it into a political manifesto with majority appeal at a time when minority opinions and loyalties seem to be in the ascendancy. How, after the dire debates on Brexit, the United Kingdom might be reunited under a new national plan, a new social contract and a new post-Brexit national vision if it is to become a better Britain, for all ages not just for the old or the better-off.

While Polly's political strategy remained firmly based on her faith in the baby boomer generation as the advanced guard for any such manifesto, she now saw the young as much a part of the silver dawn ahead as the old; as its inner light; its eternal light in guiding all ages forward. Giving Laura and her Team Z the opportunity to lead and initiate debate had been a step-change in itself and, for Polly, a personification of the spirit that had inspired the Beveridge Report in the first place. Baby boomers have changed the world before; but this time round, reflected Polly, we need to change it with and for the young too. After all, it's more their future than ours now. They are young; they still have the legs for marching and campaigning; and they have a lifetime ahead of them, not just a later life. We may instead need to step back wisely and marshal and marvel from the side lines rather than lead from the front. We may need to be there in spirit even if we cannot make it in the flesh. But whatever way round the roles and responsibilities turn out to be, time is running on as the boomer generation moves into retirement and soon – oh so soon – into old age and dependency. As David Willetts has reminded us, January 2017 was the 70th anniversary of the baby boomer boom and soon even more of us will be aged 70 and over than ever before. The 2022 British General Election is only three years away, and as Professor Laura Carsten (2009) has so forcefully reminded us: "*Aging is inevitable. HOW you age is not!... You will very likely spend about three decades of your life as an old person. Deal with it. Death is the only alternative. If you can put behind you the fantasy of eternal youth, you can begin to plan seriously for what comes next. You can think hard about the type of old person you want to be.*"

So, that's Polly's story; that's Polly's story to date. Clearly, there is more to come; clearly it is not cut 'n' dried with an oven-ready manifesto the outcome. Clearly, like Polly's campaign, the age debate has barely begun, and raising it up the British political agenda will be a Herculean task, even if some of its key themes like intergenerational fairness are now receiving national attention. Meanwhile, the world at large is moving on at mega-pace as globalisation, urbanisation and particularly new technology advance, converge and coalesce. As the website **Future Timeline** (2015) has described it: "*The world of 2050 will be a world of contrasts and paradoxes. On the one hand, science and technology have continued to advance in response to emerging crises, challenges and opportunities. This has created radical transformations in genetics, nanotechnology, biotechnology and related fields. On the other hand, many of these same technologies have been so disruptive that it has led to a more frightening, unpredictable and chaotic world than ever before. Humanity is at a cross-roads that will determine its future path for centuries to come – survival or destruction, prosperity or collapse.*"

So ultimately, the debate about ageing is not just about ageing generations or even ageing societies. It is about the future of humankind. It is about an ageing revolution within an ageing world where global forces are transforming that world at speeds currently beyond man's comprehension and where artificial intelligence is creating a whole new structure of power and control. Propelling the age agenda to the forefront of human debate, designing a new intergenerational social contract and unleashing generational power as a counterforce to untrammelled globalisation may prove to be one final attempt to re-establish human values and direction on a world apparently increasingly beyond the control of all but the most economically and politically powerful. And who better to lead, or at least instigate, this new age liberation than the generation that first put 'age rage' on the political map some 50 years ago and which now, as the new old, is most at risk from unrestrained 'Googlisation' and the Orwellian scenarios described above. Whether British baby boomers will rise up and respond to this generational swansong remains to be seen. Whether the age agenda can transcend the Brexit debate now or in the near future remains an open question; but if not, Great Britain faces a very bleak and grey future far from the silver land that longevity and generativity currently offer; far from the Britain where happiness and child welfare are high on the agenda, not low down the UNICEF scorecard as at present. Our children and grandchildren deserve and need a better legacy than this and to repeat the proverb at the beginning of this Epilogue: *"The world was not left to us by our parents. It was lent to us by our children. What survives of me are the world's children, for whose sake I act today."* Generativity: 2001.

We *"can't go back and make a brand new start (but perhaps we) can start now and make a brand new end."*

As explained in the Foreword and Preface, this book was written as an initial contribution to this much-needed debate, not its epitaph. Ageing is a mammoth issue and a gargantuan task. It is a national debate that Britain hasn't yet had; and all that a publication like this can do is set out the issues, explore some initial ideas for how this massive agenda might progress and hope someone will listen. If this contribution is in any way successful, if the age bandwagon begins to gather pace, then possibly Polly's work might be done and a real live silver (or orange) manifesto might be drafted and adopted by one of the major British political parties in the next British general election. If countries such as Norway can develop an embryonic strategy for the ageing world ahead (Appendix B), then why can't Great Britain? If the British political establishment is unwilling to take up this cause, will Polly's faith in her fellow boomers' idealism, wisdom and generativity be as well-founded as the African proverb above? Time will tell, and hopefully it will tell well.

Finally, and perhaps on a lighter note, maybe we all need an **age map** of our own, a road map for life – even later life – to give us a sense of direction, make the most of all the opportunities still before us, and make sure we don't leave a mess behind us. Maybe we all need an occasional reminder of our mortality and of the need to act *today* rather than leave it to tomorrow, particularly as we get older. So, the booklet overleaf was a particularly apt and timely present

Why we all need a new
MID-LIFE MAP

Gone are the days when middle age marked a leisurely stroll towards the finishing line of your working life. Now you're as likely to be changing your career as planning retirement. In fact, the only thing certain about midlife is that it's full of uncertainties. So where do we go from here? GH says it's time to rip up the retirement rulebook and plan for a new approach

It's up to you: plotting a new course

Figure 1: **Towards an Age Roadmap for Later Life**
(Good Housekeeping: Nov. 2013)

on my 67th birthday, not least as it came from my lovely wife, Jacqueline, rather than from HMRC. The title alone, *I'm Dead. Now What?* could have been heart-stopping, if not life-threatening, had it come from anyone else. Fortunately, it was simply part of her plan for tidying up in our later life and not leaving a mess behind for our children to clear up. A laudable ambition and one that, after extensive reassurances that happily I am still part of her plan for the future, Jacqueline and I have used to recheck our life insurances, rethink our later life and get everything in order before it is too late. If that title and that thought doesn't inspire you too, whatever your age, then nothing will. Enjoy the thought; buy the book and then enjoy the life ahead as you plan for yourselves, your children and your grandchildren in the century ahead.

APPENDIX A

The Ageing of the European Union

Europe, with over 500 million people, is already the oldest continent in the world, with parts of it about to go into demographic implosion, quite literally shrinking in terms of population.

By 2060, Europe will be the 'senior citizen' of the world as the proportion of the EU population over 65 explodes from 18% to 28%, from nearly 100 million to over 150 million by 2080 with those aged 80; an age cohort of over 66 million – the size of Britain today. By 2060, the elder population of the EU will have become almost as populous as the young population aged 0–14, while the working-age population aged 15–64 will have shrunk from 66% to 57%. The EU is undergoing a massive demographic challenge that will transform the EU, and the Western world with it, as graphically illustrated by the ageing infographic issued by the European Commission in 2016 and attached as Figure 1 on page 329.

By 2060, the 2018 EU Commission Ageing Report projected that, across the EU:

- **Life expectancy at birth** for males will have risen by 7.8 years from 78.3 years in 2016 to 86.1 by 2070, and by 6.6 years for females from 83.7 to an astonishing 90.3 years reflecting some closing of the traditional 'age gap' between men and women.

- **The old age dependency ratio** will have nearly doubled, from 29.6% in 2016 to 51.2% by 2070, a demographic 'shift' of volcanic proportions, from about four working-age people to every one person over 65 to two working-age people; the economic and social effects of such a seismic shift in population balance are yet to be fully understood.

- **The total fertility rate** is expected to rise slightly, from 1.58 in 2016 to 1.81 by 2070, across the EU but still be well below the replacement level of 2.1.

- **Annual net migration** across the EU is expected to decline, from net inflows of about 1.5 million people in 2016 to 914,000 by 2060 and 804,000 by 2070.

- **The UK** will have overtaken Germany by 2070 as the most populous European country, with 81 million people, followed by France (77m), Germany (79.2m), Italy (54.9m) and Spain (49.9m).

- **Globally**, as a proportion of the world population, the EU will have shrunk from 13.5% in 1960 to 4.5% by 2070. Africa, in contrast, is projected to grow to 32.1% of the world's population in the same period.

Moreover, *Two Europes* seem to be emerging as parts of Europe continue to grow demographically while other parts implode or shrink as the grey age wave sweeps across Southern and Eastern Europe far faster than Western and Northern Europe. While the population of Northern Europe is projected to rise sharply, increasing by 8% in the years up to 2030, the population of Eastern Europe is projected to fall by some 3% in the years up to 2030, and by 4% by 2070. Fourteen EU member states face old age dependency ratios of 2:1 or less over the next thirty years mainly in the east but with Portugal and Greece equally vulnerable. Nevertheless, Europe overall is rapidly dividing between the wealthier and healthier Western, Northern and Southern European nations and those in Eastern Europe that were formerly part of the Soviet Union. And it is likely that this demographic **age wave** that will not only profoundly affect economic relations between East and West but potentially the political and even military **balance of power**, with Russia lurking in the background but ironically facing a demographic implosion of its own.

The impact of ageing on this scale and at this rate is likely to be as *"permanent, profound and all-pervasive"* as anything the UN/WHO predicted for the rest of the world back in 2012. The EU, and Europe at large, will go through a demographic shift that will reshape it more profoundly and more permanently than any previous revolution or even global warming. It will affect not only the internal workings of the EU and the internal dynamics of the whole continent but equally its external relations with the rest of the West and, more profoundly, the developing nations of Asia, Latin America and particularly Africa, projected now to be the youngest of the world's continents and potentially the one with the greatest number of young people. A **demographic war** could potentially break out as the wealthy West and the Asian Tigers go into fierce competition for the young talent, energy and ideas that will be central to economic growth and prosperity in the mid- and late-21st century but no longer available at home from Europe's homebred youth.

The shift in the dependency ratio alone, from 4:1 to 2:1 workers to dependents, will leave most EU countries top-heavy with older people, potentially creating a huge demographic drag on their economies and a dramatic explosion in age-related spending that can only be met by massive improvements in productivity and a dramatic shift in the balance of responsibility between the state and the individual. The demographic revolution is about to present the EU with the challenge of an economic, social and political transformation that will reshape it for the rest of the century and impact on every government, household and individual across the continent – and beyond.

According to the ILC-UK fact-pack, 'Europe's Ageing Demography' (2014), the costs of ageing are likely to be dramatic if not traumatic. Pension costs will rise dramatically as a proportion of Europe's GDP, from just over 11% to 14.2% by 2060, with significant variations across member states. Healthcare expenditure across the EU is projected to rise from 7% in 2010 to anything between 8.2% of GDP to 12.6%, and long-term care is projected to double, from 1.8% to 3.6% between 2010 and 2060. Public expenditure increases of these proportions are bound to lead to intense political debates in every member state about the fair, as well as affordable, levels of age-related spending each country can and should afford to support and protect the older age groups. It is equally likely to impact profoundly on what the Europeans call **social solidarity**, on intergenerational relations, as the younger working-age groups are faced by escalating taxes to pay for their elder relations, while cuts occur in areas they need help with, be they education and training or childcare. The full impact, though, is expected to hit home from 2030 onwards as the baby boomers across Europe retire en masse and fundamentally shift the balance of the remaining workforce and the focus of the economy from the young to the older populations.

Europe, therefore, is at a demographic and political crossroads, with a dependency ratio projected to rise from nearly 28% now to over 50% by 2060: a 2:1 ratio that Vítor Constâncio, Vice-President of the European Central Bank, has described as *"collective demographic suicide"* unless addressed immediately. Spain, for example, has the lowest fertility rate in the EU, with an average 1.27 children per child-bearing woman, and a mass exodus of young people abroad in search of work. Germany and Italy are also shrinking demographically, while Portugal faces the prospect of soon being *"unsustainable in terms of economic growth, social security and the welfare state"*, according to the commission set up to investigate its demographic crisis in 2015. Sweden is one of the few countries that is likely to weather this demographic storm, aided by its generous parental leave and childcare system, its stable economy and its high net immigration. Ironically, as the rest of Europe shrinks, the UK is predicted to be the continent's largest nation; though post-Brexit and with tighter controls on immigration, it too is likely to see ageing rise dramatically.

The response to the age challenge across the EU is as rich and varied as the range of its members, with the EU Commission itself seeking to take the lead and follow the WHO vision of active ageing. The EU Commission's own Index of Active Ageing puts the Nordic and Northern nations of the EU, such as Norway, Sweden and Switzerland, at the forefront of planning for active ageing, while the poorer regions of Eastern and Southern Europe lag far behind. However, as discussed at the end of Part One, even the most advanced of the EU nations are only at the early stages in recognising the full implications and the depth of economic, social and political change ageing on this scale and at this speed represents. So, while the EU Commission has adopted a very proactive approach to ageing, and to 'smart ageing' in particular, individual member states have varied enormously in the response and long-term planning.

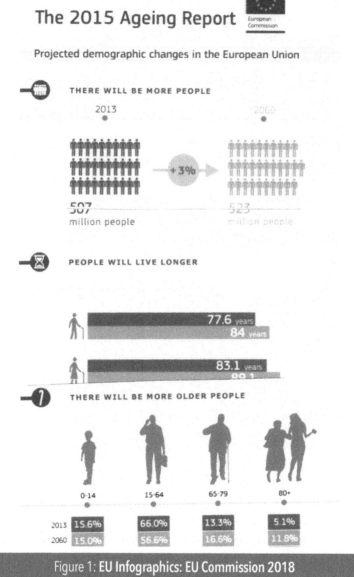

The 2015 Ageing Report

Projected demographic changes in the European Union

THERE WILL BE MORE PEOPLE

2013   2060

+3%

507   523
million people   million people

PEOPLE WILL LIVE LONGER

77.6 years
84 years

83.1 years

THERE WILL BE MORE OLDER PEOPLE

0-14   15-64   65-79   80+

2013   15.6%   66.0%   13.3%   5.1%
2060   15.0%   56.6%   16.6%   11.8%

Figure 1: **EU Infographics: EU Commission 2018**

Given the sheer size and potential impact of the demographic challenge facing Europe today, some would see the recent flood of refugees as a real opportunity to rebalance its populations and restore its youth. While Germany attempted to become a beacon of migration, a 'United States of Europe', welcoming migrants from all walks of life, it was ironically many of the EU countries who are shrinking demographically fastest, who closed their borders the quickest and the firmest. Hungary, Croatia and the Baltic States are fearful of being overrun and ethnically swamped, but in closing their borders so tightly they are also closing their economies and societies to new young blood. As Christian Bodewig of the Brookings Institution has argued (2015), the EU at large, through fear and lack of imagination, has now lost a golden opportunity to rejuvenate its population, rebuild its dependency ratio, regenerate its economy and regain its international reputation for compassion and humanity. Given the dramatic fall in their fertility rates, many of these grey states now have empty schools, nurseries and even housing that they can no longer fill or fund! Hence Hungary's proposed 'call for childbirth' offering lifetime exemption from income tax for women having four or more children.

However, it may all be too little, too late. As the UN World Population Report in 2015 and the 2016 report by the Federal Statistical Office of Germany made clear, immigration alone will not solve either Europe's demographic chasm or Germany's. Germany's elder population aged 67 and over, for example, is set to skyrocket, from 15.1 million in 2013 to 21.5 million in 2040, a 42% increase, while its working-age population, aged 20-66, is set to drop dramatically by nearly 25%, a potential loss of 13 million workers. Bridging this demographic chasm would require nearly half a million new immigrants every year for the next 25 years, and that would require a complete rethink of Germany's demographic strategy, let alone that of EU's as a whole. What the European refugee crisis has illustrated, however, is that global migration and global greying are intertwined; and that as they play out on the continent of Europe, 'doing nothing' may well prove the worst strategy of all. Finally, as the IMF Staff Development Note in January 2018 highlighted, Europe too faces an intergenerational challenge. Not possibly as severe as in the UK but nevertheless very real, as youth unemployment in some EU countries such as Spain and Greece remains exceptionally high and the resultant youth poverty is leading inexorably to the brain and skills drain of high levels of youth migration abroad, alongside high levels of youth alienation, crime and even terrorist recruitment, with severe implications for these countries' welfare systems and economies.

By 2050, Europe and the EU will be the **old man** of the known world in a global economy where the newer, younger, more vibrant continents will be fighting full force for economic and political dominance. Europe can no longer assume its political and economic pre-eminence. It will have to fight for it against younger nations determined to at last enjoy some of the wealth and prosperity that the West controlled in imperial times and since World War

II. The West no longer rules the world; European nations no longer possess vast empires overseas; Asia and the East are now challenging the economic and political power of the USA and Europe; and the internet has 'liberated' everyone and unleashed new technology that is transforming the very basis of the world economy. Europe and the EU is in danger of becoming an '**ancient continent**', left behind by the subsonic speed of globalisation and its failure to nurture tech giants capable of competing with those in America and Asia. Its failure to transform ageing and the gift of longevity from a threat into an asset could well prove its downfall; an asset that if properly managed could restore its world prominence, not maybe so much as an economic or military power but as a social and moral example of a continent where the full potential of all ages is being exploited for the common good; where the quality of life and the harmony of its intergenerational relations make it the greatest continent to grow old in; and where the older age groups feel valued and engaged, able to contribute as well as be supported and no longer discarded onto the margins of

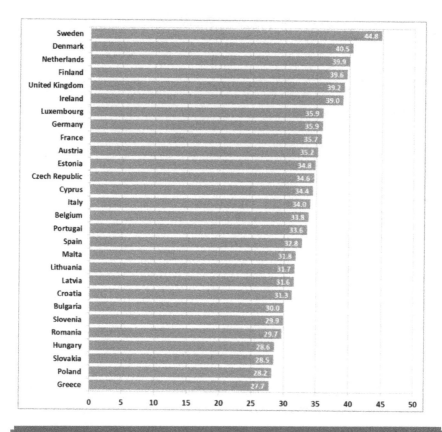

Figure 2: **Active Ageing Index (AAI): 2014**

society as before. That would be a true European legacy and an example of how human civilisations, and continents, can progress through generativity, as well as implode and decline through Darwinian economics and military conflict. McKinsey Global Institute's proposals (Dec. 2018) for a more inclusive European growth strategy based on increasing public social spending, tackling rising income inequality between and within member states and renewing the post-war European social contracts between employers and workers, citizens and government may well offer valuable lessons for a post-Brexit Britain; a Britain facing both the global megatrends above and its own need to regenerate its economy and reunite its nation after the intense debates on Brexit and the deep-seated divisions created by inequality and intergenerational tension.

APPENDIX B

The Norwegian Strategy on Ageing

The vision is that all Norwegians must be able to lead long and meaningful lives, and experience active and healthy ageing.

The goal is to make Norwegian society more age-friendly, and better harness the resources offered by older people, in terms of participation and contribution, by countering negative attitudes, reducing age discrimination, adopting new technology and providing better facilities for activity and participation.

The strategy is to continue to strengthen Norway's welfare state with its focus on pension reform and healthcare but also to keep older workers active and healthy for more years before they retire, to help them and society at large through:

- supporting longer working lives
- creating more age-friendly local communities
- engaging the voluntary sector and civil society
- developing new technology and stimulating the silver economy
- promoting a life-course approach to healthy ageing
- undertaking in-depth research into active ageing.

The aim is the top spot on the UNECE Active Ageing Index (AAI).

BIBLIOGRAPHY

A.

Abrams R. et al: Boomer Basics – Everything That You Need to Know About the Issues Facing You, Your Children and Your Parents: McGraw Hill: 2000

Acton Institute/Global Coalition for Aging: Ageing Population Strategies: 21st Century Social & Fiscal Challenges: December 2010

Aegon Retirement Readiness Surveys: 2012–2018, including The New Social Contract: a blueprint for retirement in the 21st century (2018)

AGE Platform Europe: Manifesto for the European Parliament elections: 2014

Age UK: Monthly Briefings/Reports including:

* The Economic Contribution of Older People in the United Kingdom (2018)
* Poverty in Later Life (2018)
* Health and Care of Older People in England (2017)
* Older people, fraud and scams (2017)
* Housing in Later Life (2014)
* Care in Crisis (2014)
* Age Manifestos: 2014/2015

Aguilar-Millan, Stephen: World Future Review: May 2014

Aldridge, James: *The Sunday Times* (11 Jan. 2015)

Alexander Shaw, Kate: Baby Boomers versus Millennials: rhetorical conflicts and interest-construction in the new politics of intergenerational fairness: SPERI/Sheffield Political Economy Research Institute: January 2018

Alston, Philip: Report on poverty in the UK: UN 2018

Arber Sara, Timonen Virpi (eds): Contemporary Grandparenting: Changing Family Relationships in Global Contexts: Policy Press: 2012

Arthur, W. Brian:

* The second economy: McKinsey Quarterly: 2011
* Where is technology taking the economy? McKinsey Quarterly 2017

B.

Bacon, James A. Jnr: Boomergeddon – How Runaway Deficits Will Bankrupt the Country and Ruin Retirement for Aging Baby Boomers: Oaklea Press: 2010

Barker Commission/Commission on The Future of Health and Social Care in England: Final Report: The King's Fund (2014)

Bartlett, James: The People Vs Technology: How the Internet is Killing Democracy: Penguin: 2017

BBC Radio 5: experiment on old age

Beckett, Francis: What did the baby boomers ever do for us? Why the Children of the Sixties Lived the Dream and Failed the Future: Biteback Publishing: 2010

Bedell, Geraldine: The *Observer* (8 May 2011)

Bell, Torsten: How to solve the UK's wealth inequality problem: *New Statesman*: February 2018

Berry, Craig: How the Growing Grey Vote could undermine British Democracy: openDemocracyUK (30 Apr. 2012)

The Rise of Gerontocracy: Intergenerational Foundation: 2012

Bloch, Lisa Friedman; Silverman Kirtland, Kathy: Manopause: Your Guide to Surviving His Changing Life: Hay House: 2012

Bodewig, Christian: Education is the key to integrating refugees in Europe: Nov. 2015: Brookings Institute

Bond, John et al: Ageing in Society – European Perspectives on Gerontology: Sage Publications: 2007

Bortz, WM; Stickrod, R: The Roadmap to 100 – The Breakthrough Science of Living a Long and Healthy Life: Palgrave McMillan: 2010

Bricker Darrell; Ibbitson John: Empty Planet: The Shock of Global Population Decline: Robinson:2019

Bristow, Jennie:
* Baby Boomers and Generational Conflict: Palgrave Macmillan: 2015
* The Sociology of Generations – New Directions and Challenges: Palgrave Macmillan: 2016

British Research Establishment: Design for Dementia: March 2019

Brynjolfsson, Erik; McAfee, Andrew:
* The Second Machine Age: W.W. Norton & Co: 2014
* Machine, Platform, Crowd-Harnessing our Digital Future: W.W. Norton:2017

Buchanan, Ann; Rotkirch, Anna (eds): The Role of Grandparents in the 21st Century: Routledge: 2018

Buettner, Dan: Blue Zones movement: WEF 2017

Burke, Stephen: United for All Ages: 2012

Butler, RN:
* Age-Ism – Another Form of Bigotry: The Gerontologist vol.9 (1969)
* Why Survive? Being Old in America: Harper & Row: 1975

C.

Cann, P; Dean, M (eds): Unequal Ageing – The Untold Story of Exclusion in Old Age: Policy Press: 2009

Capital Economics Report: 2010

Care Quality Commission:

* Elder Abuse: 2017
* The State of Healthcare and Adult Social Care in England: 2018

Carney, Mark: Inclusive capitalism: Creating a sense of the systemic: Speech at Conference on Inclusive Capitalism, London: Bank of England publications: May 2014

Carstensen, Laura: A Long Bright Future: PublicAffairs/Perseus Books:2009/2011
WEF article: 2018

Cass Business School Report: 2016

Cavendish, Camilla: Extra Time: 10 Lessons for an Ageing Society: Harper Collins: 2019

Center for Strategic & International Studies (CSIS):

* GAP Index (2014)
* The Graying of the Great Powers (2007)

Centre for Better Ageing:

* A silver lining for the UK economy: Feb 2018
* Inequalities in later life: Dec.2017

Centre for Progressive Policy (CPP): Further from the First Rung: May 2019

Chartered Institute for Housing Report: 2014

Chief Medical Officer's Report 2015: Baby Boomers – Fit for the Future: December 2016

Chivers Tom: The AI Does Not Hate You: Weidenfeld & Nicholson: 2019

CIPD: Generation Up – How the 4 Generations Work: Sept. 2008

Citizens Jury Report: Intergenerational Fairness: Britain Think: Feb. 2016. In association with PWC

Codrington, Graeme; Grant-Marshall Sue: Mind the Gap: Penguin Books: 2011

Commission on the Voluntary Sector & Ageing: Population Ageing and the Voluntary Sector: NPC/ILC-UK: 2014

Connolly, Billy: *Billy Connolly's Big Send Off*: ITV: May 2014

Coughlin, JF:

* How Technology will Transform Retirement: Wall Street Journal: 29 November 2015
* Technology, Aging and the Coming Fifth Wave: Next Avenue, June 20, 2016

Cowen, Tyler: Average Is Over: Powering America Beyond the Age of the Great Stagnation: Dutton Books: 2013

Cravit, David: The New Old – How the Boomers Are Changing Everything… Again: ECW Press: 2008

Credit Suisse: Global Wealth Report: 2016

Cridland Commission: Independent Review of the State Pension Age: Smoothing the Transition: Crown Copyright 2017

Croker, Richard: The Boomer Century 1946-2046 – How America's Most Influential Generation Changed Everything: Springboard Press/Hachette Books: 2007

D.

Danaher, John; McArthur, Neil (eds): Robot Sex: Social and Ethical Implications: MIT Press: 2017

Dean, Malcolm: Growing Older in the 21st Century: ESRC: 2007

De Hennezel, Marie: The Warmth of the Heart prevents your Body from Rusting: Ageing without growing old: Pan MacMillan: 2011

Deloitte Plc: Global Healthcare Strategy for the Future: 2019

Demos Publications:

- Huber, Julia; Skidmore Paul: The New Old: 2003
- Harkin, James; Huber Julia: Eternal Youth: 2004
- The Commission on Assisted Dying: Jan. 2012
- Generational Strains: Sept. 2013
- The Top of the Ladder: Sept. 2013
- Introducing Generation Citizen: Feb. 2014
- Tune In: Tune Out 2015: Dec. 2014
- Next Steps: Life Transitions in the 21st Century: 2015
- Next Generation UK: Youth attitudes and concerns: Sept.2017
- A Good Retirement: Dec. 2017

Dorling, Danny: Inequality and the 1%: Verso Books: 2015

Drake, Tim: Generation Cherry: Red Door: 2017

Driscoll, Helen: Sex with Robots will be 'the norm' in 50 years: The *Independent*: 4 Aug 2015

Dychtwald, Ken:

- Age Wave: The Challenges and Opportunities of an Aging America (with Joe Flower): Bantam Books: 1990
- Age Power: How the 21st Century Will Be Ruled by the New Old: Penguin/Putnam Books: 1999
- The Power Years – A User's Guide to the Rest of Your Life (with Daniel J Kadlec): 2005

E.

Easterbrook, Gregg: Sonic Boom – Globalization at Mach Speed: Random House: 2011

Eatwell, Roger; Goodwin, Matthew: National Populism: The Revolt Against Liberal Democracy: Pelican Books: 2018

The Economist (eds. Franklin, D with Andrews, J):

- Megachange: The World in 2050: Profile Books: 2012
  2020 Report
- Age Invaders (2014)

English Longitudinal Study of Ageing (ELSA): Reports: 2002-2015

Erikson, Erik:

- Identity and the Life Cycle: W.W. Norton & Company: 1994
- The Life Cycle Completed: W.W. Norton & Company: 1998
- Vital Involvement in Old Age: W.W. Norton & Company: 1994

EU Commission:

- Index of Active Ageing (IAA): 2014
- The 2018 Ageing Report: Nov. 2017

* Silver Economy Study by Oxford Economics & Technopolis: May 2018
European Observatory Report: 2013

F.

Family Planning Association (FPA): Safe Sex adverts for older people: 2010

Fergusson, Niall: The Ascent of Money: Penguin: 2019

Filkin Report: House of Lords Committee on Public Service and Demographic Change: Ready for Ageing: 2013

Financial Conduct Authority: Ageing Population and Financial Services: Sept. 2018

Fishel, Deirdre; Holtzberg, Diana: Still Doing It: The Intimate Lives of Women Over Sixty: Penguin: 2008

Foer, Franklin: World Without Mind: Penguin/Random House: 2018

Foresight Report: Future of an Ageing Population: Government Office for Science: 2016

Francis Report: Mid-Staffordshire NHS Foundation Trust Public Inquiry: 2013

Freedman, Marc:
* Prime Time: How Baby Boomers Will Revolutionize Retirement and Transform America: PublicAffairs: 1999
* Encore: Finding Work that Matters in the Second Half of Life: PublicAffairs: 2007
* The Big Shift: PublicAffairs: 2012
* How to Live Forever: The Enduring Power of Connecting the Generations: Public Affairs: 2018.

Frey, Carl B; Osborne, Michael A: The Future of Employment: How susceptible are jobs to computerisation? Oxford Martin School: 2013

Friedman, George: The Next 100 Years: A Forecast for the 21st Century: Double Day: 2010

Friedman, Thomas L: The World is Flat: Penguin: 2006

Fukuyama, Francis: Identity: Contemporary Identity Politics and the Struggle for Recognition: Profile: 2018

Furlong, Mary: Turning Silver into Gold: How to Profit in the New Boomer Marketplace: FT Press: 2007

Future of London Report: Are we ready for the boom? Housing older Londoners: 2018

Future Timeline: 2015

G.

Gawande, Atul: Being Mortal: Illness, Medicine and What Matters in the End: Profile Books:2014

German Federation Statistics Office Report: 2016

Gerrard, Nicci: The Twilight Hour: Penguin Books: 2014

Gibney, Bruce: A Generation of Sociopaths: How the Baby Boomers Betrayed America: Hatchette: 2017.

Giddens, Anthony: Modernity and Self-Identity: Polity: 1991

Gilleard, Chris; Higgs, Paul: Rethinking Old Age: Palgrave MacMillan: 2015

Global AgeWatch: 2015

Global Human Capital Trends Report: 2018

Global Retirement Index: Natixis Investment Managers: 2017

Goodhart, David: The Road to Somewhere: Penguin: 2017

Gordon, Robert J: The Rise and Fall of American Growth: Princeton University Press: 2017

Gott, Merryn: Sexuality, Sexual Health and Ageing: OUP: 2005

Grandparents Plus: The Poor Relation? 2009

Gratton, Lynda; Scott, Andrew: The 100-Year Life: Living and Working in an Age of Longevity: Bloomsbury: 2017

Green, Brent: Generation Reinvention: How Boomers Today are Changing Business, Marketing, Aging and the Future: Universe Inc: 2013

Grossman, Terry: The Baby Boomers' Guide to Living Forever: Hubristic Press: 2000

Grosvenor Report: Silver Cities – Planning for an Ageing Population: 2018

The Guardian: Article on Government's Civil Society Strategy: Aug. 2018

H.

Harari, Yuval Noah:
- Homo Deus: A Brief History of Tomorrow: Penguin/Vintage Books: 2015
- 21 Lessons for the 21ˢᵗ Century: Jonathan Cape: 2018

Harding, Tessa: Help the Aged Farewell Speech: 2006

Harkin, James: The backlash against baby boomers: *The Guardian*: Nov.6 2006

Harper, Sarah:
- Ageing Societies: Hodder Arnold/OUP: 2006
- Hard Brexit means retiring later: *The Guardian*: 16 Jan. 2017

Haskel, Jonathan; Westlake, Stian: Capitalism without Capital: The Rise of the Intangible Economy: Princetown University Press: 2018

Hawking, Stephen: Brief Answers to the Big Questions: John Murray: 2018

Heyman, Arlene: Scary Old Sex: Bloomsbury Paperbacks: 2017

Hills, John et al: Wealth in the UK: OUP: 2013

Hills, John: Good Times, Bad Times: The Welfare Myth of Them & Us: Policy Press: 2014

Holford, Patrick; Burne, Jerome: The 10 Secrets of Healthy Ageing: How to live longer, look younger and feel great: Piatkus: 2012

Hollis, Patricia: Foreword for The Pensions Advisory Service Report: 2010

House of Commons Reports:
- Fairness in an Ageing Society: Work & Pensions Committee: 2016
- Housing for Older People: Communities & Local Government Committee: Feb. 2018

House of Lords Reports:
- Public Services and Demographic Change: Ready for Ageing: March 2013
- Tackling Intergenerational Unfairness and Provision: April 2019

Howker, Ed: Jilted Generation: Icon Books: 2010

HSBC: Global Retirement Survey: 2013

Hutchison, Michele; Acosta, Rina Mae: The Happiest Kids in the World: Doubleday: 2017

Hutton, Will: Them and Us: Changing Britain – Why We Need a Fair Society: Abacus: 2011
Hyman-Robertson Report on Residential Care: 2017

I.

Independent Age: (Sex) Survey: Feb. 2018
I'M DEAD. NOW WHAT? Peter Pauper Press: 2015
Institute of Advanced Study of Human Sexuality: (2011)
Institute of Customer Service: The Service Generation: 2016
Institute of Fiscal Studies reports including:
* Dynamics of Ageing: 2016
* Savings after Retirement: 2016
* House of Commons Briefing: 2017
* Securing the Future: Funding health and social care to the 2030s: May 2018
* The NHS at 70: June 2018
* Living standards, poverty and inequality in the UK: June 2018
* Inequalities in the twenty-first century (introducing the Deaton Review by Robert Joyce and Xiaowei Xu): 2019

Institute of Mechanical Engineers: 2018
Institute of Policy Research (IPR)/Bath University: Death, Dying and Devolution: Sept. 2017
Institute of Public Policy Research (IPPR):
* Divided Democracies: Public Inequality in the UK and Why It Matters: 2014
* Future proof: Britain in the 2020s: Dec. 2016
* Wealth in the 21st Century (with Bath University): 2017
* Prosperity and Justice: Commission on Economic Justice: 2018

Intergenerational Commission/Resolution Foundation Reports including:
2019   Raising the equality flag: health inequalities among the older people.
2018   A new generational contract: the final report of the IGC.
       The new wealth of our nation: the case for a citizen's inheritance.
       Home improvements: action to address the housing challenges faced by young people.
       A silver lining for the UK economy? The intergenerational case for supporting longer working lives.
       A welfare generation: lifetime welfare transfers between generations.
2017   Home Affront: housing across the generations.
       The millennial bug: public attitudes on the living standards of different generations.
       As time goes by: shifting incomes and inequality between and within generations
       Live long and prosper? Demographic trends and their implications for living standards.
2016   Votey McVoteface: Understanding the growing turnout gap between the generations.
       Stagnation generation? The case for renewing the intergenerational contract.

Intergenerational Foundation Publications including:
2018   IF Fairness Index.

2017   Youthquake: Young people and the 2017 General Election.

Generation Remain: Understanding the Millennial Vote (2017).

2016   Generations Apart? The growth of age segregation in England and Wales.

2016 Intergenerational Fairness Index.

Unlocking England's Hidden homes.

The Rising Tide of Gerontocracy.

2015   What are we leaving to our children?

2012   Pensioner millionaires in the UK.

2011   Hoarding of Housing: the intergenerational crisis in the housing market.

The Poor Perception of Young people in the UK.

2008   Gerontocracy: Booth Philip.

International Longevity Centre (ILC-UK) publications including:

2018   The Future of Ageing Conference.

Inequalities Matter.

2017   Inequalities in Later Life.

When I'm 64 – Retirement Fact-pack.

The Grandparent Army.

Exploring Retirement Transitions.

How Long Will I Love You? Sex and Intimacy in Later Life.

Future of Ageing Summit.

2016   The State of the Nation's Housing: An ILC-UK Fact-pack.

Toward a New Age: The Future of the UK Welfare State.

Still Not Ready for Ageing.

Measuring State Effectiveness: an ILC-UK Index.

Tomorrow's World: The Future of Ageing in the UK.

Generation Stuck: Exploring the Reality of Downsizing in Later Life.

2015   Creating a Sustainable 21st Century Healthcare system.

The Myth of the Baby Boomer.

80 at Eighty. An ILC-UK Fact-pack .

2014   End of Life Decisions.

Getting Ready for Ageing: a Manifesto for Action.

Population Ageing & the Voluntary Sector: Key Figures & Projected Trends.

Age of Opportunity: Putting the ageing society of tomorrow on the agenda of the voluntary sector today.

2030 Vision: The best – and the worst – futures for older people in the UK.

I can't afford to die. Addressing funeral poverty.

The rise and rise of the silver separator.

Europe's Ageing Demography. An ILC-UK 2014 EU Fact-pack.

A Better Offer: The future of volunteering in an ageing society.

The Future Care Workforce.

Linking state pension age to longevity – tackling the fairness challenge.

2013   Grandparental Generosity.

2012   The cost of our ageing society.

Global Perspectives on Multigenerational Households and Intergenerational relations.

2011   Resuscitating Retirement saving: How to help today's young people plan for later life.

The last taboo: A guide to dementia, sexuality, intimacy and sexual behaviour in care homes.

Understanding the Older Entrepreneur.

'Living Beyond 100': A report on centenarians.

2010   The Golden Economy – The Consumer Marketplace in an Ageing Society.

Ageism and age discrimination.

The Future of Retirement.

International Monetary Fund (IMF):

* Advanced Economies Need Migration: April 2018

* Inequality & Poverty across the generations in the European Union: Staff Development Note: Jan. 2018

Ipsos MORI: How an Ageing Population Affects Voting Power in the UK (2010)

Ipsos MORI Social Research Institute: Beyond Binary – Communicating with Gen Z: 2018

J.

Jackson, Richard: Leading Edge Magazine interview: 2011

The Japan Times: Nov. 2011

Johnson, Michael: Why we should scrap state pensions for the rich: *Money Marketing*: April 2017

Jones, Ian Rees et al: Ageing in a Consumer Society: From passive to active consumption in Britain (Ageing and the Life-course Series): Policy Press: 2008

Joseph Rowntree Foundation (JRF) Reports:

* Retirement in the 21st Century: 2015

* UK 2017 General Election vote explained: Sept. 2017

* Living standards, poverty and inequality in the UK 2017-18 to 2021-22: Nov. 2017

K.

Kaku, Michio: Physics of the Future: The Inventions That Will Transform Our Lives: Penguin: 2012

Kalache, Alexandre: How the Baby Boomers Are Reinventing Old Age: *Huffington Post*: April 2012

Keen, Andrew: Rich List 2015: *The Sunday Times* (22 Feb. 2015)

Kennedy, Carole: Baby Boomers: The Ultimate Boomer Generation Guide: 2018

Key Retirement Report: 2017

King, Stephen D: Grave New World: The End of Globalisation: Yale University Press: 2017

The King's Fund Publications:

* Future Trends: Nov. 2012

* Time To Think Differently: 2014

* Barker Commission: The Future of Health and Social Care in England: 2014

- Futureproofing our NHS: 2018

Klein, Shelley: The Book of Senior Moments: Michael O'Mara Books: 2006

Klinenberg, Eric: Going Solo: The Extraordinary Rise and Surprising Appeal of Living Alone: Longman: 2013

Knight Frank: Reports on Housing in UK

Knight, India: In Your Prime: Older, Wiser, Happier: Penguin: 2014.

Knoll: How the Generations Compare: 2010

KPMG: Global Online Consumers Report: 2017

L.

Lanier, Jaron: Ten Arguments for Deleting Your Social Media Accounts Right Now: Bodley Head: 2018

Laslett, Peter: The World We Have Lost: Methuen & Co: 1965

Leach, Rebecca et al: Baby Boomers, consumption and social change: the bridging generation? International Review of Sociology 23(1): March 2013

Levy, David: Love and Sex with Robots: Gerald Duckworth & Co.: 2009

London School of Economics (LSE): Public lecture: Baby Boomers on Trial (part of LSE Space for Thought Literary Festival: 2014

Local Government Association (LGA): Housing our Ageing Population: Sept. 2017

Lord Wei: Why we need a national retirement service: *The Guardian*: 29 June 2012

Lukianoff, Greg; Haidt, Jonathan: The Coddling of the American Mind: Allen Lane: 2018

M.

Magnus, George: The Age of Aging: How Demographics are Changing the Global Economy and Our World: John Wiley & Sons: 2009

Manchester Institute of Collaborative Research on Ageing (MICRA): The Golden Generation? Wellbeing and inequalities in later life: June 2017

Mannheim, Karl (1928): The Problem of Generations; in Kecskemeti, Paul (ed.): Essays on the Sociology of Knowledge: Routledge: 1952

Manning, Margaret et al: Sixty and Me website

Manning Report: Migration Advisory Committee Report on EEA Migration: Sept. 2018

Mannix, Kathryn: With the End in Mind: Dying, Death and Wisdom in an Age of Denial: William Collins: 2017

Marmot Indicators Report: Institute of Health Equality: 2017

Matten, Glen; Goggins, Aidan: The Health Delusion: How to Achieve Exceptional Health in the 21st Century: Hay House Publications: 2012

Mayhew, Les:

- The Dependency Trap: are we fit enough to face the future? Centre for Study of Financial Innovation/Cass Business School: Jan. 2018

- The Last-Time Buyer: housing and finance for an ageing society: Centre for the Study of Financial Innovation: Feb.2019

McCarthy & Stone: Colour Report: 2015

McKinsey Global Institute reports and articles including:

- Global Flows in a Digital Age (2014)
- No Ordinary Disruption: Dobbs R; Manyika J; Woetzel J: PublicAffairs/Perseus: 2015
- Poorer than their Parents: 2016
- Global Migration
- Urbanisation and Global Consumer: 2016
- Urban World: 2017
- A Future that Works: 2017
- AI, Automation, and the Future of Work: 2018
- The Promise and Challenge of the Age of Artificial intelligence: 2018
- Inclusive Growth: Six global megatrends testing the EU model: 2018.
- Confronting the risks of artificial intelligence: 2019
- Globalisation's next chapter (podcast): 2019
- Asia's Future is Now: July 2019

McNamee, Roger: Zucked: Waking Up to the Facebook Catastrophe: Penguin:2019

Melbourne Mercer Institute: Global Pension Index Reports (GRI): 2017

Meister, Jeanne C; Willyerd, Karie: The 2020 Workplace: How Innovative Companies Attract, Develop, and Keep Tomorrow's Employees Today: Harper Collins: 2010

Mercer Workforce Monitor Report: 2018: The Impact of Brexit, Migration and Ageing on the UK Workforce: March 2018

Merrill Lynch:

- Age Wave Report: Americans' Perspectives on New Retirement Realities and the Longevity Bonus: 2013
- Family and Retirement: The Elephant in the Room: 2013

Modern Family Index: 2018 Report: Working Families/Bright Horizons

Morland, Paul: The Human Tide: How Population Shaped the Modern World: John Murray: 2019

N.

National Citizen Service: Youth Report: Welcome to our world: life as a teen in 2017

National Housing Federation on Housing and Intergenerational Inequality: 2017

National Survey (3rd) of Sexual Attitudes and Lifestyles: *The Lancet*: 25 Nov. 2013

Neuberger, Julia: Not Dead Yet: A Manifesto for Old Age: Harper Collins: 2008

New Economic Foundation: Nothing Personal. Replacing the personal tax allowance with a weekly national allowance: April 2019

New Labour: Building a Society for all Ages: 2009

New Policy Institute: Market Assessment of Housing Options for Older People: April 2012

Next Steps Project: Learning from your Generation: 2018 Update: Centre for Longitudinal Studies/ UCL Institute of Education.

Nielsen: BoomAgers: A Thought Leadership Collaboration:2012

Norwegian National Government: More Years – More Opportunities: 2016

Nottingham Trent University/ESRC Report: Young People and Politics in Britain: 2012

O.

Office for Budget Responsibility (OBR): Fiscal Sustainability Reports: 2015–2018

O'Connell, Mark: To be a Machine: Doubleday Books: 2017

OECD Publications including:

* Retirement, Past, Present & Future

* Society at a Glance: 2014

* Inequality: 2017

* Child Happiness: 2017

* Preventing Ageing Unequally: 2017

* Understanding the Socio-Economic Divide in Europe: 2017

* Pensions at a Glance: 2018

* Generational Solidarity: 2018

Odgers Berndtson: Talentocalpse: After the Baby Boomers: The next generation of leadership: 2013

Office of National Statistics: Statistical Reports (ONS):

* UK Population Reports 2017/18

* All publications relating to ageing: 2013–2018

* Population Tomorrow

* Life After Sixty Informatics

* Health Inequalities: 2017

* Family Types

* ONS/Cebr Report

Onward: Generation Why: April 2019

Oxfam Publications

* Reward Work, Not Wealth (2018)

* An Economy for the 99% (2017)

* Even It Up (2017)

* An Economy for the 1% (2016)

* Wealth-Having It All and Wanting More (2015)

Oxford Economics Report on:

* UK Economy: 2017

* The State of the Nation: The UK Family Business Sector 2017-18 (2018)

Oxford & Durham University: Grandparents influence where you are on the social ladder: 2017

P.

Pensions Policy Institute: Living the future life: 2018

Perel, Esther: The State of Affairs: Rethinking Infidelity: Yellow Kite: 2017

Phillipson, Chris: Re-thinking ageing populations: The British Academy: 23 May 2014

Piketty, Thomas et al:

- Capital in the twenty-first century: Belknap Press: 2014
- World Inequality Report: Harvard University Press: 2018

Policy Exchange: Building for the Baby Boomers. Making a housing market for an ageing population: December 2018

Portsmouth City Council: Myths & Outdated Assumptions of Older People in Portsmouth

Pressley, Alison: The 50s & 60s; The Best of Times: Growing up and Being Young in Britain: Michael O'Mara Books: 2003

PricewaterhouseCoopers (PwC): Will robots really steal our jobs? An international analysis of the potential long-term impact of automation: 2018

The Prince's Trust: Macquarie Youth Index Annual Report: 2018

Prudential: 2018 Retirement Preparedness Survey: A Generational Challenge

R.

Rand Europe: An Analysis of Global Societal Trends to 2030 and Their Impact on the EU (2015)

Raynsford, Nick: Planning 2020: Review of Planning in England: 2018

Rees, Martin:

- Our Final Hour: A Scientist's Warning: Basic Books: 2004
- Our Final Century: Will Civilisation Survive the Twenty-first Century? Arrow Books: 2004
- On the Future: Prospects for Humanity: Princetown University Press: 2018

Resolution Foundation Reports on:

- Inequality: 2017
- Living Standards Outlook: 2018

Richards, Amanda: Getting help for elderly loved ones: *Good Housekeeping*: 2013

Richardson, Kathleen: Sex Robots: The End of Love: Polity Press: 2019

Royal College of Nursing: Older people in care homes: Sex, Sexuality and Intimate Relationships (Guidelines on Patient Sexuality): 2011/2018

Royal London: The Death of Retirement Report: 2016

Royal Society for Public Health (RSPH): Survey on Ageism: That Age Old Question: June 2018

Royal Society of Arts (RSA): Collective Defined Contribution Pensions: 2018

S.

Saga/Cebr Report: Consumer spending key trends among the over 50s: Feb.2014

Savills Spotlight Report: Housing An Ageing Population: 2015

Schwab, Klaus: The Fourth Industrial Revolution: Crown Publishing Group: 2017

Schwalbe, Robert: Sixty, Sexy, and Successful: A Guide for Aging Male Baby Boomers: Praeger Books: 2008

Scott, John: quoted in WEF Global Risks Report: 2018

Scottish Widows: Retirement Report 2018: Adequate Savings Index

Seoul City: Ageing Strategy & 50 plus policy: cited in OECD Future of Work project: 2018

Shaxson, Nick: The Finance Curse: How global finance is making us all poorer: Bodley Head: 2018

Shelter:

- A better fit? Creating housing choices for an ageing population: 2012
- Far From Alone: 2018
- Building for our future: A vision for social housing: 2019

Singh, Sarwant: New Mega Trends: Implications for our Future Lives : Palgrave MacMillan: 2012

SIRC/Friends Provident: The Freetirement Generation: 2007

Smith Institute:
- Housing associations and the NHS: new thinking, new partnerships (2014)
- Are housing associations ready for an ageing population? (2015)

Social Mobility Commission Reports:
- Downward mobility and opportunity hoarding: June 2015
- State of the Nation: 2015/2017
- Social Mobility Barometer: 2017

Standard & Poor:
- Global Aging 2010: An Irreversible Truth
- Global Aging 2013: Rising to the Challenge

Stiglitz, Joseph: Freefall: America, Free Markets, and the Sinking of the World Economy: Penguin Books: 2009

Strauss, William; Howe, Neil:
- The Fourth Turning: an American Prophecy: Bantam Books: 1997
- Generations: William Morrow: 1998

Strittmatter Kai: We Have Been Harmonised: Old Street Publishing: 2018

Stroud, Dick; Walker, Kim: Marketing to the Ageing Consumer: The Secrets to Building an Age-Friendly Business: Palgrave MacMillan: 2013

The Sunday Times reports, articles & quotations (by author)
- Cybersecurity: Raconteur independent publication: 24 February 2019
- Female Entrepreneurs: 2014
- Ferguson, Niall: 26 June 2016
- Harris, Tristan: 7 July 2019
- Marsh, Henry: A Time to Die:1 July 2018)
- Milburn, Alan: 7 July 2019
- Nineties glamazons: 24 Feb.2019
- Precisely because we thought we would never get old: ST Magazine: 15 Oct. 2010
- Retirement: 28 Oct. 2018
- Rich List: Phillip Beresford in 2015 edition
- Rich Lists: 2017/18/19
- Seddon, Anthony: Don't Forget the Young (23 Nov. 2014)
- Stelzer, Irwin: 2013
- Surveillance: 4 Nov. 2018
- Willetts, David: 1 Jan. 2017

T.

Takarajima: Japan-Suicide Archipelago: Dec. 2013

Technopolis Report: A Mapping of Smart Ageing Activity in Ireland and An Assessment of the Potential Smart ageing Opportunity Areas: April 2015

Theobald, Stephanie: Sex Drive: On the Road to a Pleasure Revolution: Unbound: 2018

Timonen, Virpi: Ageing Societies: A Comparative Introduction: OUP: 2008

TUC: Life Expectancy, Inequality & State Pensions (2013)

Turner, Claire: JRF quotation: 2014

Turner Commission: Final Report: 2004/05

U.

UBS: 2017

UCL Report by Dustmann, Christian; Frattini, Tommaso: The Fiscal Effects of Immigration to the UK: 2014

UKCES: The future of work: jobs and skills in 2030: 2014

UNECE: Active Ageing Index: 2018

UNICEF:

Innocenti Report Card 13: Fairness for Children: A league table of inequality in child well-being in rich countries: 2016

Innocenti Report Card 14: Building the Future: Children and the Sustainable Development Goals in Rich Countries: 2018

United Nations Organization (UNO): World Population Reports on Ageing:2013-2018

United For All Ages: Fairness for all ages: 2016

University of Birmingham Policy Commission: The Distribution of Wealth in the UK: Sharing Our Good Fortune: Understanding and Responding to Wealth Inequality: 2013

University of Strathclyde: Global Entrepreneurship Monitor (2011)

V.

Victor, Christina R: Ageing, Health and Care: Policy Press: 2010

Vincent, John A:

- Politics, Power and Old Age: OUP: 1999
- The Future of Old Age: Sage Publications: 2006

W.

Walker, Alan: Ageing: The best years of our lives? British Academy Debates: 2014

Walker-Smith, J; Clurman, A: Generation Ageless: Yankelovich Survey: Harper Collins: 2007

Weigelt, David; Boehman, Jonathan: Dot Boom: Marketing to Baby Boomers Through Meaningful Online Engagement: Linx: 2009

Westendorp, Rudi: Growing Older Without Feeling Older: Scribe: 2014

Which: Report on Pensions (2014)

Wilkinson, Richard; Pickett, Kate: The Spirit Level: Why More Equal Societies Almost Always Do Better: Penguin Books: 2009

Willetts, David: The Pinch: How the Baby Boomers Took Their Children's Future – And Why They Should Give It Back: Atlantic books: 2011

Williams, Gervais: The Retreat of Globalisation: Anticipating radical change in the culture of financial markets: Harriman House: 2016

Williams, James: Stand out of our Light: Freedom and Resistance in the Attention Economy: CUP 2018

Worcester, Robert (Founder of Ipsos MORI): Grey Power to Decide? Ipsos MORI: 2003

World Economic Forum (WEF) publications including:

* Global Population Ageing: Peril or Promise? 2012
* How the 21st- Century Longevity Can Create Markets and Drive Economic Growth: Oct. 2015
* Technological Innovations for Health and Wealth for an Ageing Global Population: 2016
* We'll Live to 100: How Can We Afford It? May 2017
* Global Pensions Time Bomb (incl. Michael Dexler quote): May 2017
* Global Risks Report: 2017 & 2018
* Global Competitiveness Report & Index: 2018
* What robots mean for the future of work: Jan. 2018
* Silver Entrepreneurs: 2018
* The Inclusive Development Index (IDI): 2018

World Family Map: Mapping Family Change and Child Well-Being Outcomes: Child Trends: 2015

World Happiness Report 2018: Helliwell, J; Layard, R; Sachs, J: Sustainable Development Solutions Network: 2018

World Health Organization (WHO): publications including:

* Active Ageing: a policy framework: 2002
* World report on Ageing and Health: 2015
* WHO/Imperial College International Longevity Study: Future life expectancy in 35 industrialised countries: *The Lancet*: 21 Feb. 2017

Y.

YouGov: 2017 Survey
Young Foundation Report: 2018
Youth Parliament Manifesto: 2015/2016
Yueh, Linda: BBC News: 18 Dec. 2013

Z.

Zucman, Gabriel: The Hidden Wealth of Nations: University of Chicago Press: 2015

ORGANISATIONAL TITLES & ACRONYMS

AARP: American Association for Retired Persons
BPAS: British Pregnancy Advisory Service
CARP: Canadian Association for Retired Persons
CSFI: Centre for the Study of Financial Innovation
EFTA: European Free Trade Association
ESRC: Economic and Social Research Council
EU: European Union
FCA: Financial Conduct Authority
IF: Intergenerational Foundation
IGC/RF: Intergenerational Commission/Resolution Foundation
ILC-UK: International Longevity Centre-UK
IMF: International Monetary Fund
IPPR: Institute of Public Policy Research
IPR;   Institute of Policy Research
JRF: Joseph Rowntree Foundation
MGI: McKinsey Global Institute:
MICRA: Manchester Institute of Collaborative Research on Ageing
NCVP: National Council for Voluntary Organisations.
OBR: Office of Budget Responsibility (UK)
OECD: Organisation for Economic Co-operation and Development
ONS: Office of National Statistics (UK)
RCN: Royal College of Nursing
RSPH: Royal Society for Public Health
RVS: Royal Voluntary Service
TCF: The Citizens Foundation
UKCES: UK Commission for Employment & Skills
UNECE: United Nations Economic Commission for Europe
UNICEF: United Nations International Children's Emergency Fund
UNO: United Nations Organisation
WEF: World Economic Forum
WHO: World Health Organization

LIST OF ILLUSTRATIONS

A. Figures

PART ONE

Appendix A: The European Union